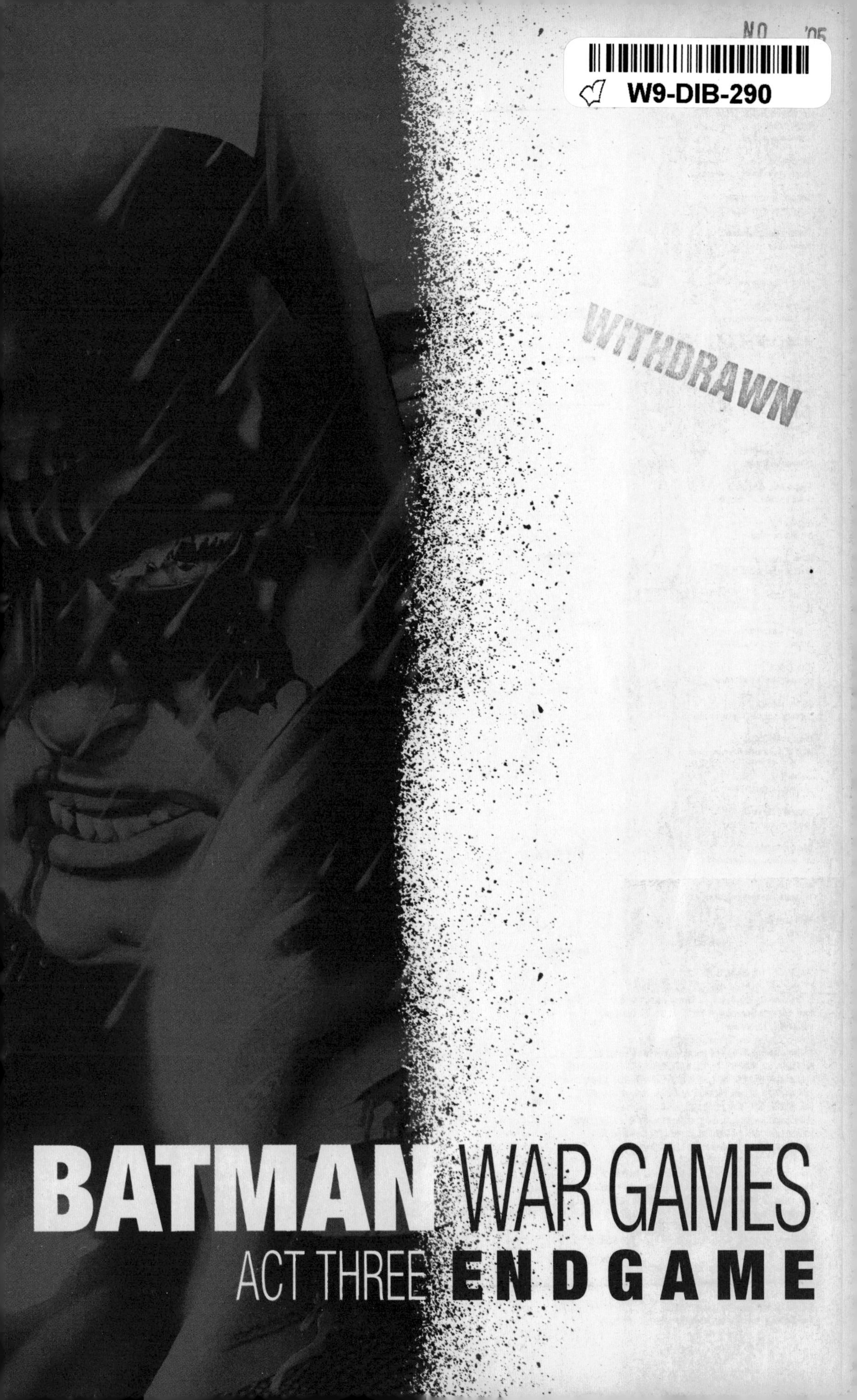
BATMAN WAR GAMES
ACT THREE ENDGAME

BATMAN WAR GAMES ACT 3

Published by DC Comics. Cover, introduction
and compilation copyright © 2005 DC Comics.
All Rights Reserved.

Originally published in single magazine form as
BATGIRL 57, BATMAN 633, BATMAN: GOTHAM KNIGHTS
58, BATMAN: LEGENDS OF THE DARK KNIGHT #184,
CATWOMAN 36, DETECTIVE COMICS 799, NIGHTWING
98, ROBIN 131. Copyright © 2004 DC Comics.
All Rights Reserved. All characters, their distinctive
likenesses and related elements featured in this
publication are trademarks of DC Comics.

The stories, characters and incidents featured in
this publication are entirely fictional. DC Comics does
not read or accept unsolicited submissions of ideas,
stories or artwork.

DC Comics, 1700 Broadway, New York, NY 10019

A Warner Bros. Entertainment Company
Printed in Canada. First Printing.
ISBN: 1-4012-0431-7
Cover illustration by James Jean.
Publication design by Amie Brockway-Metcalf.

ED BRUBAKER
ANDERSEN GABRYCH
DEVIN GRAYSON
DYLAN HORROCKS
A.J. LEIBERMAN
BILL WILLINGHAM

WRITERS

AL BARRIONUEVO
THOMAS DERENICK
PAUL GULACY
MIKE HUDDLESTON
KINSUN
SEAN PHILLIPS
BRAD WALKER
PETE WOODS
PENCILLERS

ROBERT CAMPANELLA
ADAM DEKRAKER
JESSE DELPERDANG
TROY NIXEY
JIMMY PALMIOTTI
SEAN PHILLIPS
FRANCIS PORTELLA
RODNEY RAMOS
CAM SMITH
AARON SOWD
INKERS

PAT BROSSEAU
JARED K. FLETCHER
ROB LEIGH
KEN LOPEZ
CLEM ROBINS
LETTERERS

BRAD ANDERSON
TONY AVINA
LAURIE KRONENBERG
GUY MAJOR
JAVIER RODRIGUEZ
GREGORY WRIGHT
JASON WRIGHT
COLORISTS

BATMAN CREATED BY
BOB KANE

BATMAN
WAR GAMES
ACT THREE

WHAT HAS GONE BEFORE

The Underworld crime bosses in Gotham City have been executed, leaving the criminal element rudderless and out of control. Everything was going according to plan – a plan Batman conceived but never imagined would be executed.

Stephanie Brown, the Spoiler, unleashed the plan in hopes of proving to her mentor that she was worthy of his trust. Instead, things spiraled out of control despite the best efforts of Batman, Robin, Nightwing, Tarantula, Catwoman, Orpheus and Onyx.

Batman convinces Police Commissioner Akins to call a curfew, hoping to herd the run-amok criminals into a stadium, where Orpheus is to take control, and through him, Batman would ultimately pull the strings. But first, the Penguin plunges the city into a blackout, hoping to take advantage of the carnage. Tarantula, though, put a crimp in those plans, going through Killer Croc, Trickster and Deadshot to reach the Penguin.

Worse, Stephanie has been in the clutches of a foe long thought dead, Black Mask. Back in Gotham, Black Mask tortures Stephanie for information and then kills Orpheus. After killing Batman's agent, Black Mask is visited by Hush, who provides him with key, albeit erroneous, information. Meantime, despite her wounds, Stephanie manages to escape. Black Mask then disguises himself as Orpheus, the pivotal player in Batman's scenario.

Batman meets with "Orpheus" in an attempt to restore power to the city. They are met by Zeiss who nearly kills them both until Orpheus gets him alone. Zeiss is allowed to run free, carrying with him a message from the disguised criminal mastermind to all the other crime organizations.

With power restored, the media put out a call for Batman to submit to the oversight of the law.

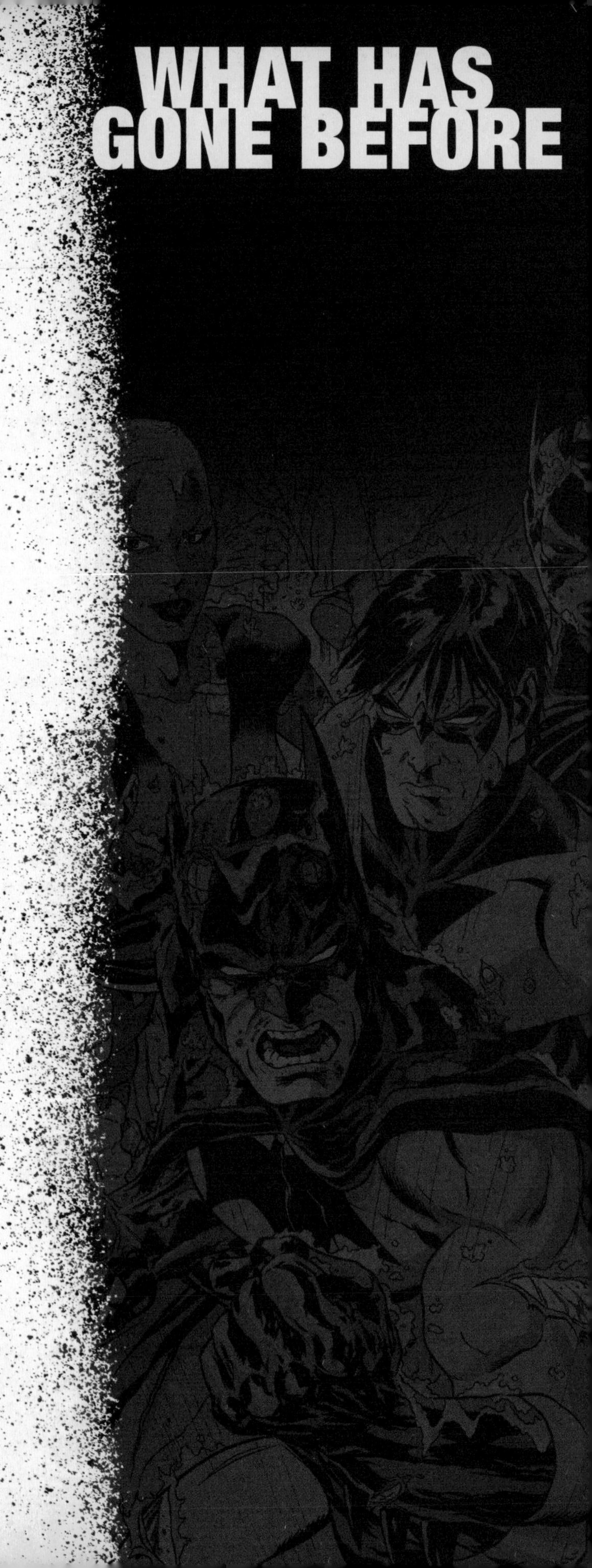

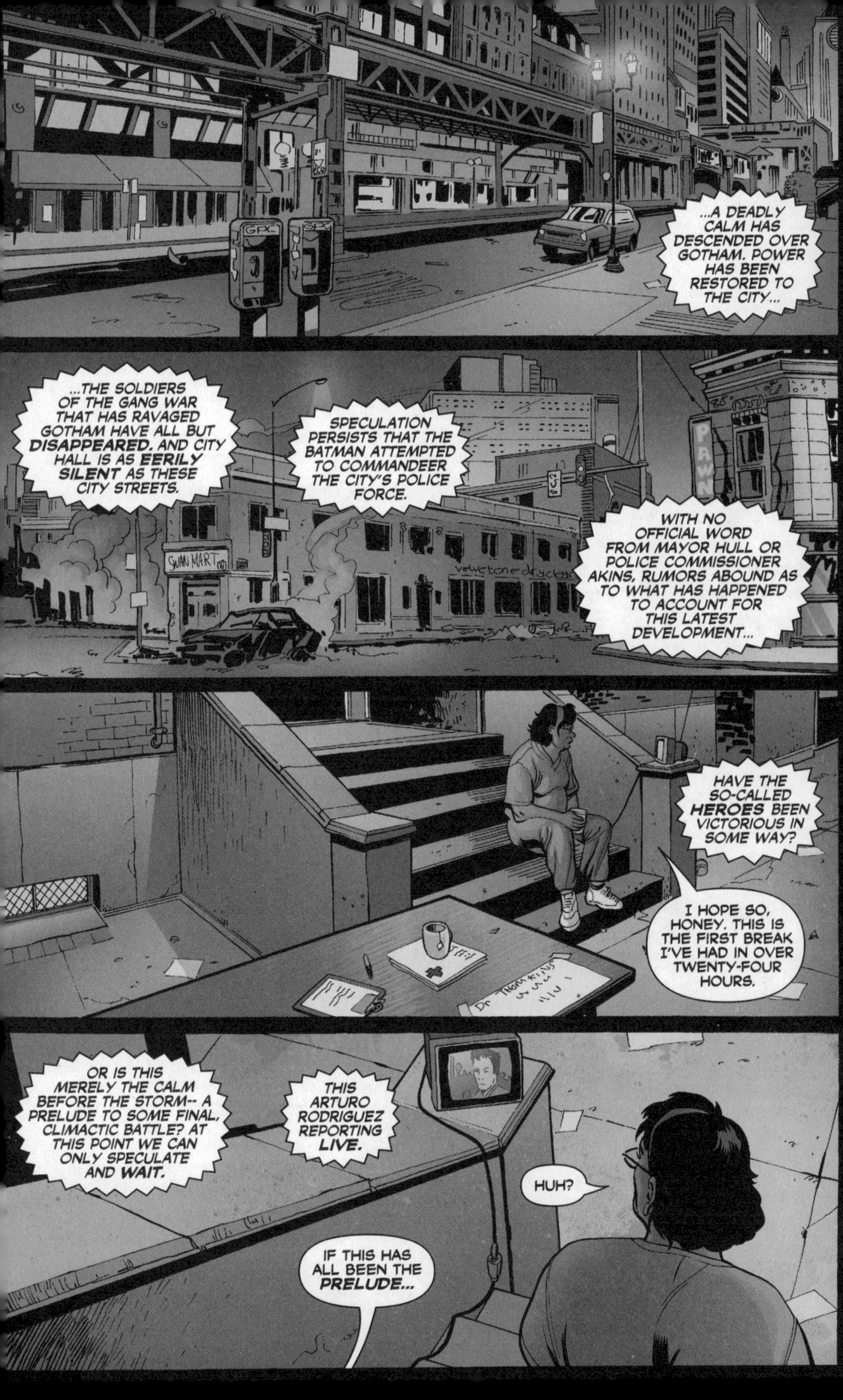

GPC
GPC
...A DEADLY CALM HAS DESCENDED OVER GOTHAM. POWER HAS BEEN RESTORED TO THE CITY...
...THE SOLDIERS OF THE GANG WAR THAT HAS RAVAGED GOTHAM HAVE ALL BUT DISAPPEARED. AND CITY HALL IS AS EERILY SILENT AS THESE CITY STREETS.
SPECULATION PERSISTS THAT THE BATMAN ATTEMPTED TO COMMANDEER THE CITY'S POLICE FORCE.
PAWN
SWAN MART
WITH NO OFFICIAL WORD FROM MAYOR HULL OR POLICE COMMISSIONER AKINS, RUMORS ABOUND AS TO WHAT HAS HAPPENED TO ACCOUNT FOR THIS LATEST DEVELOPMENT...
HAVE THE SO-CALLED HEROES BEEN VICTORIOUS IN SOME WAY?
I HOPE SO, HONEY. THIS IS THE FIRST BREAK I'VE HAD IN OVER TWENTY-FOUR HOURS.
OR IS THIS MERELY THE CALM BEFORE THE STORM-- A PRELUDE TO SOME FINAL, CLIMACTIC BATTLE? AT THIS POINT WE CAN ONLY SPECULATE AND WAIT.
THIS ARTURO RODRIGUEZ REPORTING LIVE.
HUH?
IF THIS HAS ALL BEEN THE PRELUDE...

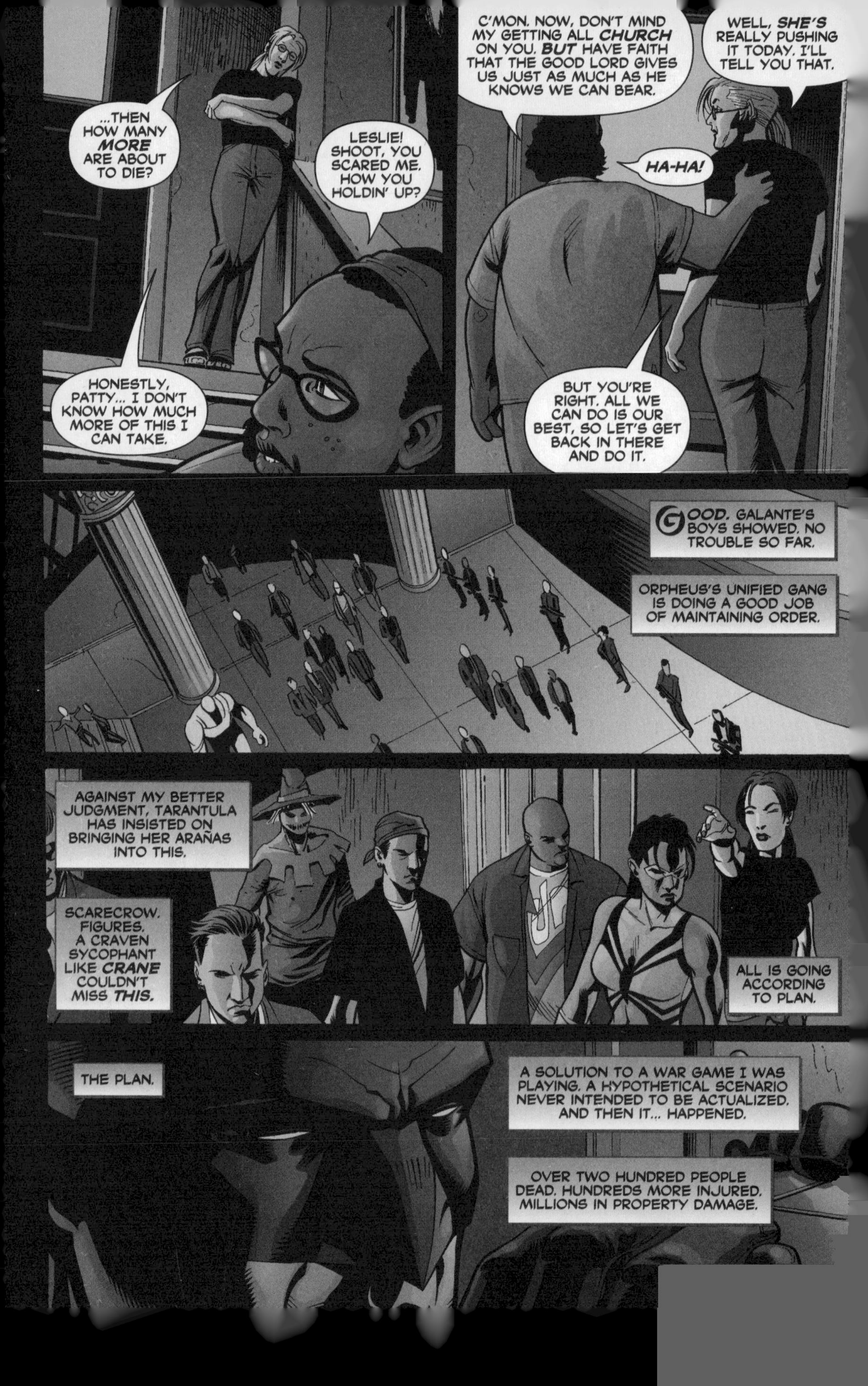
...THEN HOW MANY MORE ARE ABOUT TO DIE?
LESLIE! SHOOT, YOU SCARED ME. HOW YOU HOLDIN' UP?
HONESTLY, PATTY... I DON'T KNOW HOW MUCH MORE OF THIS I CAN TAKE.
C'MON. NOW, DON'T MIND MY GETTING ALL CHURCH ON YOU. BUT HAVE FAITH THAT THE GOOD LORD GIVES US JUST AS MUCH AS HE KNOWS WE CAN BEAR.
WELL, SHE'S REALLY PUSHING IT TODAY. I'LL TELL YOU THAT.
HA-HA!
BUT YOU'RE RIGHT. ALL WE CAN DO IS OUR BEST, SO LET'S GET BACK IN THERE AND DO IT.
GOOD. GALANTE'S BOYS SHOWED. NO TROUBLE SO FAR.
ORPHEUS'S UNIFIED GANG IS DOING A GOOD JOB OF MAINTAINING ORDER.
AGAINST MY BETTER JUDGMENT, TARANTULA HAS INSISTED ON BRINGING HER ARAÑAS INTO THIS.
SCARECROW. FIGURES. A CRAVEN SYCOPHANT LIKE CRANE COULDN'T MISS THIS.
ALL IS GOING ACCORDING TO PLAN.
THE PLAN.
A SOLUTION TO A WAR GAME I WAS PLAYING. A HYPOTHETICAL SCENARIO NEVER INTENDED TO BE ACTUALIZED. AND THEN IT... HAPPENED.
OVER TWO HUNDRED PEOPLE DEAD. HUNDREDS MORE INJURED. MILLIONS IN PROPERTY DAMAGE.

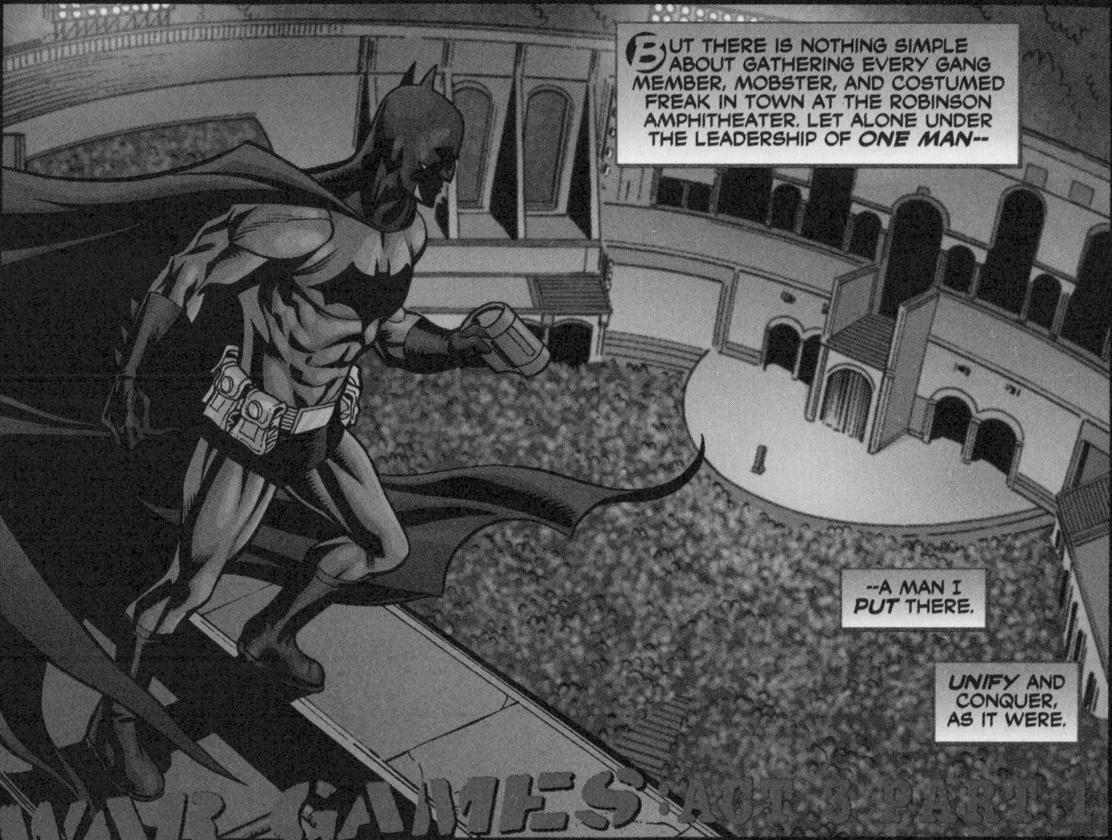
BUT THERE IS NOTHING SIMPLE ABOUT GATHERING EVERY GANG MEMBER, MOBSTER, AND COSTUMED FREAK IN TOWN AT THE ROBINSON AMPHITHEATER. LET ALONE UNDER THE LEADERSHIP OF *ONE MAN*--
--A MAN I *PUT* THERE.
UNIFY AND CONQUER, AS IT WERE.
WAR GAMES: ACT 3 PART 1

GOOD INTENTIONS

ANDERSEN GABRYCH- Writer **PETE WOODS**- Penciller **CAM SMITH**- Inker
JASON WRIGHT- Colorist **JARED K. FLETCHER**- Letterer **MICHAEL WRIGHT**- Assoc. Editor **BOB SCHRECK**- Editor
BATMAN created by **BOB KANE**

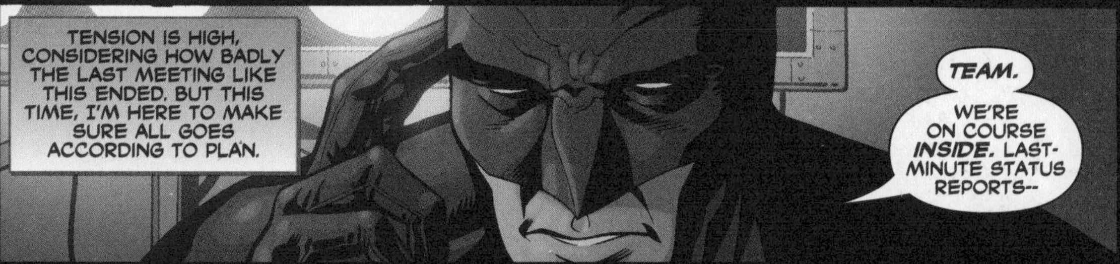
TENSION IS HIGH, CONSIDERING HOW BADLY THE LAST MEETING LIKE THIS ENDED. BUT THIS TIME, I'M HERE TO MAKE SURE ALL GOES ACCORDING TO PLAN.
TEAM.
WE'RE ON COURSE *INSIDE.* LAST-MINUTE STATUS REPORTS--

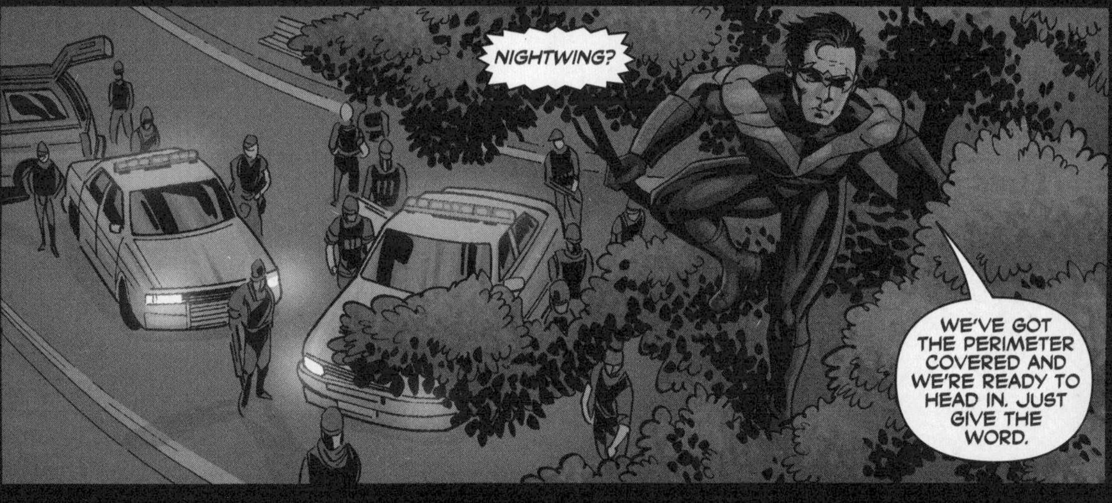
NIGHTWING?
WE'VE GOT THE PERIMETER COVERED AND WE'RE READY TO HEAD IN. JUST GIVE THE WORD.

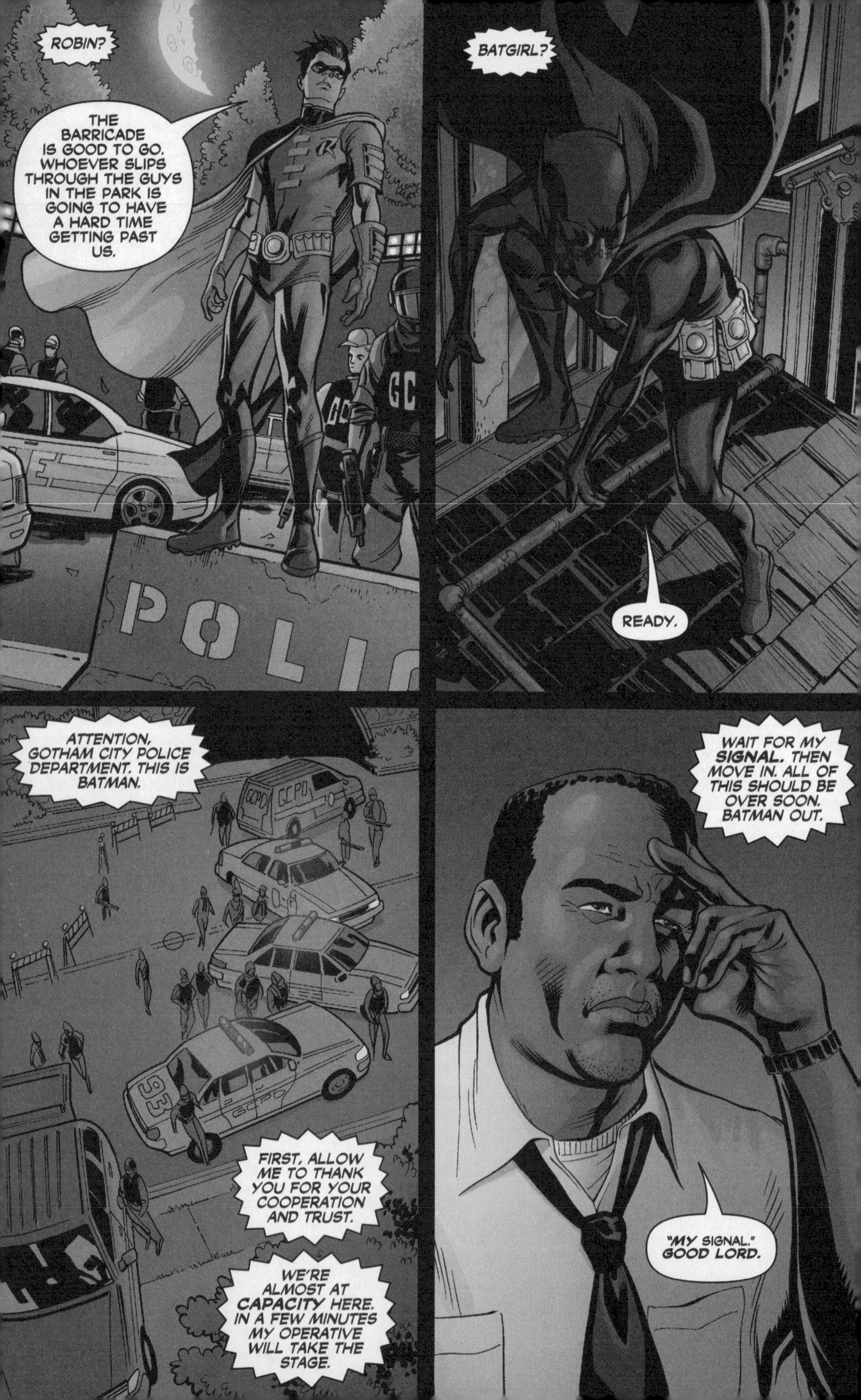
ROBIN?
THE BARRICADE IS GOOD TO GO. WHOEVER SLIPS THROUGH THE GUYS IN THE PARK IS GOING TO HAVE A HARD TIME GETTING PAST US.
POLIC
BATGIRL?
READY.
ATTENTION, GOTHAM CITY POLICE DEPARTMENT. THIS IS BATMAN.
FIRST, ALLOW ME TO THANK YOU FOR YOUR COOPERATION AND TRUST.
WE'RE ALMOST AT CAPACITY HERE. IN A FEW MINUTES MY OPERATIVE WILL TAKE THE STAGE.
WAIT FOR MY SIGNAL. THEN MOVE IN. ALL OF THIS SHOULD BE OVER SOON. BATMAN OUT.
"MY SIGNAL." GOOD LORD.

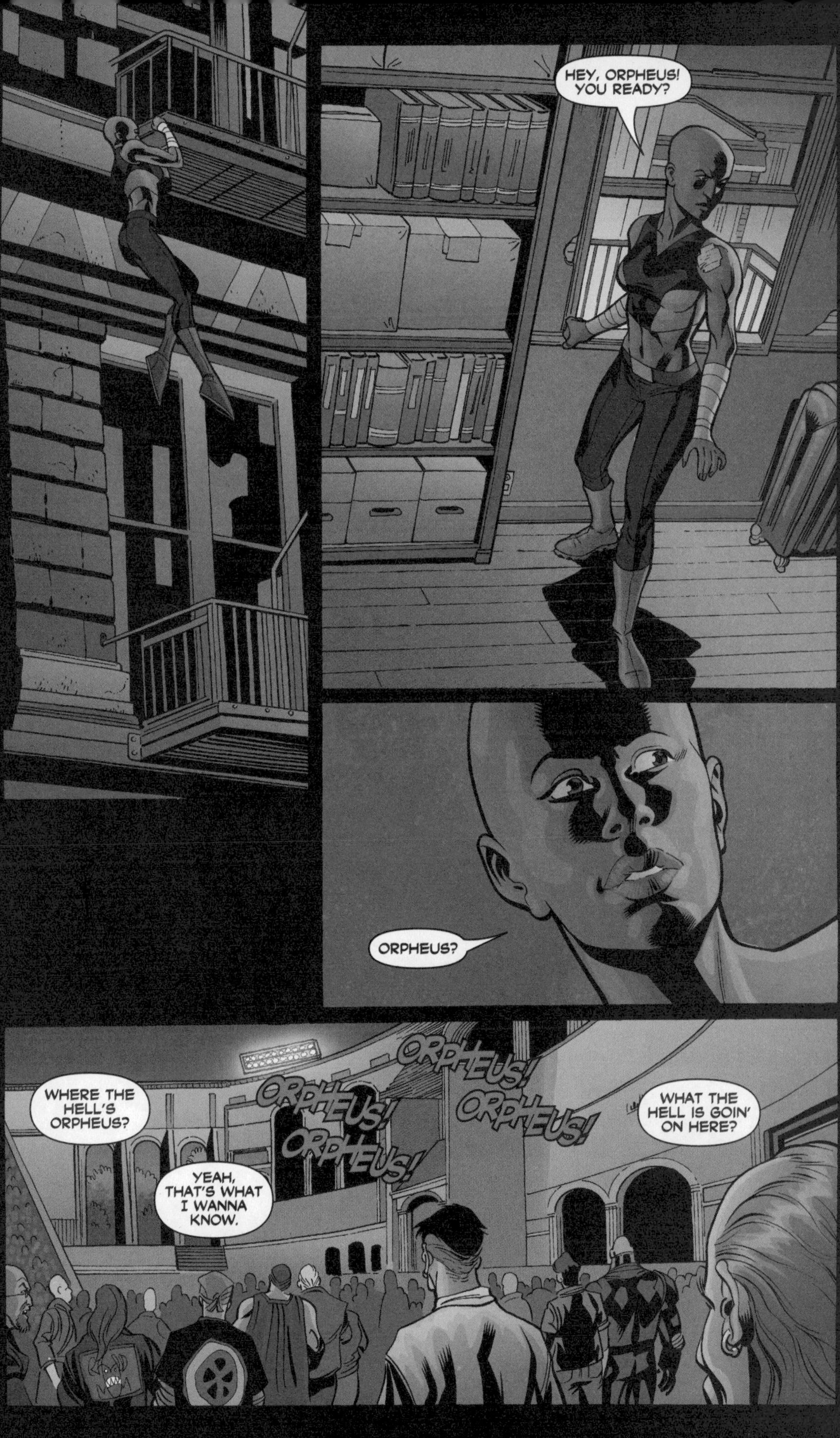
HEY, ORPHEUS! YOU READY?
ORPHEUS?
WHERE THE HELL'S ORPHEUS?
YEAH, THAT'S WHAT I WANNA KNOW.
ORPHEUS!
ORPHEUS!
ORPHEUS!
ORPHEUS!
WHAT THE HELL IS GOIN' ON HERE?

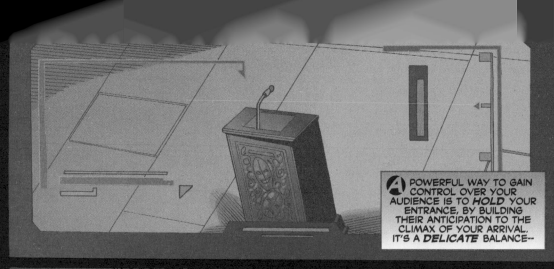

A POWERFUL WAY TO GAIN CONTROL OVER YOUR AUDIENCE IS TO *HOLD* YOUR ENTRANCE, BY BUILDING THEIR ANTICIPATION TO THE CLIMAX OF YOUR ARRIVAL. IT'S A *DELICATE* BALANCE--

SHOWTIME.

HE SHOULD BE--

--HOLD TOO LONG AND YOU RUN THE RISK OF *LOSING* THEM.

YES. RIGHT ON TIME. GOOD MAN.

LADIES AND GENTLEMEN--

IN THE LAST TWENTY-FOUR HOURS WE HAVE ALL SUFFERED THE LOSS OF FRIENDS, COMPATRIOTS, AND *FAMILY*--

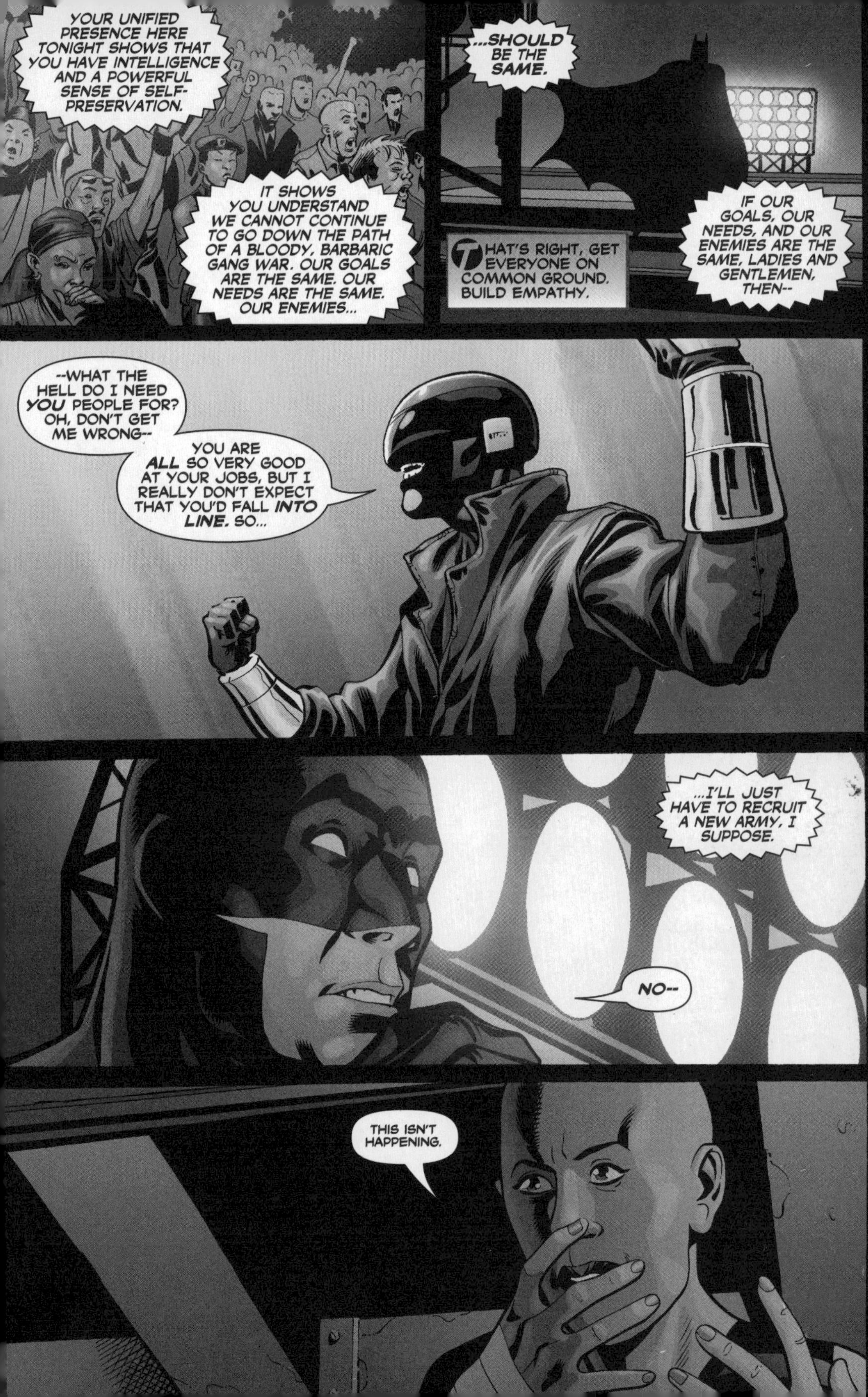
YOUR UNIFIED PRESENCE HERE TONIGHT SHOWS THAT YOU HAVE INTELLIGENCE AND A POWERFUL SENSE OF SELF-PRESERVATION.
IT SHOWS YOU UNDERSTAND WE CANNOT CONTINUE TO GO DOWN THE PATH OF A BLOODY, BARBARIC GANG WAR. OUR GOALS ARE THE SAME. OUR NEEDS ARE THE SAME. OUR ENEMIES...
...SHOULD BE THE SAME.
THAT'S RIGHT, GET EVERYONE ON COMMON GROUND. BUILD EMPATHY.
IF OUR GOALS, OUR NEEDS, AND OUR ENEMIES ARE THE SAME, LADIES AND GENTLEMEN, THEN--
--WHAT THE HELL DO I NEED YOU PEOPLE FOR? OH, DON'T GET ME WRONG--
YOU ARE ALL SO VERY GOOD AT YOUR JOBS, BUT I REALLY DON'T EXPECT THAT YOU'D FALL INTO LINE. SO...
...I'LL JUST HAVE TO RECRUIT A NEW ARMY, I SUPPOSE.
NO--
THIS ISN'T HAPPENING.

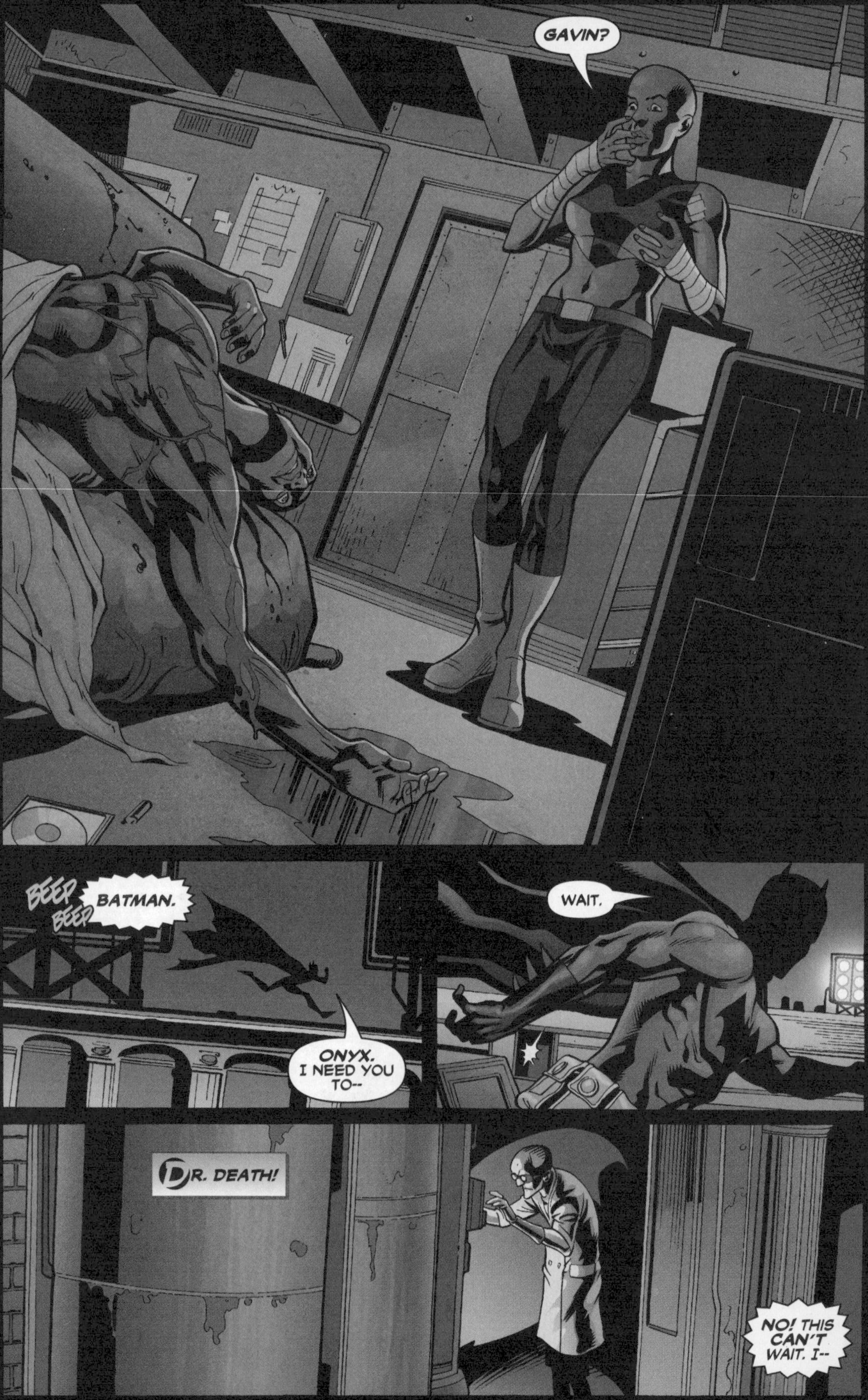
GAVIN?
BEEP BEEP
BATMAN.
ONYX. I NEED YOU TO--
WAIT.
DR. DEATH!
NO! THIS CAN'T WAIT. I--

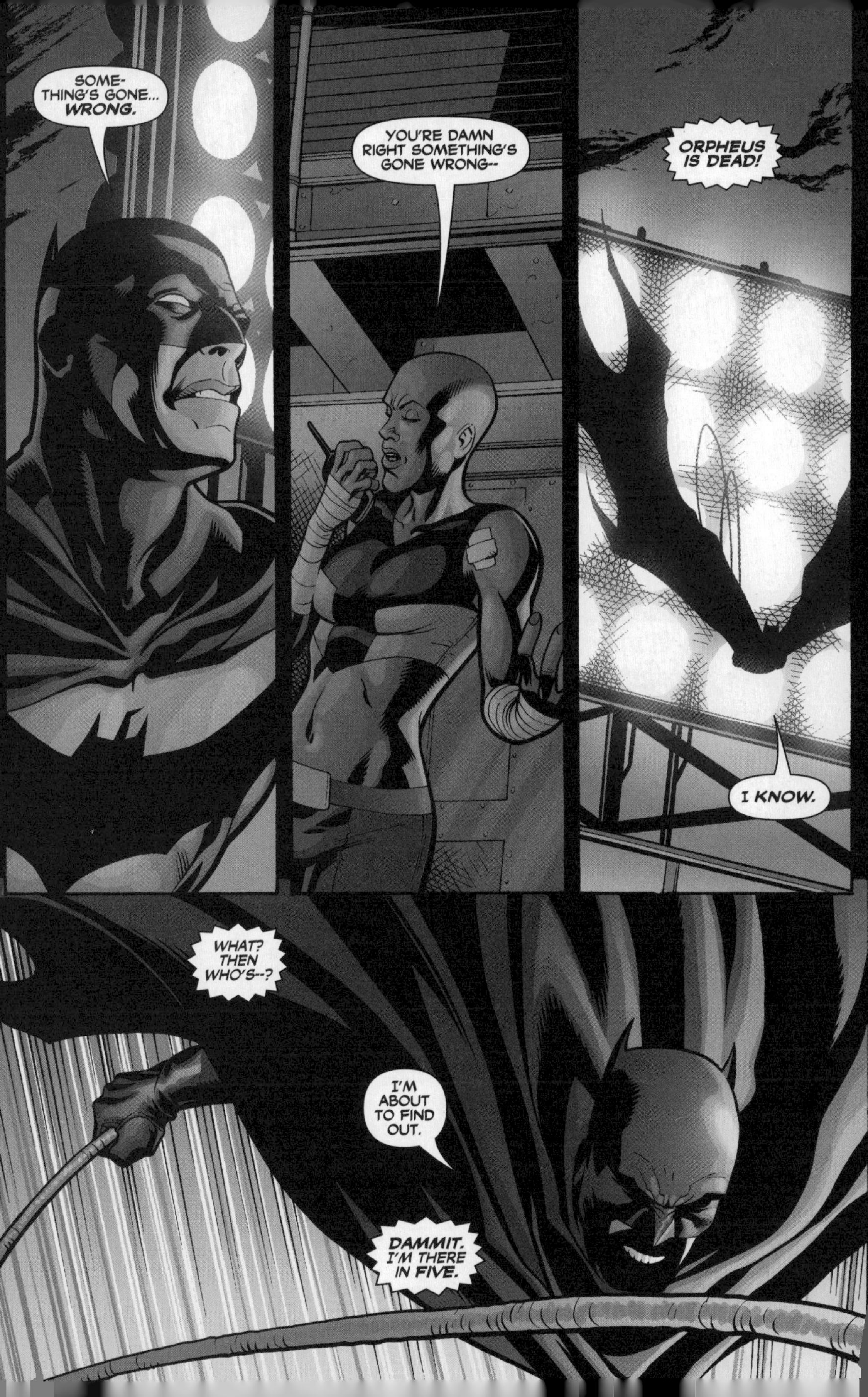
SOME-THING'S GONE... WRONG.
YOU'RE DAMN RIGHT SOMETHING'S GONE WRONG--
ORPHEUS IS DEAD!
I KNOW.
WHAT? THEN WHO'S--?
I'M ABOUT TO FIND OUT.
DAMMIT. I'M THERE IN FIVE.

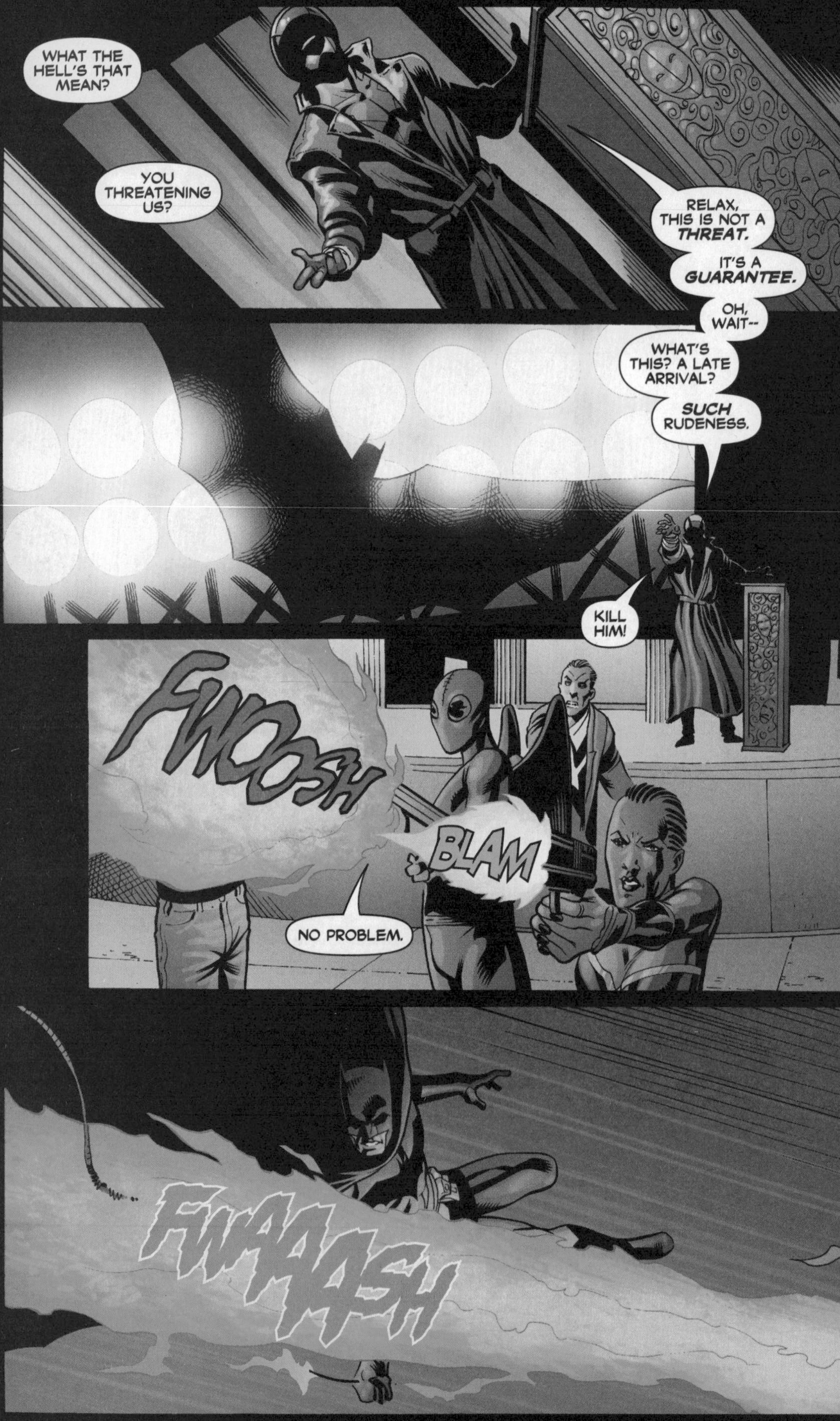
WHAT THE HELL'S THAT MEAN?
YOU THREATENING US?
RELAX, THIS IS NOT A *THREAT.*
IT'S A *GUARANTEE.*
OH, WAIT--
WHAT'S THIS? A LATE ARRIVAL?
SUCH RUDENESS.
KILL HIM!
FWOOSH
BLAM
NO PROBLEM.
FWAAASH

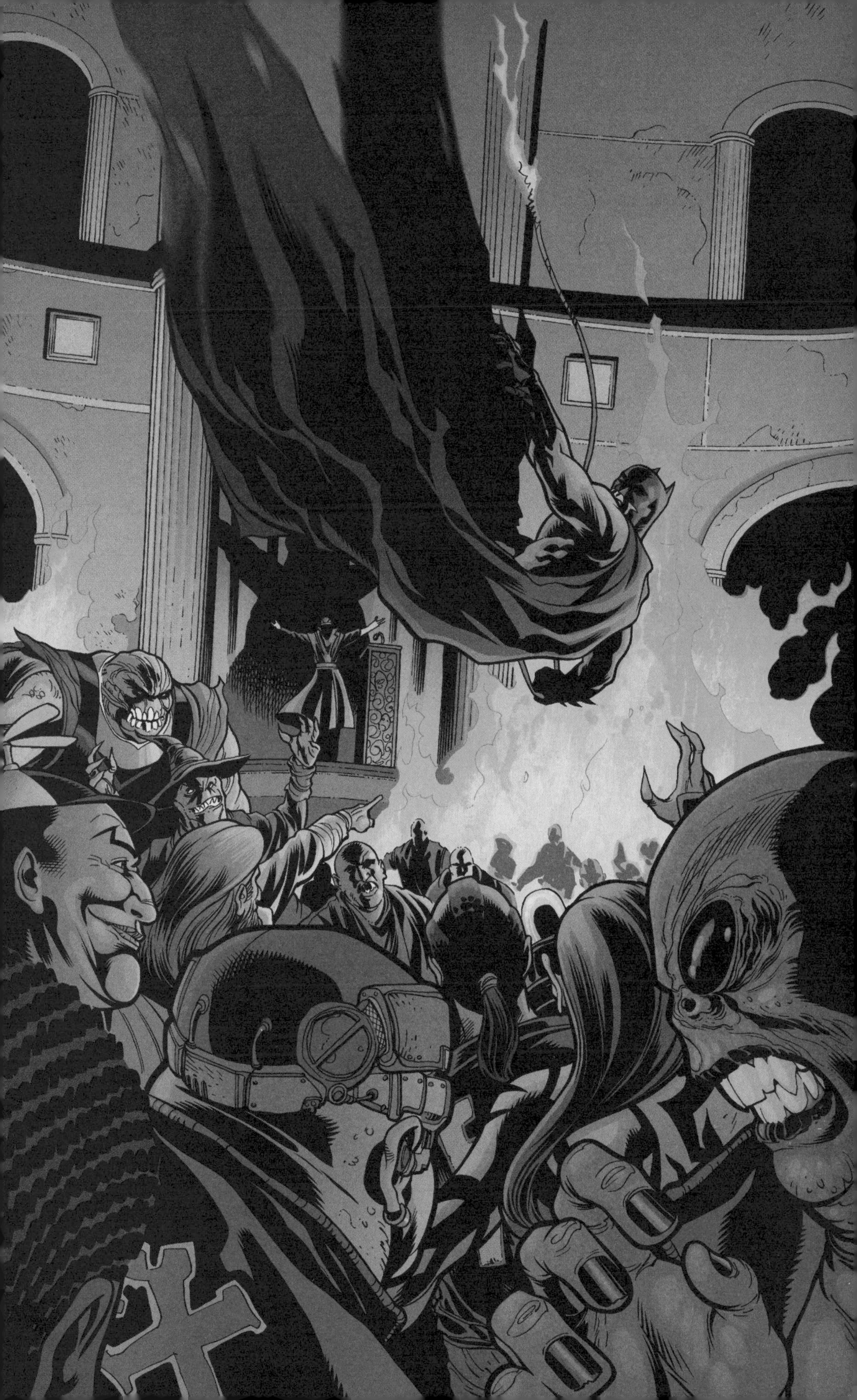

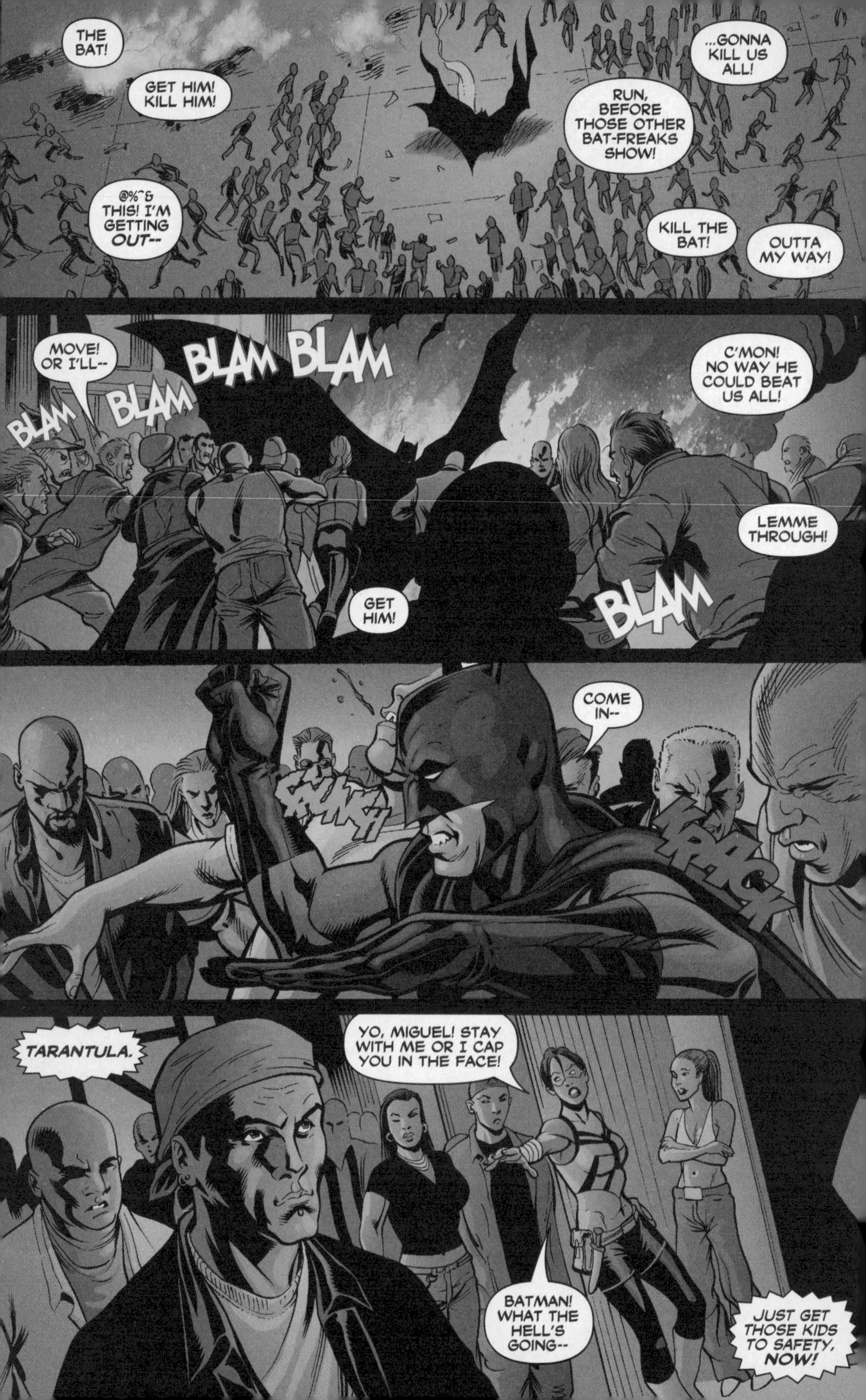

THE BAT!
GET HIM! KILL HIM!
@%^& THIS! I'M GETTING OUT--
RUN, BEFORE THOSE OTHER BAT-FREAKS SHOW!
...GONNA KILL US ALL!
KILL THE BAT!
OUTTA MY WAY!
MOVE! OR I'LL--
BLAM
BLAM
BLAM
BLAM
C'MON! NO WAY HE COULD BEAT US ALL!
LEMME THROUGH!
GET HIM!
BLAM
COME IN--
TARANTULA.
YO, MIGUEL! STAY WITH ME OR I CAP YOU IN THE FACE!
BATMAN! WHAT THE HELL'S GOING--
JUST GET THOSE KIDS TO SAFETY, NOW!

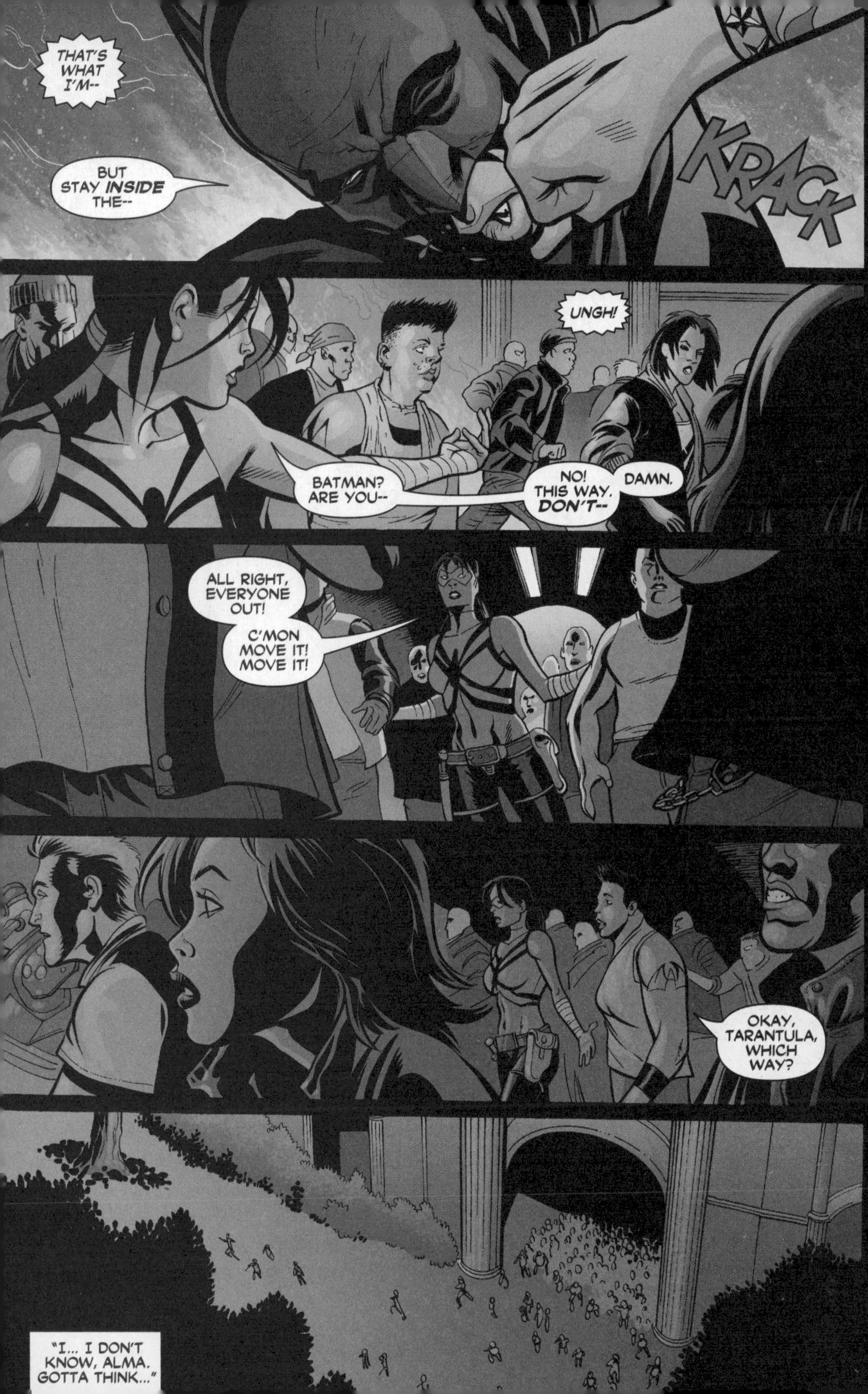
THAT'S WHAT I'M--
BUT STAY INSIDE THE--
KRACK
UNGH!
BATMAN? ARE YOU--
NO! THIS WAY. DON'T--
DAMN.
ALL RIGHT, EVERYONE OUT!
C'MON MOVE IT! MOVE IT!
OKAY, TARANTULA, WHICH WAY?
"I... I DON'T KNOW, ALMA. GOTTA THINK..."

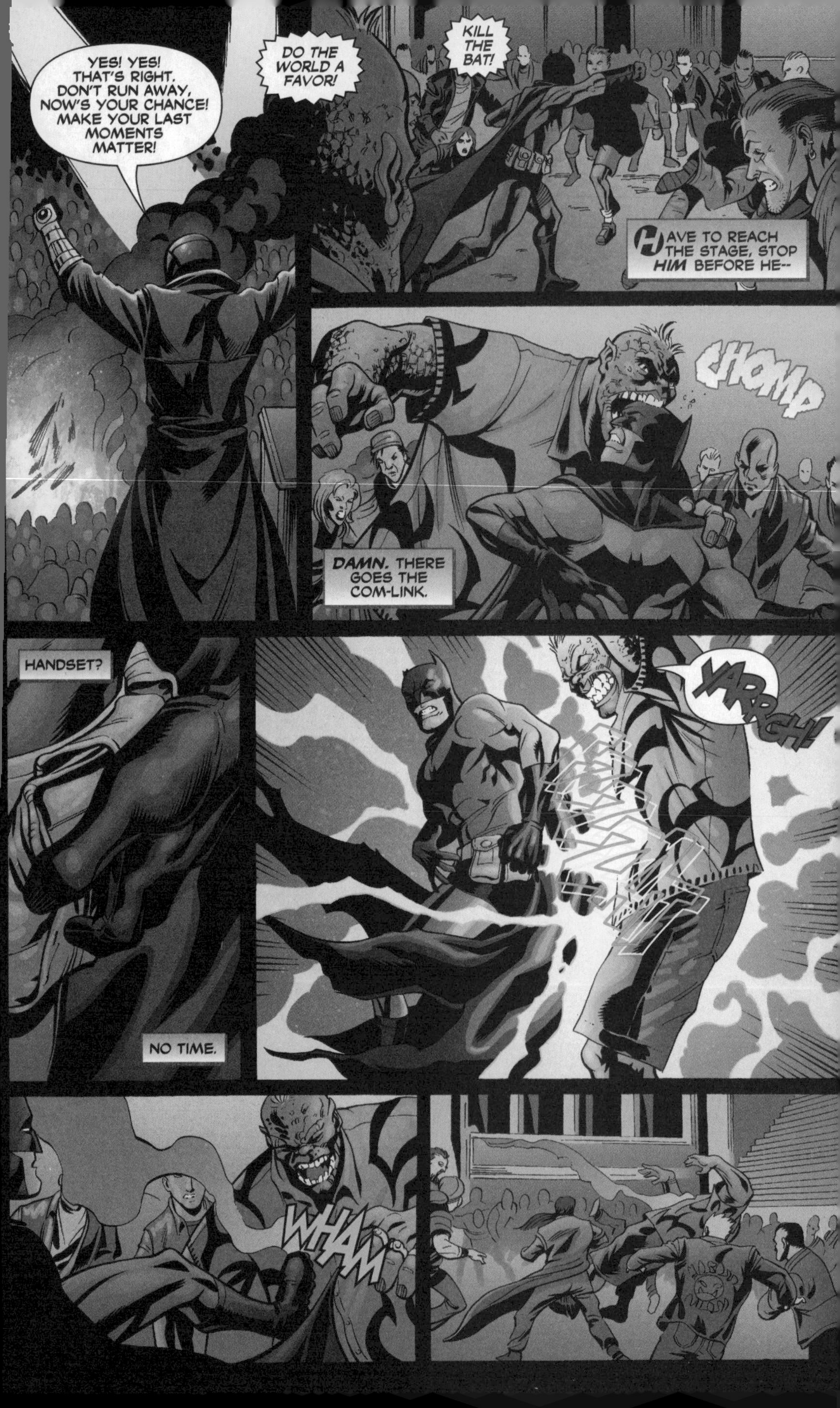
YES! YES! THAT'S RIGHT. DON'T RUN AWAY, NOW'S YOUR CHANCE! MAKE YOUR LAST MOMENTS MATTER!
DO THE WORLD A FAVOR!
KILL THE BAT!
HAVE TO REACH THE STAGE, STOP HIM BEFORE HE--
CHOMP
DAMN. THERE GOES THE COM-LINK.
HANDSET?
NO TIME.
YARRGH!
WHAM

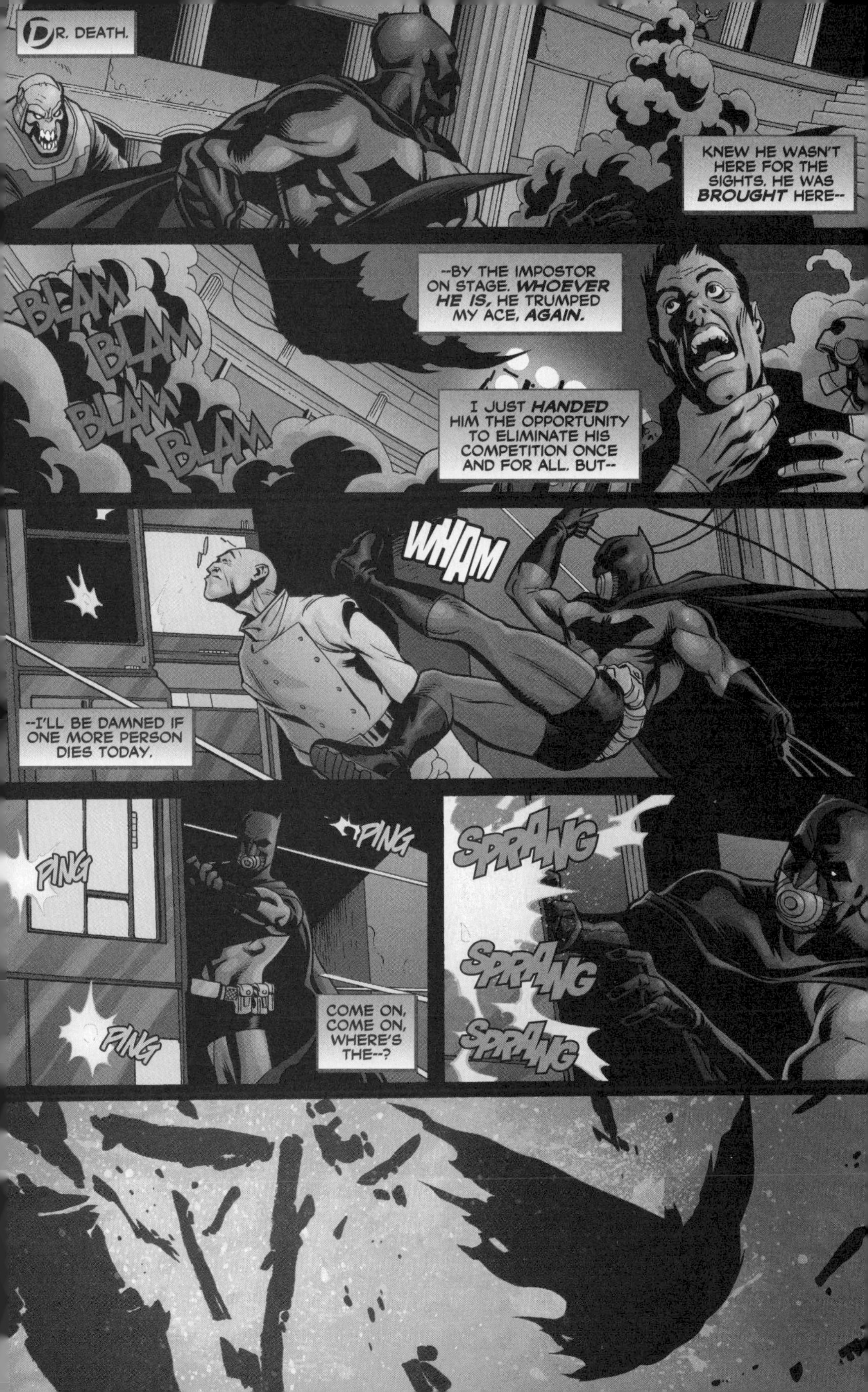

DR. DEATH.
KNEW HE WASN'T HERE FOR THE SIGHTS. HE WAS BROUGHT HERE--
BLAM BLAM BLAM BLAM
--BY THE IMPOSTOR ON STAGE. WHOEVER HE IS, HE TRUMPED MY ACE, AGAIN.
I JUST HANDED HIM THE OPPORTUNITY TO ELIMINATE HIS COMPETITION ONCE AND FOR ALL. BUT--
WHAM
--I'LL BE DAMNED IF ONE MORE PERSON DIES TODAY.
PING
PING
PING
COME ON, COME ON, WHERE'S THE--?
SPRANG
SPRANG
SPRANG

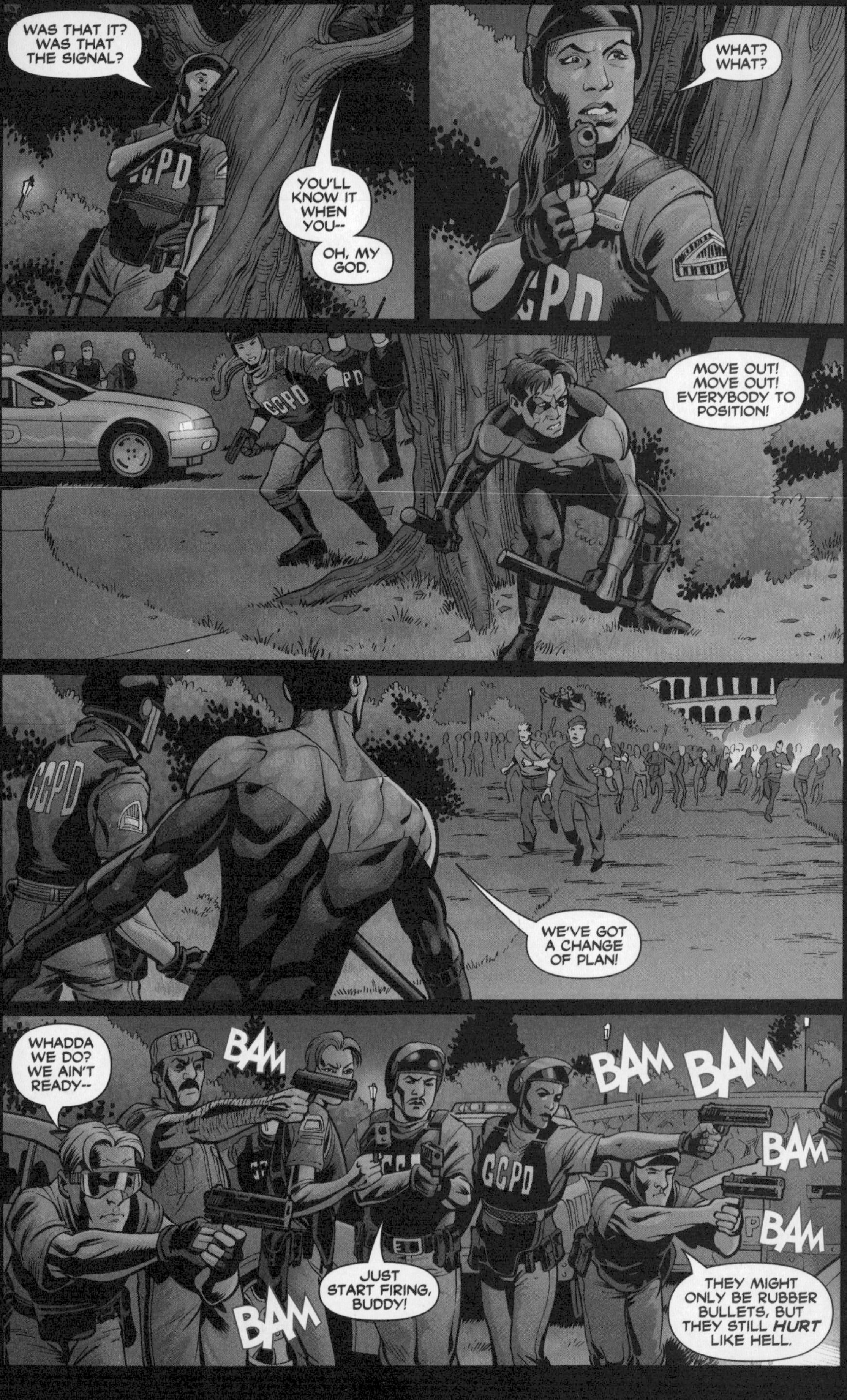
WAS THAT IT? WAS THAT THE SIGNAL?
YOU'LL KNOW IT WHEN YOU--
OH, MY GOD.
WHAT? WHAT?
MOVE OUT! MOVE OUT! EVERYBODY TO POSITION!
WE'VE GOT A CHANGE OF PLAN!
WHADDA WE DO? WE AIN'T READY--
BAM
JUST START FIRING, BUDDY!
BAM
BAM BAM
BAM
BAM
THEY MIGHT ONLY BE RUBBER BULLETS, BUT THEY STILL HURT LIKE HELL.

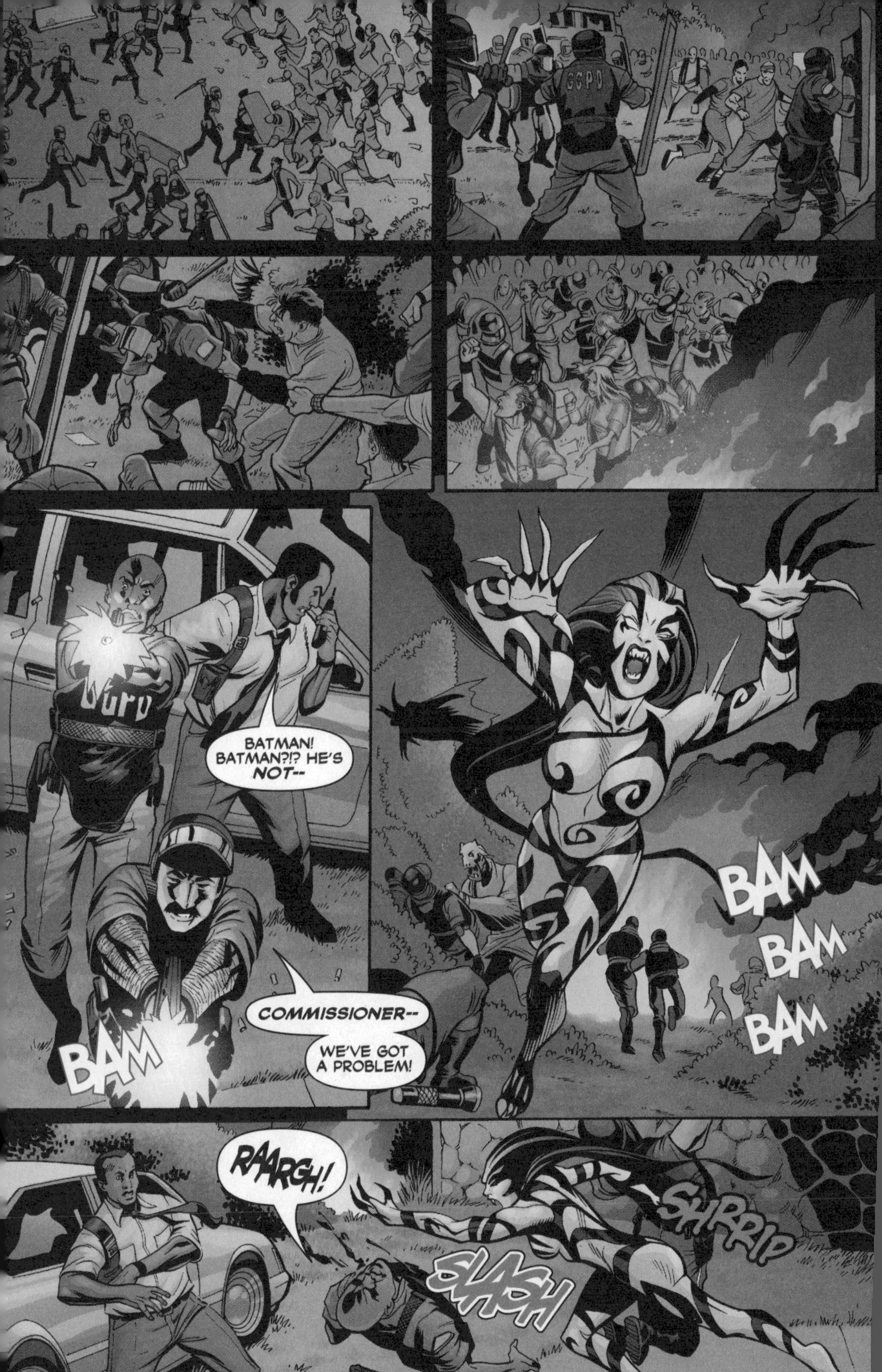
GCPD
BATMAN! BATMAN?!? HE'S NOT--
BAM
COMMISSIONER--
WE'VE GOT A PROBLEM!
BAM
BAM
BAM
RAARGH!
SHRRIP
SLASH

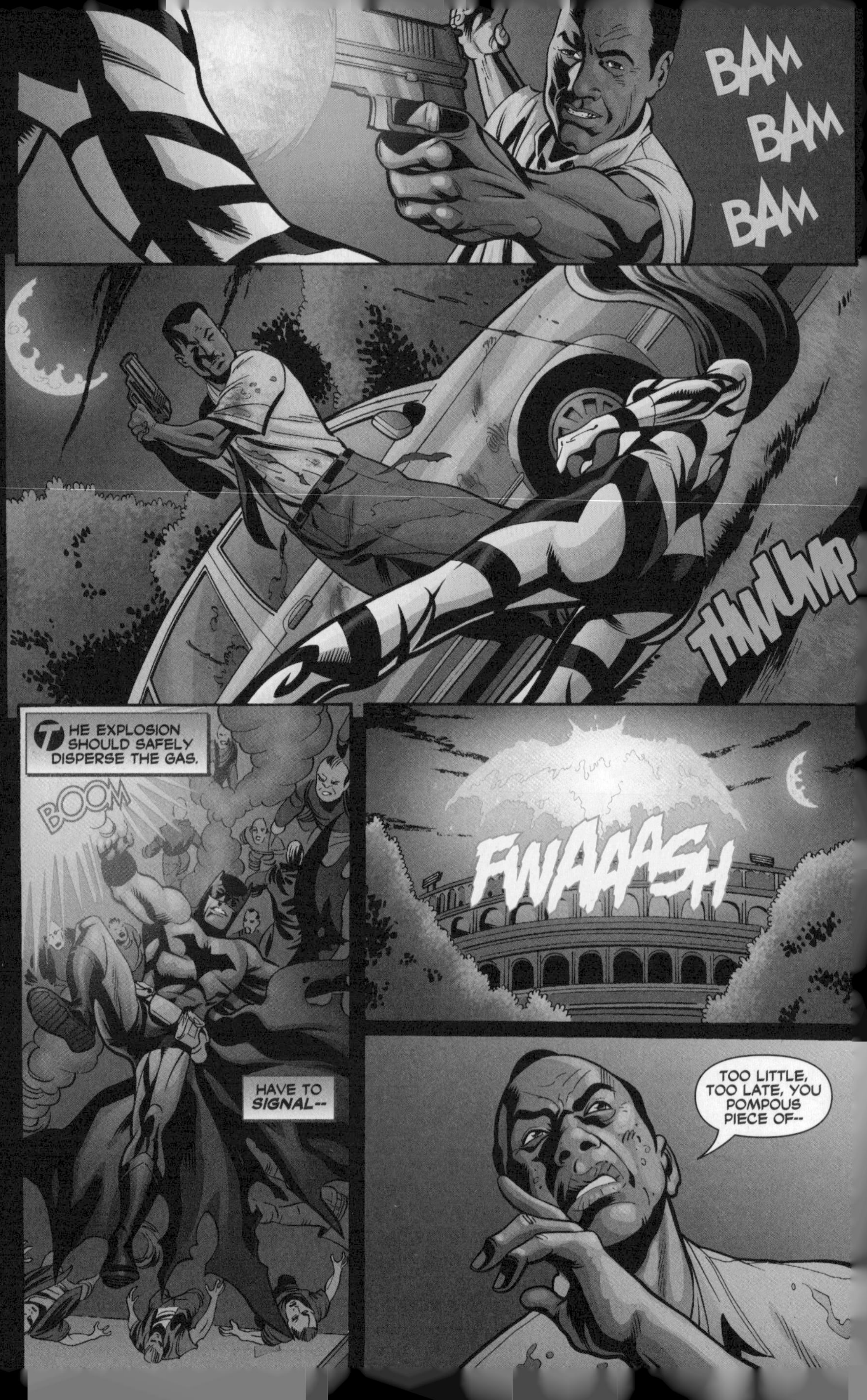
BAM
BAM
BAM
THWUMP
THE EXPLOSION SHOULD SAFELY DISPERSE THE GAS.
BOOM
HAVE TO SIGNAL--
FWAAASH
TOO LITTLE, TOO LATE, YOU POMPOUS PIECE OF--

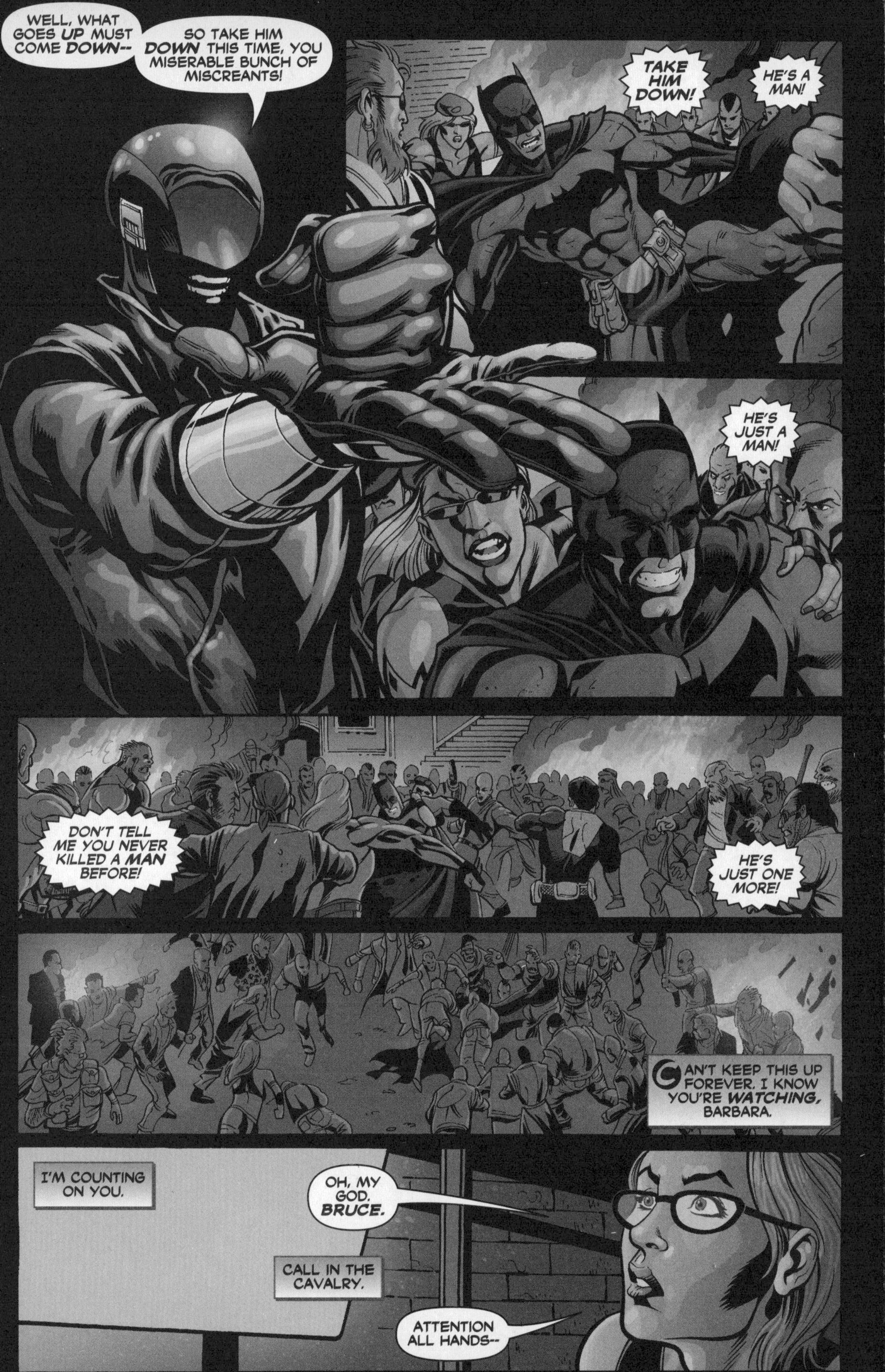
WELL, WHAT GOES UP MUST COME DOWN--
SO TAKE HIM DOWN THIS TIME, YOU MISERABLE BUNCH OF MISCREANTS!
TAKE HIM DOWN!
HE'S A MAN!
HE'S JUST A MAN!
DON'T TELL ME YOU NEVER KILLED A MAN BEFORE!
HE'S JUST ONE MORE!
CAN'T KEEP THIS UP FOREVER. I KNOW YOU'RE WATCHING, BARBARA.
I'M COUNTING ON YOU.
OH, MY GOD. BRUCE.
CALL IN THE CAVALRY.
ATTENTION ALL HANDS--

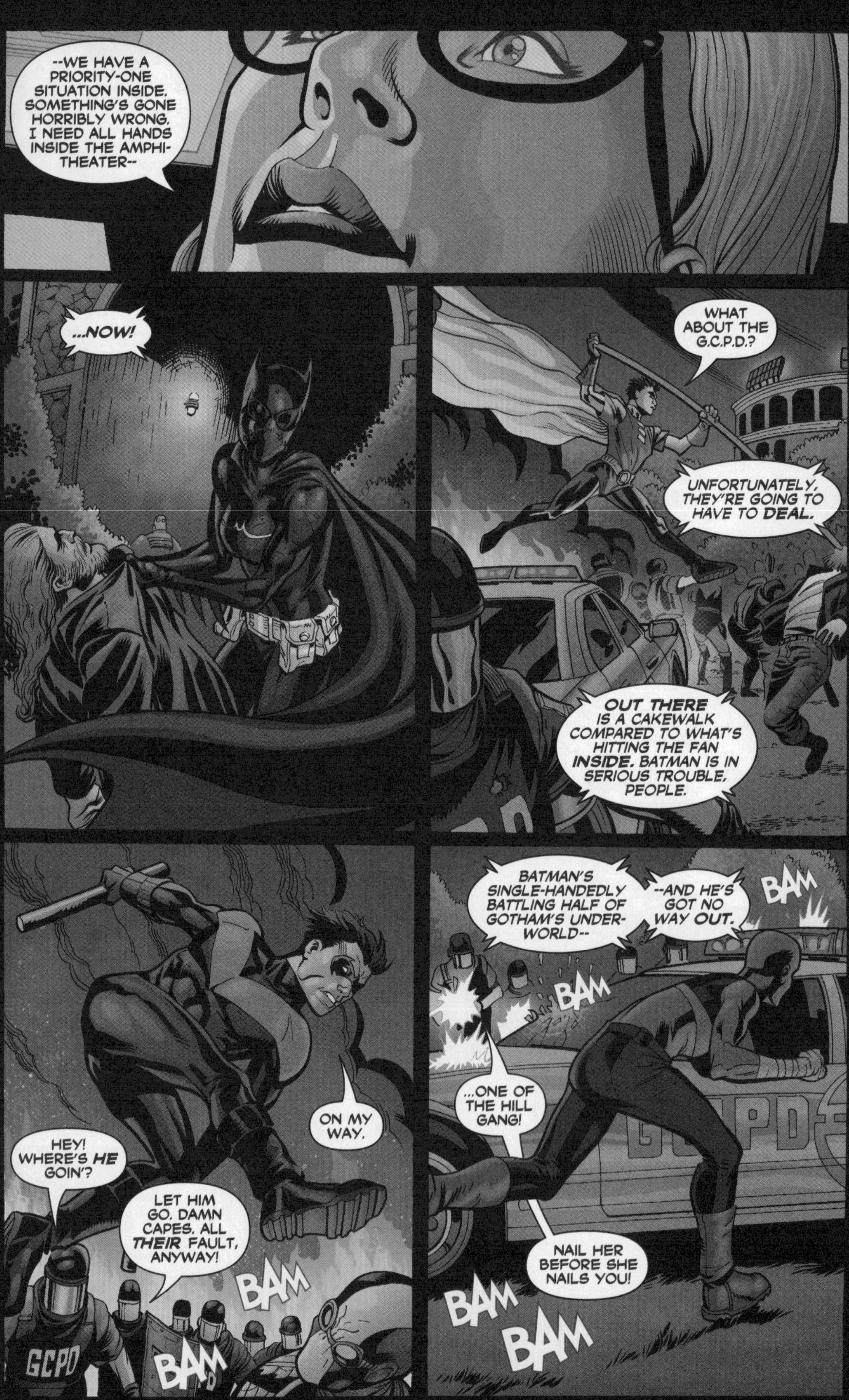
--WE HAVE A PRIORITY-ONE SITUATION INSIDE. SOMETHING'S GONE HORRIBLY WRONG. I NEED ALL HANDS INSIDE THE AMPHI-THEATER--
...NOW!
WHAT ABOUT THE G.C.P.D.?
UNFORTUNATELY, THEY'RE GOING TO HAVE TO DEAL.
OUT THERE IS A CAKEWALK COMPARED TO WHAT'S HITTING THE FAN INSIDE. BATMAN IS IN SERIOUS TROUBLE, PEOPLE.
ON MY WAY.
HEY! WHERE'S HE GOIN'?
LET HIM GO. DAMN CAPES. ALL THEIR FAULT, ANYWAY!
BAM
BAM
GCPD
BATMAN'S SINGLE-HANDEDLY BATTLING HALF OF GOTHAM'S UNDER-WORLD--
--AND HE'S GOT NO WAY OUT.
BAM
BAM
...ONE OF THE HILL GANG!
NAIL HER BEFORE SHE NAILS YOU!
BAM
BAM

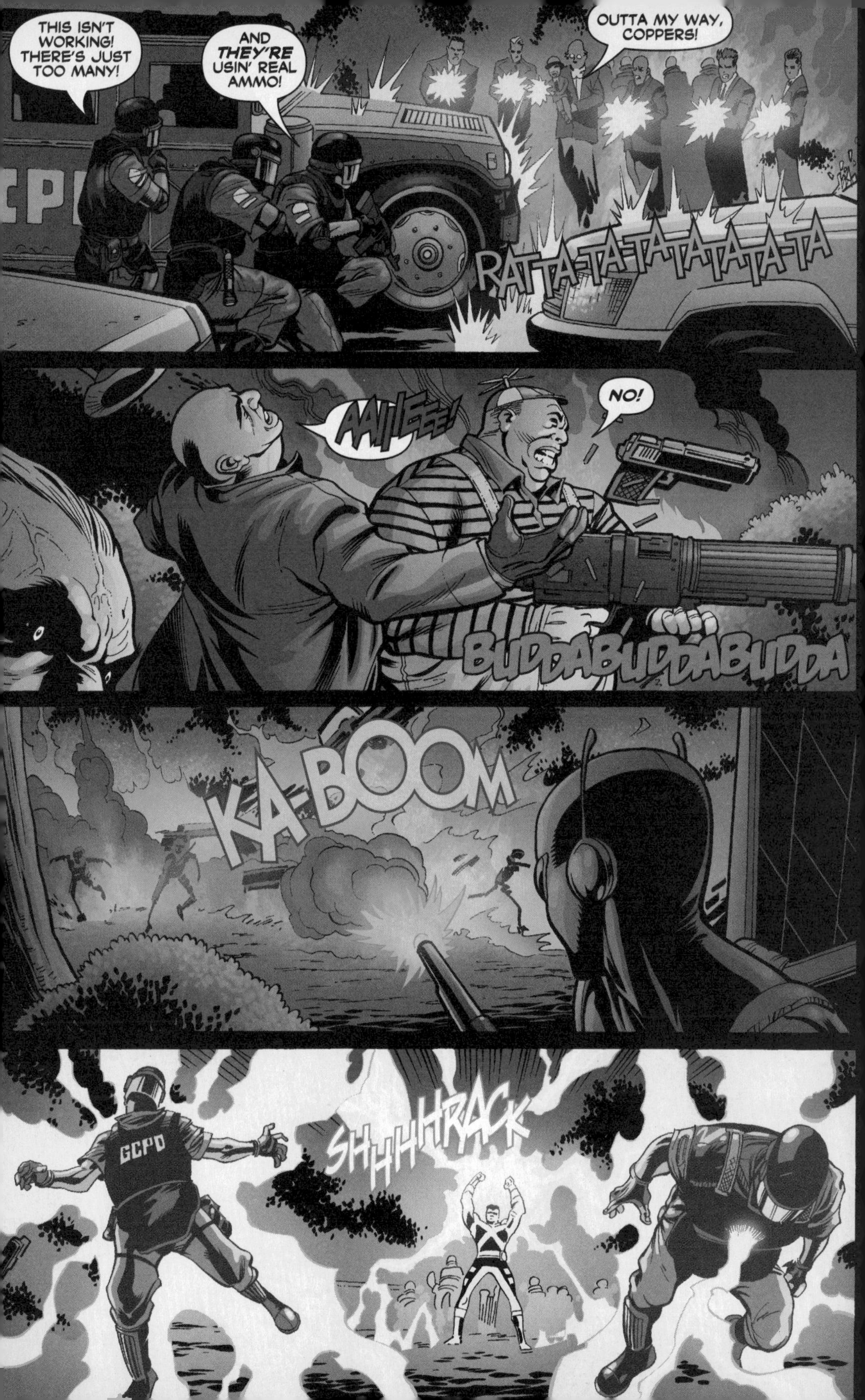
THIS ISN'T WORKING! THERE'S JUST TOO MANY!
AND THEY'RE USIN' REAL AMMO!
OUTTA MY WAY, COPPERS!
RATTA-TA-TA-TA-TA-TA-TA-TA
AAIIIEEE!
NO!
BUDDABUDDABUDDA
KA-BOOM
GCPD
SHHHHRACK

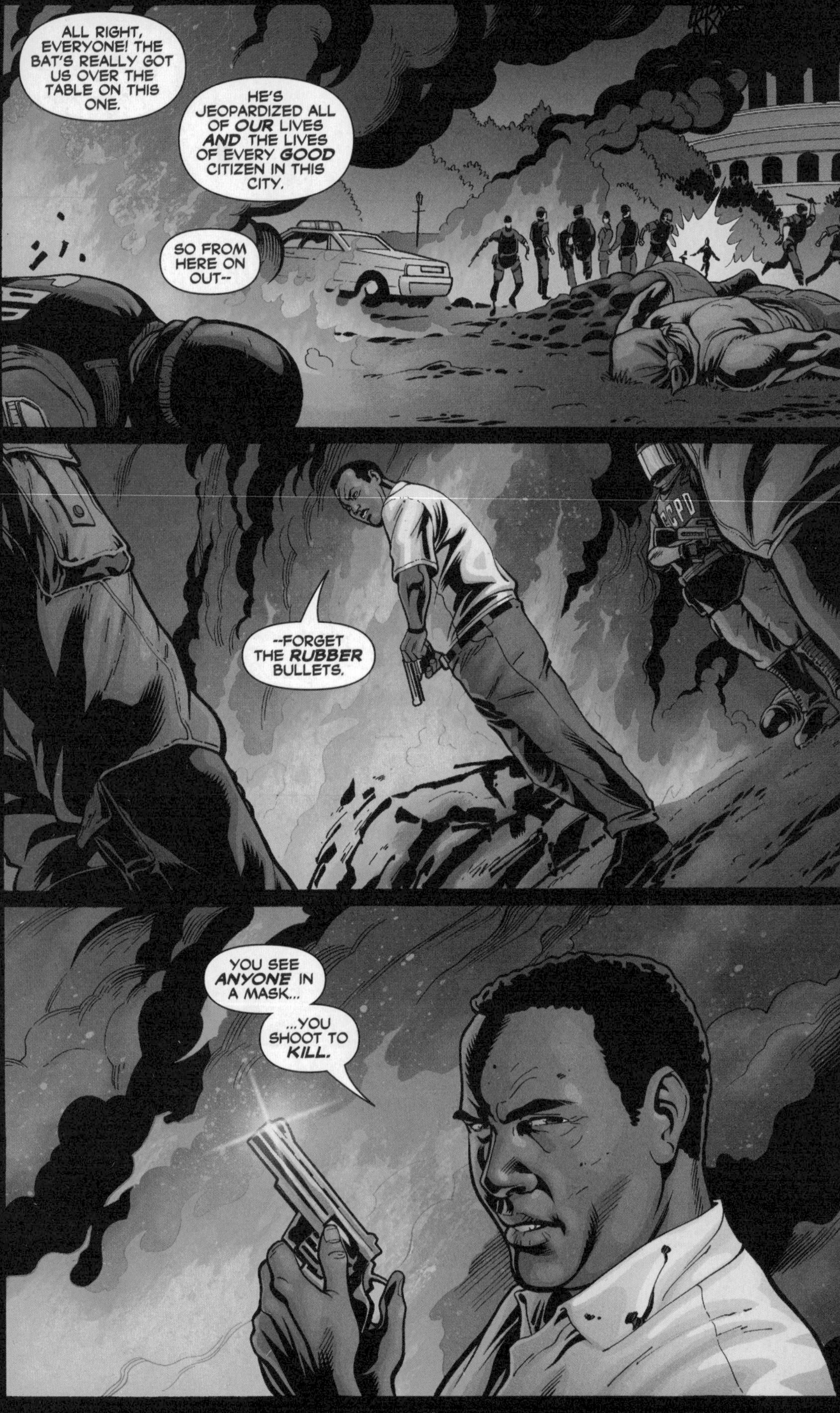
ALL RIGHT, EVERYONE! THE BAT'S REALLY GOT US OVER THE TABLE ON THIS ONE.
HE'S JEOPARDIZED ALL OF *OUR* LIVES *AND* THE LIVES OF EVERY *GOOD* CITIZEN IN THIS CITY.
SO FROM HERE ON OUT--
GCPD
--FORGET THE *RUBBER* BULLETS.
YOU SEE *ANYONE* IN A MASK...
...YOU SHOOT TO *KILL.*

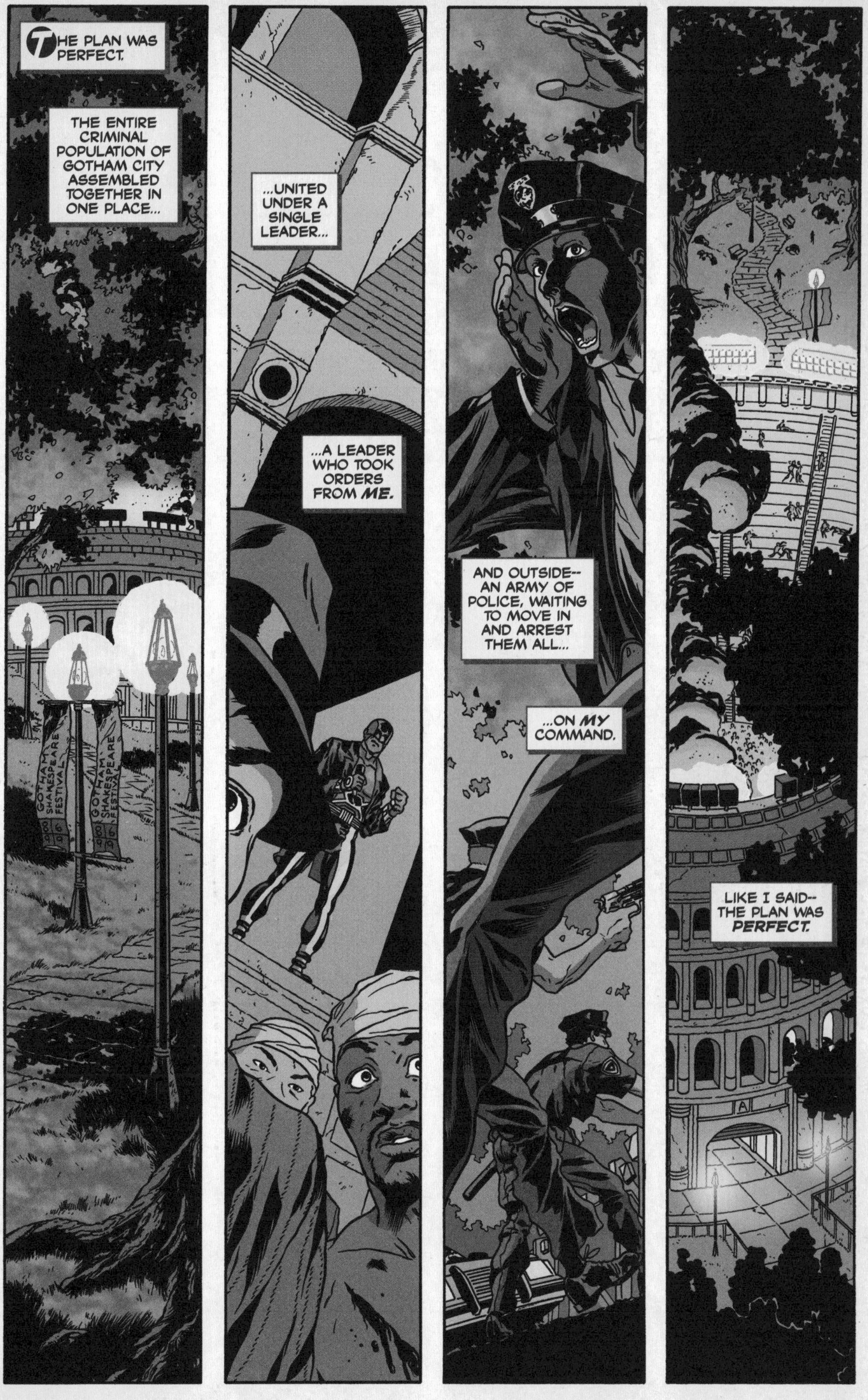
THE PLAN WAS PERFECT.
THE ENTIRE CRIMINAL POPULATION OF GOTHAM CITY ASSEMBLED TOGETHER IN ONE PLACE...
GOTHAM SHAKESPEARE FESTIVAL
...UNITED UNDER A SINGLE LEADER...
...A LEADER WHO TOOK ORDERS FROM ME.
AND OUTSIDE-- AN ARMY OF POLICE, WAITING TO MOVE IN AND ARREST THEM ALL...
...ON MY COMMAND.
LIKE I SAID-- THE PLAN WAS PERFECT.

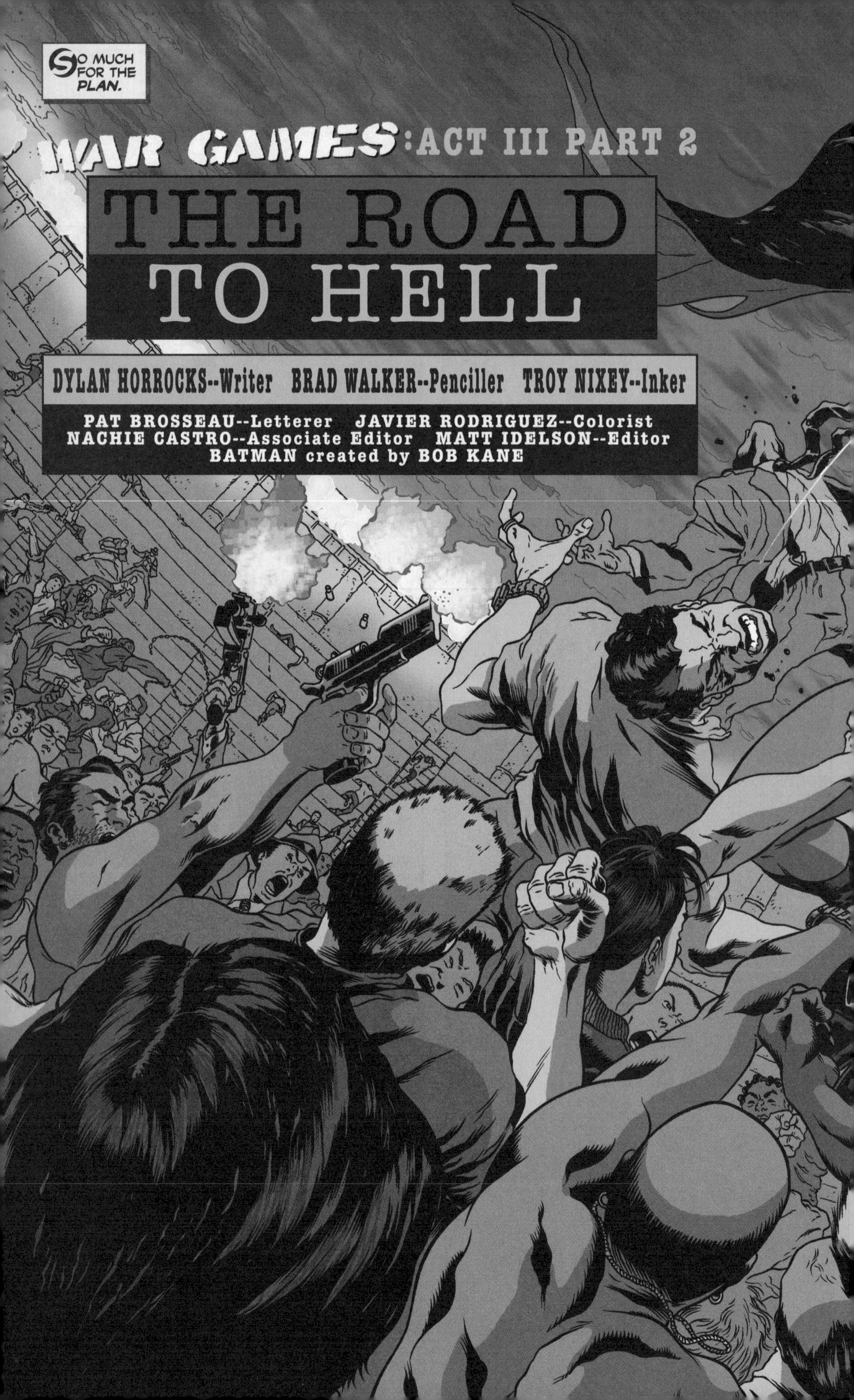
SO MUCH FOR THE PLAN.
WAR GAMES: ACT III PART 2
THE ROAD TO HELL
DYLAN HORROCKS--Writer BRAD WALKER--Penciller TROY NIXEY--Inker
PAT BROSSEAU--Letterer JAVIER RODRIGUEZ--Colorist
NACHIE CASTRO--Associate Editor MATT IDELSON--Editor
BATMAN created by BOB KANE

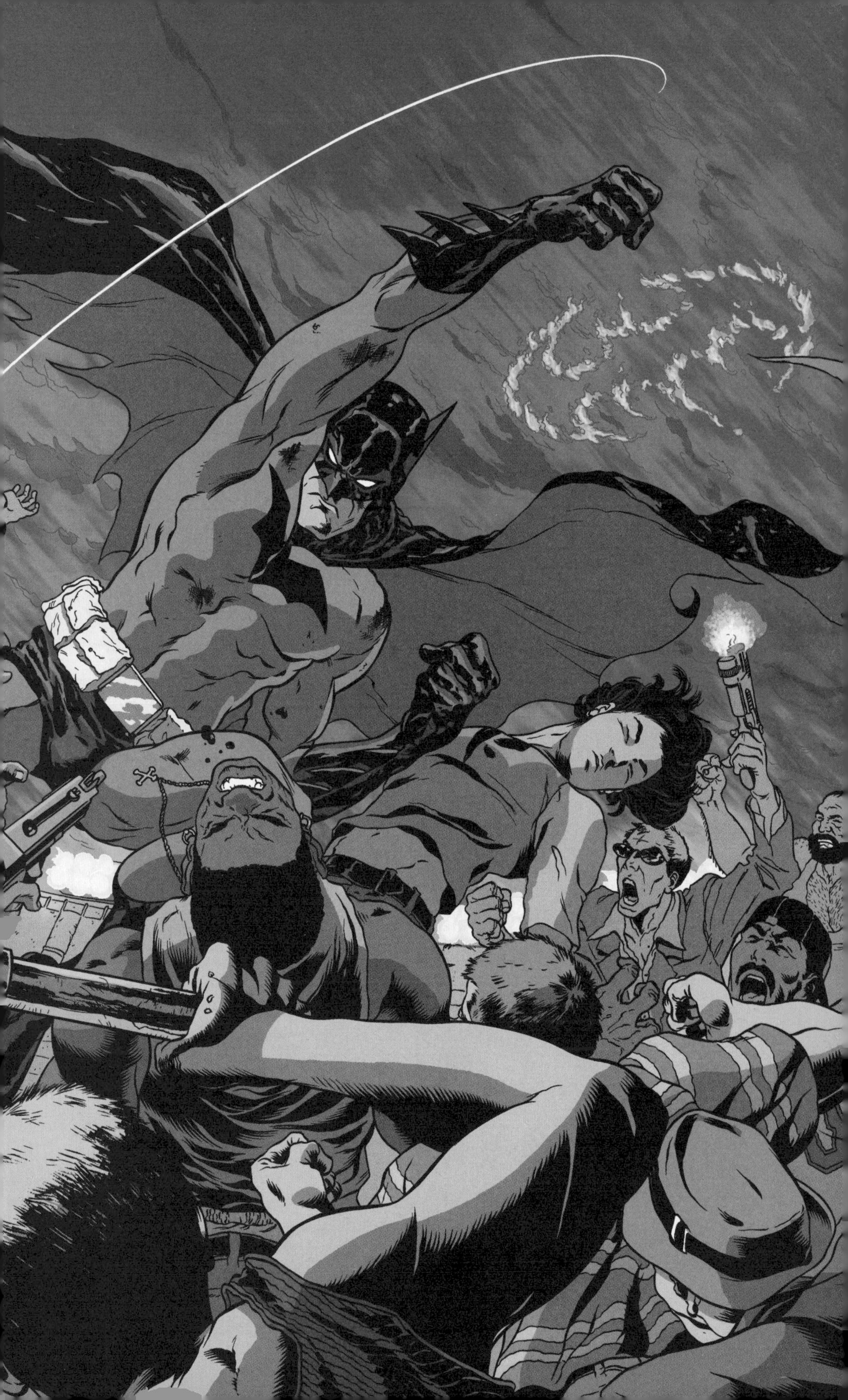

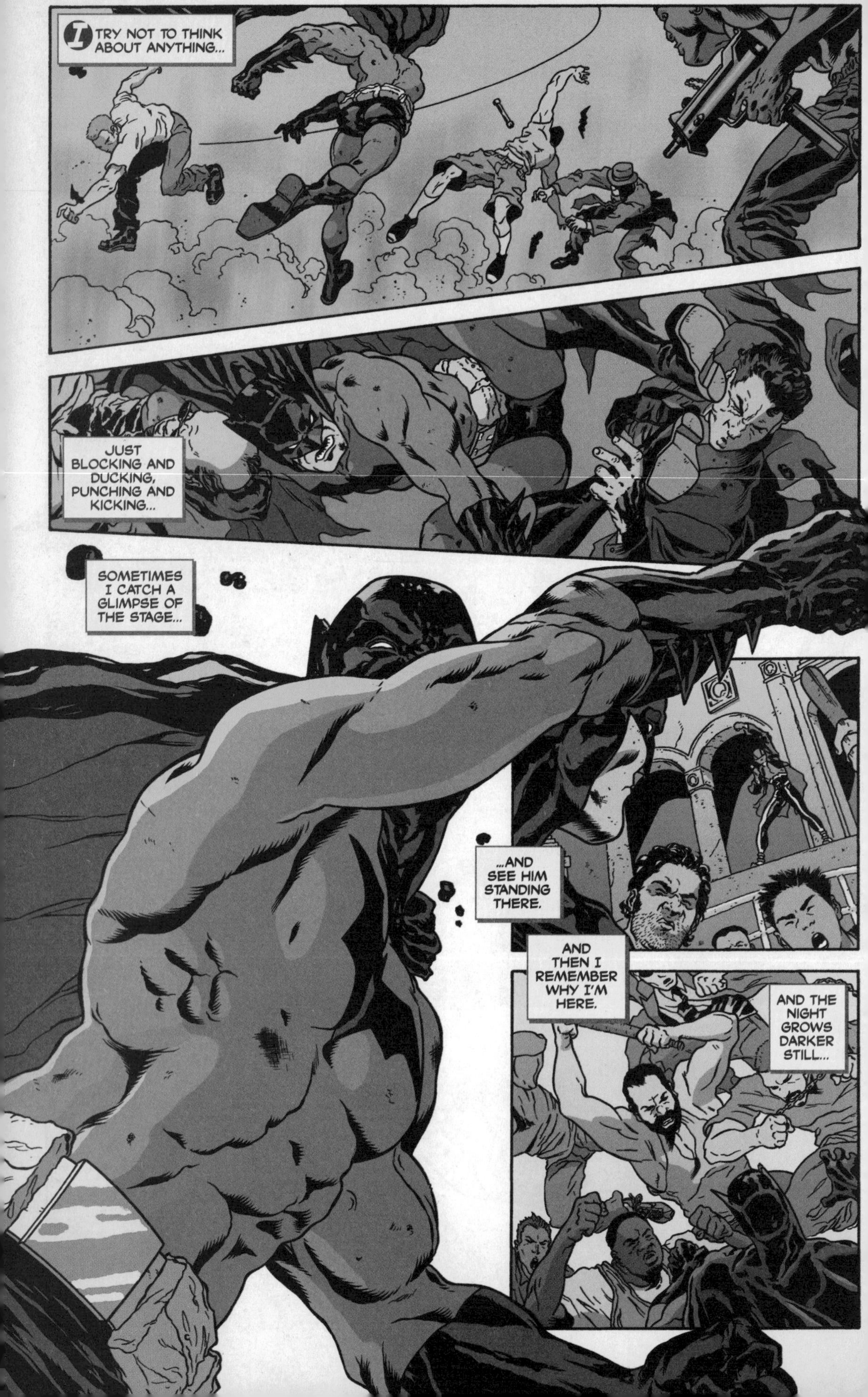
I TRY NOT TO THINK ABOUT ANYTHING...
JUST BLOCKING AND DUCKING, PUNCHING AND KICKING...
SOMETIMES I CATCH A GLIMPSE OF THE STAGE...
...AND SEE HIM STANDING THERE.
AND THEN I REMEMBER WHY I'M HERE.
AND THE NIGHT GROWS DARKER STILL...

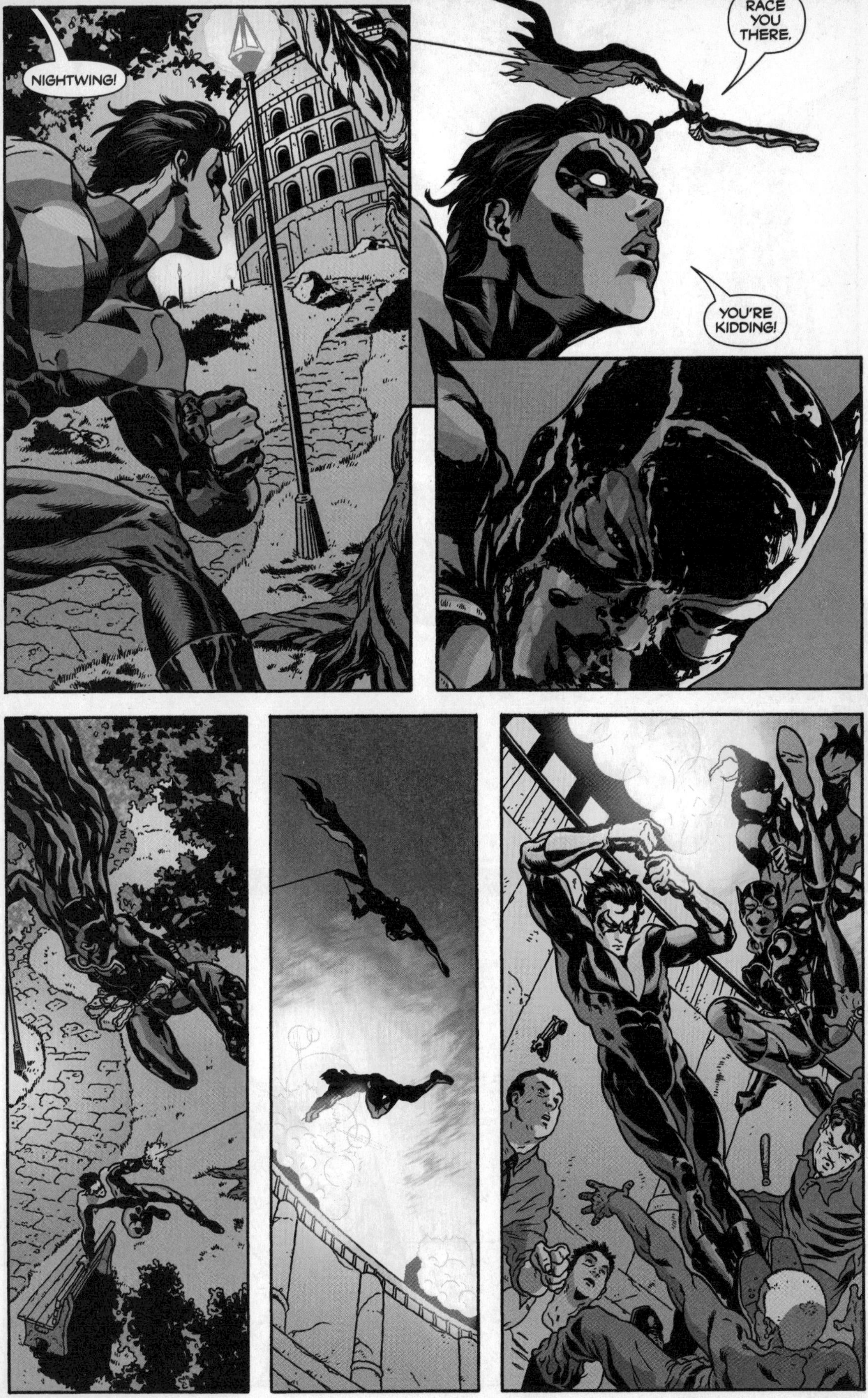
NIGHTWING!
RACE YOU THERE.
YOU'RE KIDDING!

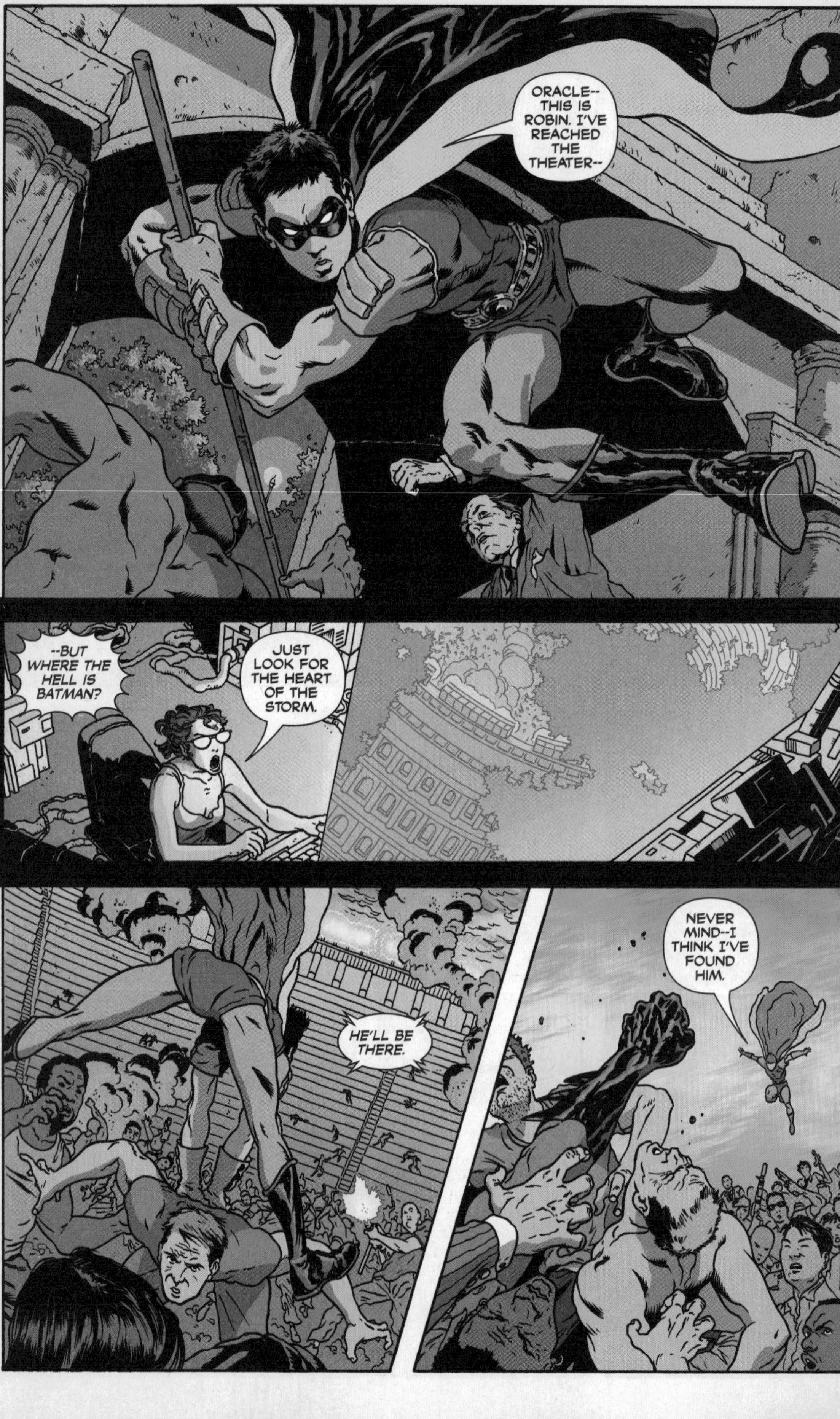
ORACLE--
THIS IS
ROBIN. I'VE
REACHED
THE
THEATER--
--BUT
WHERE THE
HELL IS
BATMAN?
JUST
LOOK FOR
THE HEART
OF THE
STORM.
HE'LL BE
THERE.
NEVER
MIND--I
THINK I'VE
FOUND
HIM.

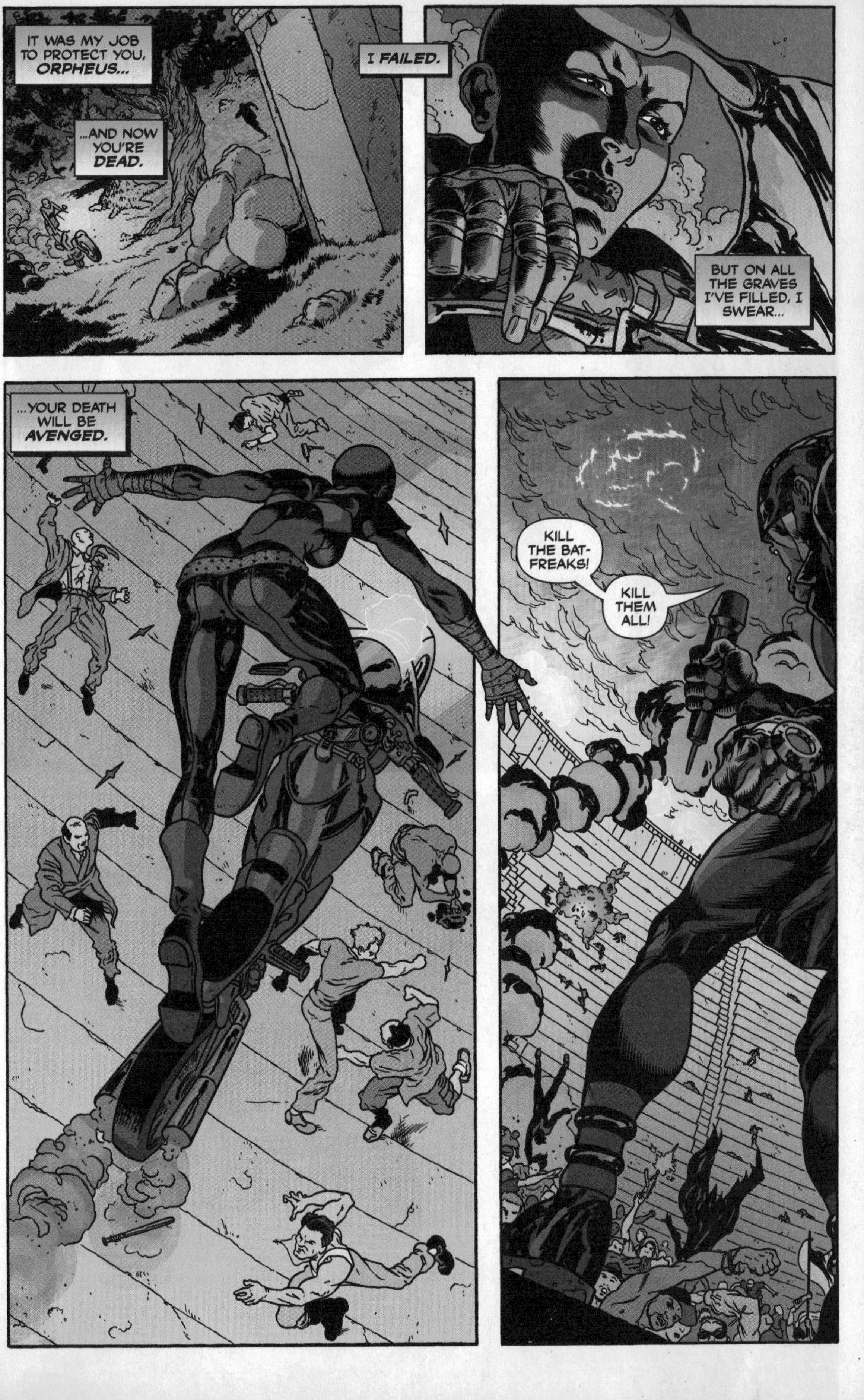
IT WAS MY JOB TO PROTECT YOU, ORPHEUS...
...AND NOW YOU'RE DEAD.
I FAILED.
BUT ON ALL THE GRAVES I'VE FILLED, I SWEAR...
...YOUR DEATH WILL BE AVENGED.
KILL THE BAT-FREAKS!
KILL THEM ALL!

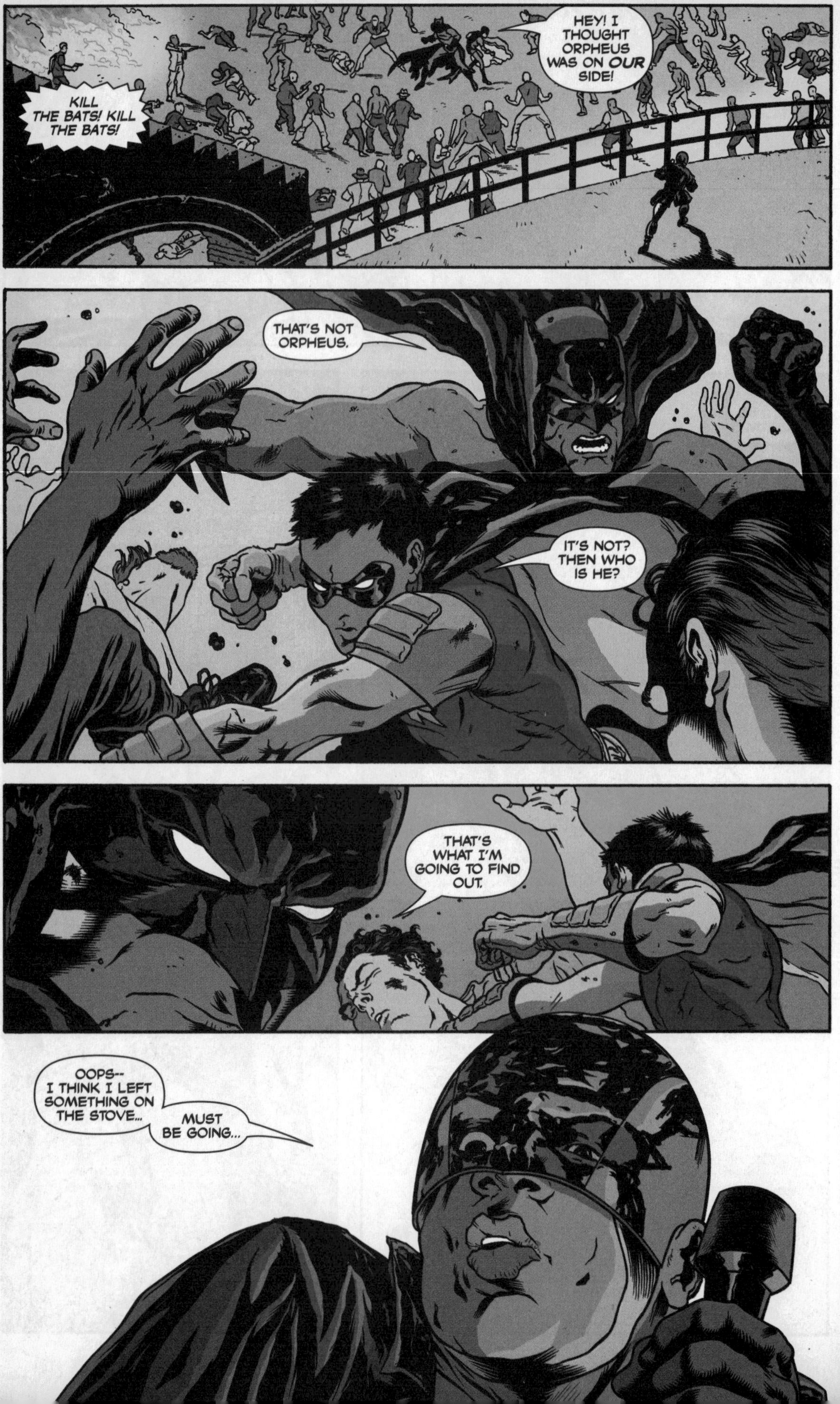
HEY! I THOUGHT ORPHEUS WAS ON OUR SIDE!
KILL THE BATS! KILL THE BATS!
THAT'S NOT ORPHEUS.
IT'S NOT? THEN WHO IS HE?
THAT'S WHAT I'M GOING TO FIND OUT.
OOPS-- I THINK I LEFT SOMETHING ON THE STOVE...
MUST BE GOING...

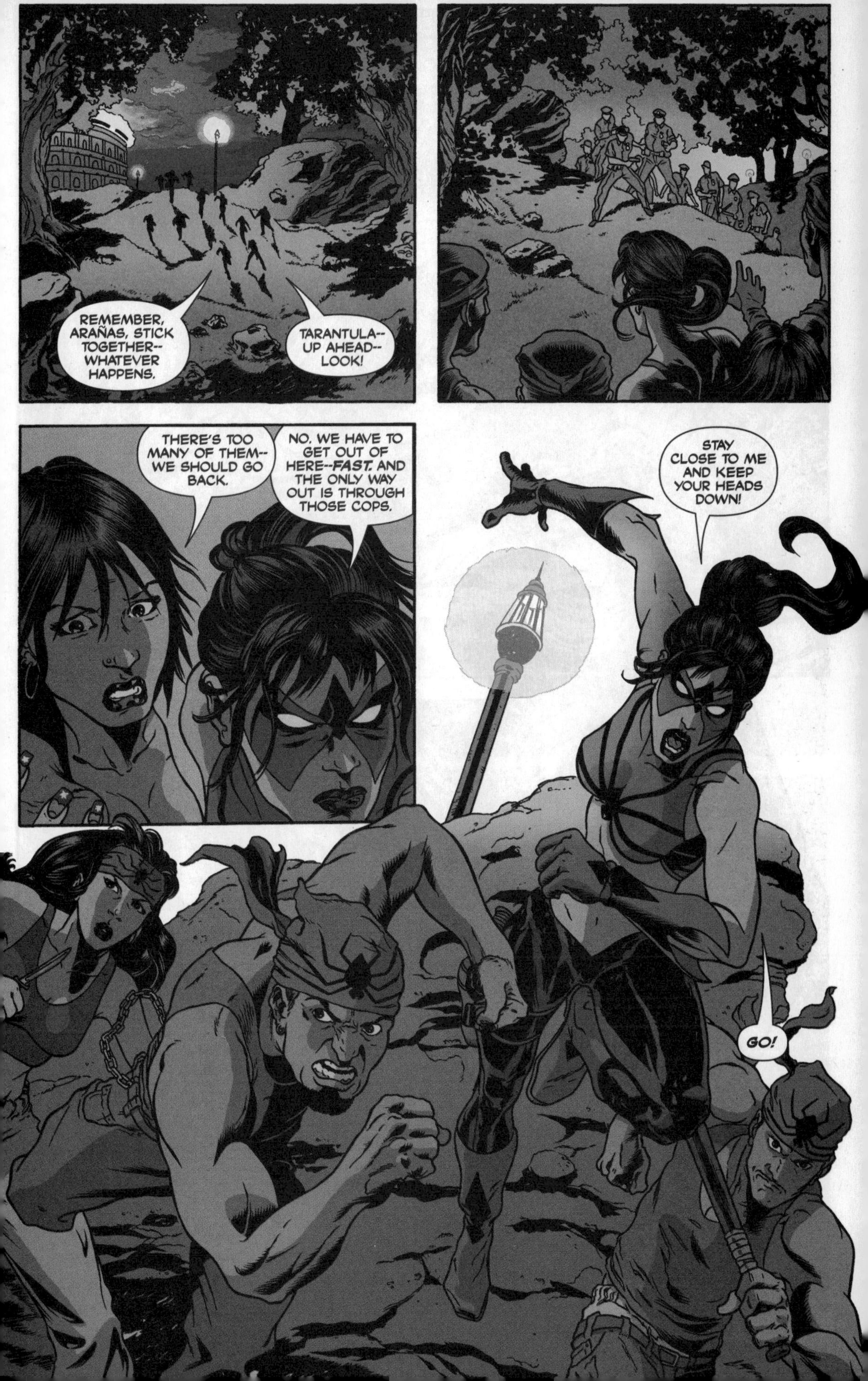
REMEMBER, ARAÑAS, STICK TOGETHER-- WHATEVER HAPPENS.
TARANTULA-- UP AHEAD-- LOOK!
THERE'S TOO MANY OF THEM-- WE SHOULD GO BACK.
NO. WE HAVE TO GET OUT OF HERE--*FAST.* AND THE ONLY WAY OUT IS THROUGH THOSE COPS.
STAY CLOSE TO ME AND KEEP YOUR HEADS DOWN!
GO!

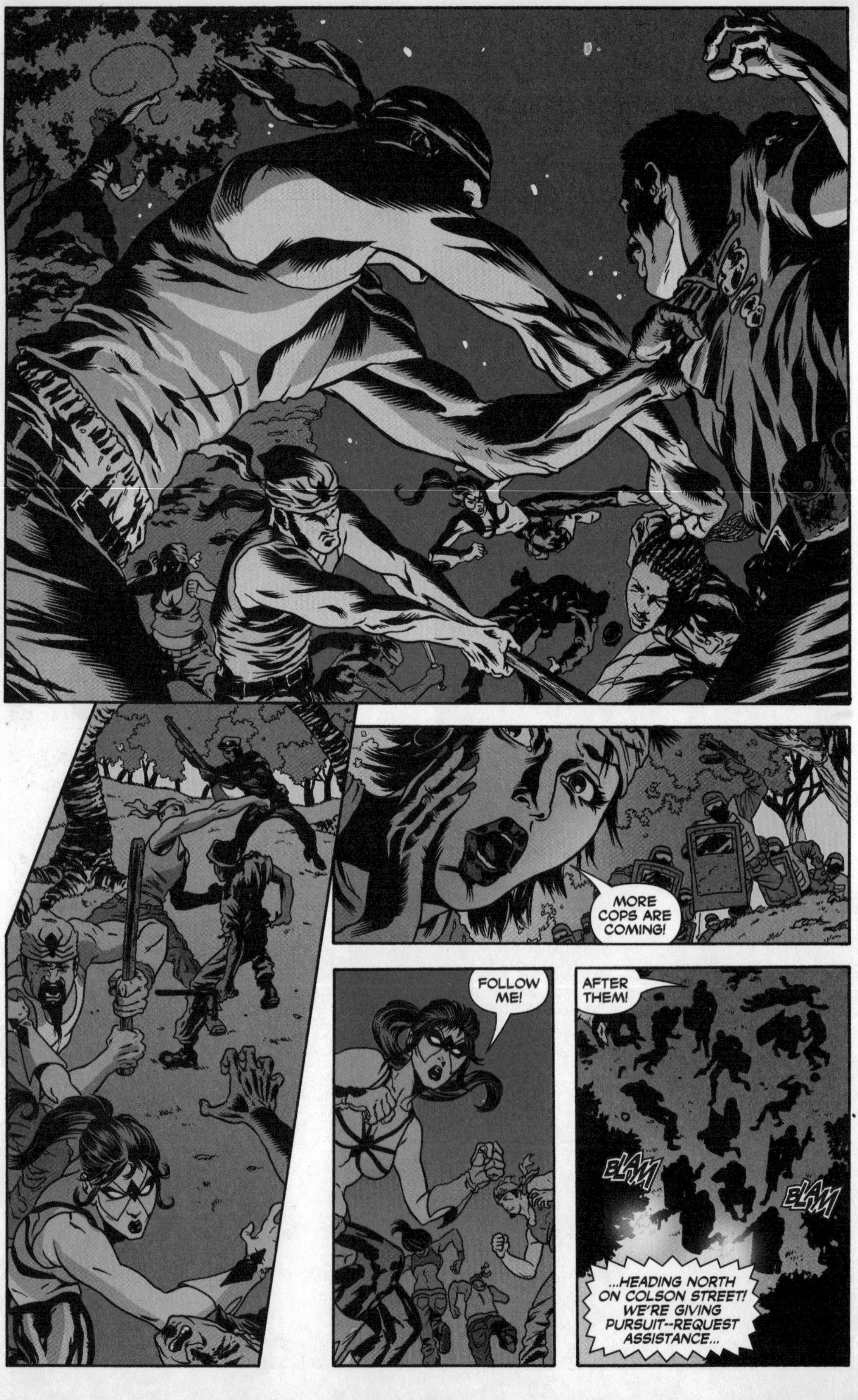
MORE COPS ARE COMING!
FOLLOW ME!
AFTER THEM!
BLAM
BLAM
...HEADING NORTH ON COLSON STREET! WE'RE GIVING PURSUIT--REQUEST ASSISTANCE...

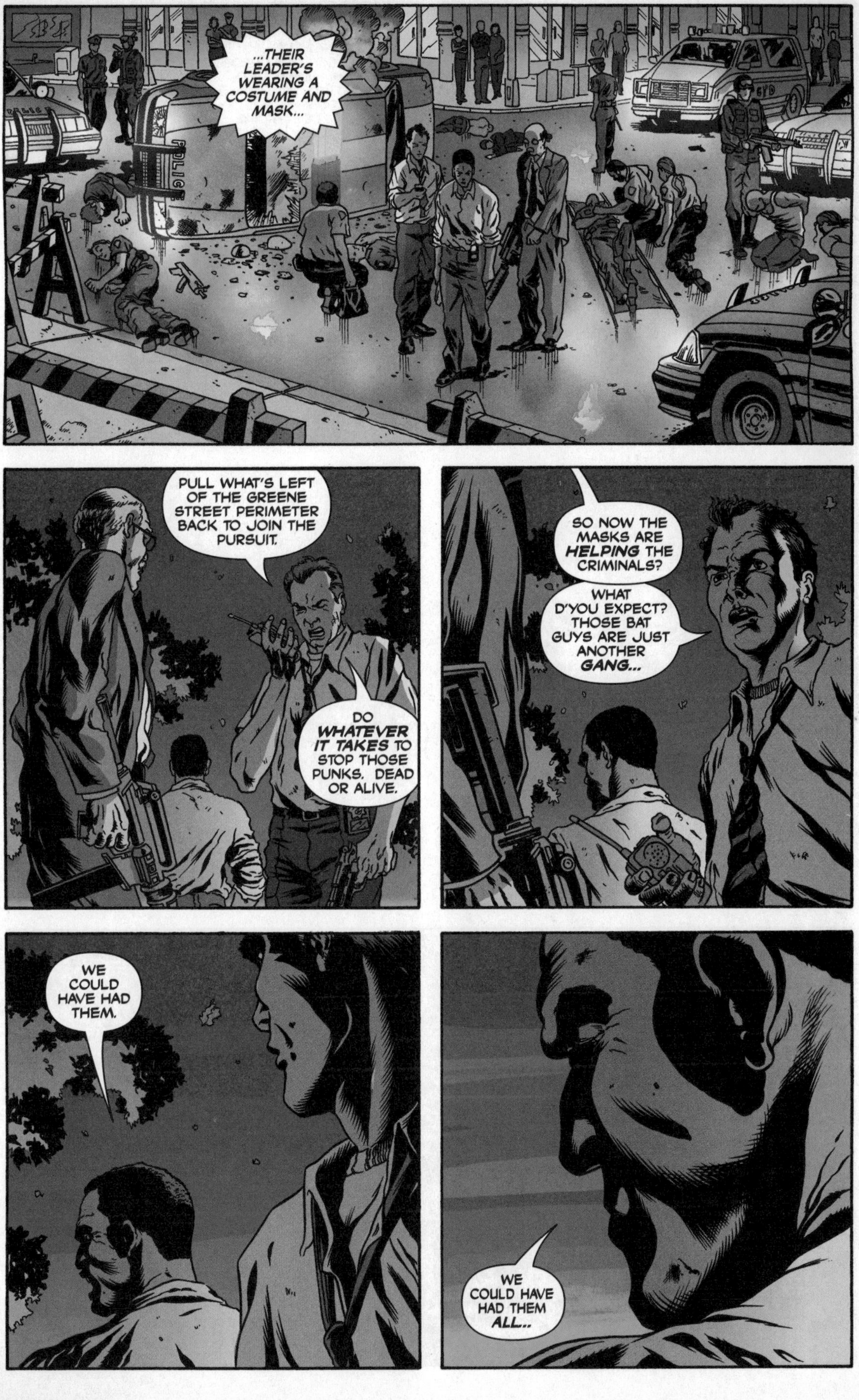
...THEIR LEADER'S WEARING A COSTUME AND MASK...
PULL WHAT'S LEFT OF THE GREENE STREET PERIMETER BACK TO JOIN THE PURSUIT.
DO *WHATEVER IT TAKES* TO STOP THOSE PUNKS. DEAD OR ALIVE.
SO NOW THE MASKS ARE *HELPING* THE CRIMINALS?
WHAT D'YOU EXPECT? THOSE BAT GUYS ARE JUST ANOTHER *GANG*...
WE COULD HAVE HAD THEM.
WE COULD HAVE HAD THEM *ALL*...

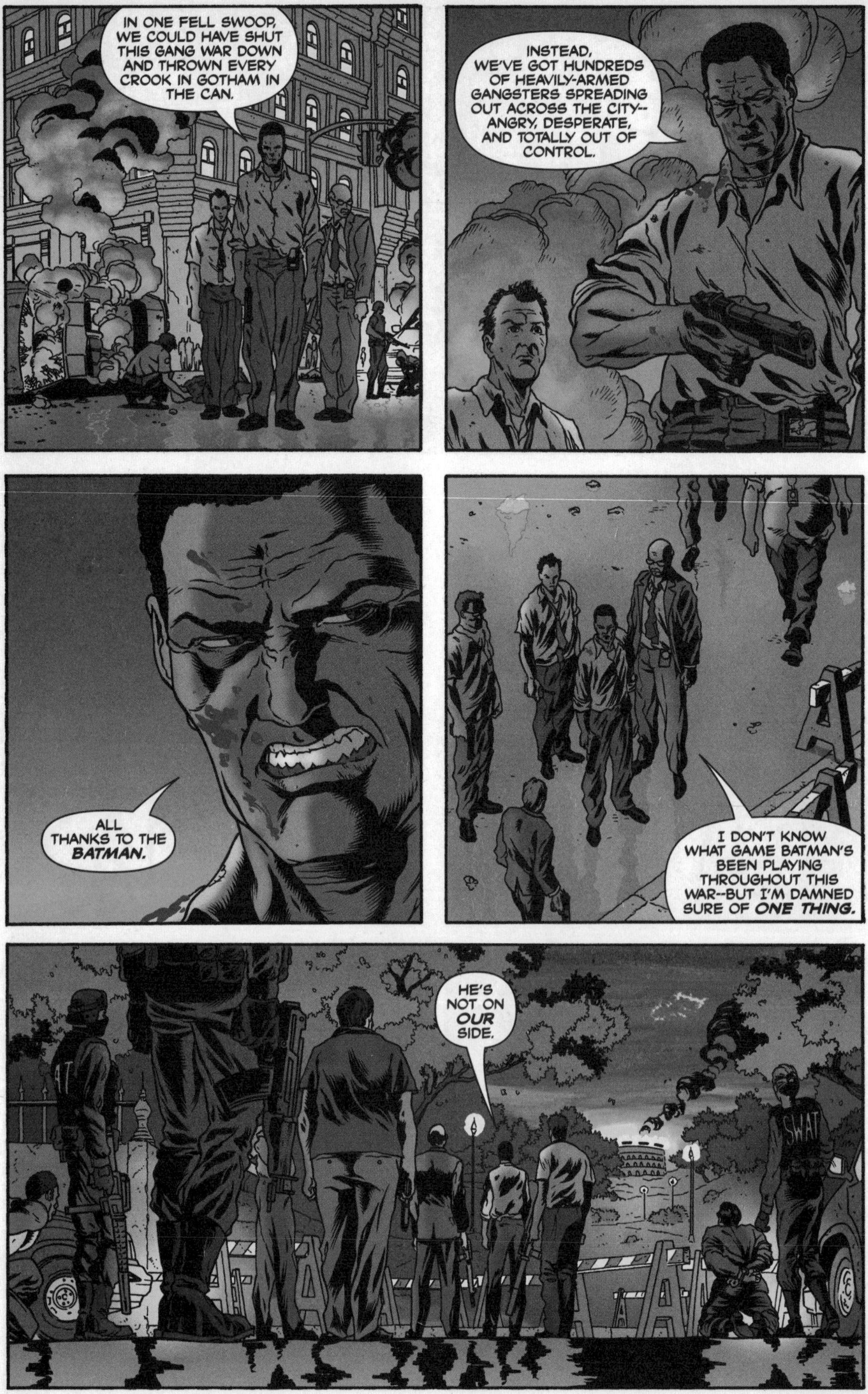
IN ONE FELL SWOOP, WE COULD HAVE SHUT THIS GANG WAR DOWN AND THROWN EVERY CROOK IN GOTHAM IN THE CAN.
INSTEAD, WE'VE GOT HUNDREDS OF HEAVILY-ARMED GANGSTERS SPREADING OUT ACROSS THE CITY--ANGRY, DESPERATE, AND TOTALLY OUT OF CONTROL.
ALL THANKS TO THE *BATMAN.*
I DON'T KNOW WHAT GAME BATMAN'S BEEN PLAYING THROUGHOUT THIS WAR--BUT I'M DAMNED SURE OF *ONE THING.*
HE'S NOT ON *OUR* SIDE.
SWAT

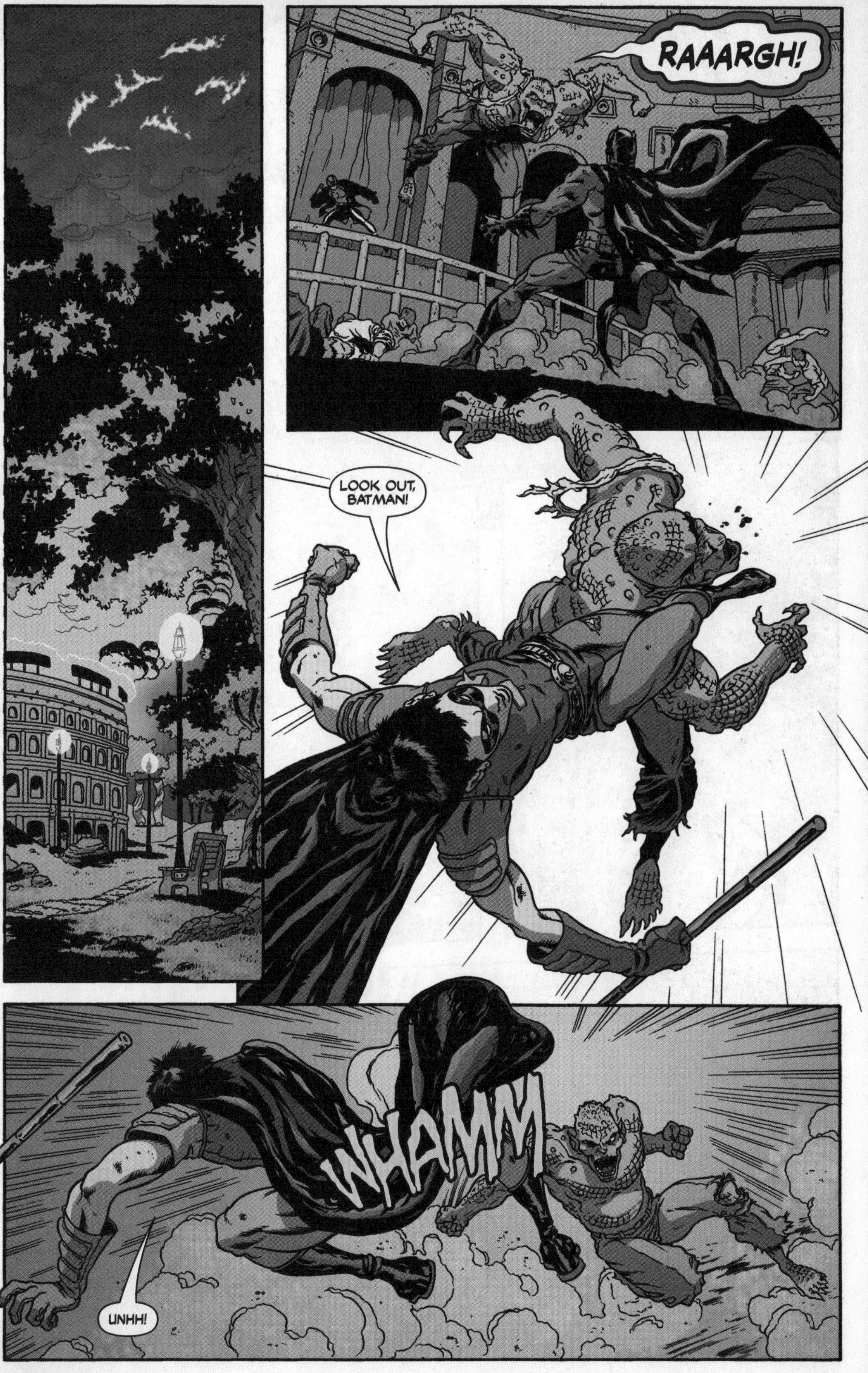
RAAARGH!
LOOK OUT, BATMAN!
WHAMM
UNHH!

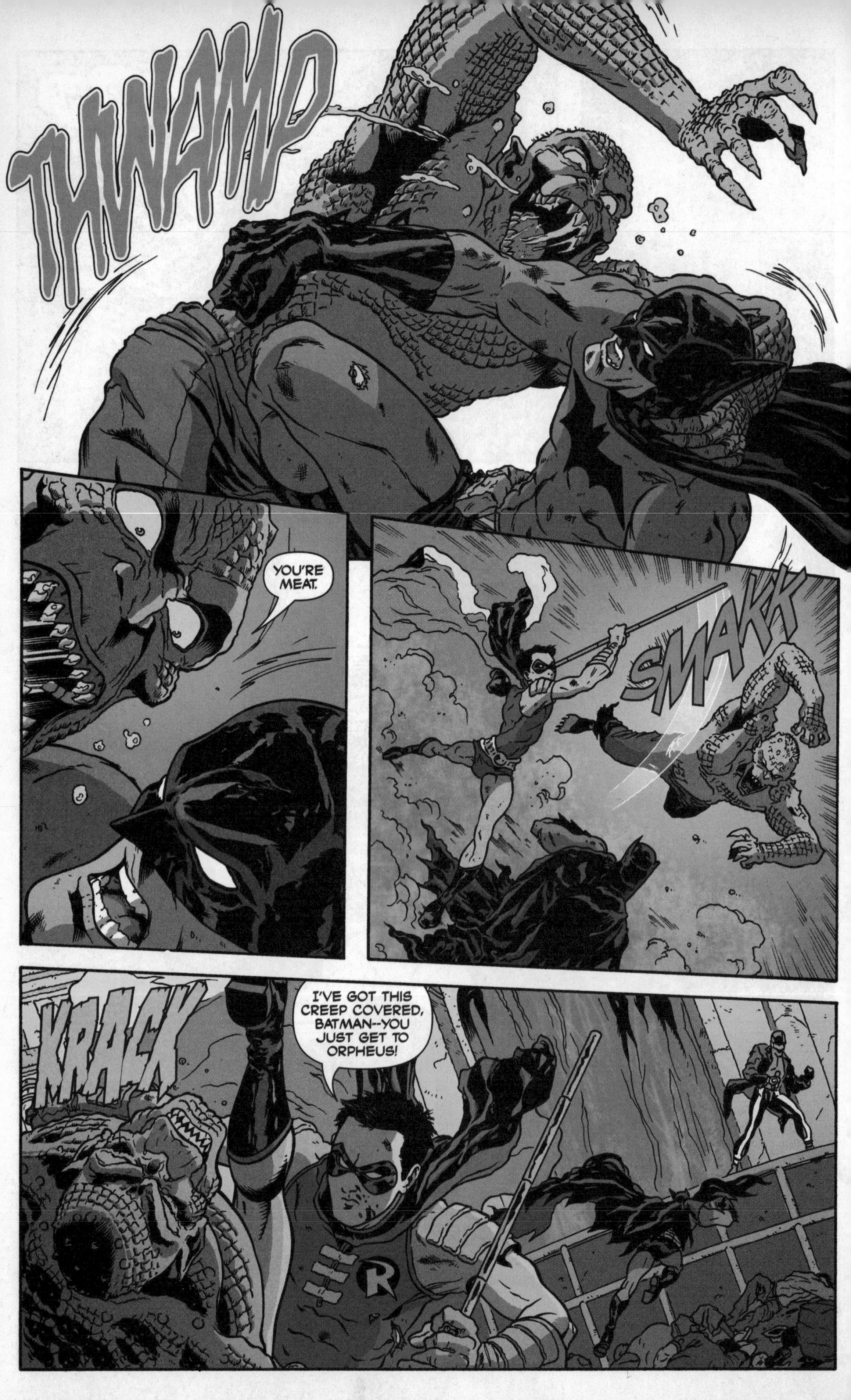
THWAMP
YOU'RE MEAT.
SMAKK
KRACK
I'VE GOT THIS CREEP COVERED, BATMAN--YOU JUST GET TO ORPHEUS!

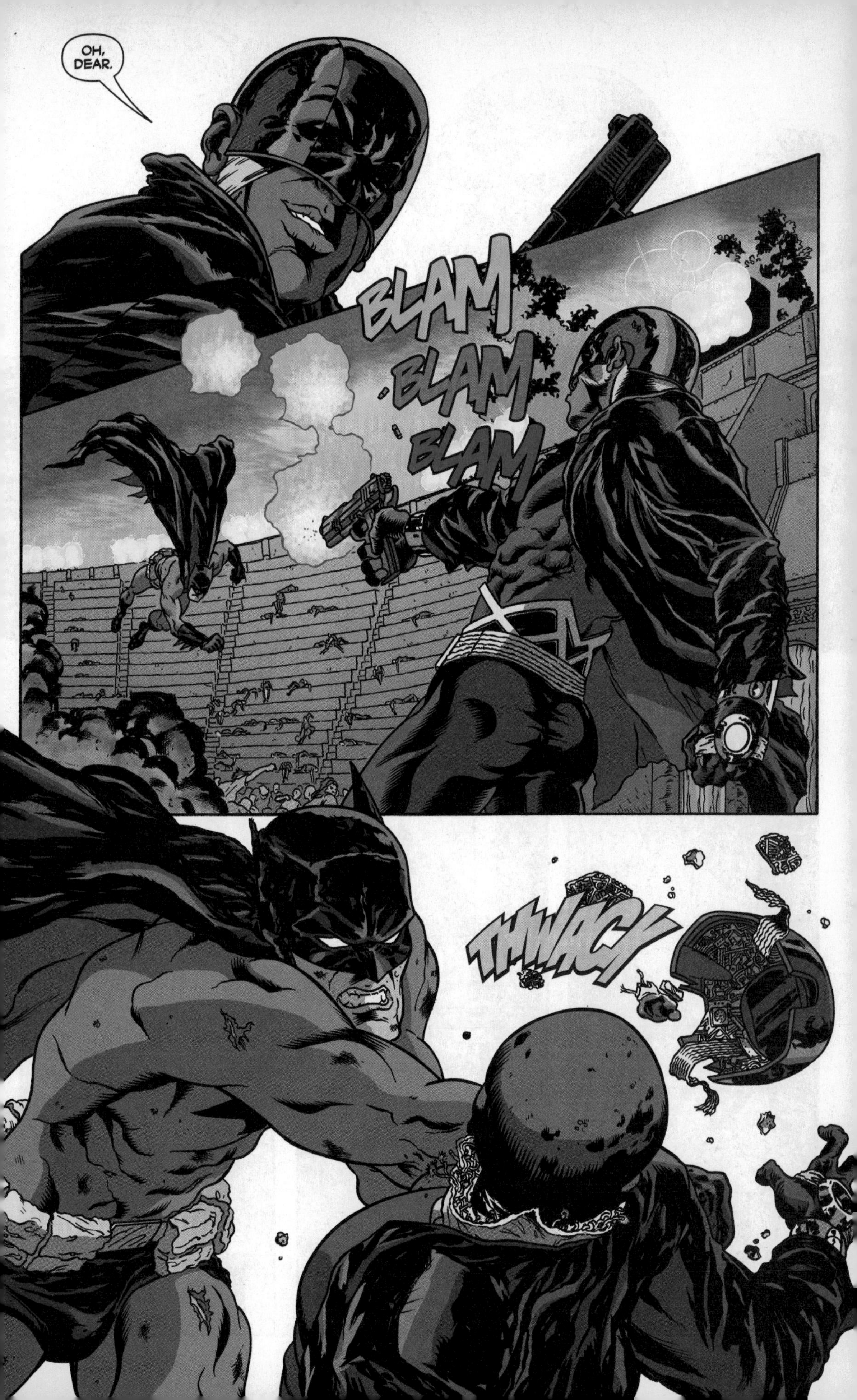
OH, DEAR.
BLAM
BLAM
BLAM
THWACK

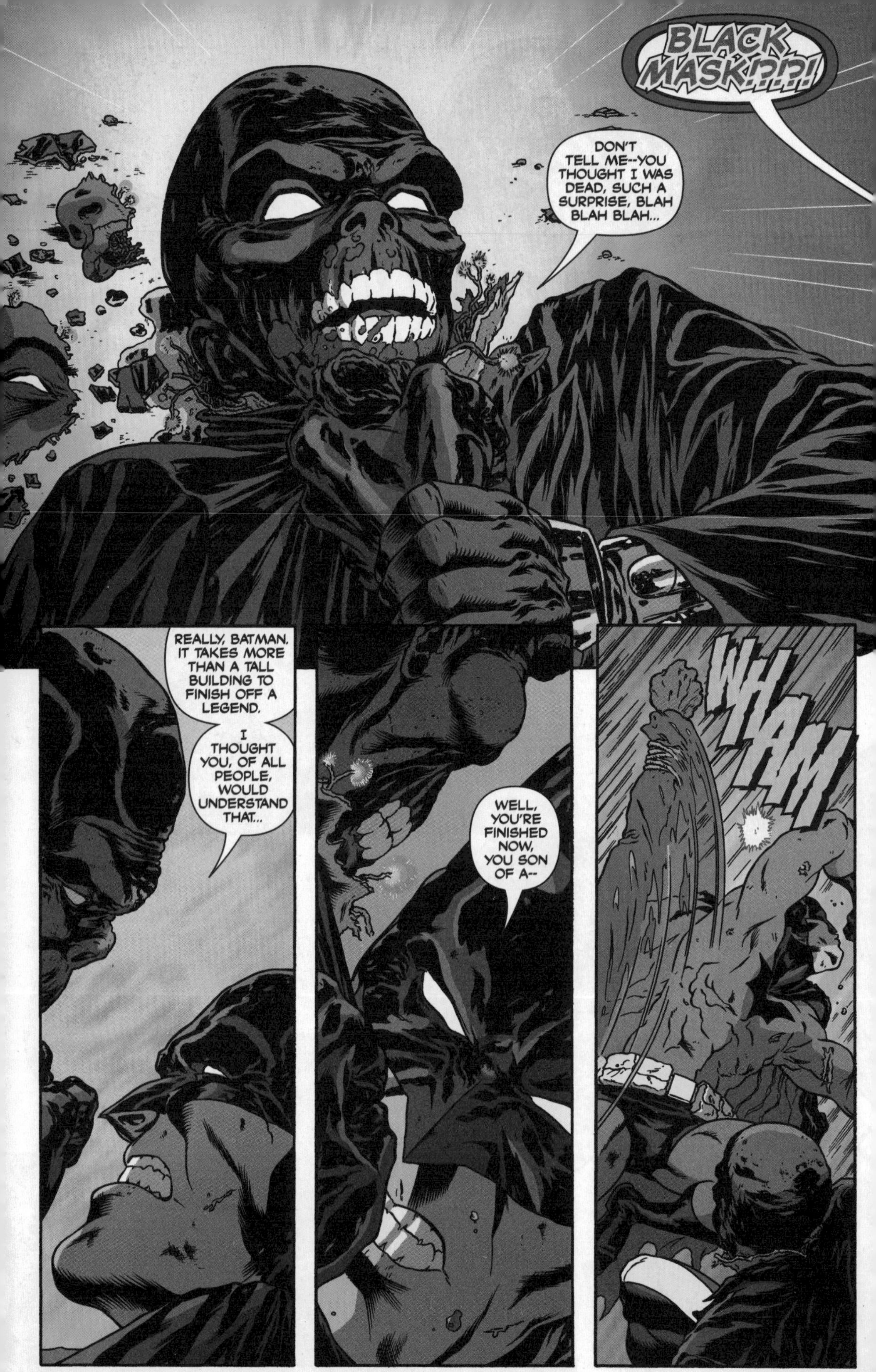
BLACK MASK!?!?!
DON'T TELL ME--YOU THOUGHT I WAS DEAD, SUCH A SURPRISE, BLAH BLAH BLAH...
REALLY, BATMAN. IT TAKES MORE THAN A TALL BUILDING TO FINISH OFF A LEGEND.
I THOUGHT YOU, OF ALL PEOPLE, WOULD UNDERSTAND THAT...
WELL, YOU'RE FINISHED NOW, YOU SON OF A--
WHAM

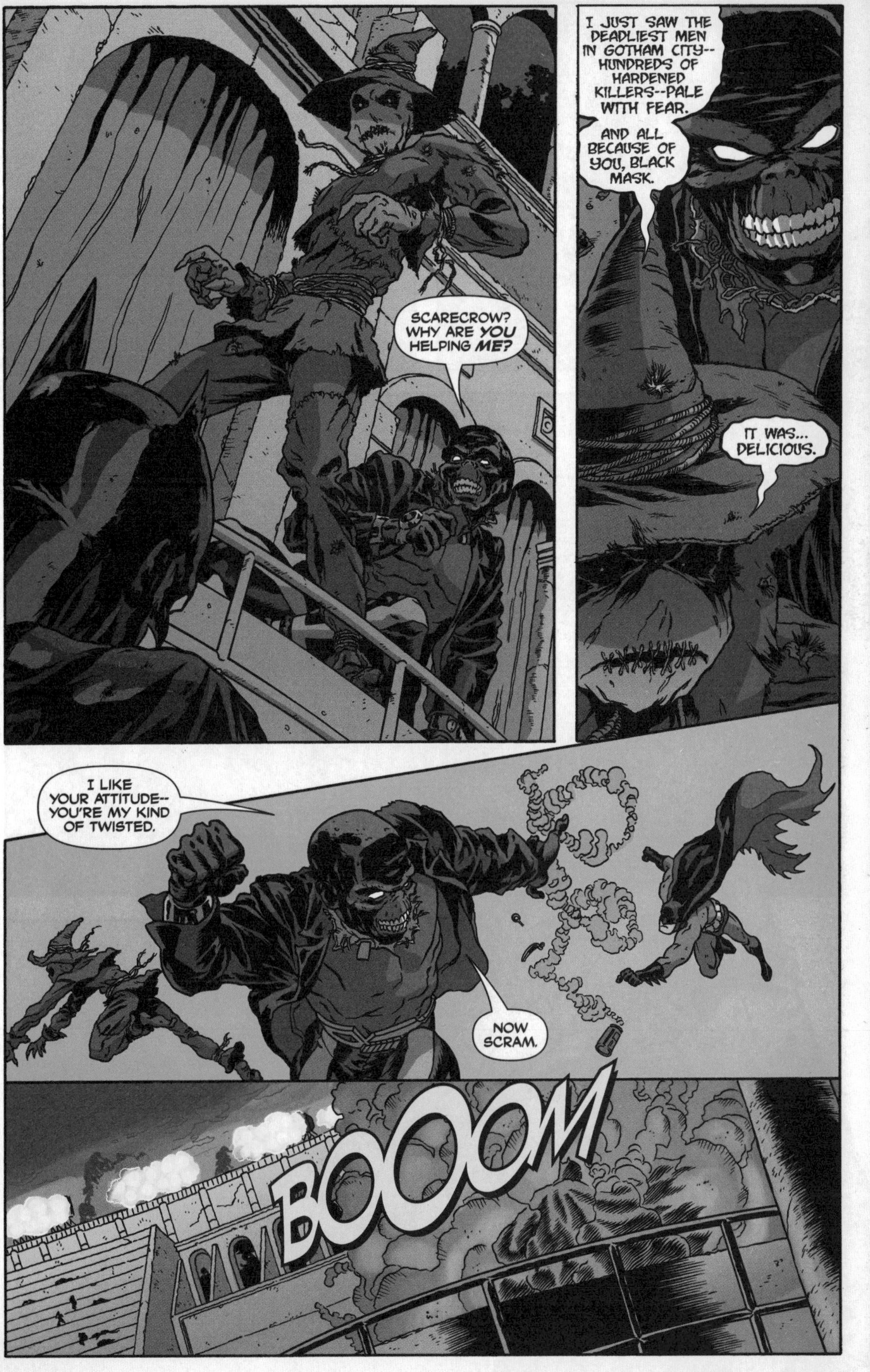
SCARECROW? WHY ARE YOU HELPING ME?
I JUST SAW THE DEADLIEST MEN IN GOTHAM CITY-- HUNDREDS OF HARDENED KILLERS--PALE WITH FEAR.
AND ALL BECAUSE OF YOU, BLACK MASK.
IT WAS... DELICIOUS.
I LIKE YOUR ATTITUDE-- YOU'RE MY KIND OF TWISTED.
NOW SCRAM.
BOOOOM

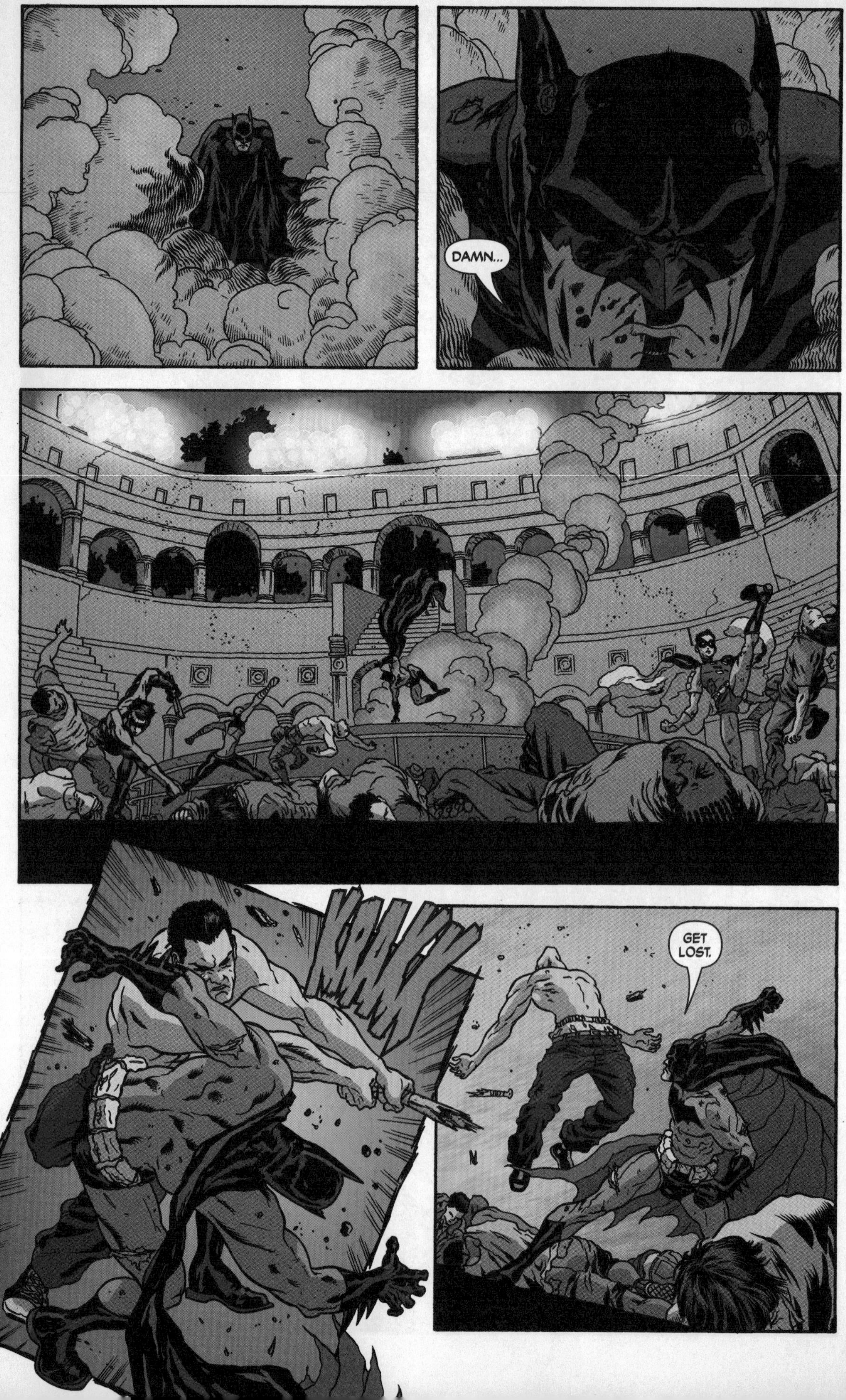
DAMN...
GET LOST.

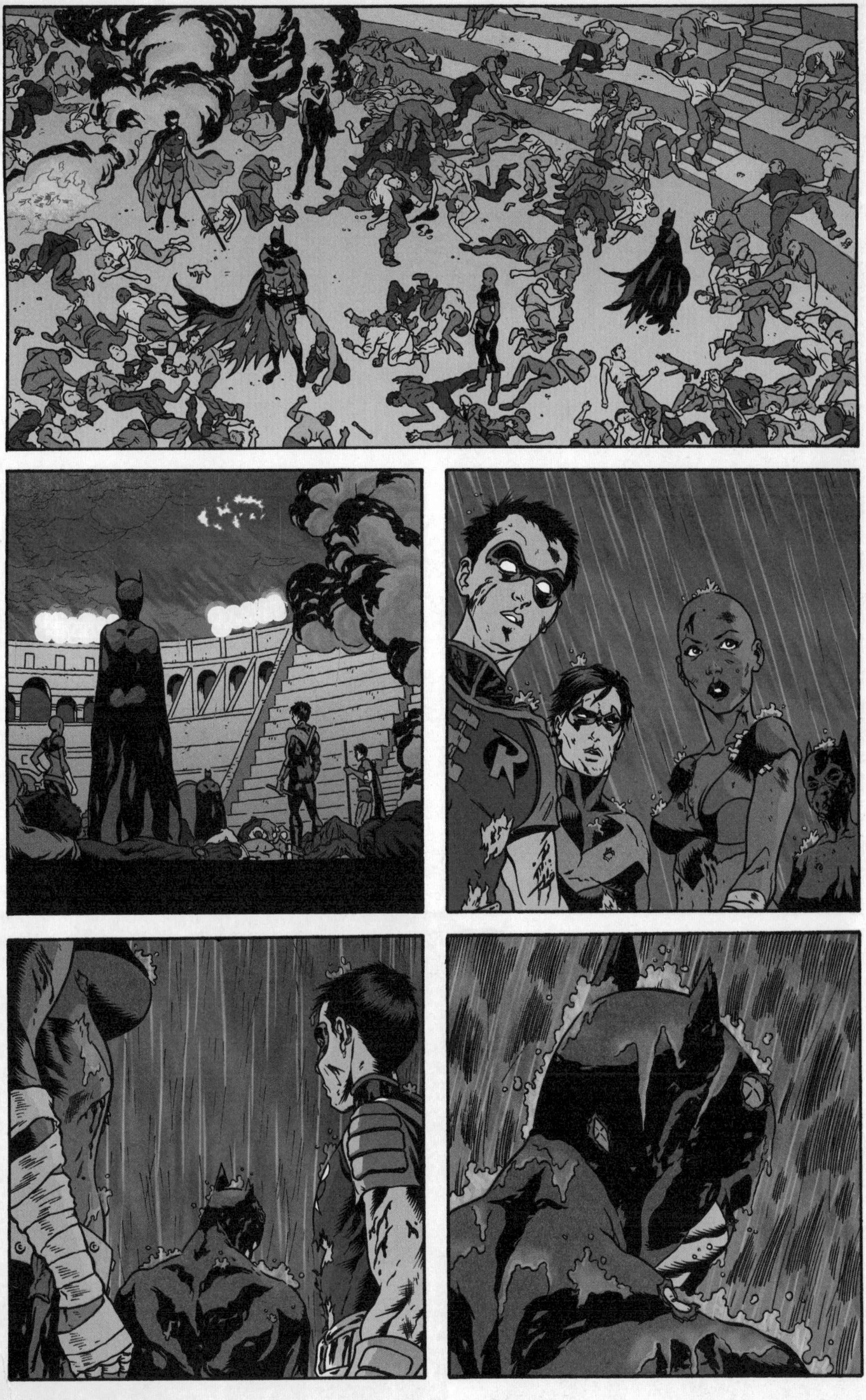

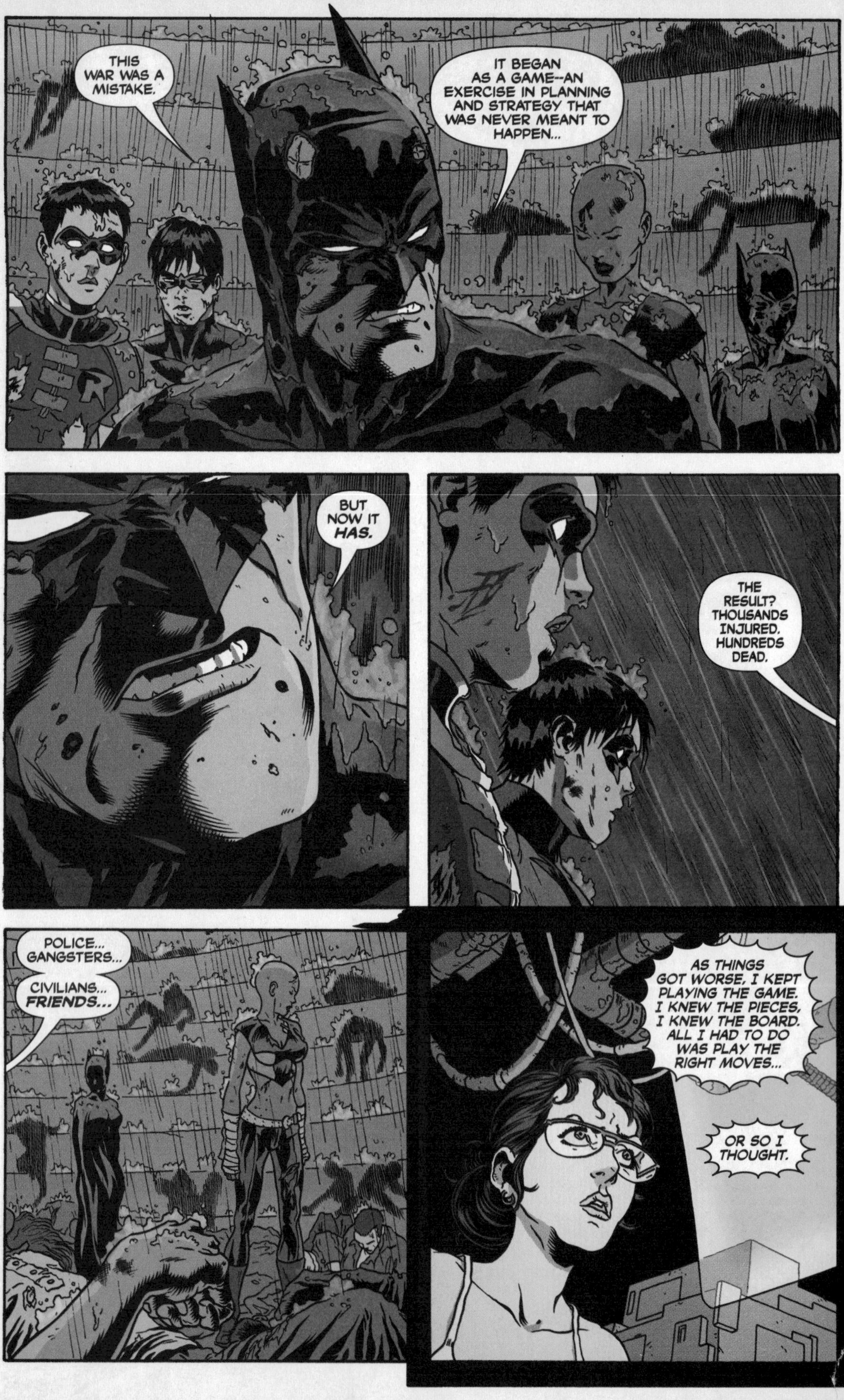
THIS WAR WAS A MISTAKE.
IT BEGAN AS A GAME--AN EXERCISE IN PLANNING AND STRATEGY THAT WAS NEVER MEANT TO HAPPEN...
BUT NOW IT *HAS.*
THE RESULT? THOUSANDS INJURED. HUNDREDS DEAD.
POLICE... GANGSTERS...
CIVILIANS... *FRIENDS...*
AS THINGS GOT WORSE, I KEPT PLAYING THE GAME. I KNEW THE PIECES, I KNEW THE BOARD. ALL I HAD TO DO WAS PLAY THE RIGHT MOVES...
OR SO I THOUGHT.

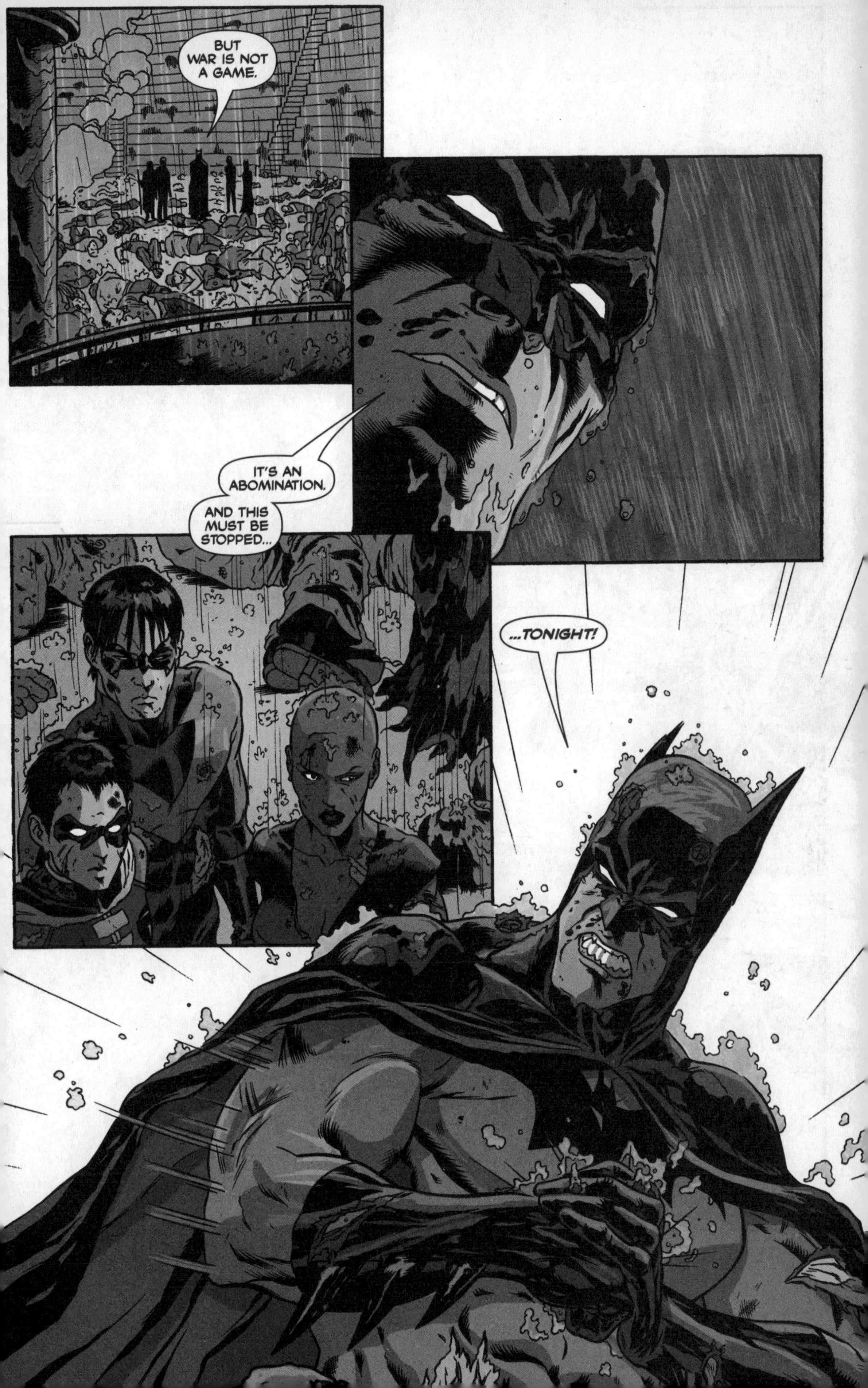
BUT WAR IS NOT A GAME.
IT'S AN ABOMINATION.
AND THIS MUST BE STOPPED...
...TONIGHT!

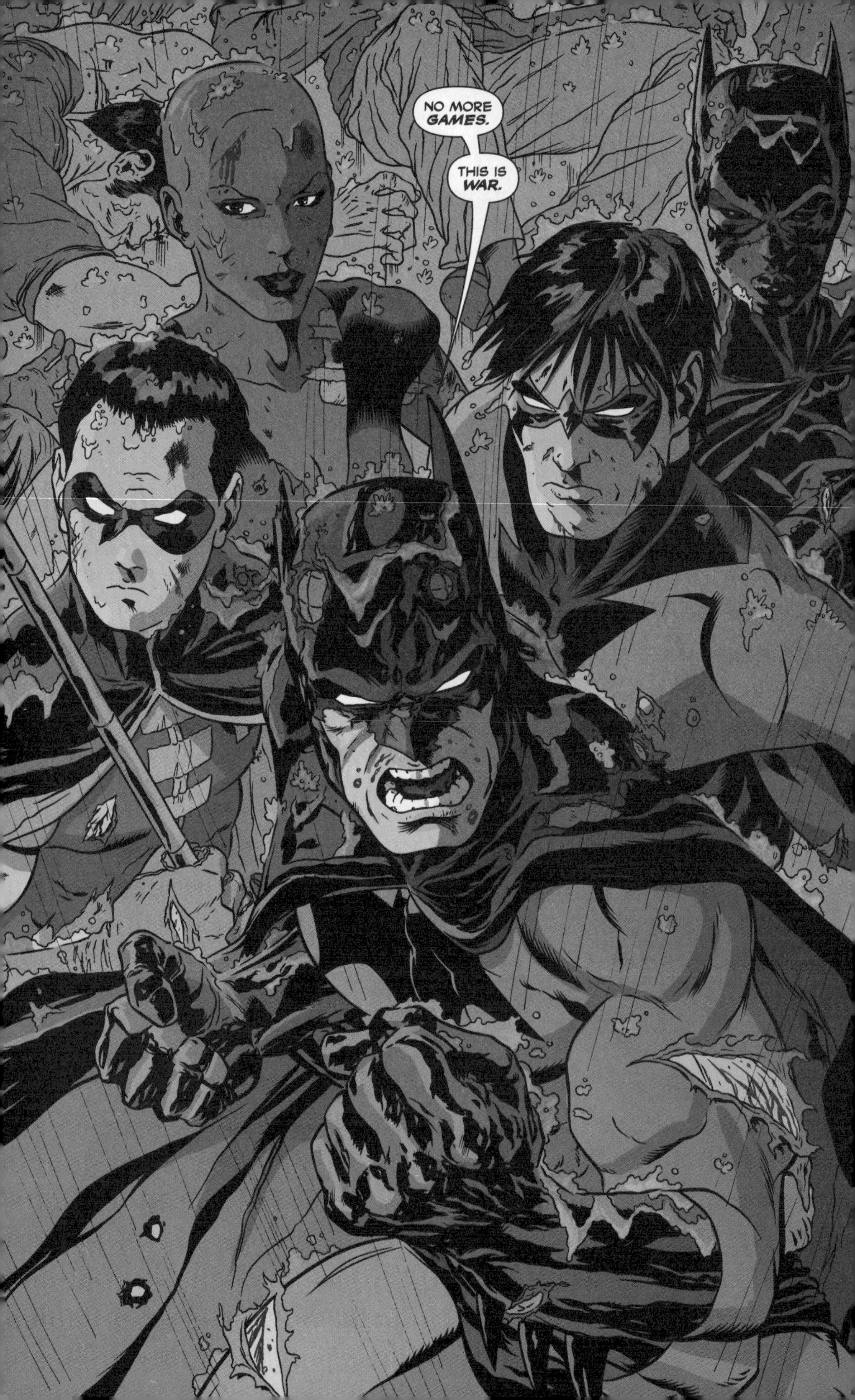
NO MORE GAMES.
THIS IS WAR.

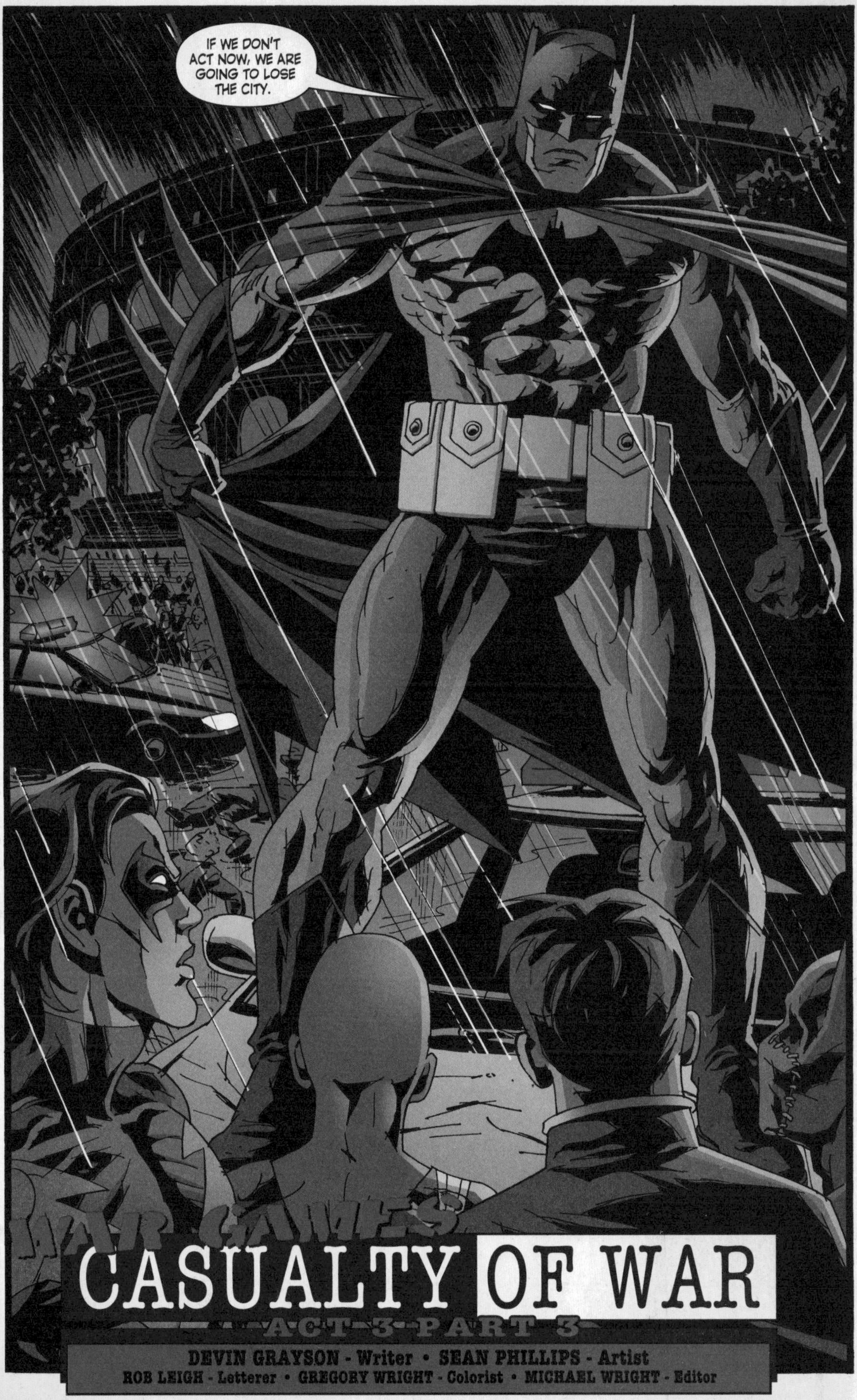
IF WE DON'T ACT NOW, WE ARE GOING TO LOSE THE CITY.
WAR GAMES
CASUALTY OF WAR
ACT 3 PART 3
DEVIN GRAYSON - Writer • SEAN PHILLIPS - Artist
ROB LEIGH - Letterer • GREGORY WRIGHT - Colorist • MICHAEL WRIGHT - Editor

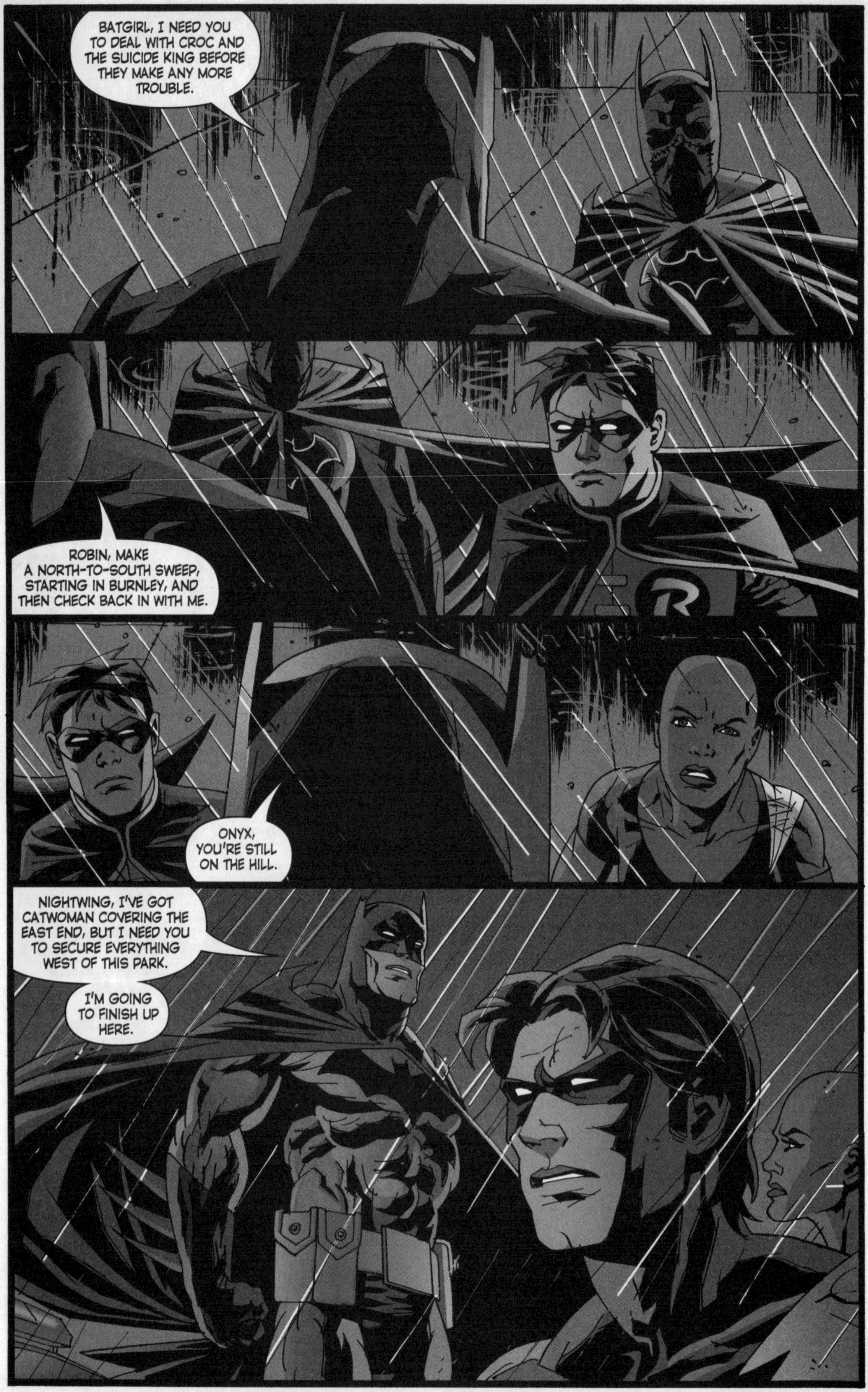
BATGIRL, I NEED YOU TO DEAL WITH CROC AND THE SUICIDE KING BEFORE THEY MAKE ANY MORE TROUBLE.
ROBIN, MAKE A NORTH-TO-SOUTH SWEEP, STARTING IN BURNLEY, AND THEN CHECK BACK IN WITH ME.
ONYX, YOU'RE STILL ON THE HILL.
NIGHTWING, I'VE GOT CATWOMAN COVERING THE EAST END, BUT I NEED YOU TO SECURE EVERYTHING WEST OF THIS PARK.
I'M GOING TO FINISH UP HERE.

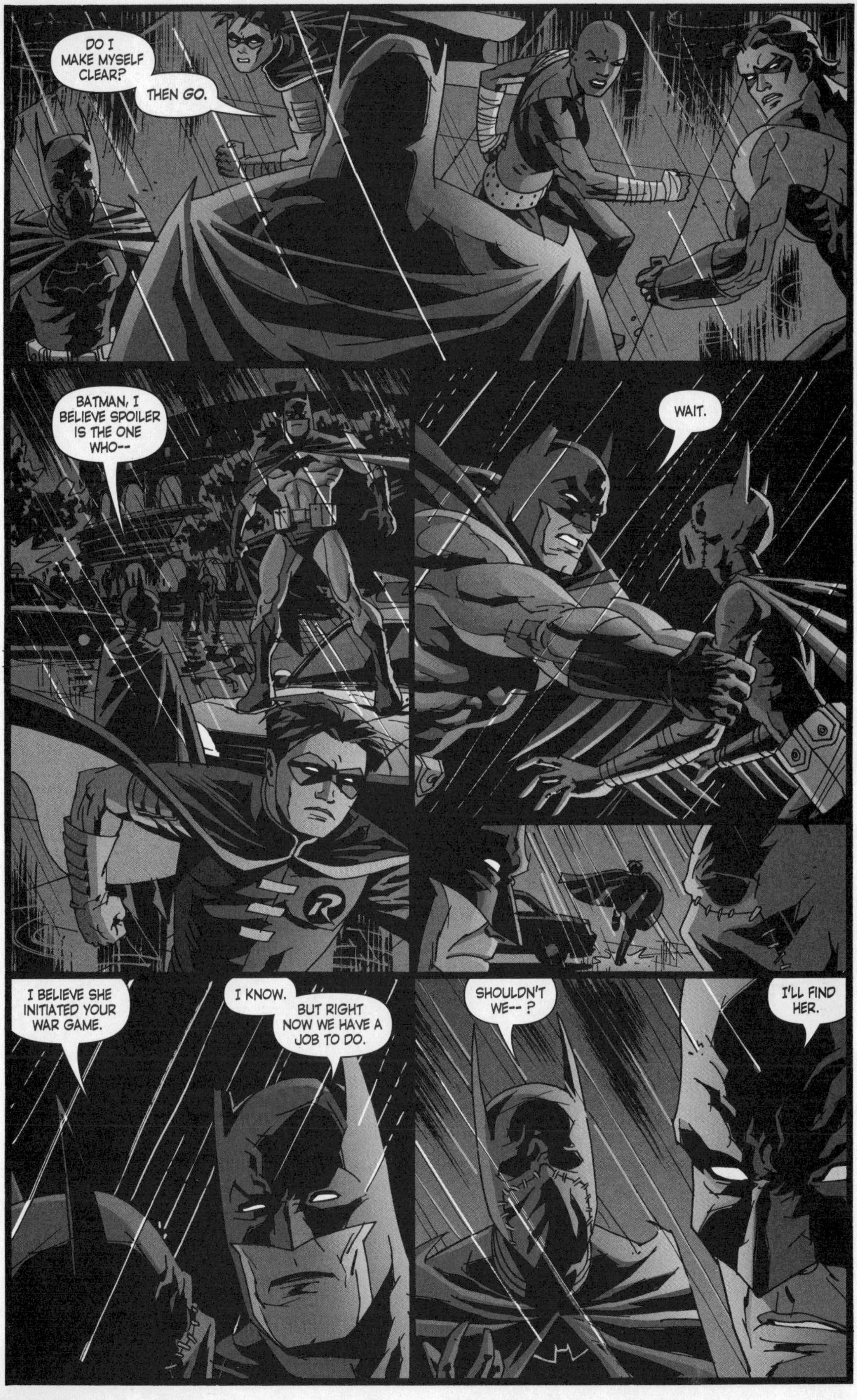
DO I MAKE MYSELF CLEAR?
THEN GO.
BATMAN, I BELIEVE SPOILER IS THE ONE WHO--
WAIT.
I BELIEVE SHE INITIATED YOUR WAR GAME.
I KNOW.
BUT RIGHT NOW WE HAVE A JOB TO DO.
SHOULDN'T WE-- ?
I'LL FIND HER.

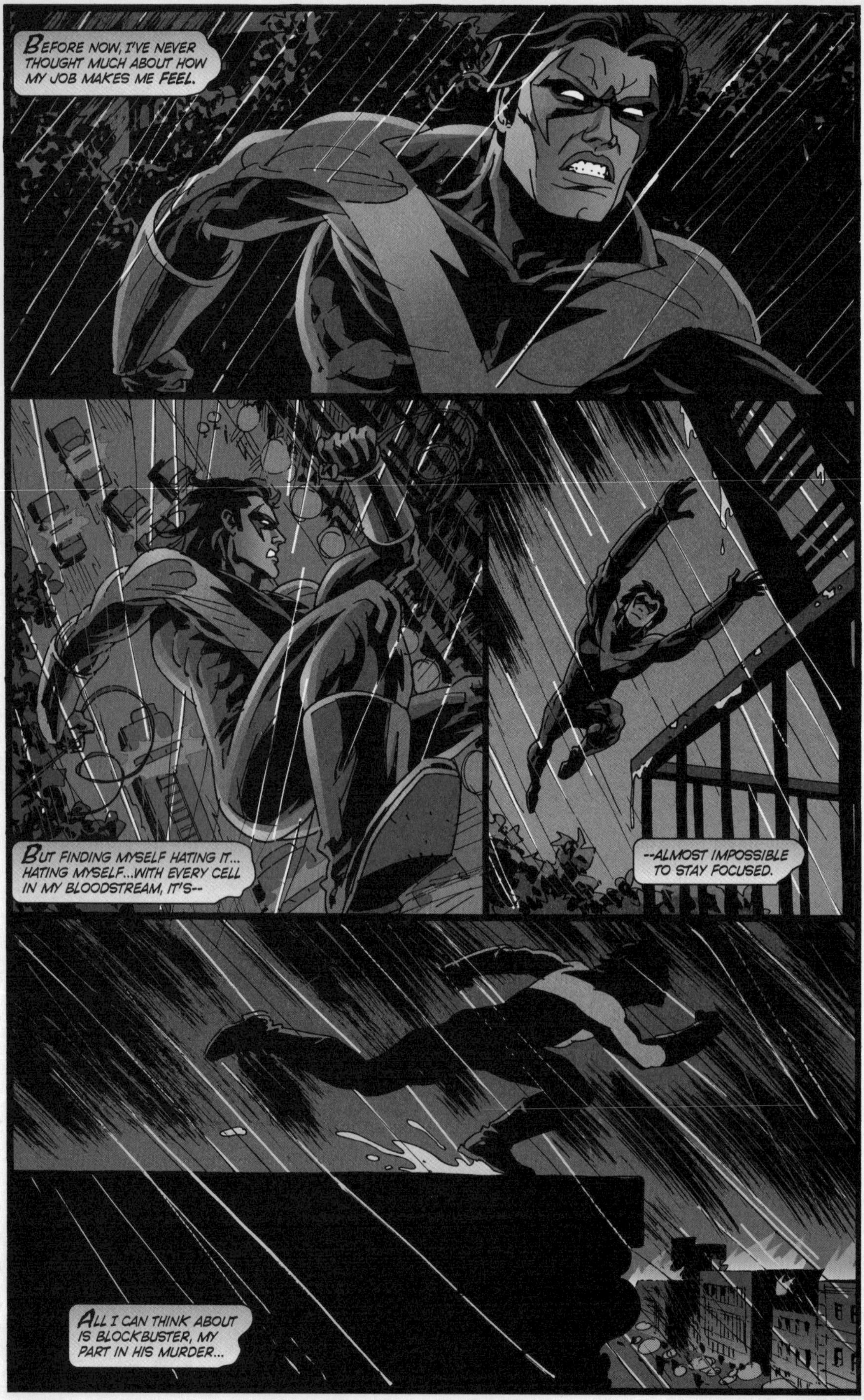
BEFORE NOW, I'VE NEVER THOUGHT MUCH ABOUT HOW MY JOB MAKES ME FEEL.
BUT FINDING MYSELF HATING IT... HATING MYSELF...WITH EVERY CELL IN MY BLOODSTREAM, IT'S--
--ALMOST IMPOSSIBLE TO STAY FOCUSED.
ALL I CAN THINK ABOUT IS BLOCKBUSTER, MY PART IN HIS MURDER...

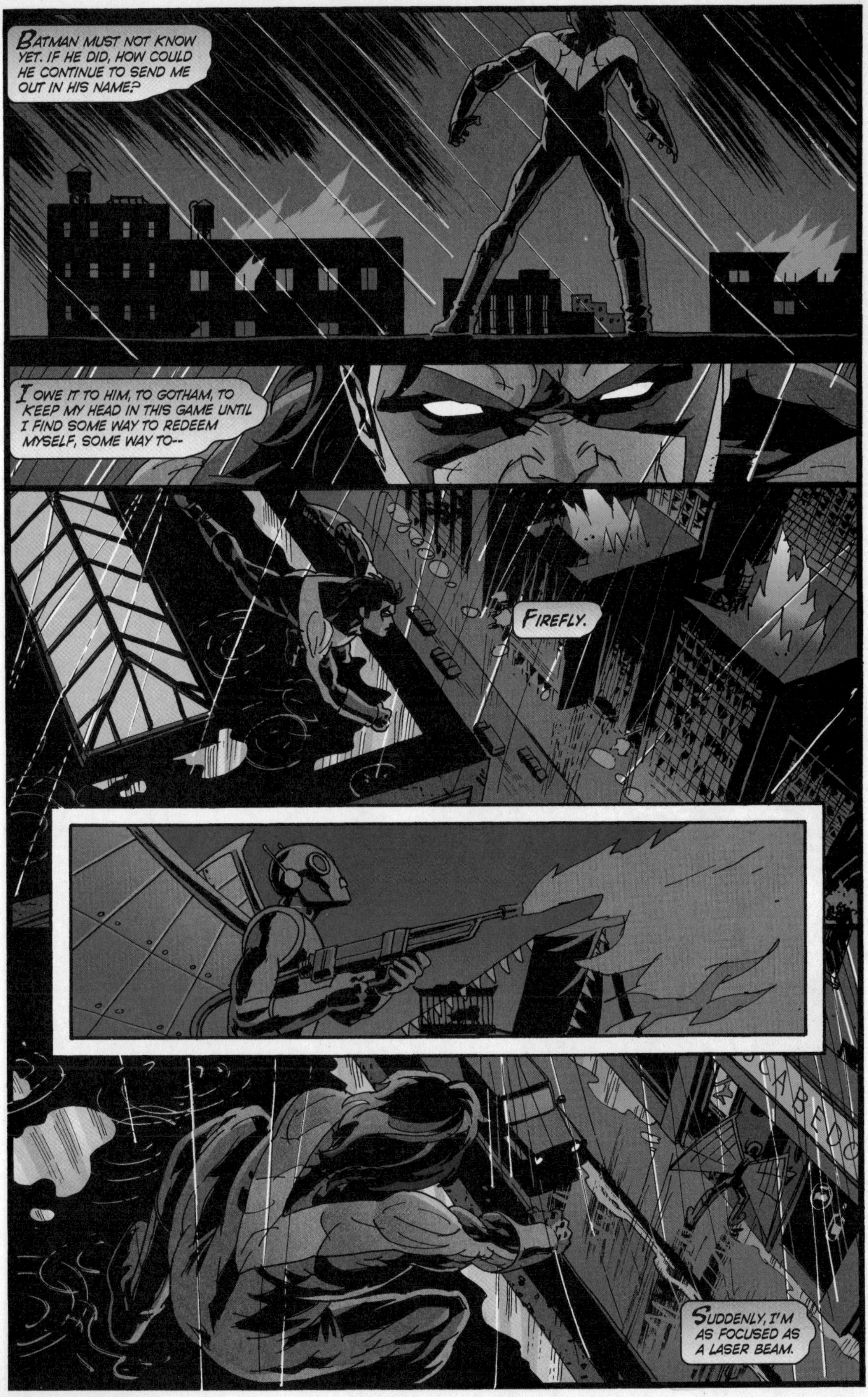
BATMAN MUST NOT KNOW YET. IF HE DID, HOW COULD HE CONTINUE TO SEND ME OUT IN HIS NAME?
I OWE IT TO HIM, TO GOTHAM, TO KEEP MY HEAD IN THIS GAME UNTIL I FIND SOME WAY TO REDEEM MYSELF, SOME WAY TO--
FIREFLY.
SUDDENLY, I'M AS FOCUSED AS A LASER BEAM.

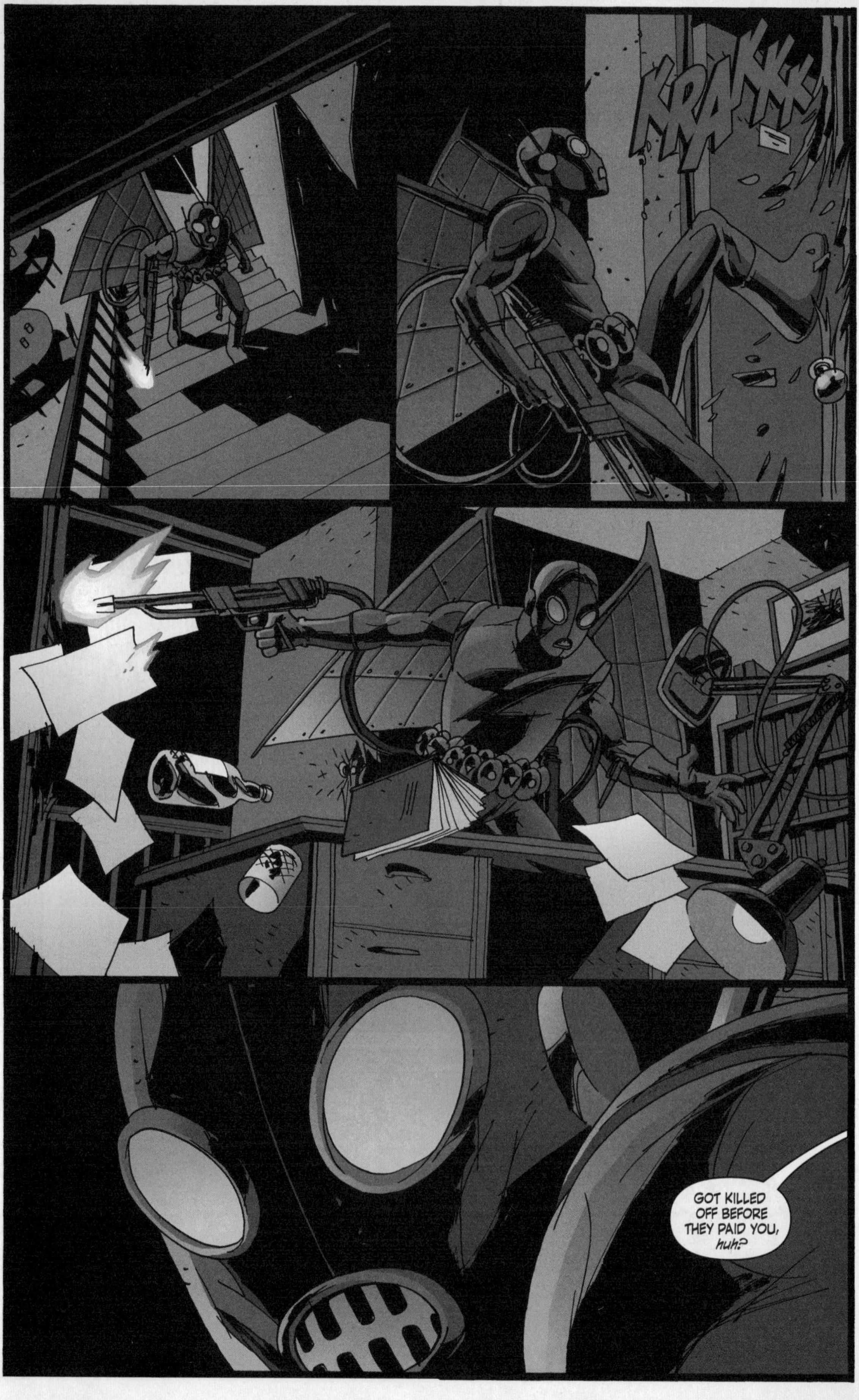
KRAKKK
GOT KILLED OFF BEFORE THEY PAID YOU, *huh?*

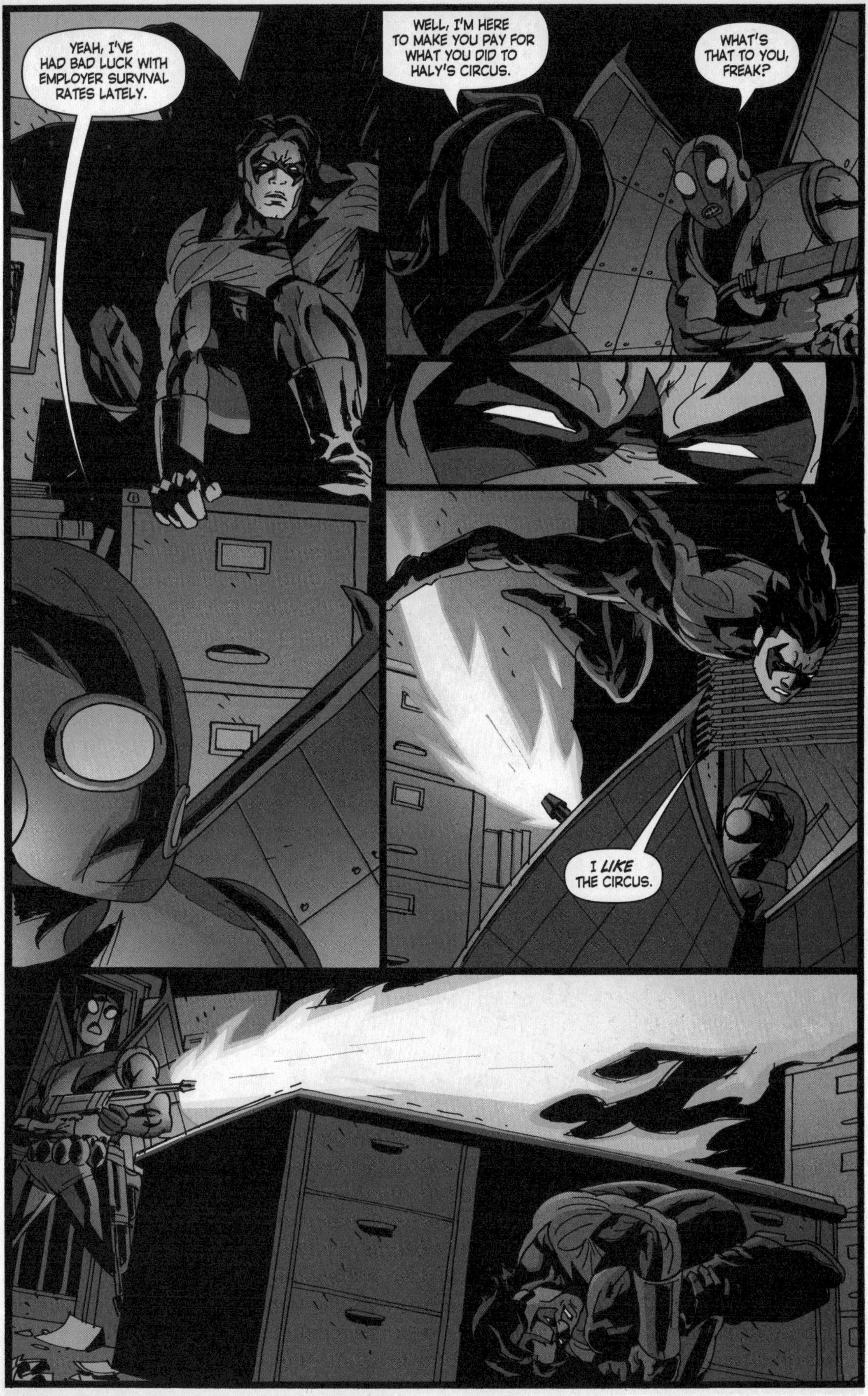
YEAH, I'VE HAD BAD LUCK WITH EMPLOYER SURVIVAL RATES LATELY.
WELL, I'M HERE TO MAKE YOU PAY FOR WHAT YOU DID TO HALY'S CIRCUS.
WHAT'S THAT TO YOU, FREAK?
I *LIKE* THE CIRCUS.

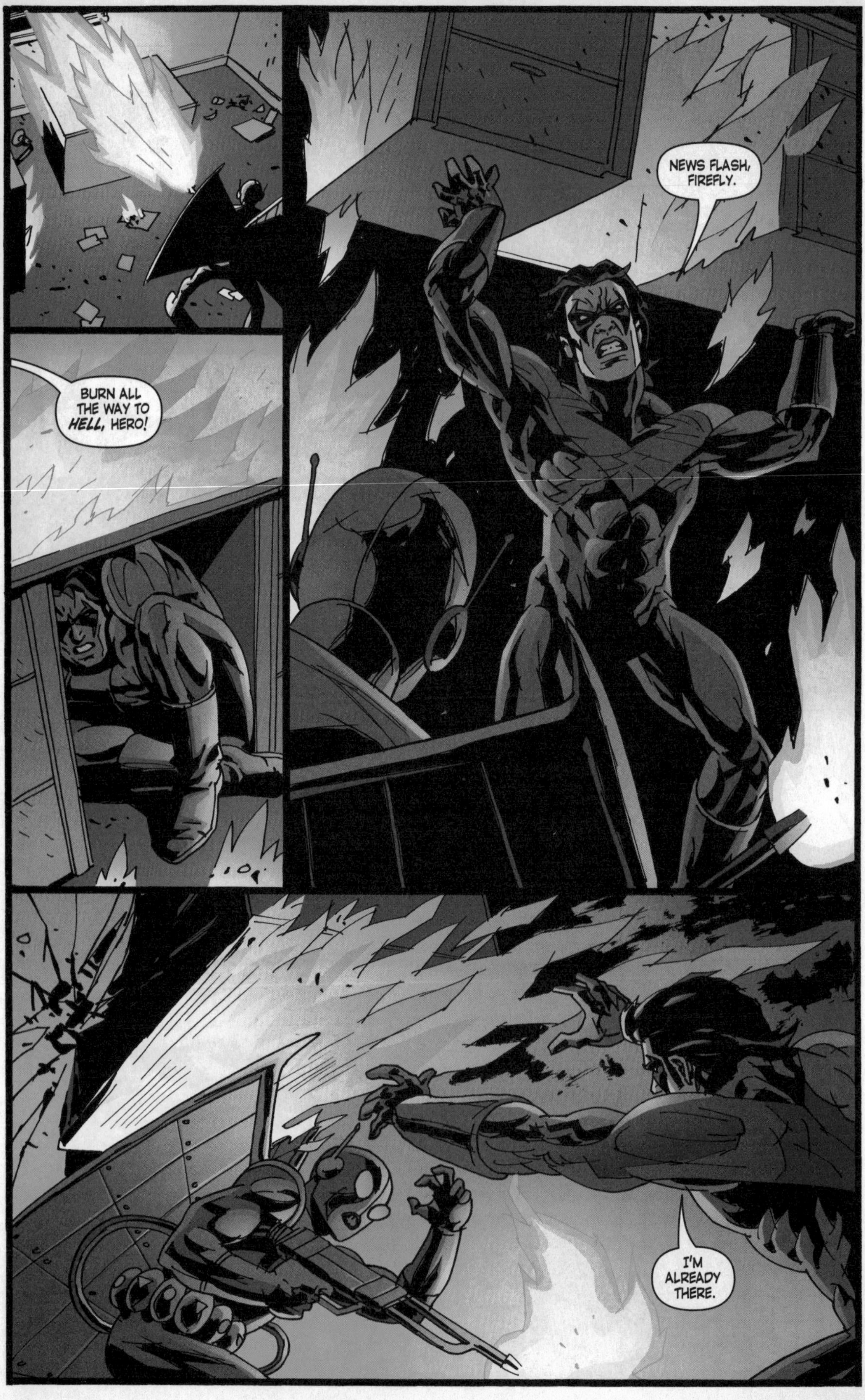
NEWS FLASH, FIREFLY.
BURN ALL THE WAY TO HELL, HERO!
I'M ALREADY THERE.

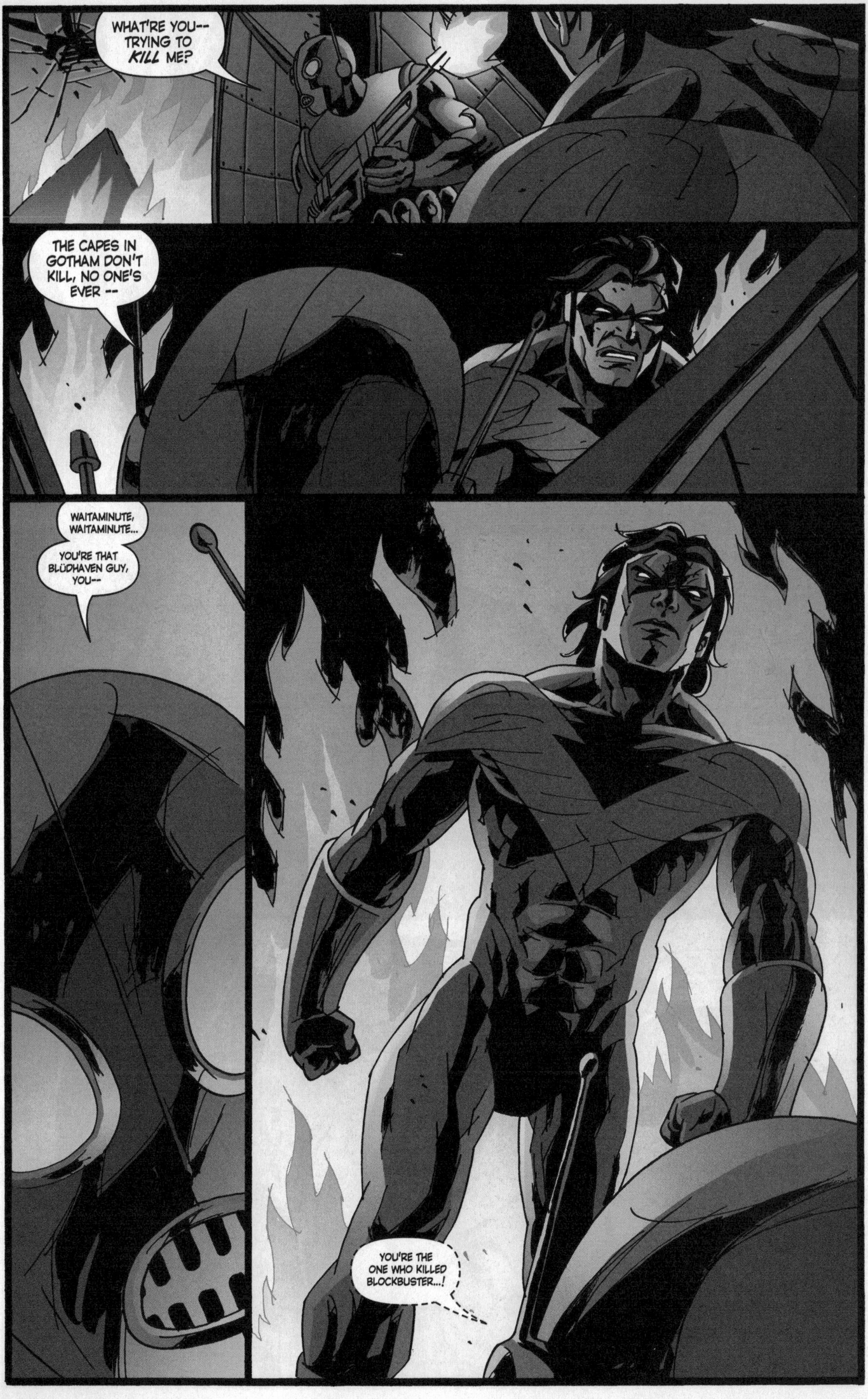
WHAT'RE YOU-- TRYING TO KILL ME?
THE CAPES IN GOTHAM DON'T KILL, NO ONE'S EVER --
WAITAMINUTE, WAITAMINUTE...
YOU'RE THAT BLÜDHAVEN GUY, YOU--
YOU'RE THE ONE WHO KILLED BLOCKBUSTER...!

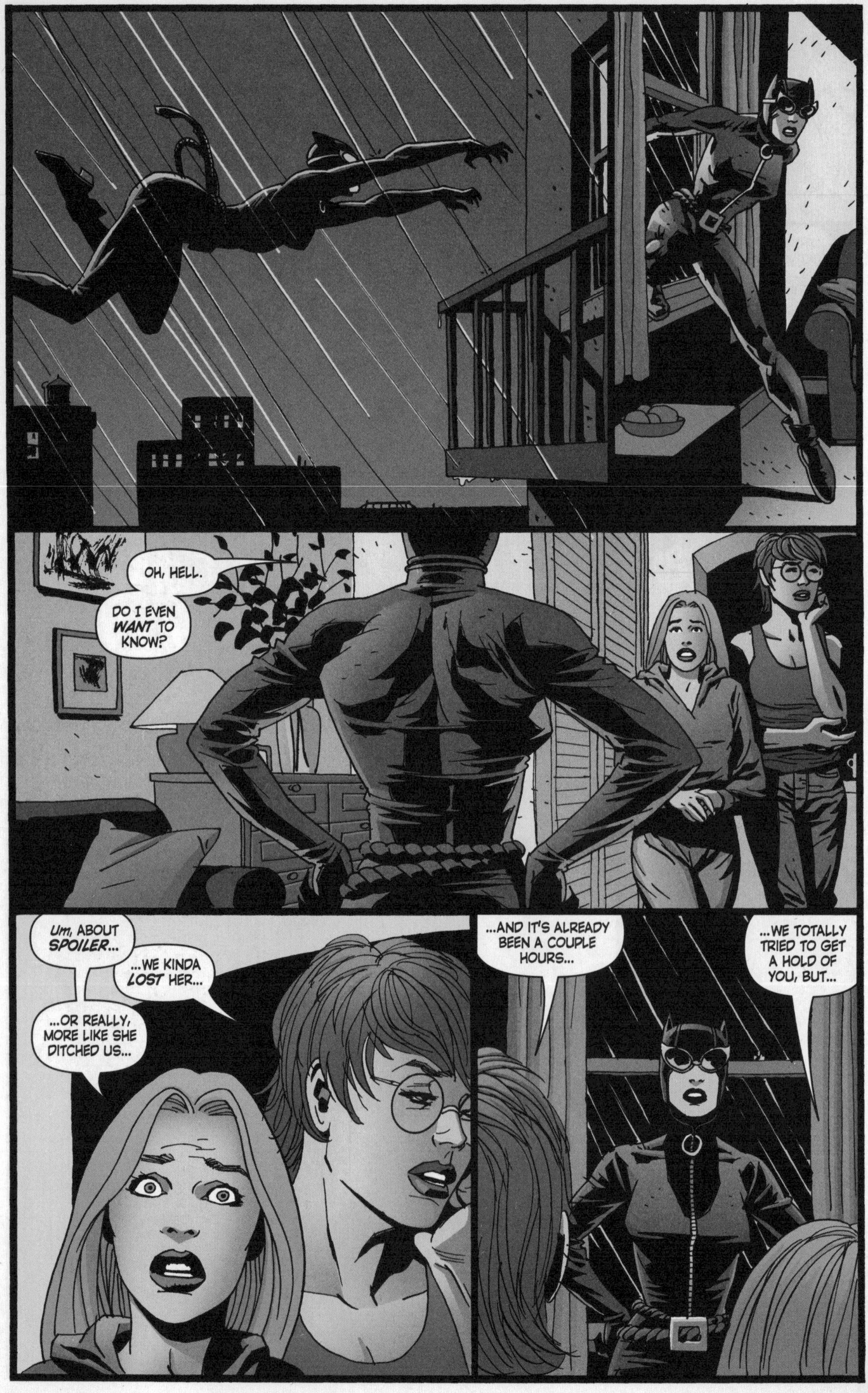
OH, HELL.
DO I EVEN WANT TO KNOW?
Um, ABOUT SPOILER...
...WE KINDA LOST HER...
...OR REALLY, MORE LIKE SHE DITCHED US...
...AND IT'S ALREADY BEEN A COUPLE HOURS...
...WE TOTALLY TRIED TO GET A HOLD OF YOU, BUT...

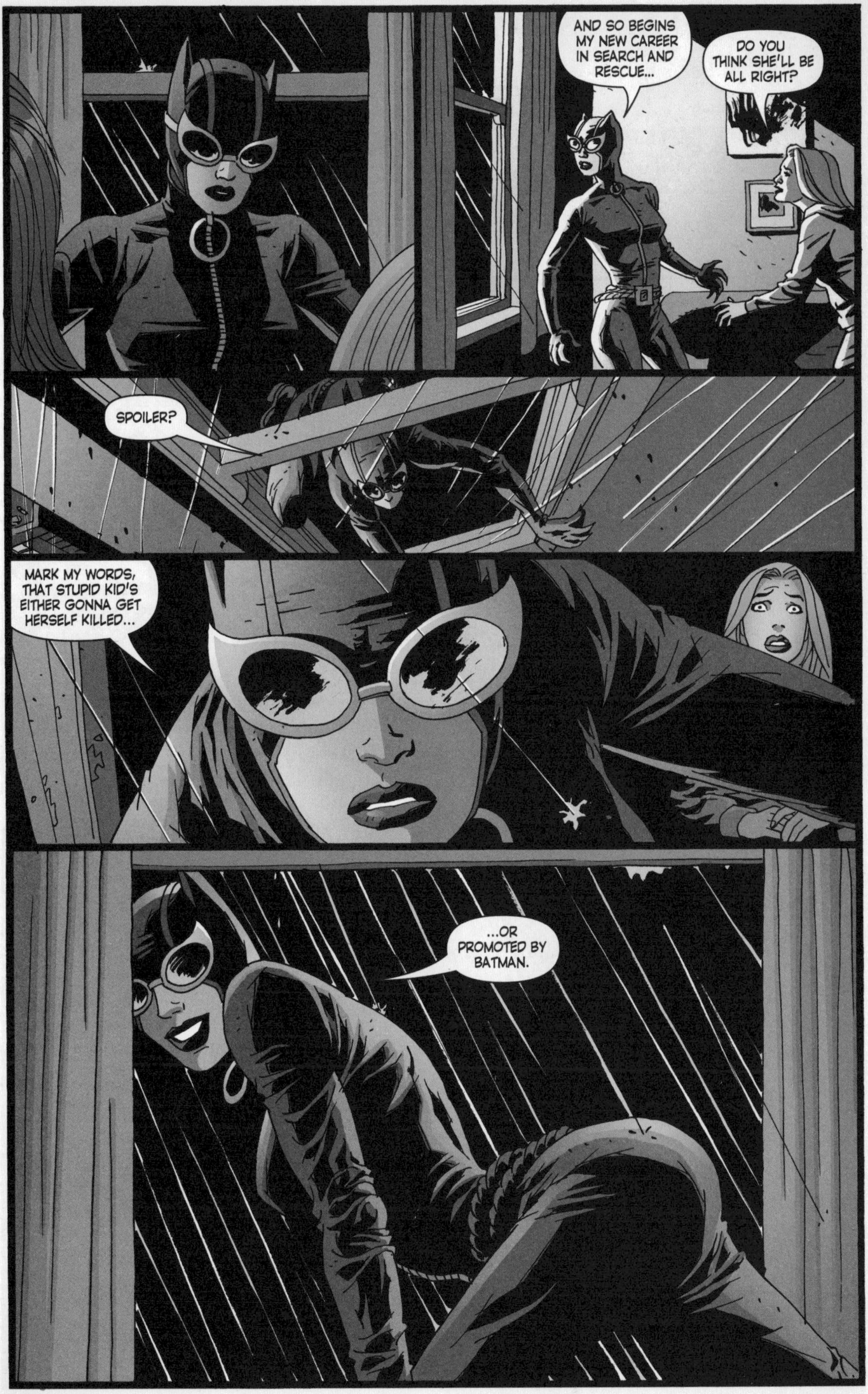
AND SO BEGINS MY NEW CAREER IN SEARCH AND RESCUE...
DO YOU THINK SHE'LL BE ALL RIGHT?
SPOILER?
MARK MY WORDS, THAT STUPID KID'S EITHER GONNA GET HERSELF KILLED...
...OR PROMOTED BY BATMAN.

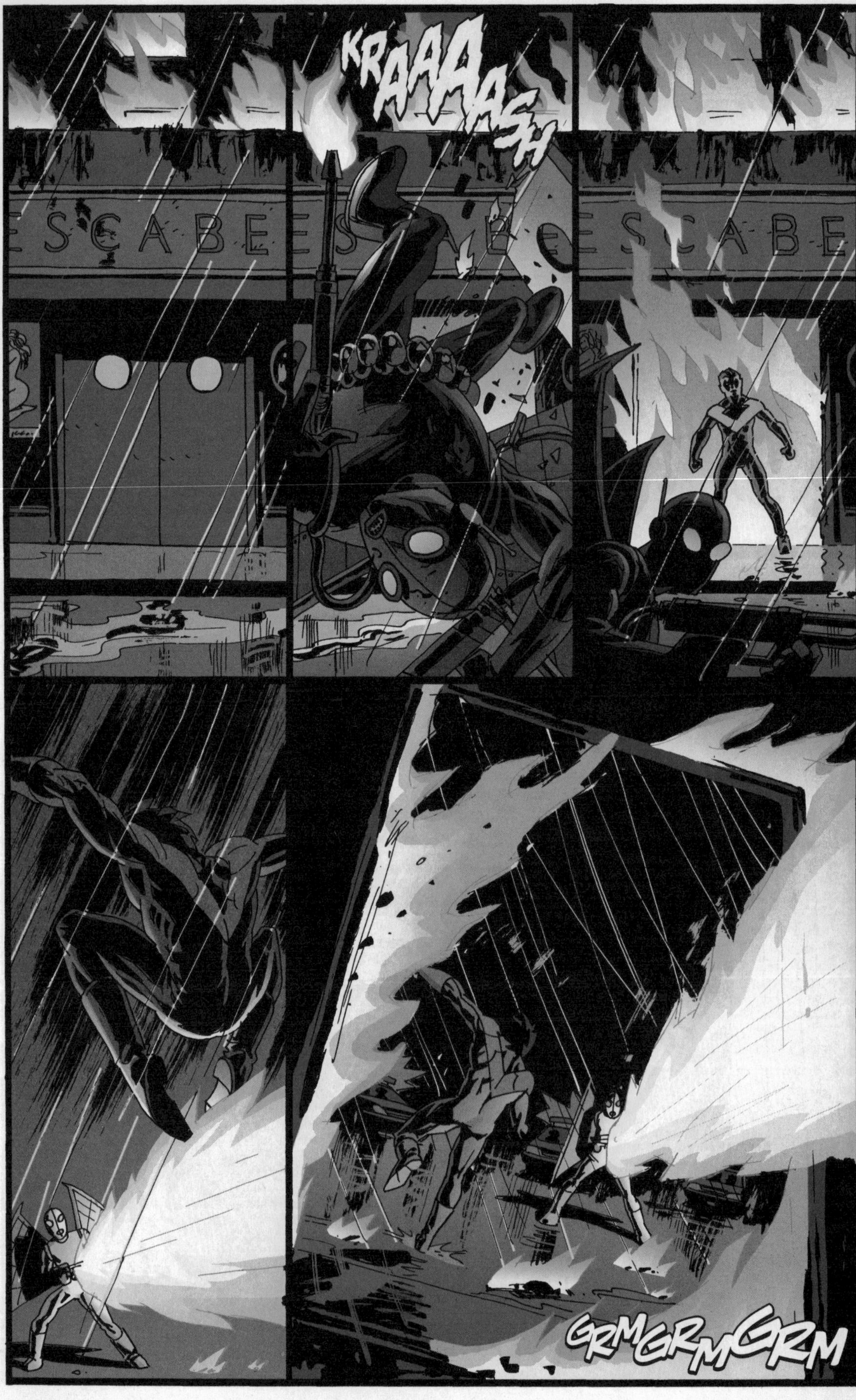
ESÇABE
KRAAAASH
GRMGRMGRM

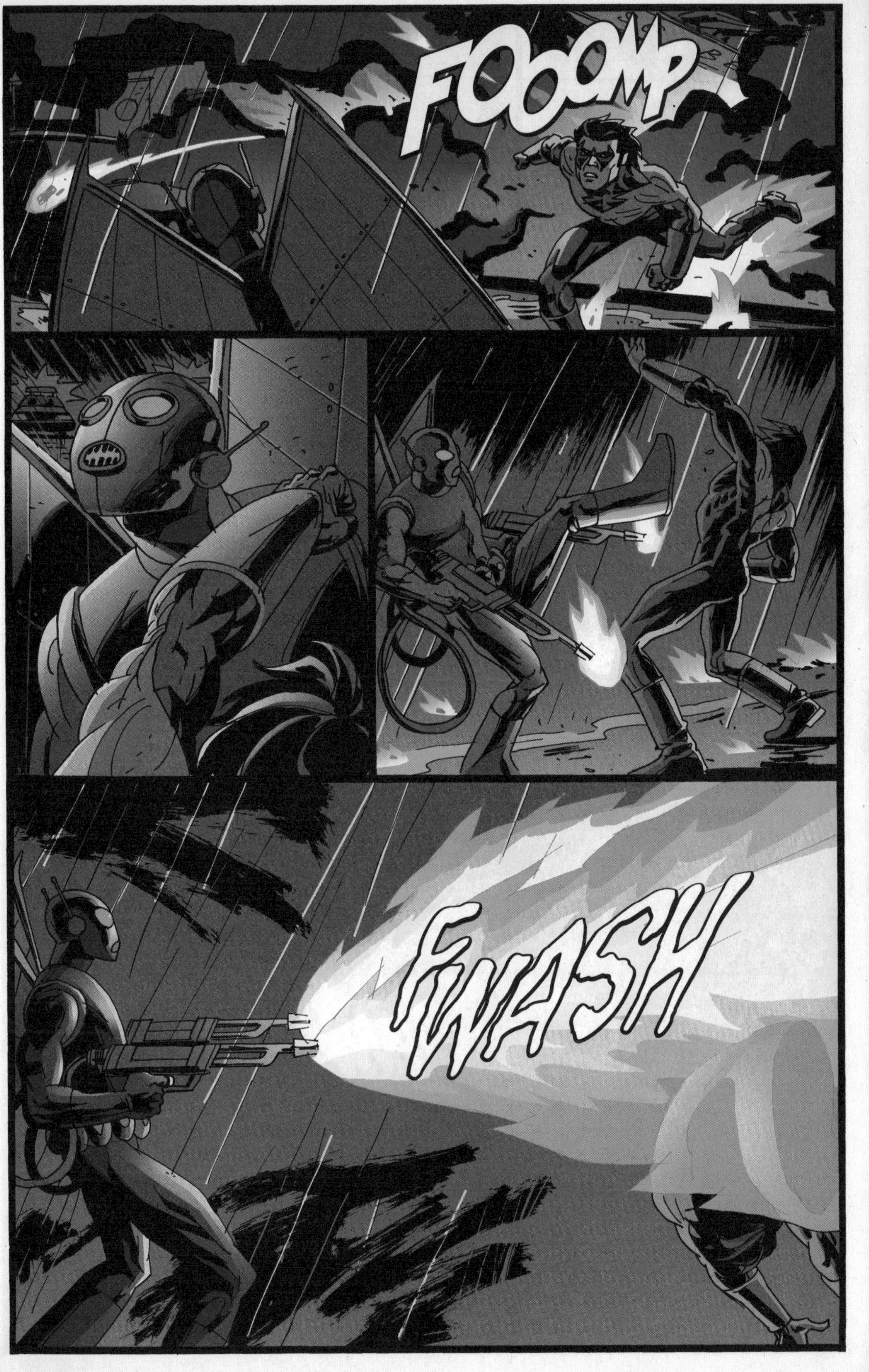
FOOOMP
FWASH

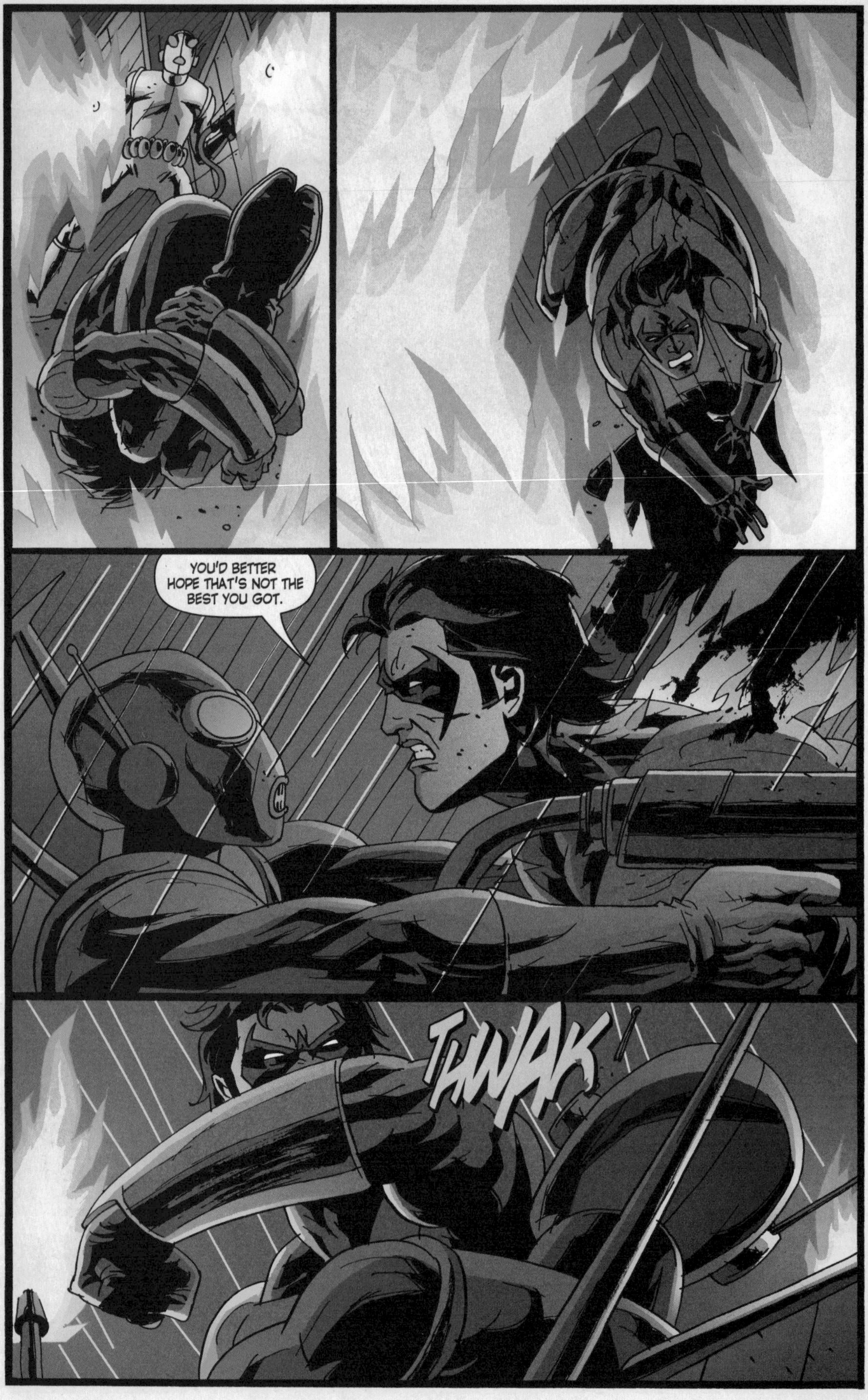
YOU'D BETTER
HOPE THAT'S NOT THE
BEST YOU GOT.
THWAK

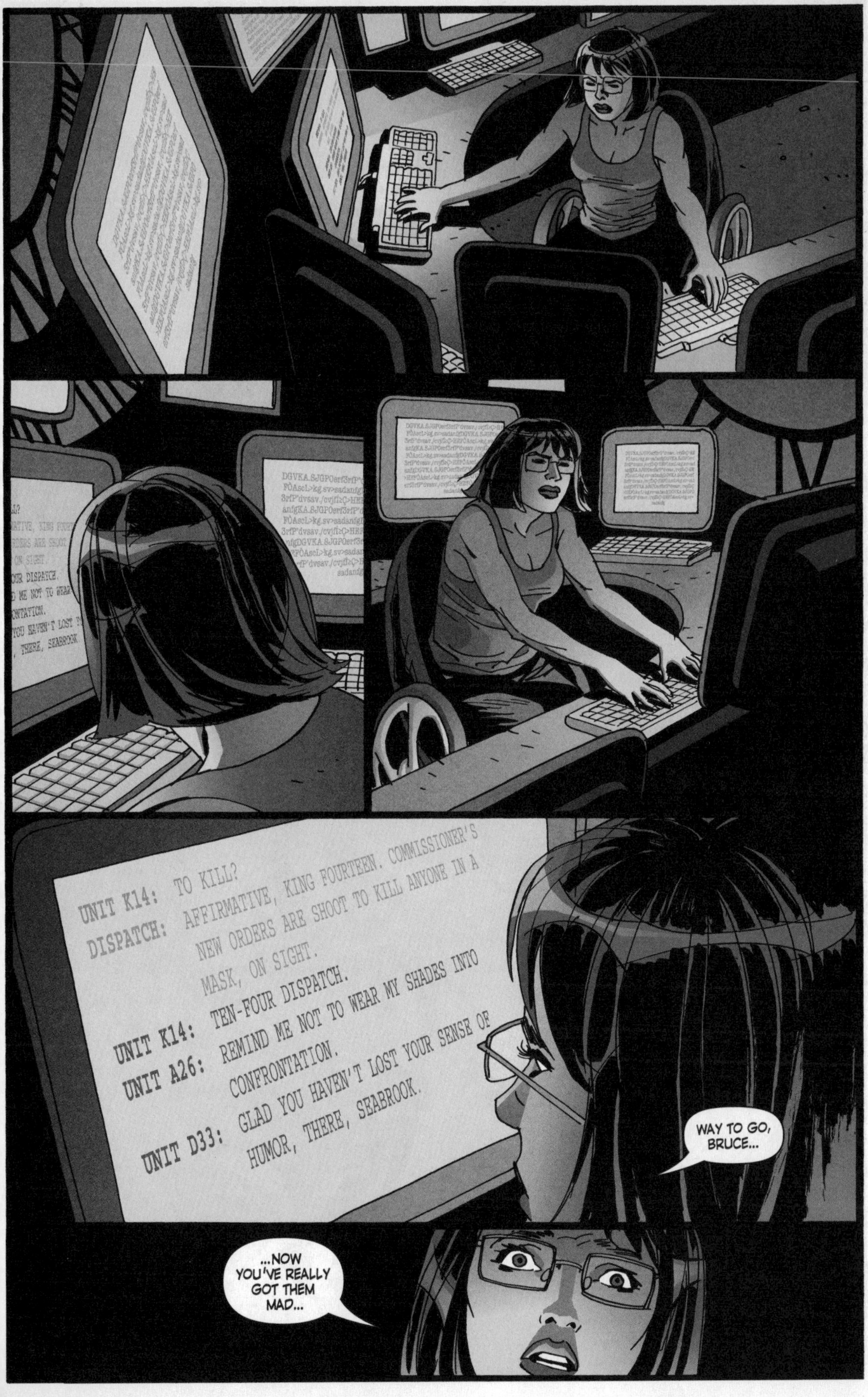
UNIT K14: TO KILL?
DISPATCH: AFFIRMATIVE, KING FOURTEEN. COMMISSIONER'S NEW ORDERS ARE SHOOT TO KILL ANYONE IN A MASK, ON SIGHT.
UNIT K14: TEN-FOUR DISPATCH.
UNIT A26: REMIND ME NOT TO WEAR MY SHADES INTO CONFRONTATION.
UNIT D33: GLAD YOU HAVEN'T LOST YOUR SENSE OF HUMOR, THERE, SEABROOK.
WAY TO GO, BRUCE...
...NOW YOU'VE REALLY GOT THEM MAD...

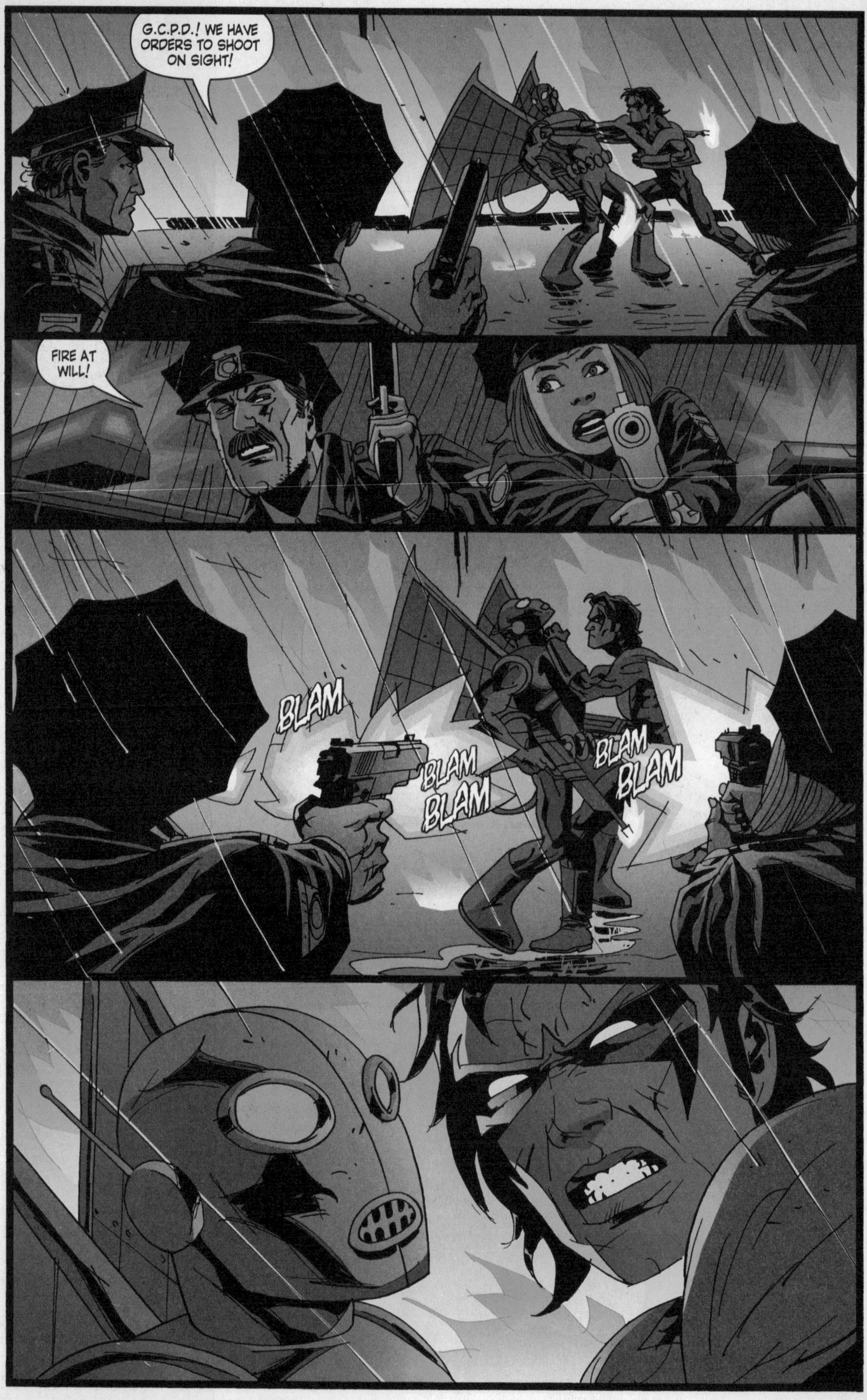
G.C.P.D.! WE HAVE ORDERS TO SHOOT ON SIGHT!
FIRE AT WILL!
BLAM
BLAM BLAM
BLAM BLAM

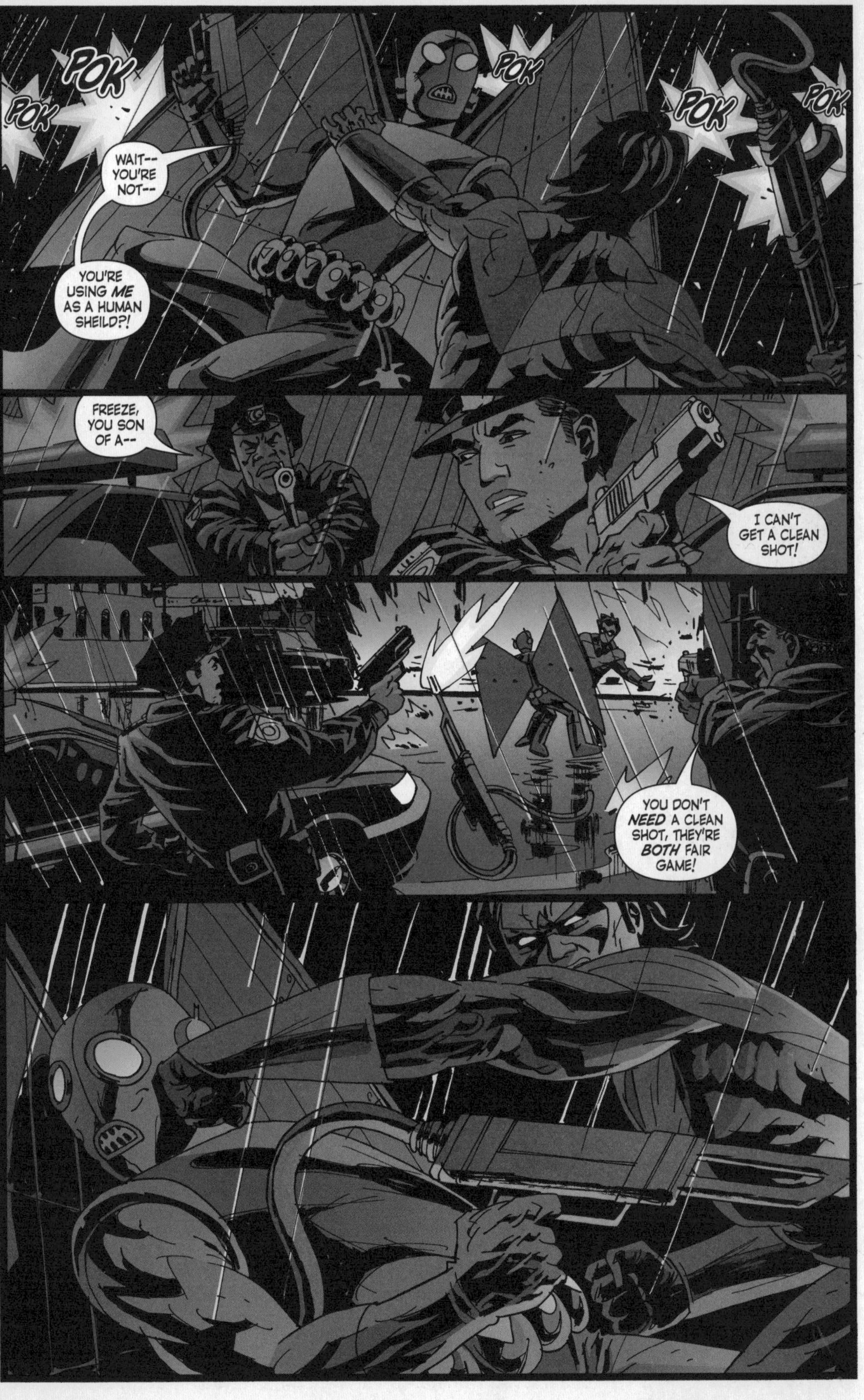
POK
POK
POK
POK
POK
WAIT-- YOU'RE NOT--
YOU'RE USING ME AS A HUMAN SHEILD?!
FREEZE, YOU SON OF A--
I CAN'T GET A CLEAN SHOT!
YOU DON'T NEED A CLEAN SHOT, THEY'RE BOTH FAIR GAME!

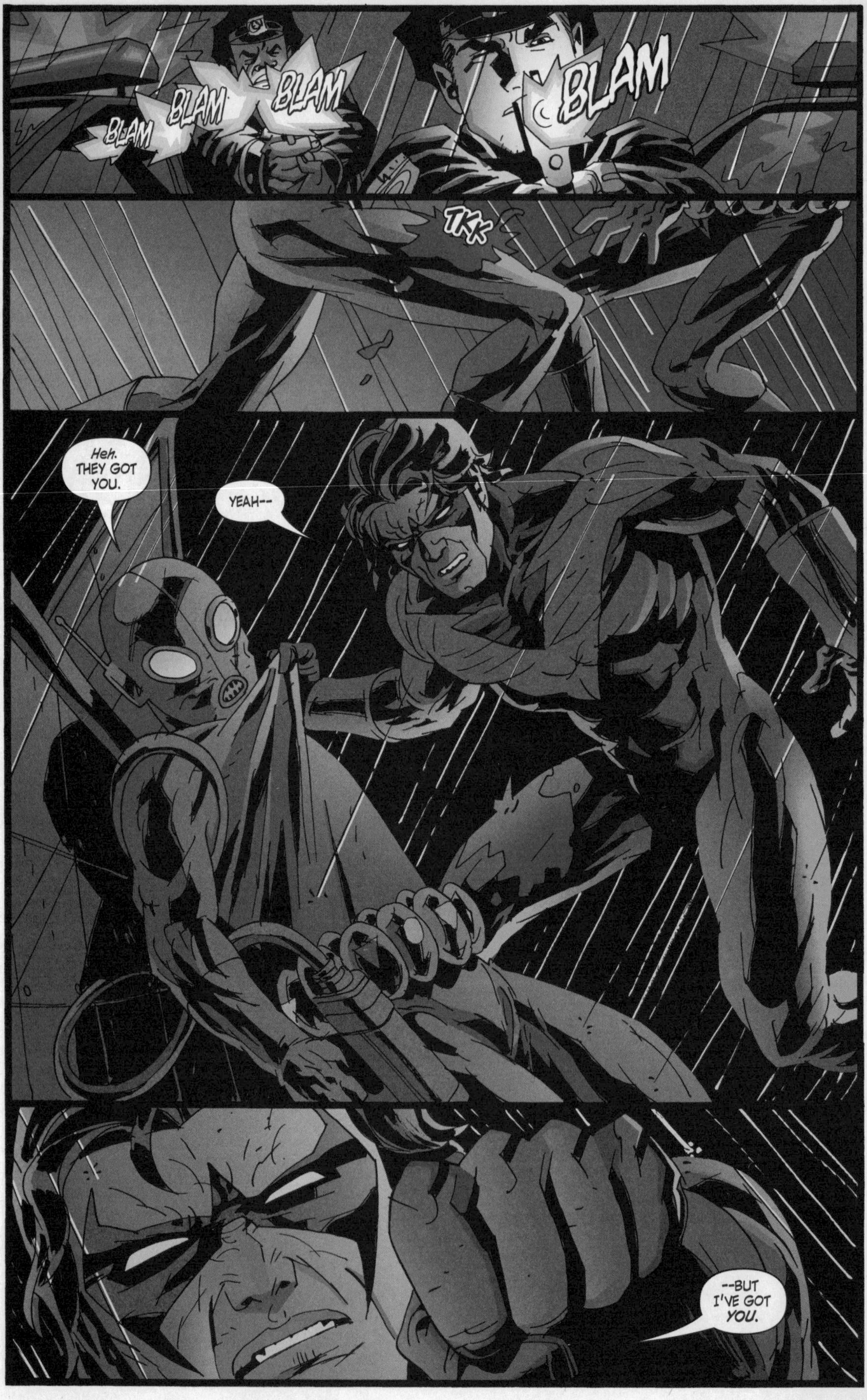
BLAM
BLAM
BLAM
BLAM
TKK
Heh. THEY GOT YOU.
YEAH--
--BUT I'VE GOT YOU.

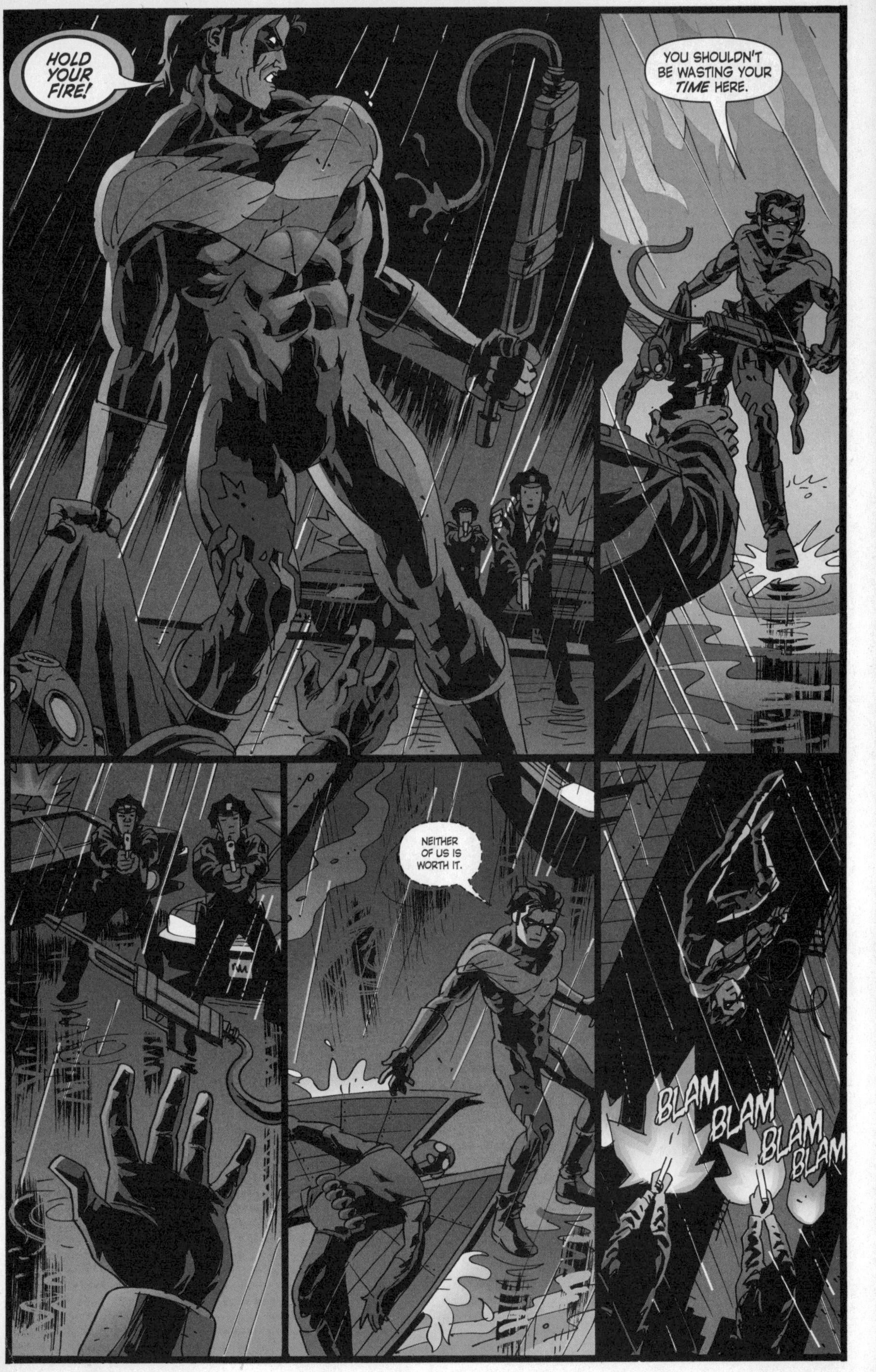
HOLD YOUR FIRE!
YOU SHOULDN'T BE WASTING YOUR *TIME* HERE.
NEITHER OF US IS WORTH IT.
BLAM
BLAM
BLAM
BLAM

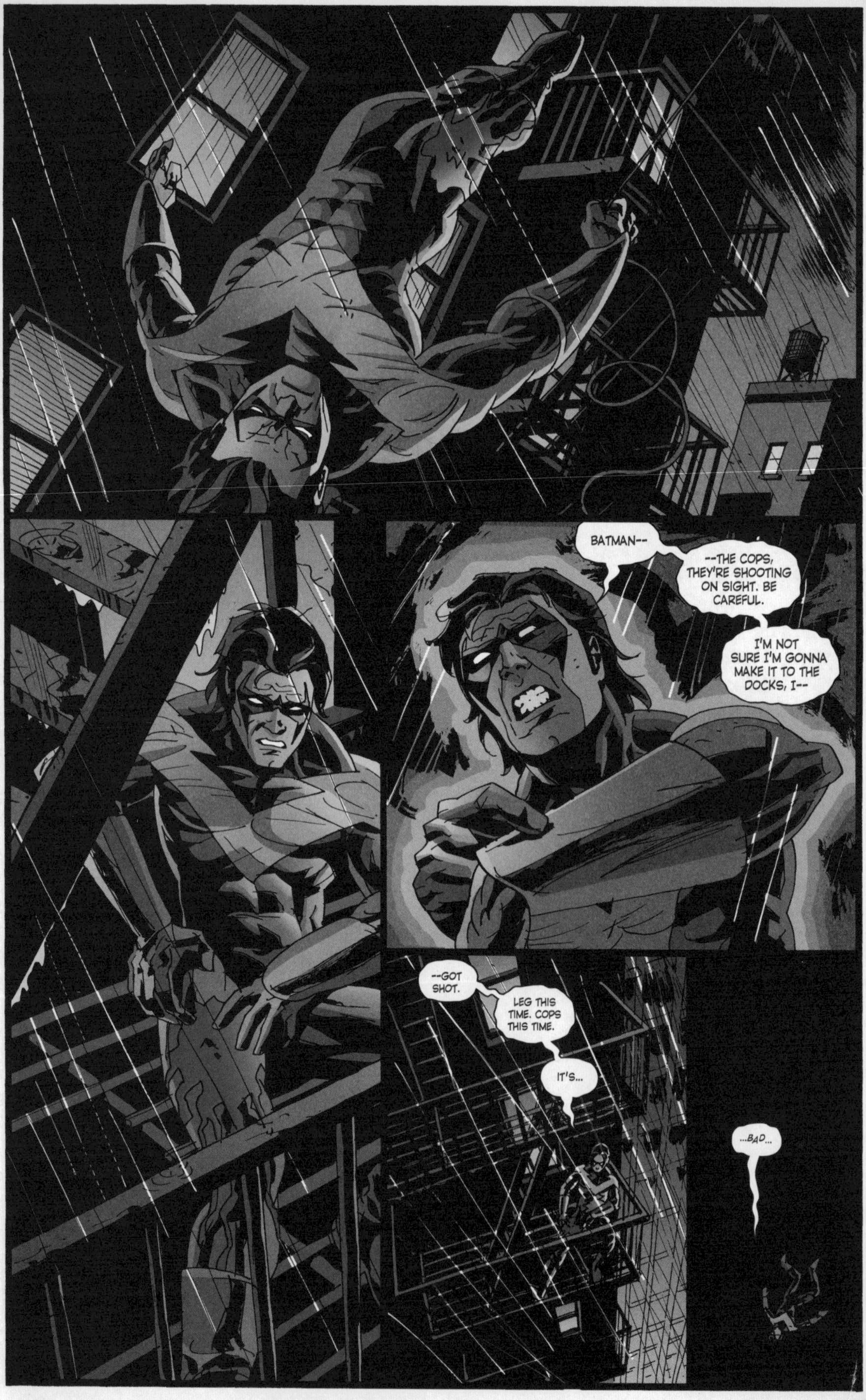
BATMAN--
--THE COPS, THEY'RE SHOOTING ON SIGHT. BE CAREFUL.
I'M NOT SURE I'M GONNA MAKE IT TO THE DOCKS, I--
--GOT SHOT.
LEG THIS TIME. COPS THIS TIME.
IT'S...
...BAD...

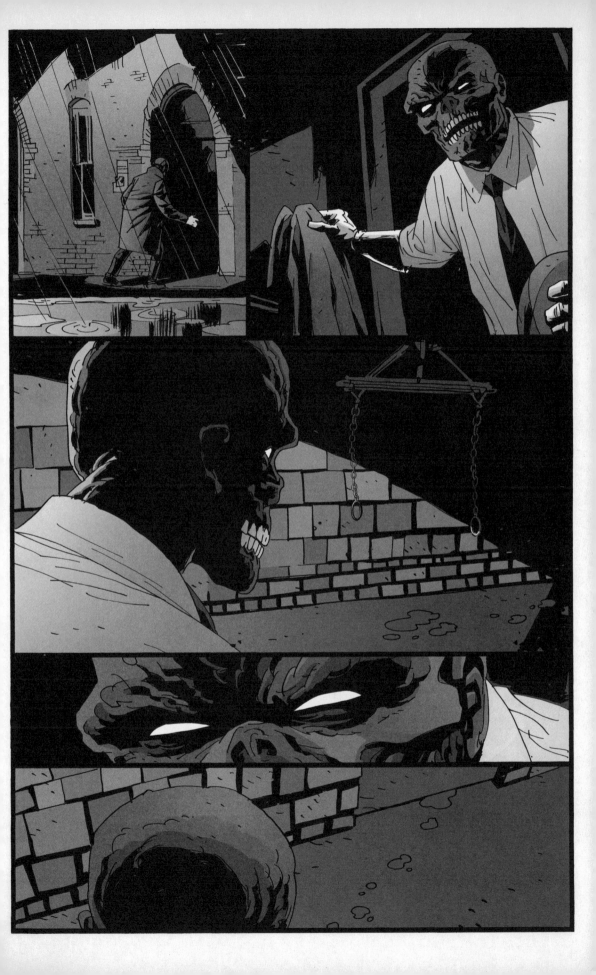

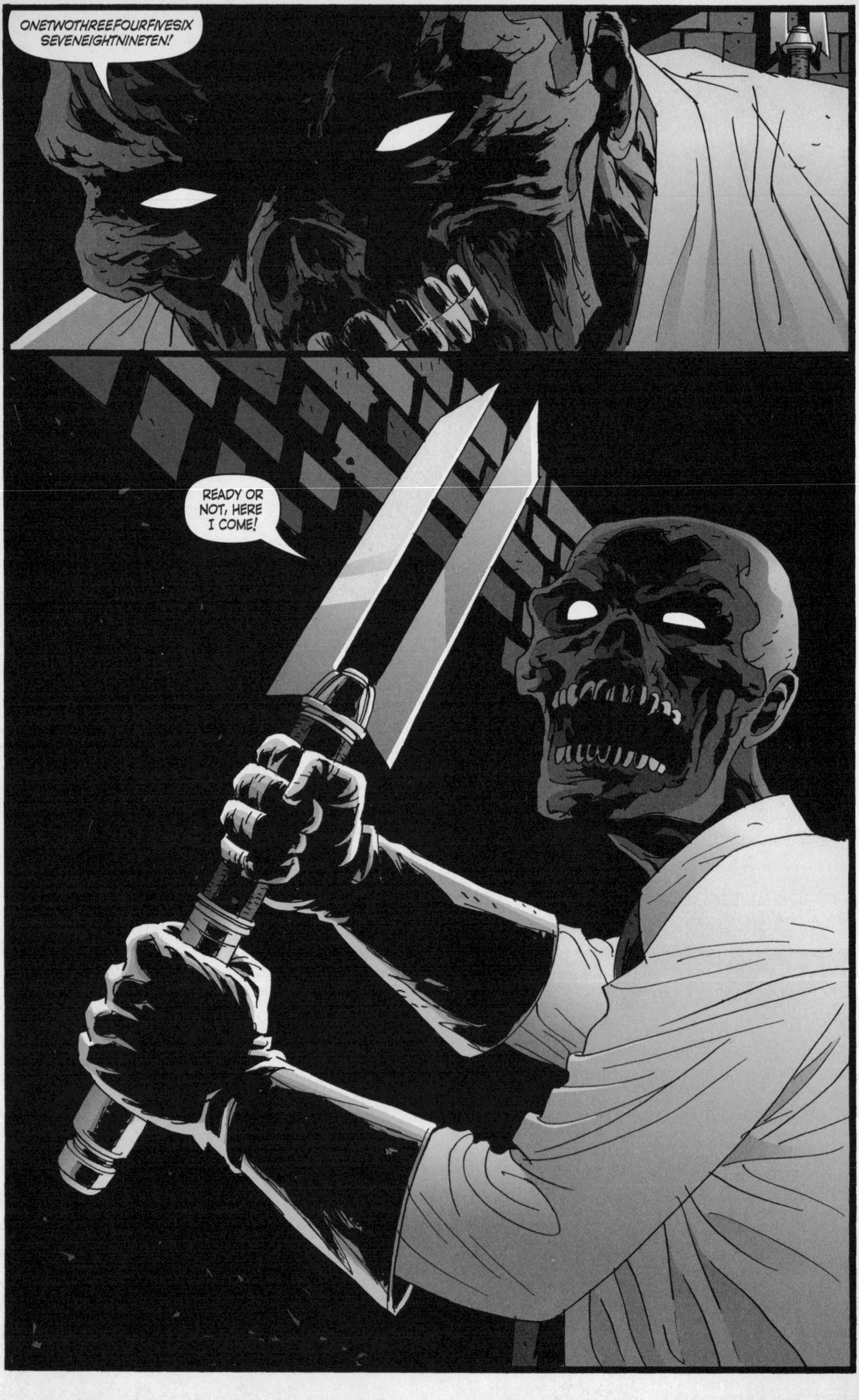
ONETWOTHREEFOURFIVESIX SEVENEIGHTNINETEN!
READY OR NOT, HERE I COME!

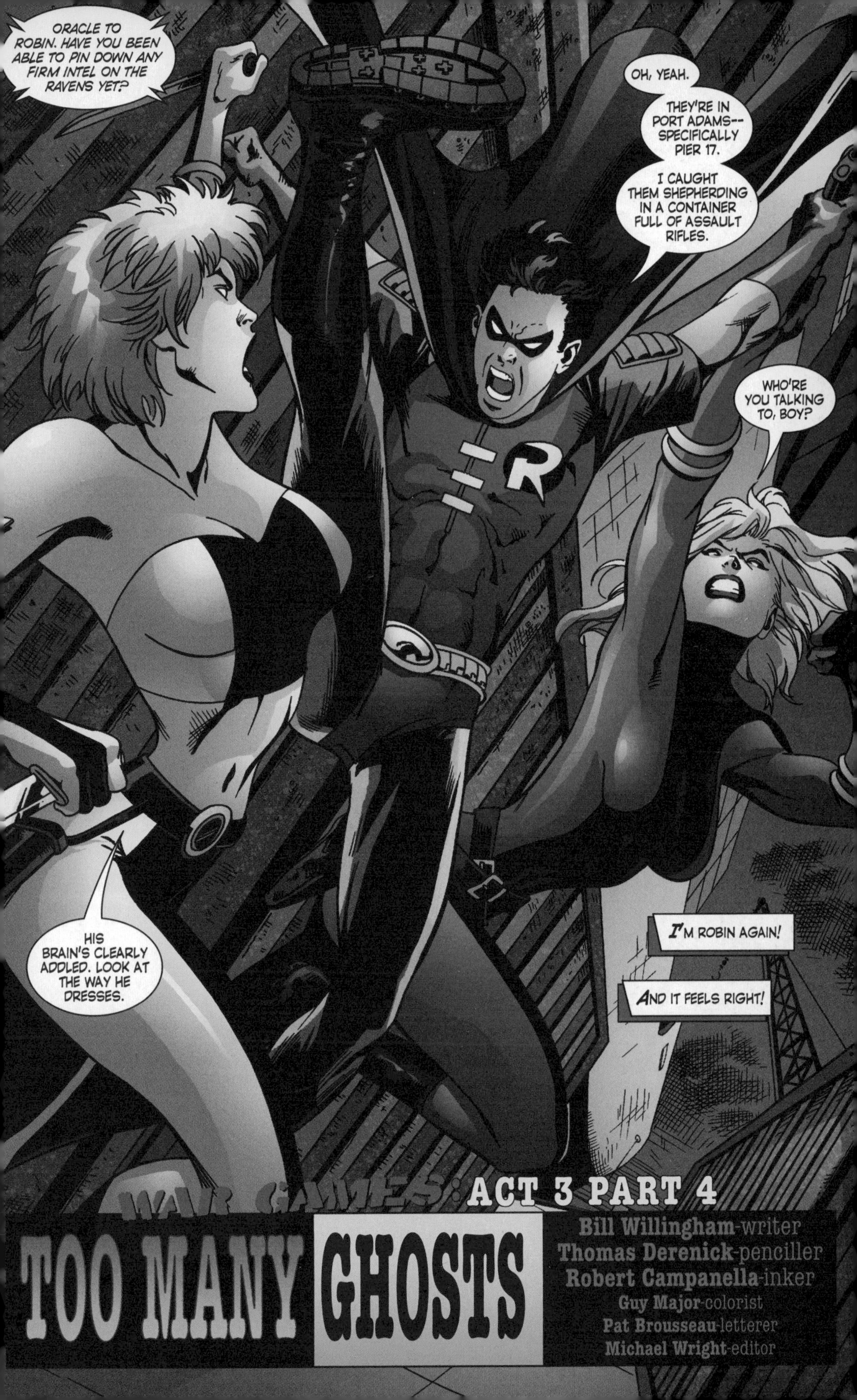

ORACLE TO ROBIN. HAVE YOU BEEN ABLE TO PIN DOWN ANY FIRM INTEL ON THE RAVENS YET?
OH, YEAH.
THEY'RE IN PORT ADAMS-- SPECIFICALLY PIER 17.
I CAUGHT THEM SHEPHERDING IN A CONTAINER FULL OF ASSAULT RIFLES.
WHO'RE YOU TALKING TO, BOY?
HIS BRAIN'S CLEARLY ADDLED. LOOK AT THE WAY HE DRESSES.
I'M ROBIN AGAIN!
AND IT FEELS RIGHT!
WAR GAMES: ACT 3 PART 4
TOO MANY GHOSTS
Bill Willingham-writer
Thomas Derenick-penciller
Robert Campanella-inker
Guy Major-colorist
Pat Brousseau-letterer
Michael Wright-editor

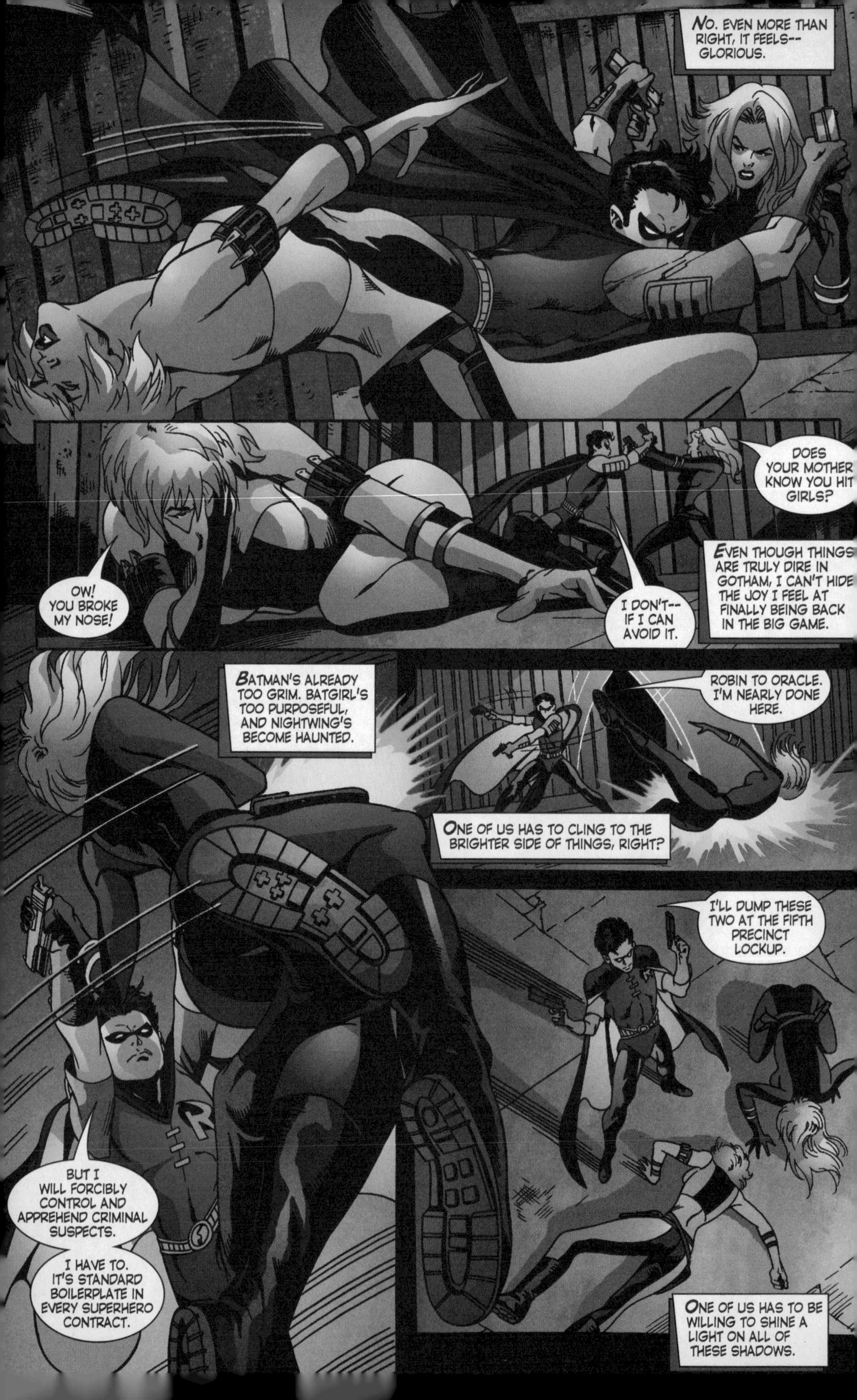
NO. EVEN MORE THAN RIGHT, IT FEELS-- GLORIOUS.
OW! YOU BROKE MY NOSE!
DOES YOUR MOTHER KNOW YOU HIT GIRLS?
I DON'T-- IF I CAN AVOID IT.
EVEN THOUGH THINGS ARE TRULY DIRE IN GOTHAM, I CAN'T HIDE THE JOY I FEEL AT FINALLY BEING BACK IN THE BIG GAME.
BATMAN'S ALREADY TOO GRIM. BATGIRL'S TOO PURPOSEFUL, AND NIGHTWING'S BECOME HAUNTED.
ROBIN TO ORACLE. I'M NEARLY DONE HERE.
ONE OF US HAS TO CLING TO THE BRIGHTER SIDE OF THINGS, RIGHT?
BUT I WILL FORCIBLY CONTROL AND APPREHEND CRIMINAL SUSPECTS.
I HAVE TO. IT'S STANDARD BOILERPLATE IN EVERY SUPERHERO CONTRACT.
I'LL DUMP THESE TWO AT THE FIFTH PRECINCT LOCKUP.
ONE OF US HAS TO BE WILLING TO SHINE A LIGHT ON ALL OF THESE SHADOWS.

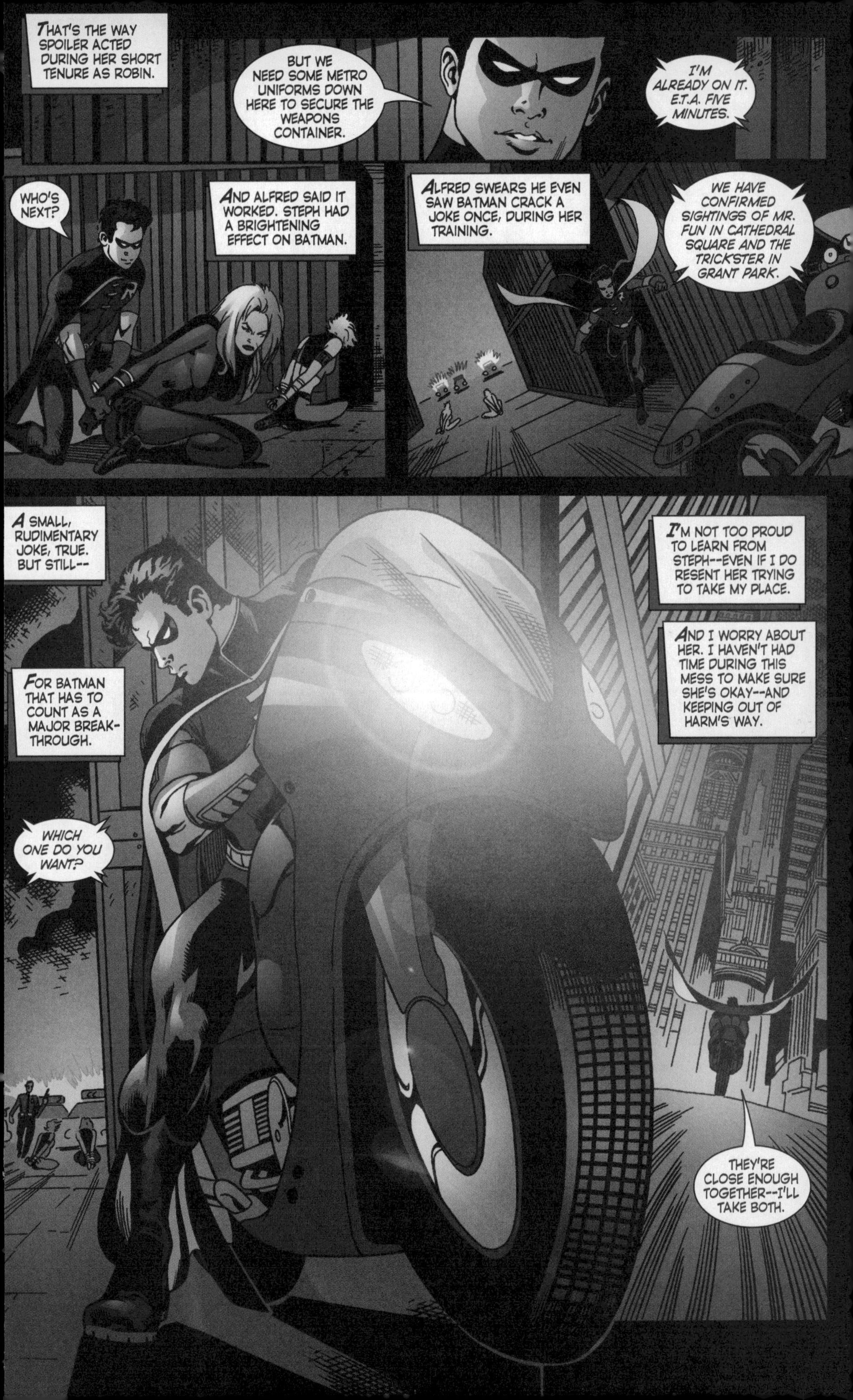
THAT'S THE WAY SPOILER ACTED DURING HER SHORT TENURE AS ROBIN.
BUT WE NEED SOME METRO UNIFORMS DOWN HERE TO SECURE THE WEAPONS CONTAINER.
I'M ALREADY ON IT. E.T.A. FIVE MINUTES.
WHO'S NEXT?
AND ALFRED SAID IT WORKED. STEPH HAD A BRIGHTENING EFFECT ON BATMAN.
ALFRED SWEARS HE EVEN SAW BATMAN CRACK A JOKE ONCE, DURING HER TRAINING.
WE HAVE CONFIRMED SIGHTINGS OF MR. FUN IN CATHEDRAL SQUARE AND THE TRICKSTER IN GRANT PARK.
A SMALL, RUDIMENTARY JOKE, TRUE. BUT STILL--
FOR BATMAN THAT HAS TO COUNT AS A MAJOR BREAK-THROUGH.
WHICH ONE DO YOU WANT?
I'M NOT TOO PROUD TO LEARN FROM STEPH--EVEN IF I DO RESENT HER TRYING TO TAKE MY PLACE.
AND I WORRY ABOUT HER. I HAVEN'T HAD TIME DURING THIS MESS TO MAKE SURE SHE'S OKAY--AND KEEPING OUT OF HARM'S WAY.
THEY'RE CLOSE ENOUGH TOGETHER--I'LL TAKE BOTH.

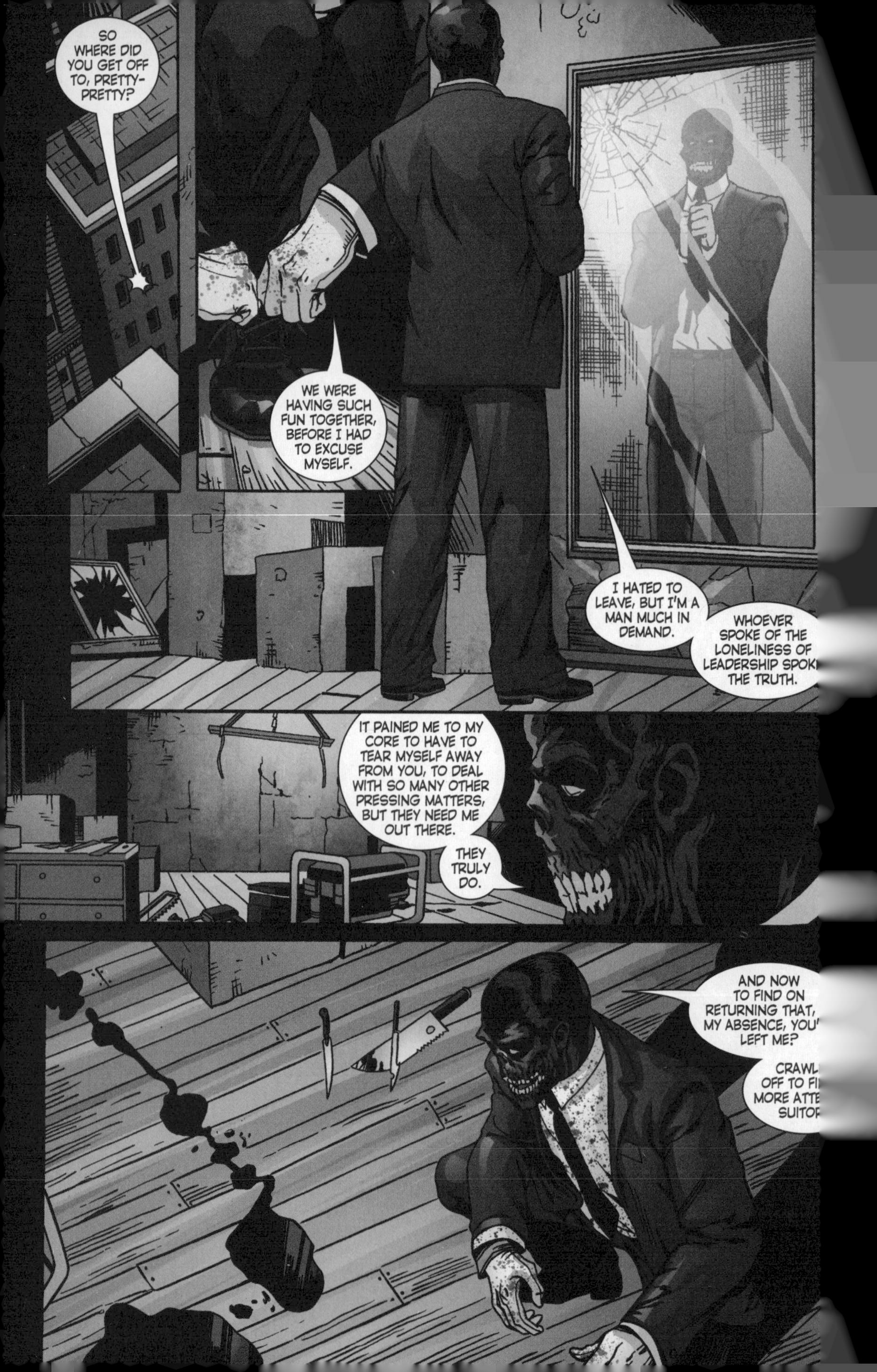
SO WHERE DID YOU GET OFF TO, PRETTY-PRETTY?
WE WERE HAVING SUCH FUN TOGETHER, BEFORE I HAD TO EXCUSE MYSELF.
I HATED TO LEAVE, BUT I'M A MAN MUCH IN DEMAND.
WHOEVER SPOKE OF THE LONELINESS OF LEADERSHIP SPOK THE TRUTH.
IT PAINED ME TO MY CORE TO HAVE TO TEAR MYSELF AWAY FROM YOU, TO DEAL WITH SO MANY OTHER PRESSING MATTERS, BUT THEY NEED ME OUT THERE.
THEY TRULY DO.
AND NOW TO FIND ON RETURNING THAT, MY ABSENCE, YOU' LEFT ME?
CRAWL OFF TO FI MORE ATTE SUITOR

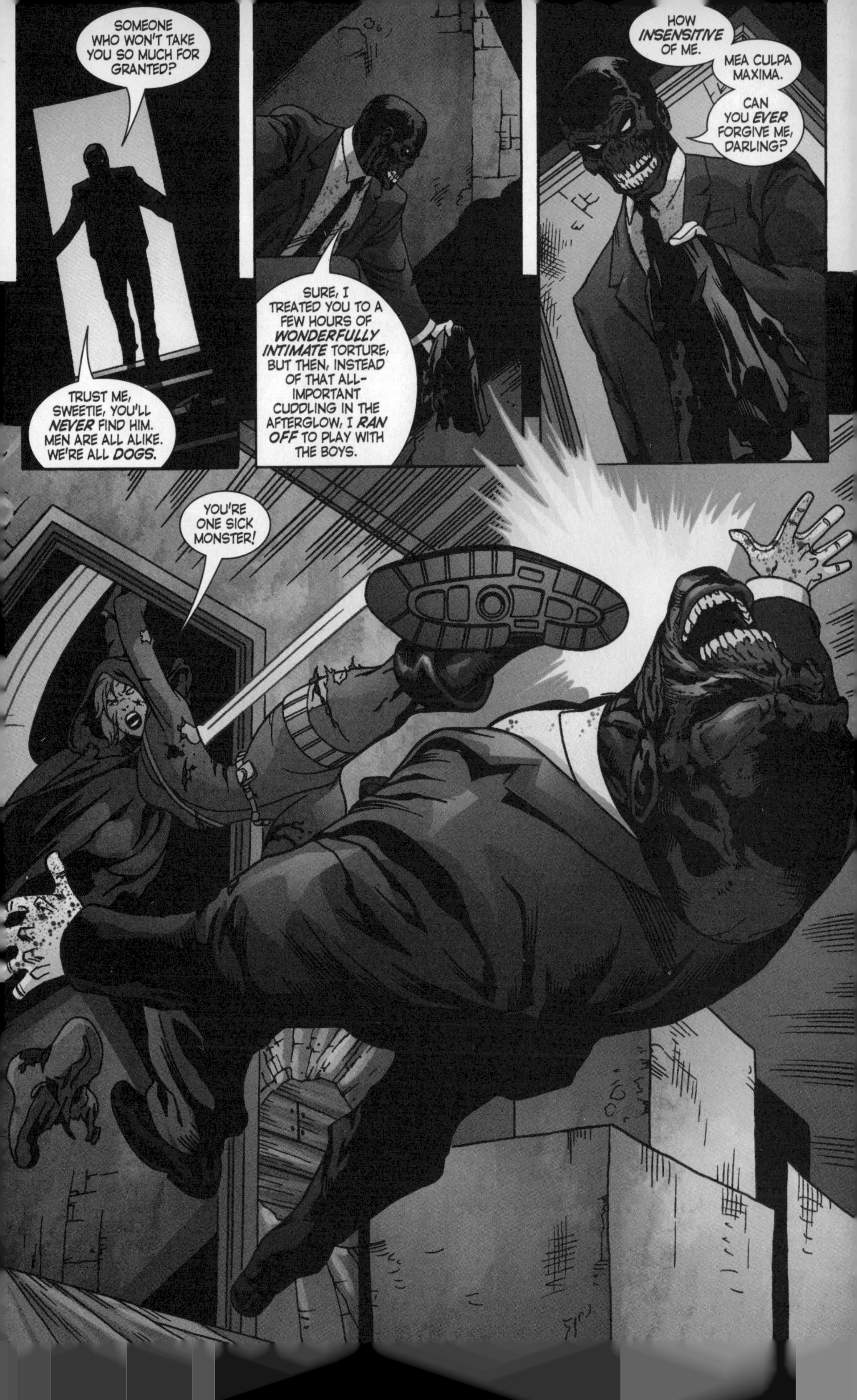
SOMEONE WHO WON'T TAKE YOU SO MUCH FOR GRANTED?
TRUST ME, SWEETIE, YOU'LL NEVER FIND HIM. MEN ARE ALL ALIKE. WE'RE ALL DOGS.
SURE, I TREATED YOU TO A FEW HOURS OF WONDERFULLY INTIMATE TORTURE, BUT THEN, INSTEAD OF THAT ALL-IMPORTANT CUDDLING IN THE AFTERGLOW, I RAN OFF TO PLAY WITH THE BOYS.
HOW INSENSITIVE OF ME.
MEA CULPA MAXIMA.
CAN YOU EVER FORGIVE ME, DARLING?
YOU'RE ONE SICK MONSTER!

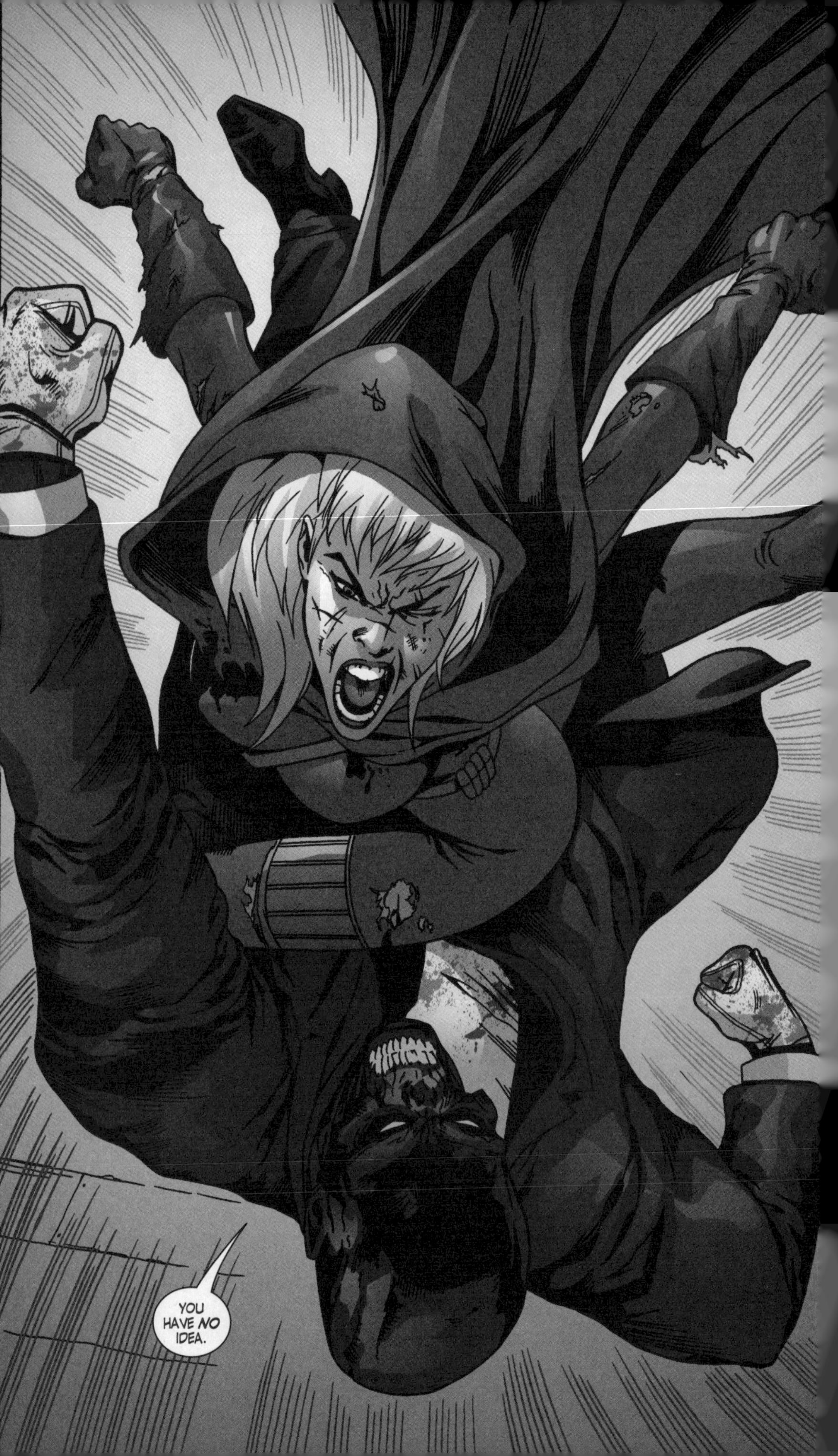
YOU HAVE NO IDEA.

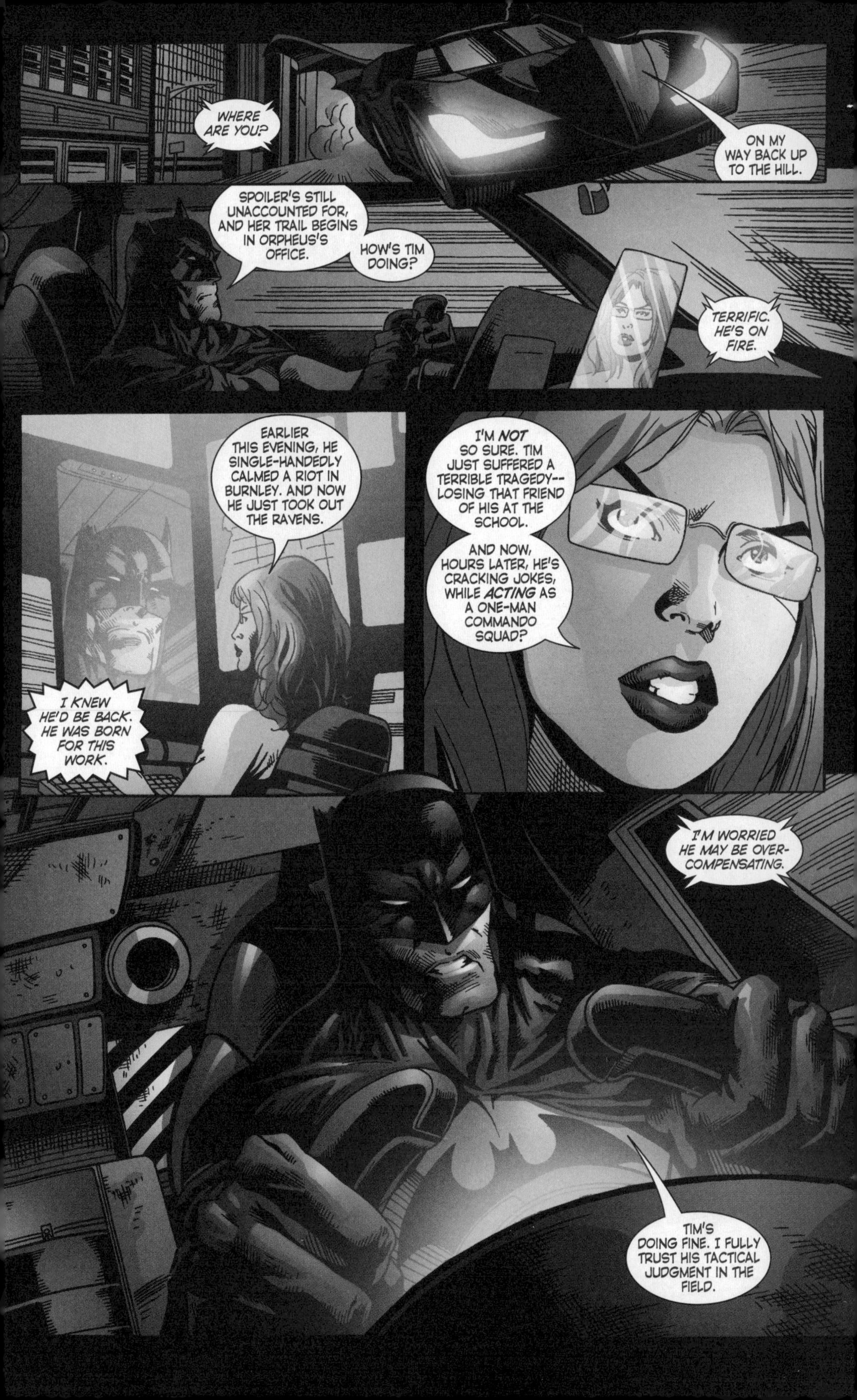
WHERE ARE YOU?
ON MY WAY BACK UP TO THE HILL.
SPOILER'S STILL UNACCOUNTED FOR, AND HER TRAIL BEGINS IN ORPHEUS'S OFFICE.
HOW'S TIM DOING?
TERRIFIC. HE'S ON FIRE.
EARLIER THIS EVENING, HE SINGLE-HANDEDLY CALMED A RIOT IN BURNLEY. AND NOW HE JUST TOOK OUT THE RAVENS.
I KNEW HE'D BE BACK. HE WAS BORN FOR THIS WORK.
I'M NOT SO SURE. TIM JUST SUFFERED A TERRIBLE TRAGEDY-- LOSING THAT FRIEND OF HIS AT THE SCHOOL.
AND NOW, HOURS LATER, HE'S CRACKING JOKES, WHILE ACTING AS A ONE-MAN COMMANDO SQUAD?
I'M WORRIED HE MAY BE OVER-COMPENSATING.
TIM'S DOING FINE. I FULLY TRUST HIS TACTICAL JUDGMENT IN THE FIELD.

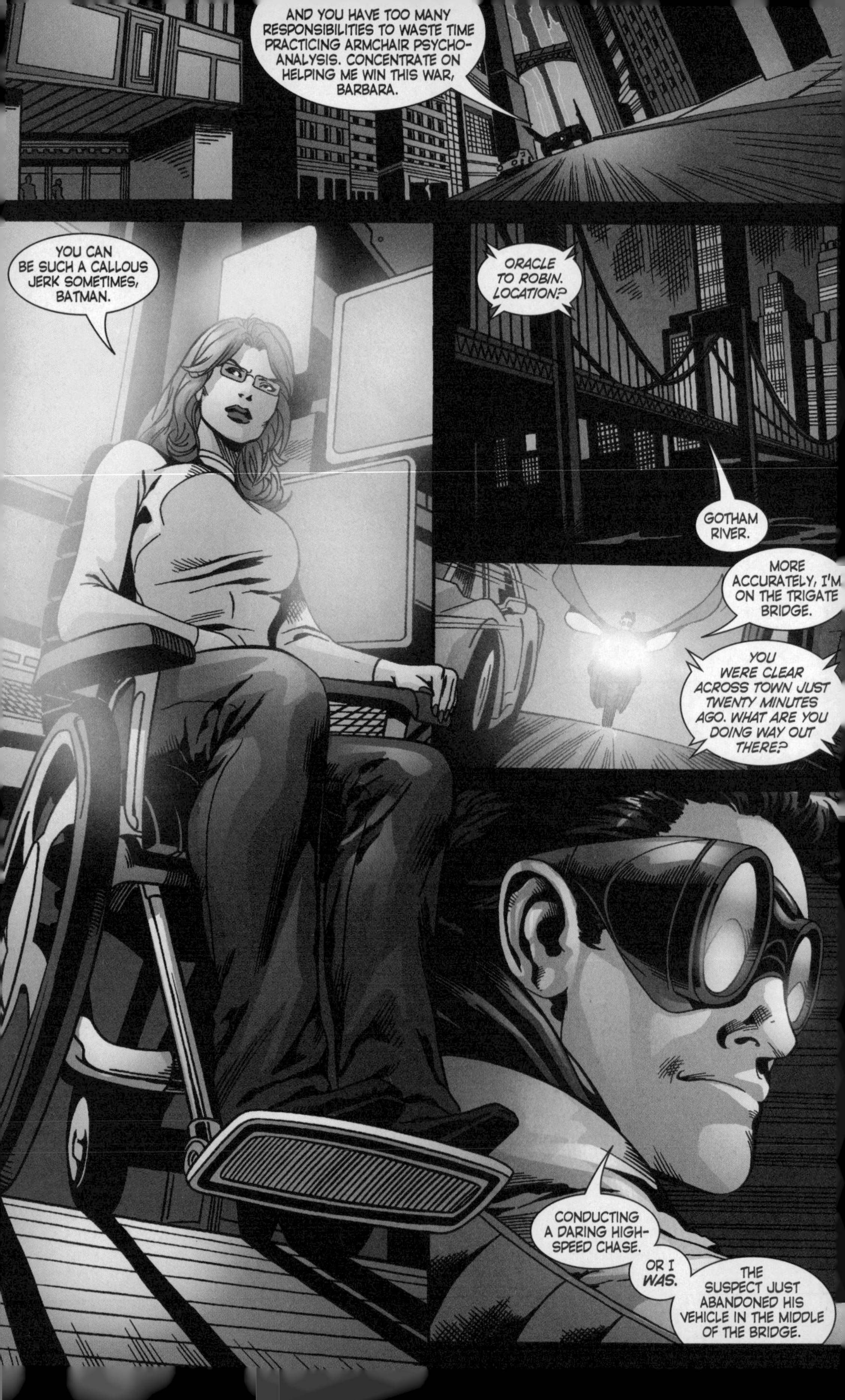
AND YOU HAVE TOO MANY RESPONSIBILITIES TO WASTE TIME PRACTICING ARMCHAIR PSYCHO-ANALYSIS. CONCENTRATE ON HELPING ME WIN THIS WAR, BARBARA.
YOU CAN BE SUCH A CALLOUS JERK SOMETIMES, BATMAN.
ORACLE TO ROBIN. LOCATION?
GOTHAM RIVER.
MORE ACCURATELY, I'M ON THE TRIGATE BRIDGE.
YOU WERE CLEAR ACROSS TOWN JUST TWENTY MINUTES AGO. WHAT ARE YOU DOING WAY OUT THERE?
CONDUCTING A DARING HIGH-SPEED CHASE.
OR I WAS.
THE SUSPECT JUST ABANDONED HIS VEHICLE IN THE MIDDLE OF THE BRIDGE.

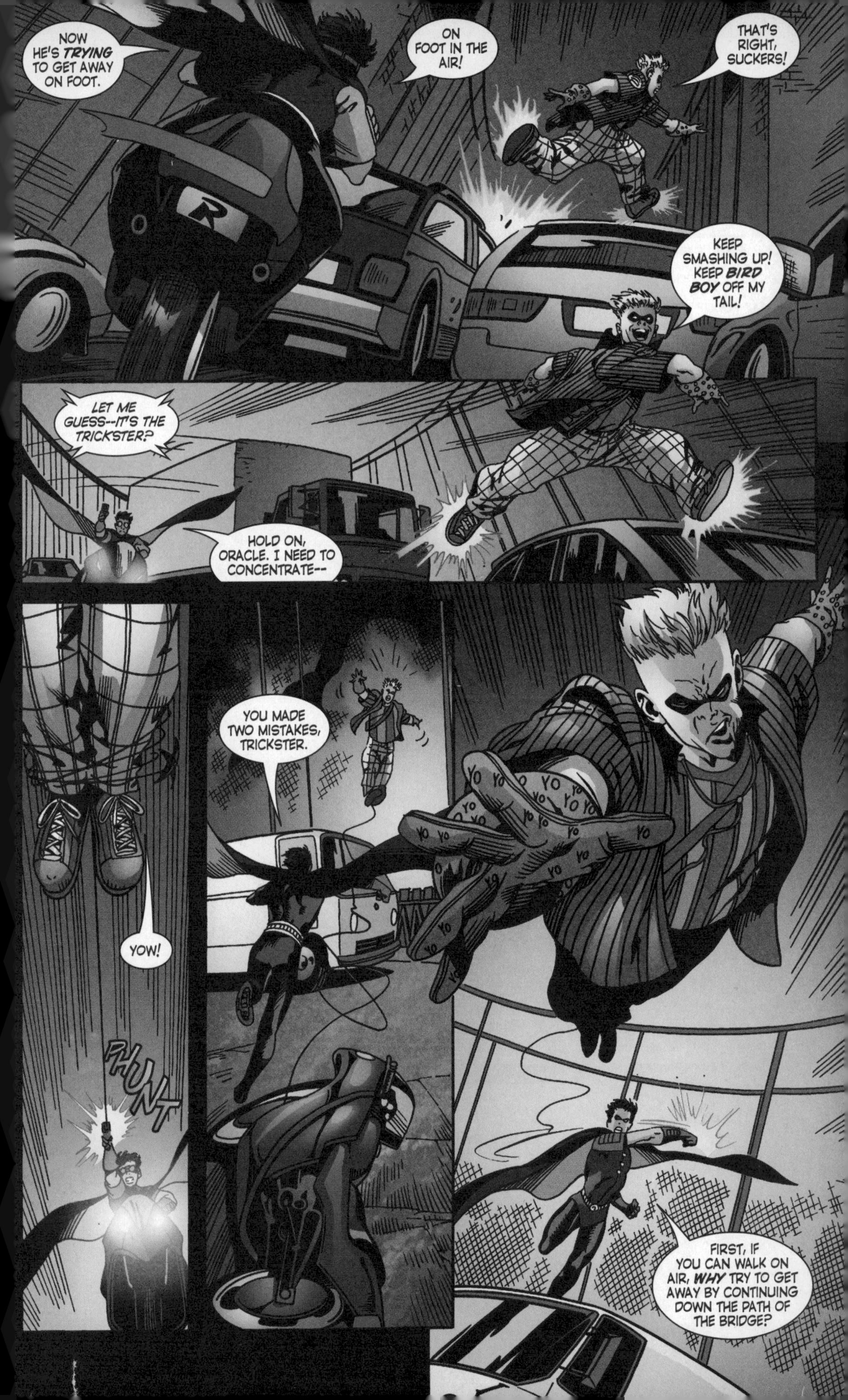
NOW HE'S TRYING TO GET AWAY ON FOOT.
ON FOOT IN THE AIR!
THAT'S RIGHT, SUCKERS!
KEEP SMASHING UP! KEEP BIRD BOY OFF MY TAIL!
LET ME GUESS--IT'S THE TRICKSTER?
HOLD ON, ORACLE. I NEED TO CONCENTRATE--
YOW!
PHUNT
YOU MADE TWO MISTAKES, TRICKSTER.
FIRST, IF YOU CAN WALK ON AIR, WHY TRY TO GET AWAY BY CONTINUING DOWN THE PATH OF THE BRIDGE?

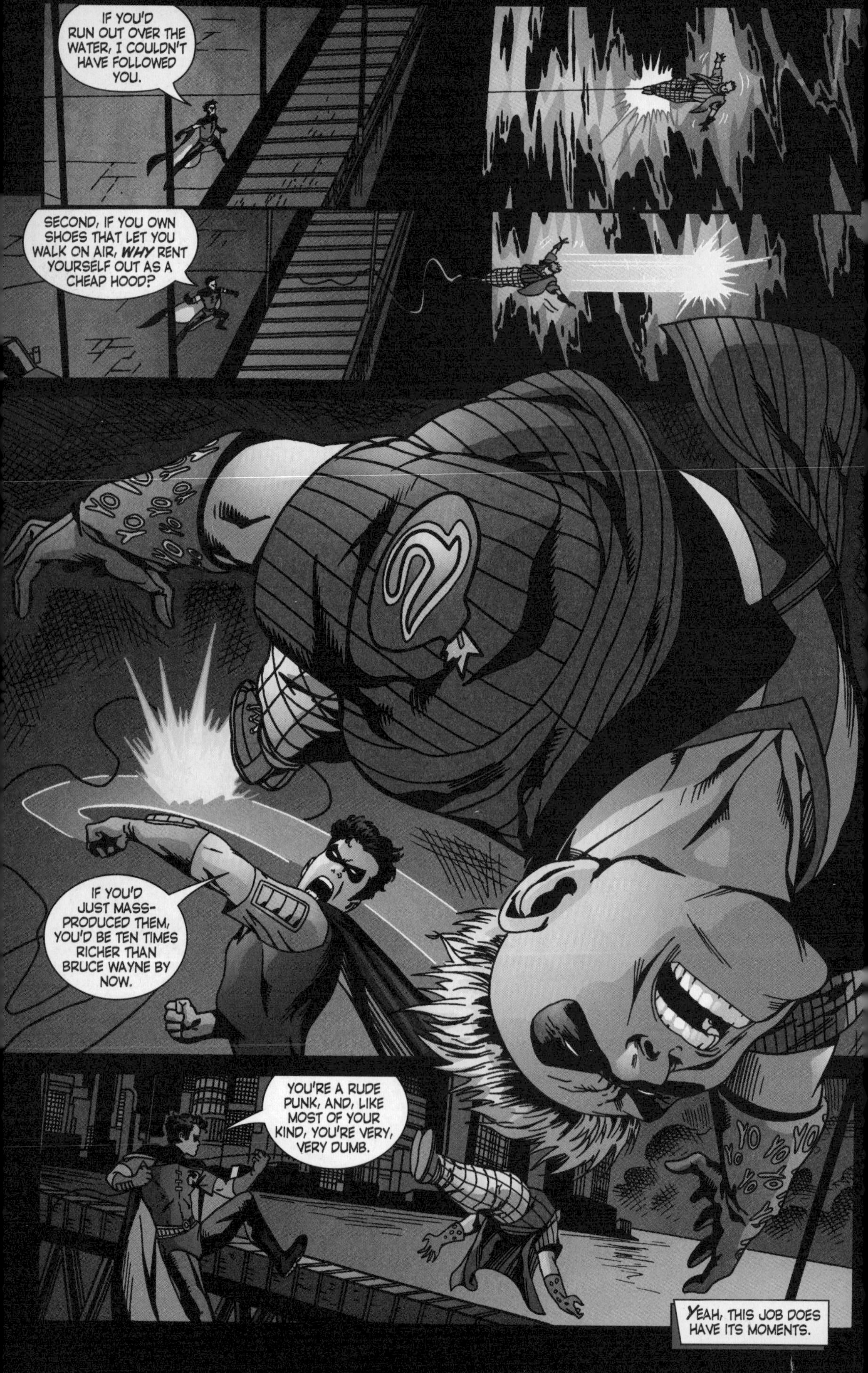
IF YOU'D RUN OUT OVER THE WATER, I COULDN'T HAVE FOLLOWED YOU.
SECOND, IF YOU OWN SHOES THAT LET YOU WALK ON AIR, *WHY* RENT YOURSELF OUT AS A CHEAP HOOD?
IF YOU'D JUST MASS-PRODUCED THEM, YOU'D BE TEN TIMES RICHER THAN BRUCE WAYNE BY NOW.
YOU'RE A RUDE PUNK, AND, LIKE MOST OF YOUR KIND, YOU'RE VERY, VERY DUMB.
YEAH, THIS JOB DOES HAVE ITS MOMENTS.

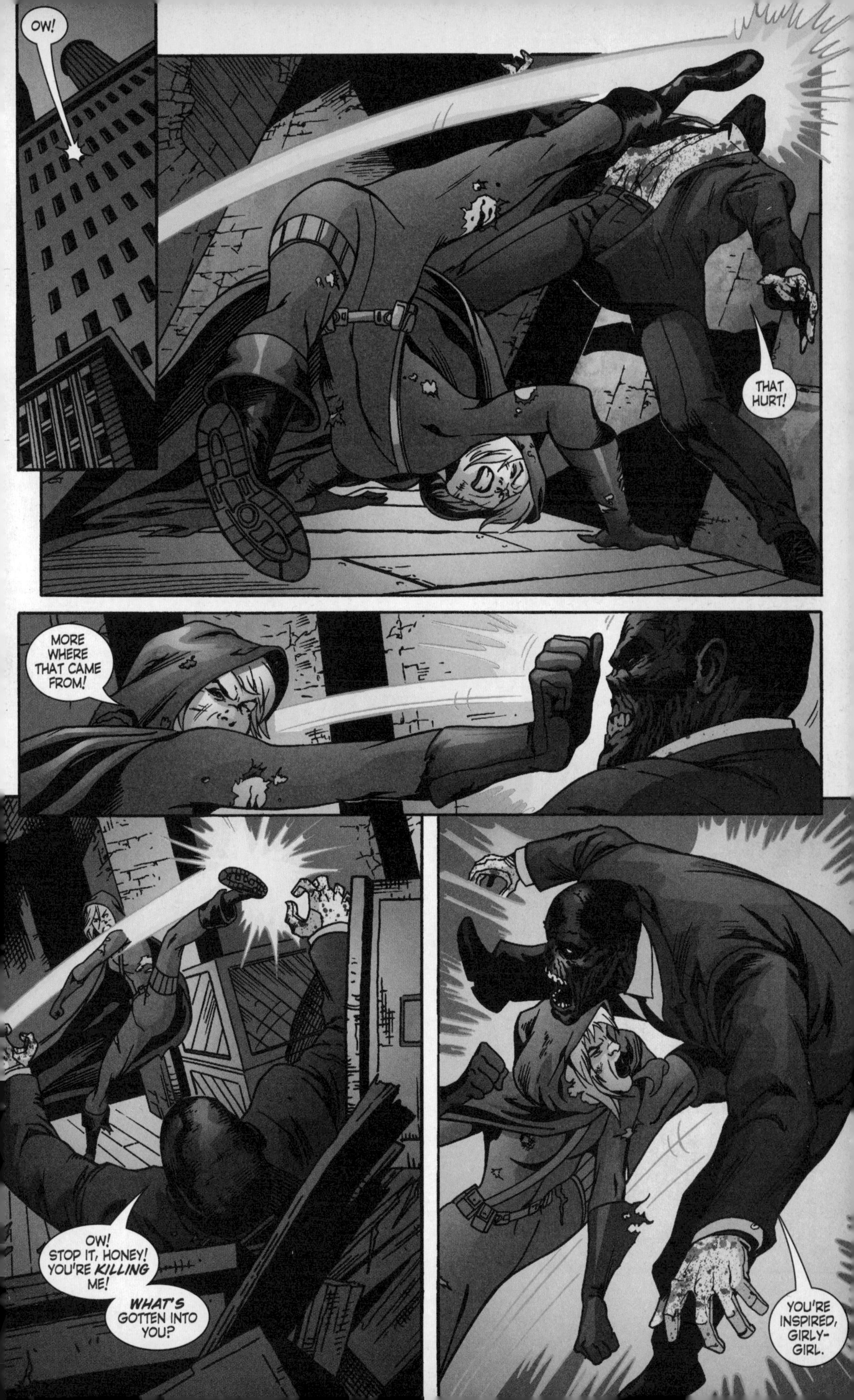
OW!
THAT HURT!
MORE WHERE THAT CAME FROM!
OW! STOP IT, HONEY! YOU'RE KILLING ME!
WHAT'S GOTTEN INTO YOU?
YOU'RE INSPIRED, GIRLY-GIRL.

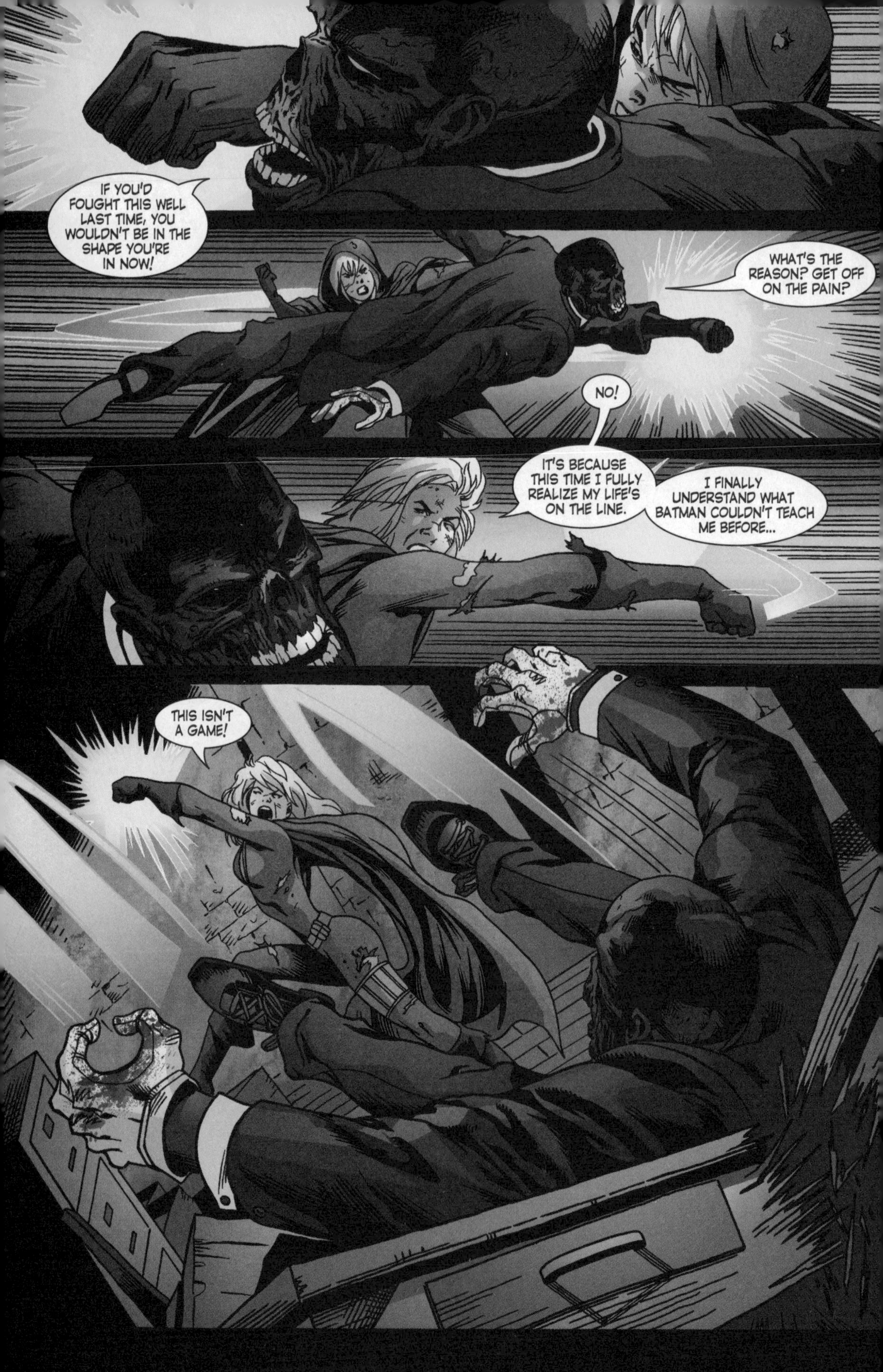
IF YOU'D FOUGHT THIS WELL LAST TIME, YOU WOULDN'T BE IN THE SHAPE YOU'RE IN NOW!
WHAT'S THE REASON? GET OFF ON THE PAIN?
NO!
IT'S BECAUSE THIS TIME I FULLY REALIZE MY LIFE'S ON THE LINE.
I FINALLY UNDERSTAND WHAT BATMAN COULDN'T TEACH ME BEFORE...
THIS ISN'T A GAME!

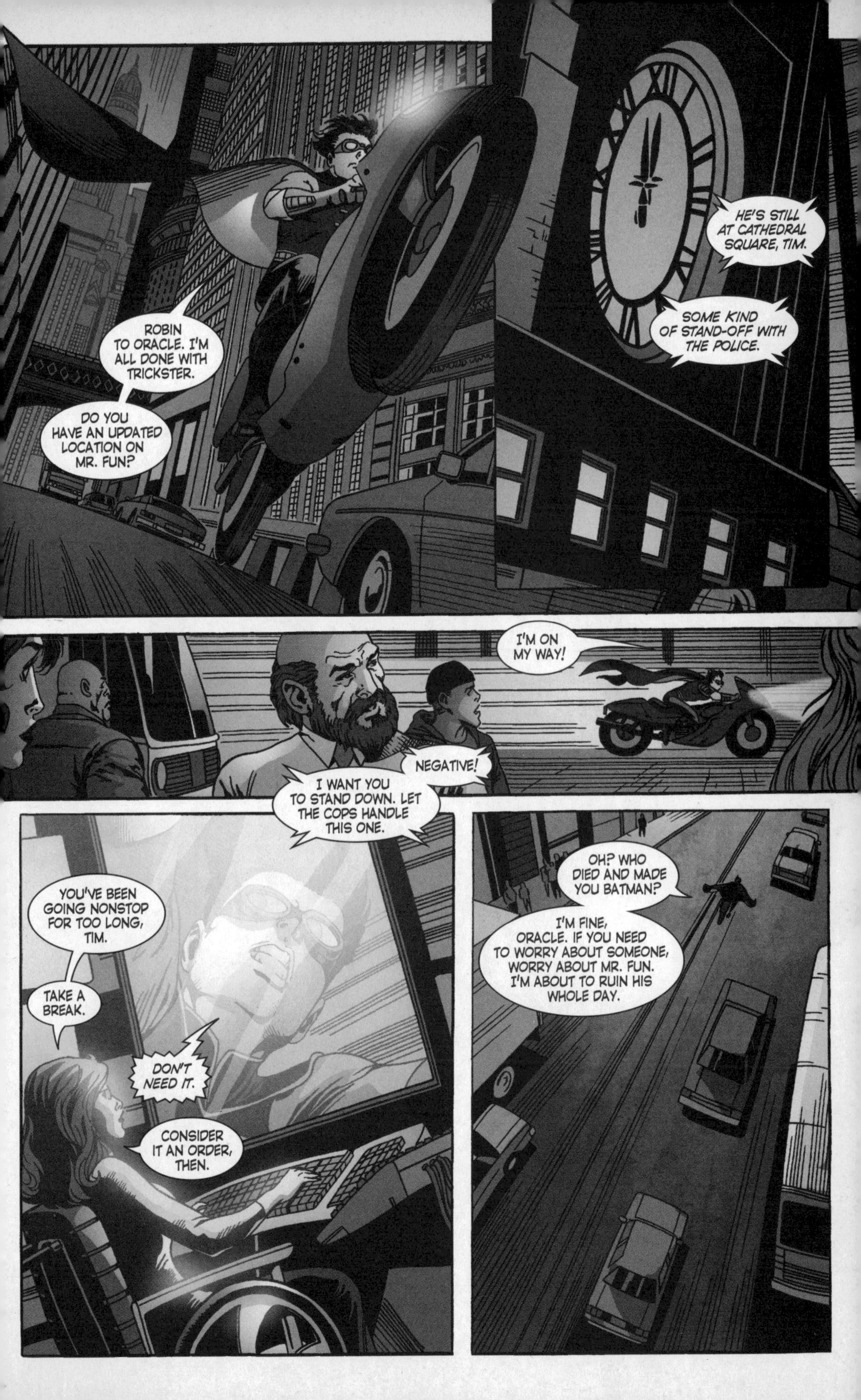
ROBIN TO ORACLE. I'M ALL DONE WITH TRICKSTER.
DO YOU HAVE AN UPDATED LOCATION ON MR. FUN?
HE'S STILL AT CATHEDRAL SQUARE, TIM.
SOME KIND OF STAND-OFF WITH THE POLICE.
I'M ON MY WAY!
NEGATIVE!
I WANT YOU TO STAND DOWN. LET THE COPS HANDLE THIS ONE.
YOU'VE BEEN GOING NONSTOP FOR TOO LONG, TIM.
TAKE A BREAK.
DON'T NEED IT.
CONSIDER IT AN ORDER, THEN.
OH? WHO DIED AND MADE YOU BATMAN?
I'M FINE, ORACLE. IF YOU NEED TO WORRY ABOUT SOMEONE, WORRY ABOUT MR. FUN. I'M ABOUT TO RUIN HIS WHOLE DAY.

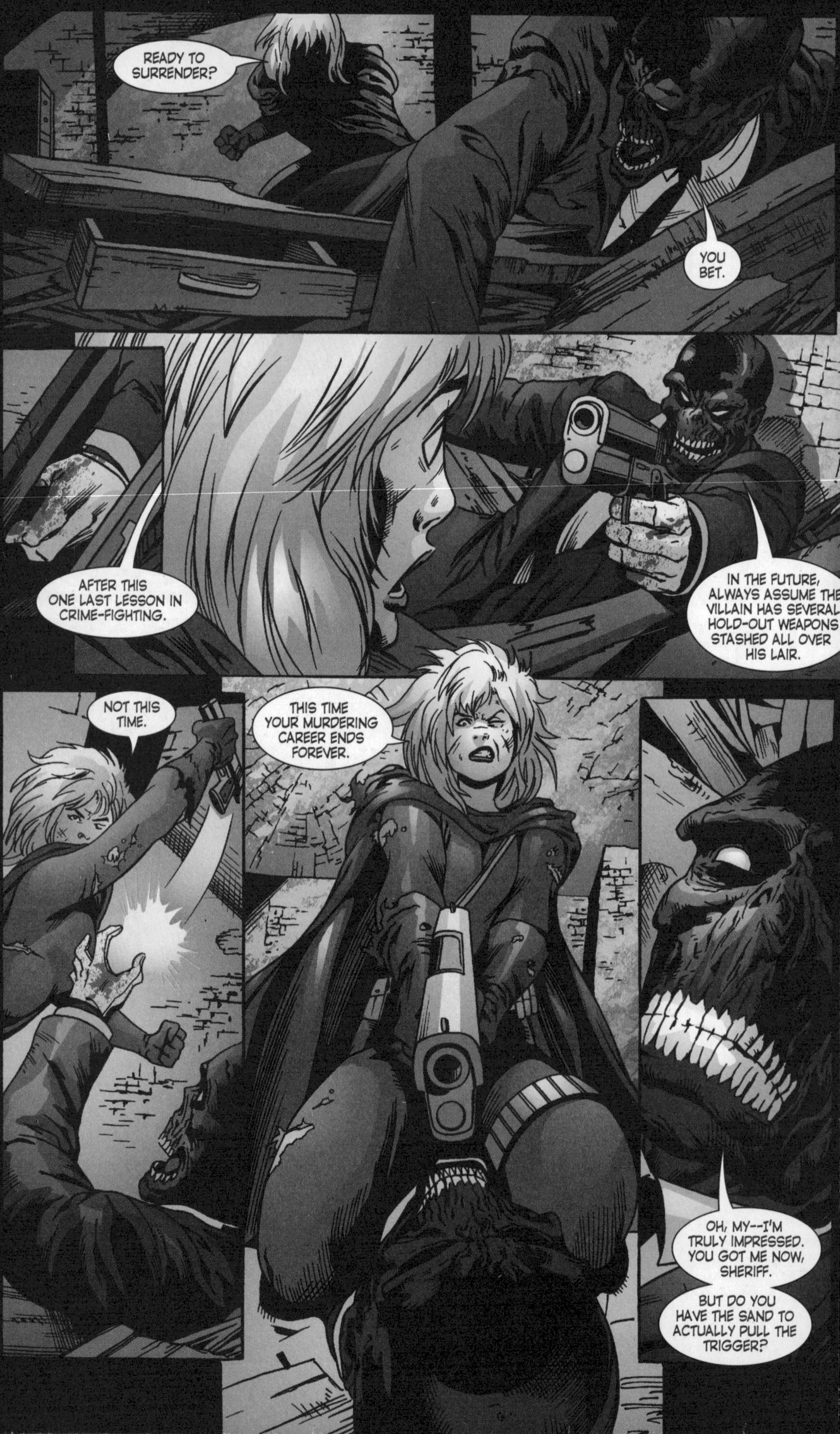
READY TO SURRENDER?
YOU BET.
AFTER THIS ONE LAST LESSON IN CRIME-FIGHTING.
IN THE FUTURE, ALWAYS ASSUME THE VILLAIN HAS SEVERAL HOLD-OUT WEAPONS STASHED ALL OVER HIS LAIR.
NOT THIS TIME.
THIS TIME YOUR MURDERING CAREER ENDS FOREVER.
OH, MY--I'M TRULY IMPRESSED. YOU GOT ME NOW, SHERIFF.
BUT DO YOU HAVE THE SAND TO ACTUALLY PULL THE TRIGGER?

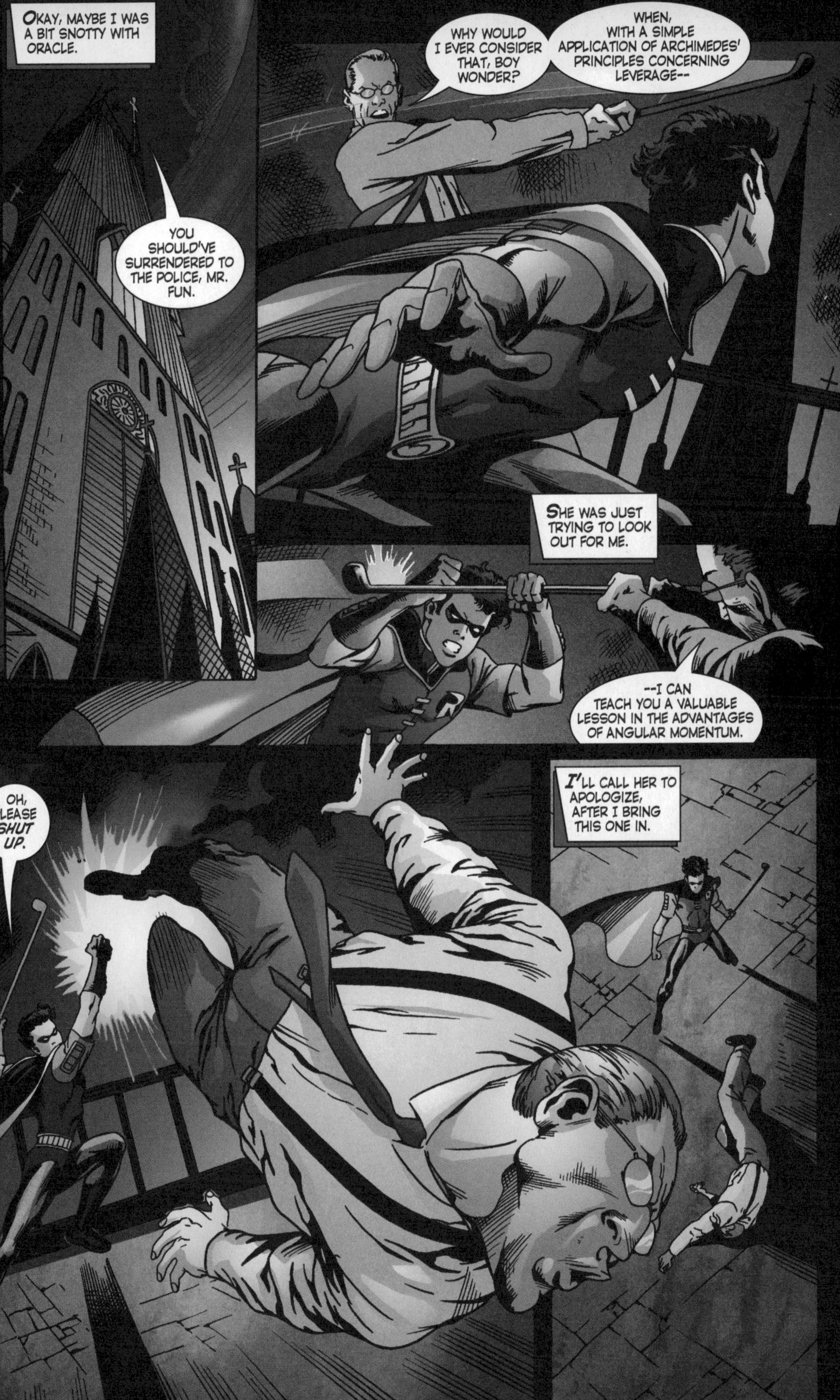
OKAY, MAYBE I WAS A BIT SNOTTY WITH ORACLE.
YOU SHOULD'VE SURRENDERED TO THE POLICE, MR. FUN.
WHY WOULD I EVER CONSIDER THAT, BOY WONDER?
WHEN, WITH A SIMPLE APPLICATION OF ARCHIMEDES' PRINCIPLES CONCERNING LEVERAGE--
SHE WAS JUST TRYING TO LOOK OUT FOR ME.
--I CAN TEACH YOU A VALUABLE LESSON IN THE ADVANTAGES OF ANGULAR MOMENTUM.
OH, PLEASE SHUT UP.
I'LL CALL HER TO APOLOGIZE, AFTER I BRING THIS ONE IN.

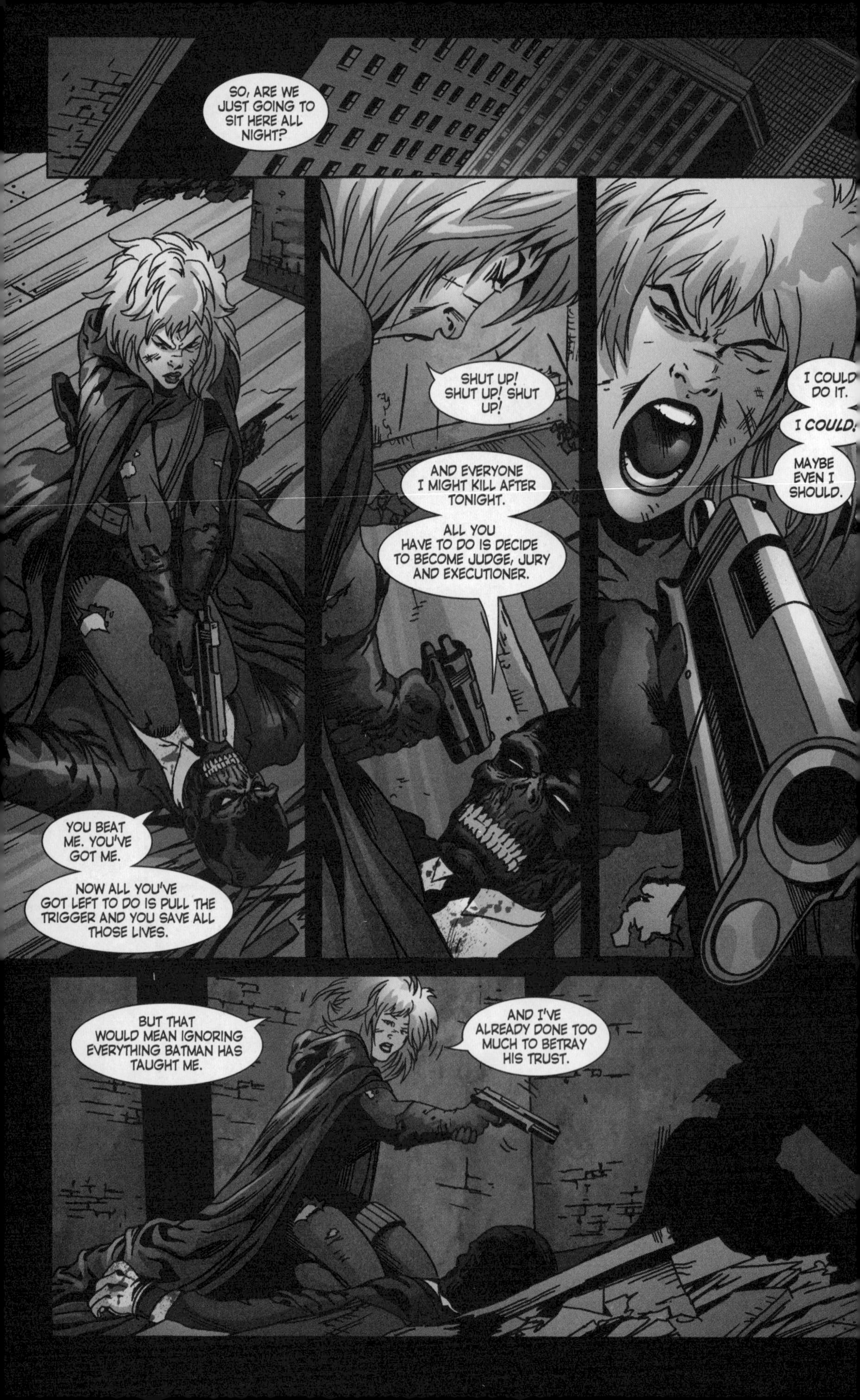
SO, ARE WE JUST GOING TO SIT HERE ALL NIGHT?
YOU BEAT ME. YOU'VE GOT ME.
NOW ALL YOU'VE GOT LEFT TO DO IS PULL THE TRIGGER AND YOU SAVE ALL THOSE LIVES.
SHUT UP! SHUT UP! SHUT UP!
AND EVERYONE I MIGHT KILL AFTER TONIGHT.
ALL YOU HAVE TO DO IS DECIDE TO BECOME JUDGE, JURY AND EXECUTIONER.
I COULD DO IT.
I *COULD.*
MAYBE EVEN I SHOULD.
BUT THAT WOULD MEAN IGNORING EVERYTHING BATMAN HAS TAUGHT ME.
AND I'VE ALREADY DONE TOO MUCH TO BETRAY HIS TRUST.

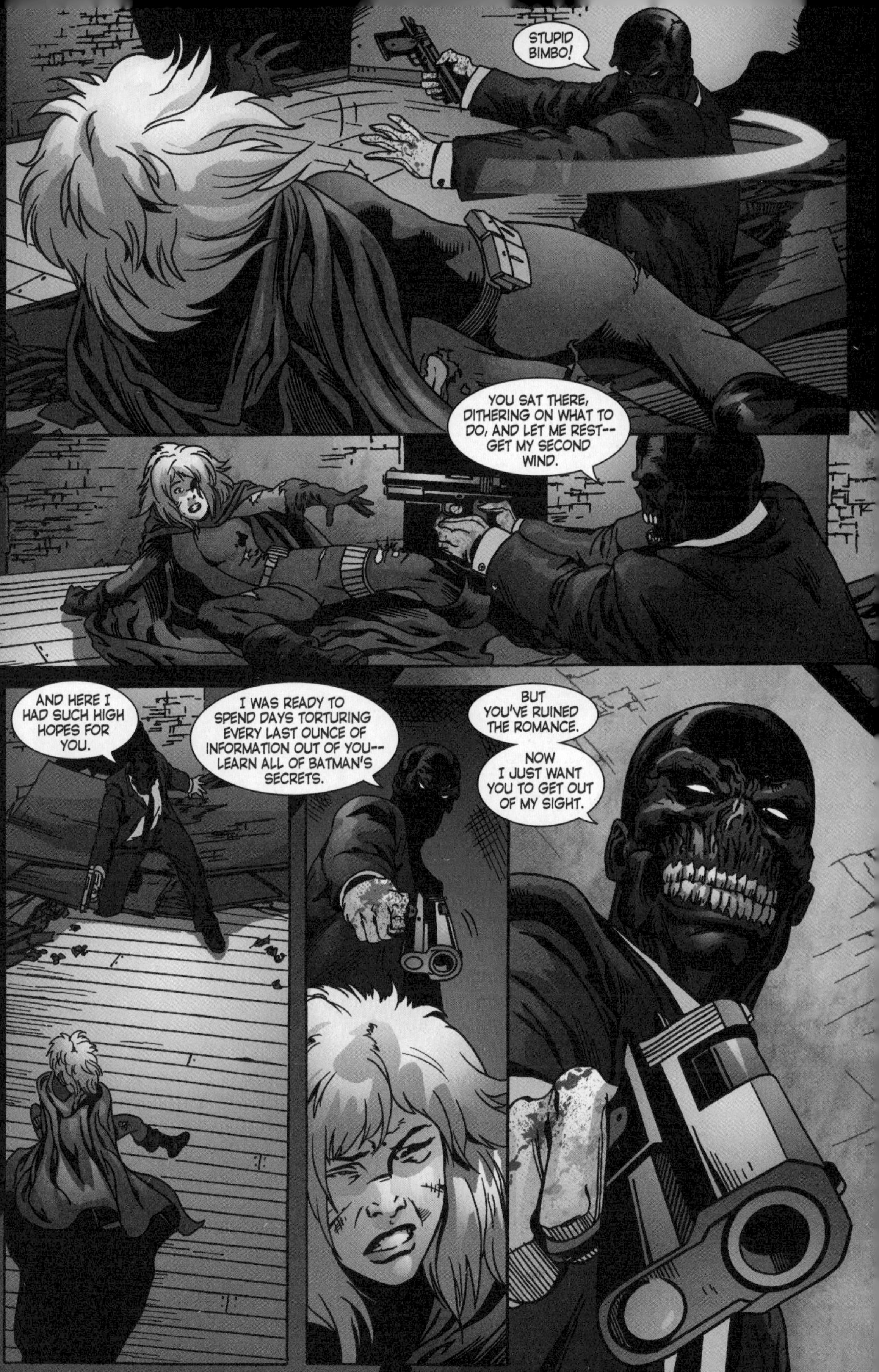
STUPID BIMBO!
YOU SAT THERE, DITHERING ON WHAT TO DO, AND LET ME REST-- GET MY SECOND WIND.
AND HERE I HAD SUCH HIGH HOPES FOR YOU.
I WAS READY TO SPEND DAYS TORTURING EVERY LAST OUNCE OF INFORMATION OUT OF YOU-- LEARN ALL OF BATMAN'S SECRETS.
BUT YOU'VE RUINED THE ROMANCE.
NOW I JUST WANT YOU TO GET OUT OF MY SIGHT.

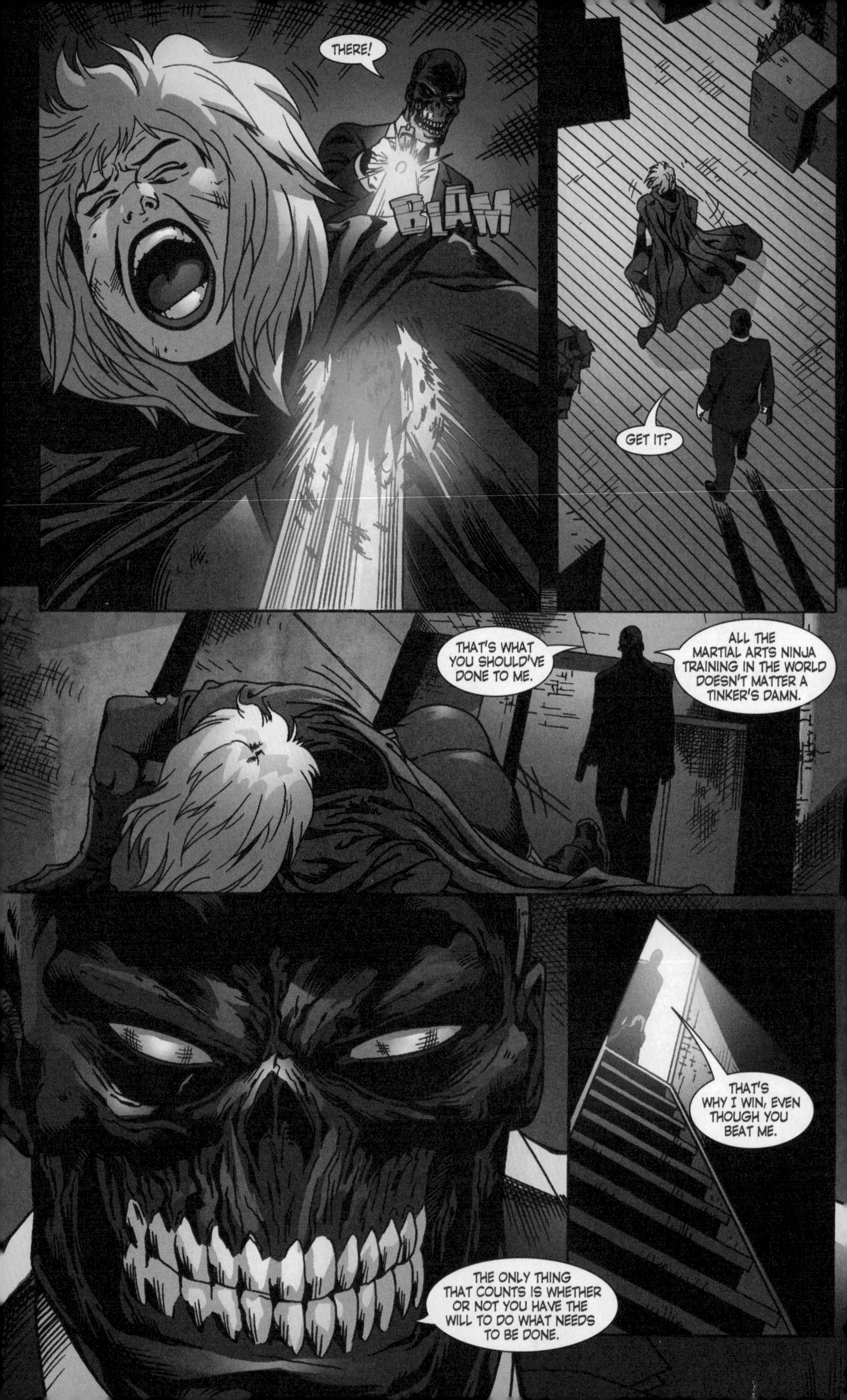
THERE!
BLAM
GET IT?
THAT'S WHAT YOU SHOULD'VE DONE TO ME.
ALL THE MARTIAL ARTS NINJA TRAINING IN THE WORLD DOESN'T MATTER A TINKER'S DAMN.
THE ONLY THING THAT COUNTS IS WHETHER OR NOT YOU HAVE THE WILL TO DO WHAT NEEDS TO BE DONE.
THAT'S WHY I WIN, EVEN THOUGH YOU BEAT ME.

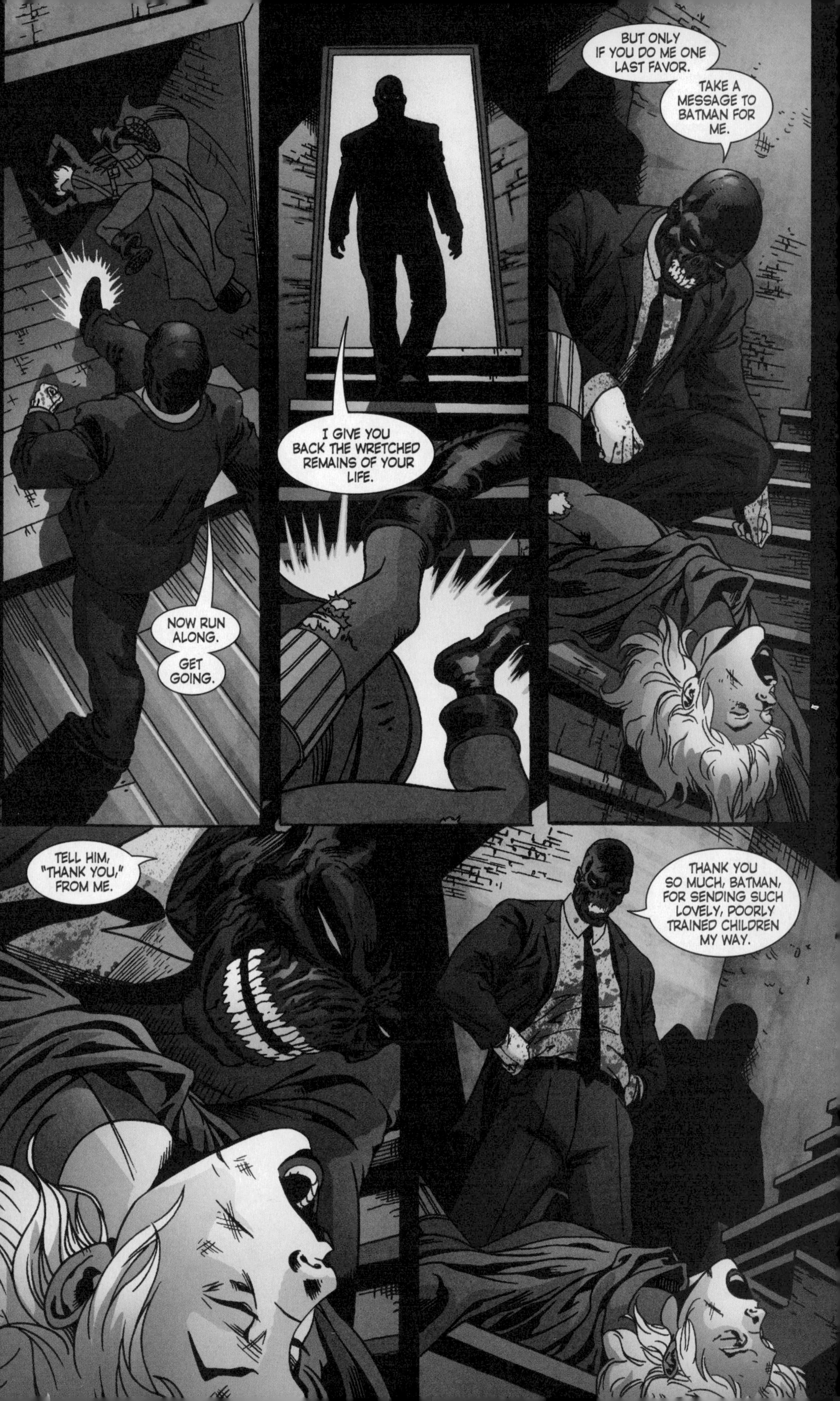
NOW RUN ALONG.
GET GOING.
I GIVE YOU BACK THE WRETCHED REMAINS OF YOUR LIFE.
BUT ONLY IF YOU DO ME ONE LAST FAVOR.
TAKE A MESSAGE TO BATMAN FOR ME.
TELL HIM, "THANK YOU," FROM ME.
THANK YOU SO MUCH, BATMAN, FOR SENDING SUCH LOVELY, POORLY TRAINED CHILDREN MY WAY.

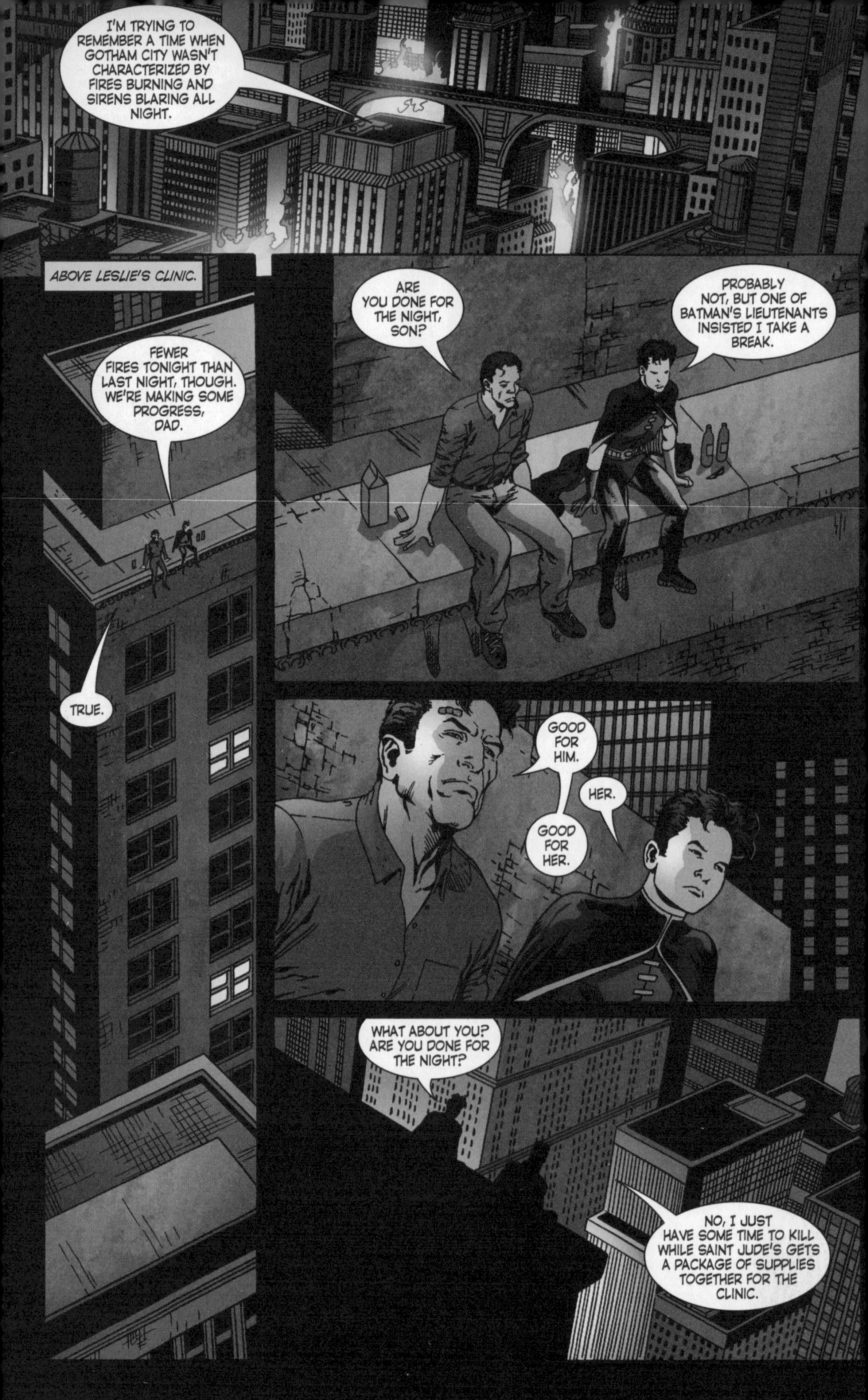
I'M TRYING TO REMEMBER A TIME WHEN GOTHAM CITY WASN'T CHARACTERIZED BY FIRES BURNING AND SIRENS BLARING ALL NIGHT.
ABOVE LESLIE'S CLINIC.
FEWER FIRES TONIGHT THAN LAST NIGHT, THOUGH. WE'RE MAKING SOME PROGRESS, DAD.
TRUE.
ARE YOU DONE FOR THE NIGHT, SON?
PROBABLY NOT, BUT ONE OF BATMAN'S LIEUTENANTS INSISTED I TAKE A BREAK.
GOOD FOR HIM.
HER.
GOOD FOR HER.
WHAT ABOUT YOU? ARE YOU DONE FOR THE NIGHT?
NO, I JUST HAVE SOME TIME TO KILL WHILE SAINT JUDE'S GETS A PACKAGE OF SUPPLIES TOGETHER FOR THE CLINIC.

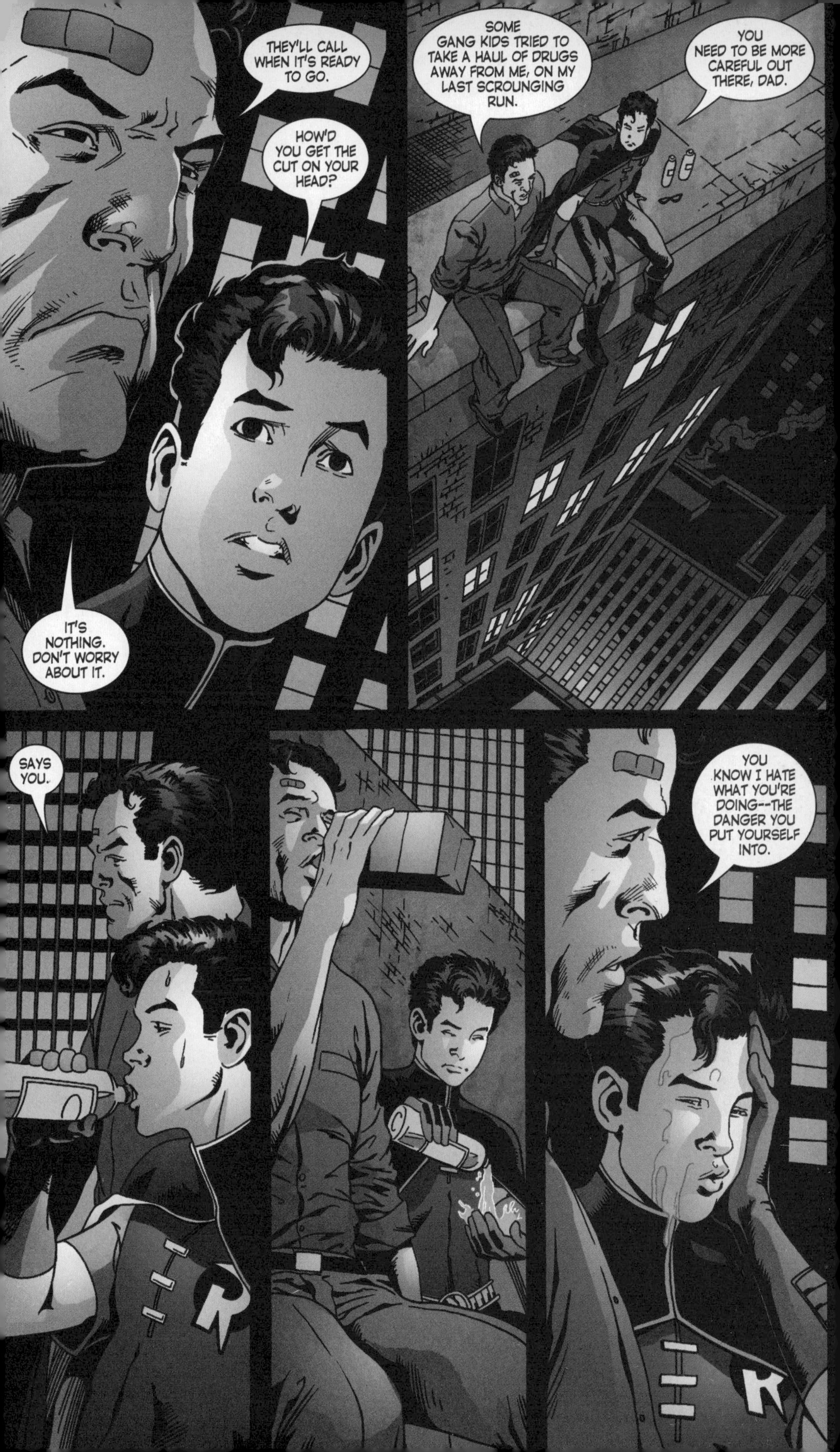
THEY'LL CALL WHEN IT'S READY TO GO.
HOW'D YOU GET THE CUT ON YOUR HEAD?
IT'S NOTHING. DON'T WORRY ABOUT IT.
SOME GANG KIDS TRIED TO TAKE A HAUL OF DRUGS AWAY FROM ME, ON MY LAST SCROUNGING RUN.
YOU NEED TO BE MORE CAREFUL OUT THERE, DAD.
SAYS YOU.
YOU KNOW I HATE WHAT YOU'RE DOING--THE DANGER YOU PUT YOURSELF INTO.

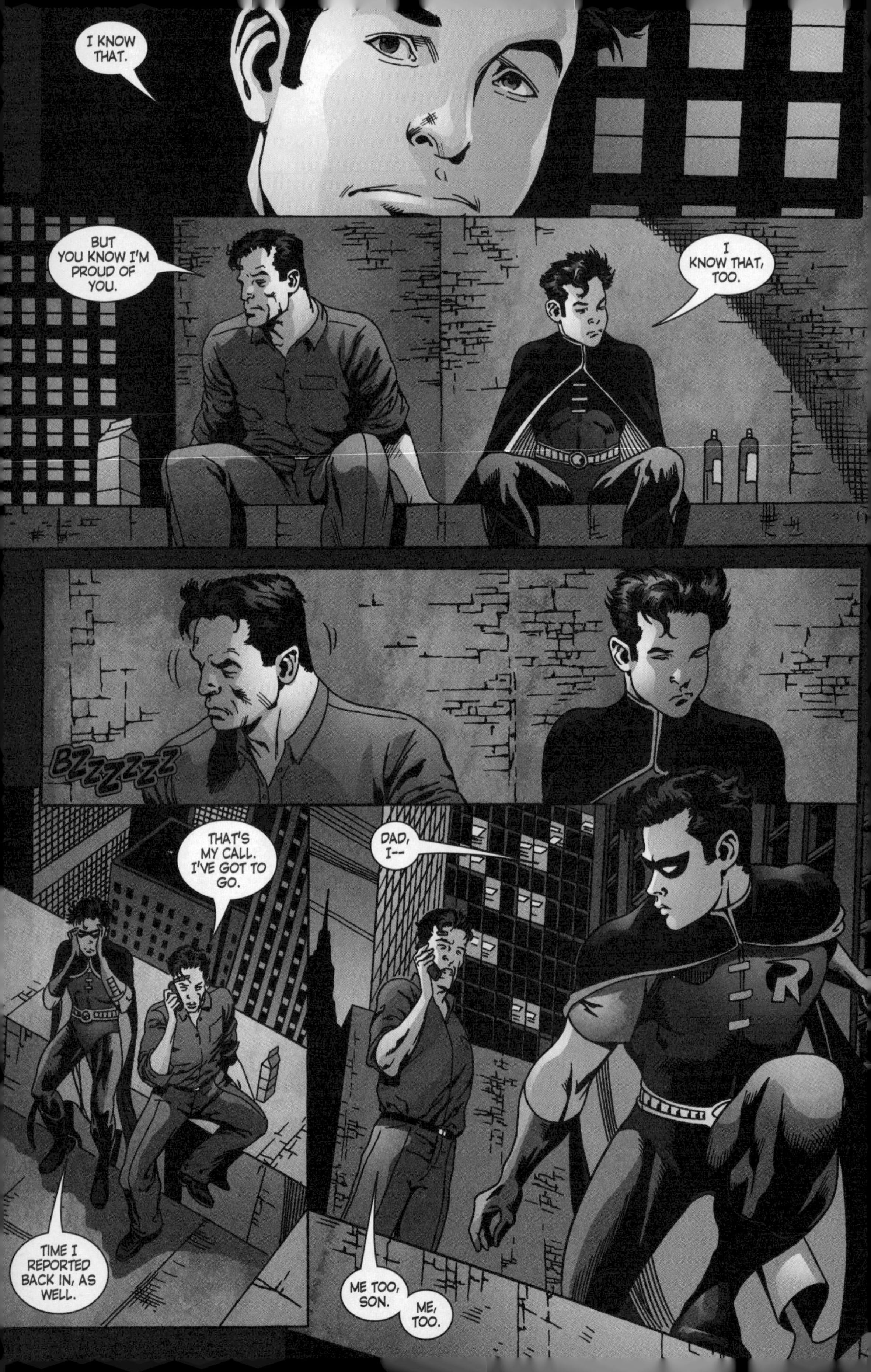
I KNOW THAT.
BUT YOU KNOW I'M PROUD OF YOU.
I KNOW THAT, TOO.
BZZZZZZ
THAT'S MY CALL. I'VE GOT TO GO.
TIME I REPORTED BACK IN, AS WELL.
DAD, I--
ME TOO, SON.
ME, TOO.

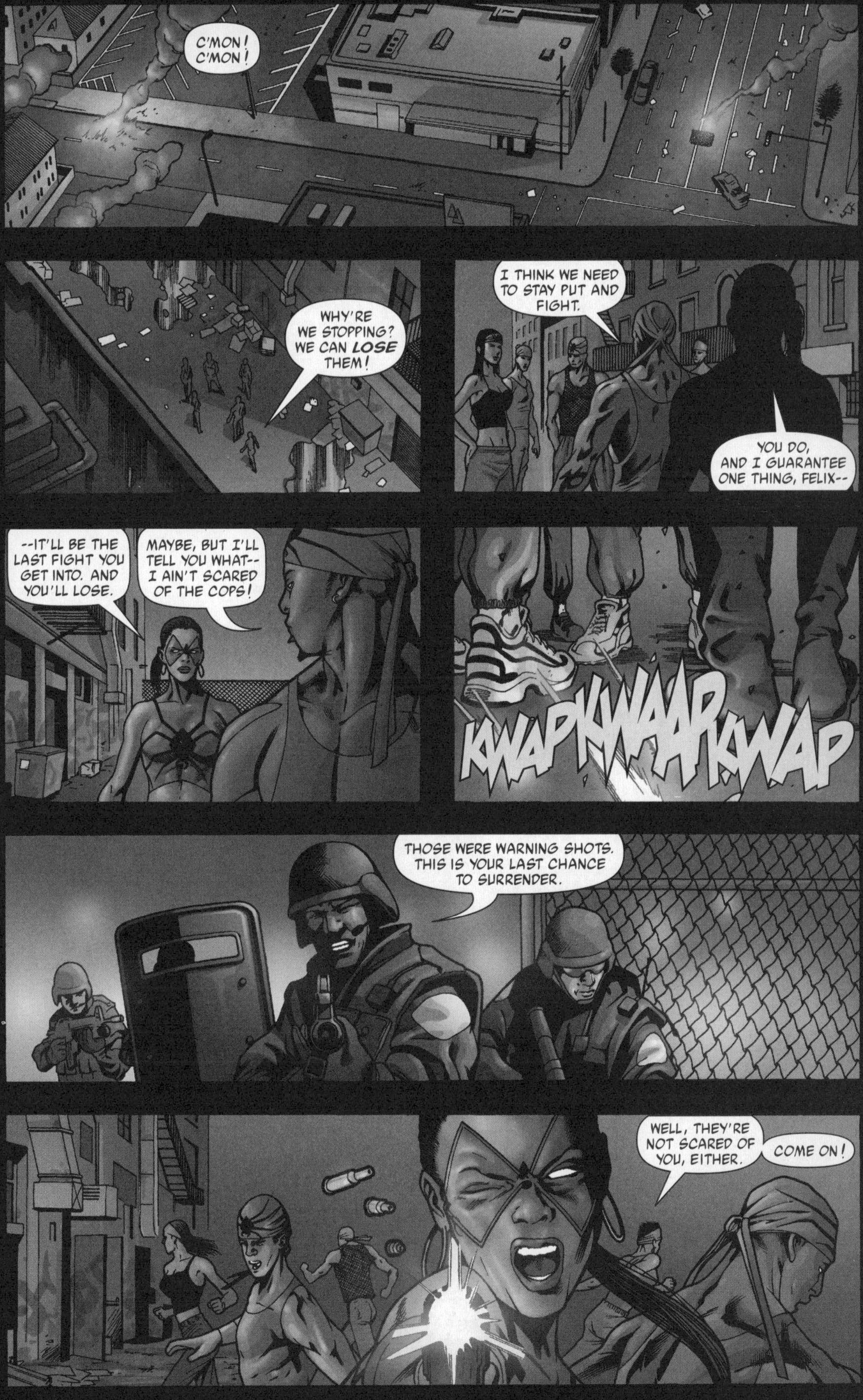
C'MON! C'MON!
WHY'RE WE STOPPING? WE CAN LOSE THEM!
I THINK WE NEED TO STAY PUT AND FIGHT.
YOU DO, AND I GUARANTEE ONE THING, FELIX--
--IT'LL BE THE LAST FIGHT YOU GET INTO. AND YOU'LL LOSE.
MAYBE, BUT I'LL TELL YOU WHAT-- I AIN'T SCARED OF THE COPS!
KWAPKWAAPKWAP
THOSE WERE WARNING SHOTS. THIS IS YOUR LAST CHANCE TO SURRENDER.
WELL, THEY'RE NOT SCARED OF YOU, EITHER.
COME ON!

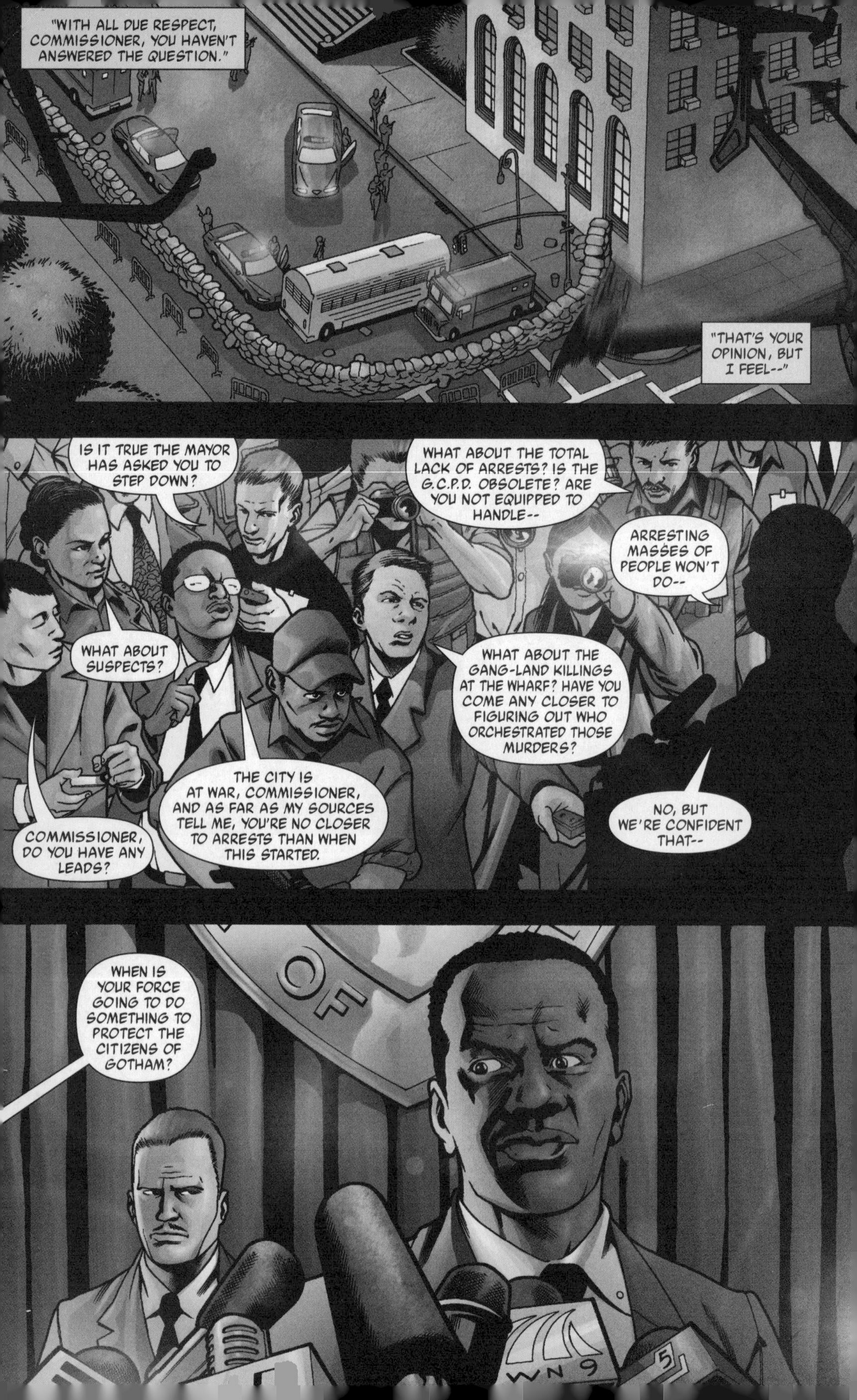
"WITH ALL DUE RESPECT, COMMISSIONER, YOU HAVEN'T ANSWERED THE QUESTION."
"THAT'S YOUR OPINION, BUT I FEEL--"
IS IT TRUE THE MAYOR HAS ASKED YOU TO STEP DOWN?
WHAT ABOUT THE TOTAL LACK OF ARRESTS? IS THE G.C.P.D. OBSOLETE? ARE YOU NOT EQUIPPED TO HANDLE--
ARRESTING MASSES OF PEOPLE WON'T DO--
WHAT ABOUT SUSPECTS?
WHAT ABOUT THE GANG-LAND KILLINGS AT THE WHARF? HAVE YOU COME ANY CLOSER TO FIGURING OUT WHO ORCHESTRATED THOSE MURDERS?
THE CITY IS AT WAR, COMMISSIONER, AND AS FAR AS MY SOURCES TELL ME, YOU'RE NO CLOSER TO ARRESTS THAN WHEN THIS STARTED.
COMMISSIONER, DO YOU HAVE ANY LEADS?
NO, BUT WE'RE CONFIDENT THAT--
WHEN IS YOUR FORCE GOING TO DO SOMETHING TO PROTECT THE CITIZENS OF GOTHAM?

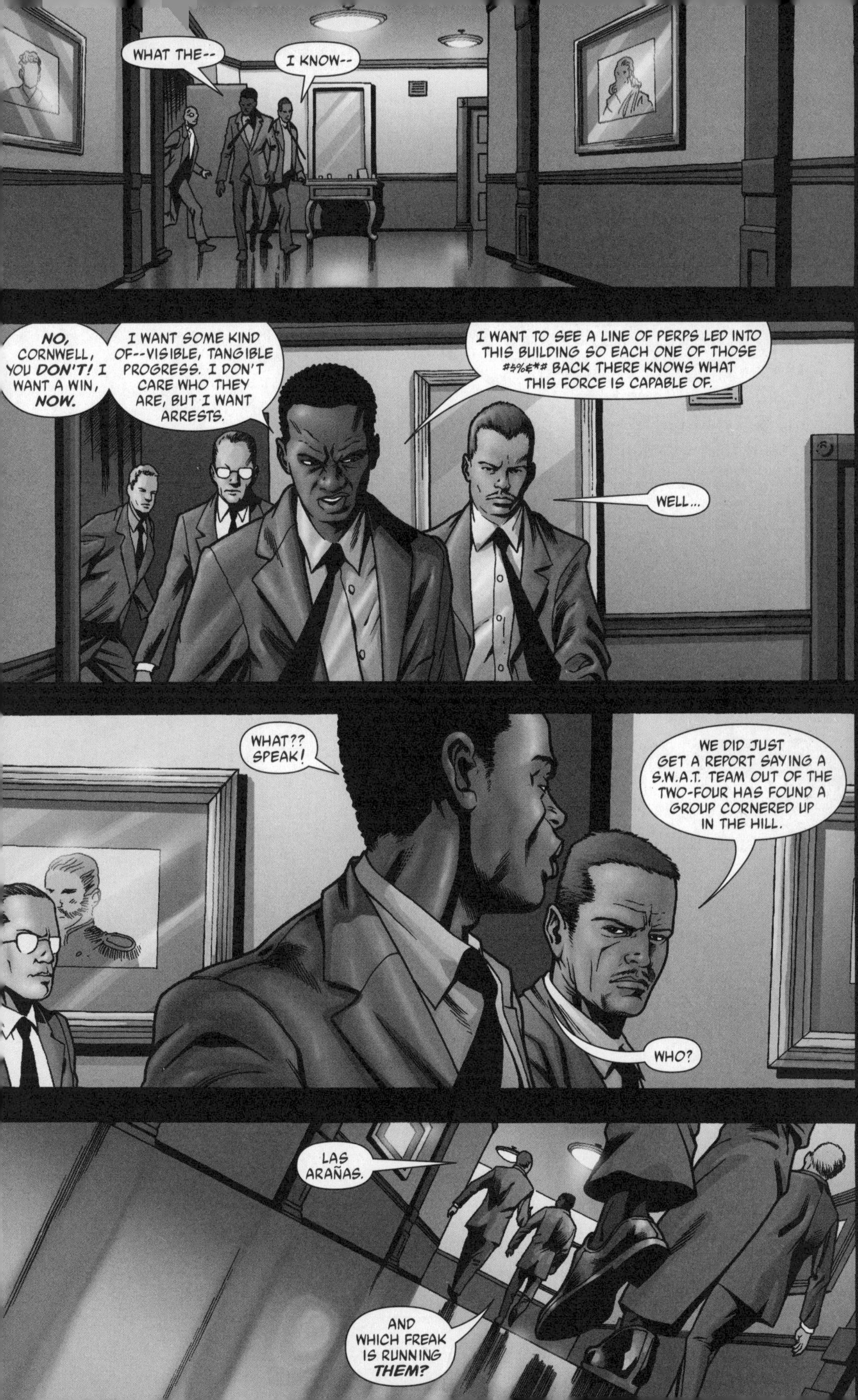

WHAT THE--
I KNOW--
NO, CORNWELL, YOU **DON'T!** I WANT A WIN, **NOW.**
I WANT SOME KIND OF--VISIBLE, TANGIBLE PROGRESS. I DON'T CARE WHO THEY ARE, BUT I WANT ARRESTS.
I WANT TO SEE A LINE OF PERPS LED INTO THIS BUILDING SO EACH ONE OF THOSE #$%€*# BACK THERE KNOWS WHAT THIS FORCE IS CAPABLE OF.
WELL...
WHAT?? SPEAK!
WE DID JUST GET A REPORT SAYING A S.W.A.T. TEAM OUT OF THE TWO-FOUR HAS FOUND A GROUP CORNERED UP IN THE HILL.
WHO?
LAS ARAÑAS.
AND WHICH FREAK IS RUNNING **THEM?**

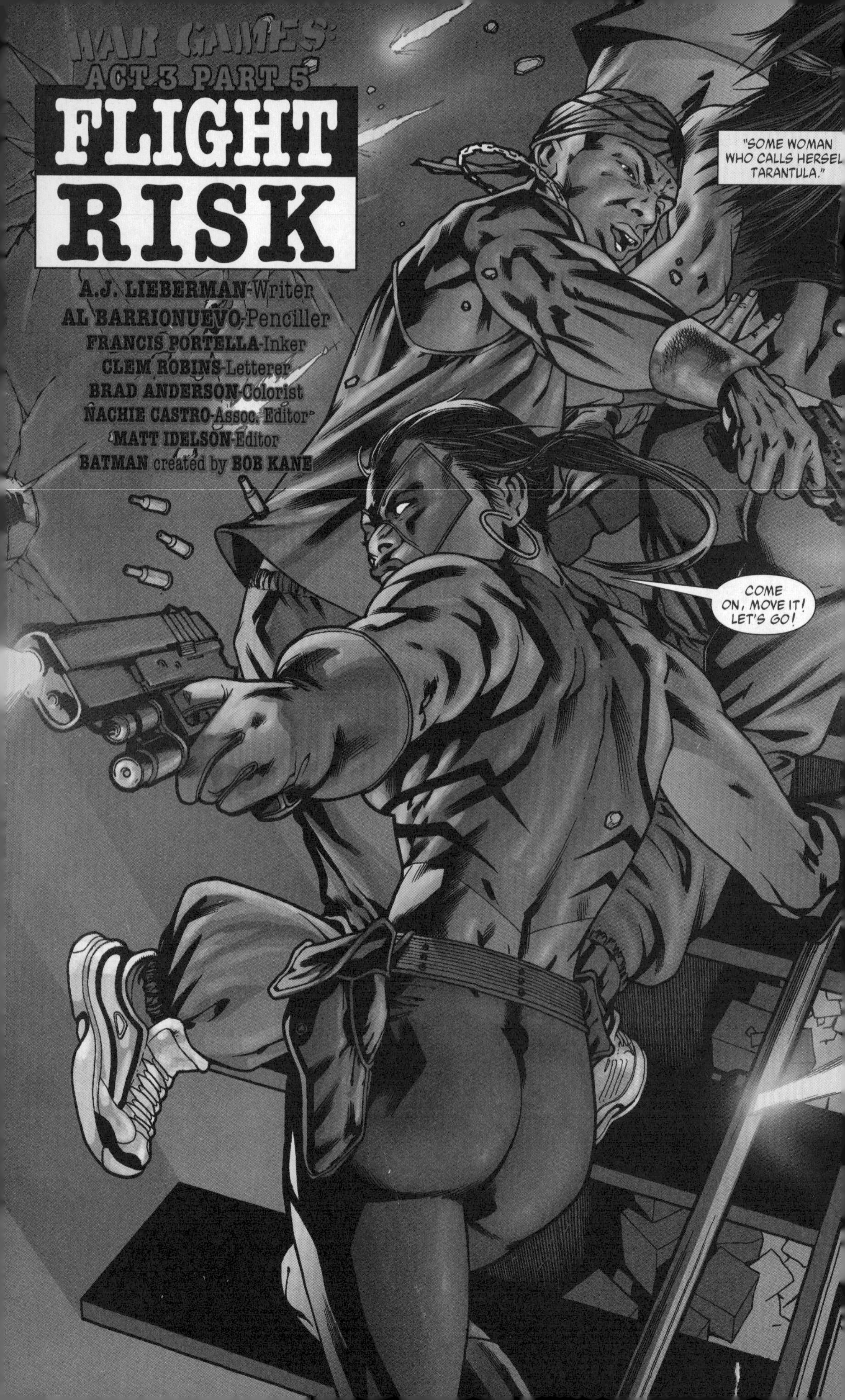
WAR GAMES:
ACT 3 PART 5
FLIGHT
RISK
A.J. LIEBERMAN-Writer
AL BARRIONUEVO-Penciller
FRANCIS PORTELLA-Inker
CLEM ROBINS-Letterer
BRAD ANDERSON-Colorist
ÑACHIE CASTRO-Assoc. Editor
MATT IDELSON-Editor
BATMAN created by BOB KANE
"SOME WOMAN WHO CALLS HERSEL TARANTULA."
COME ON, MOVE IT! LET'S GO!

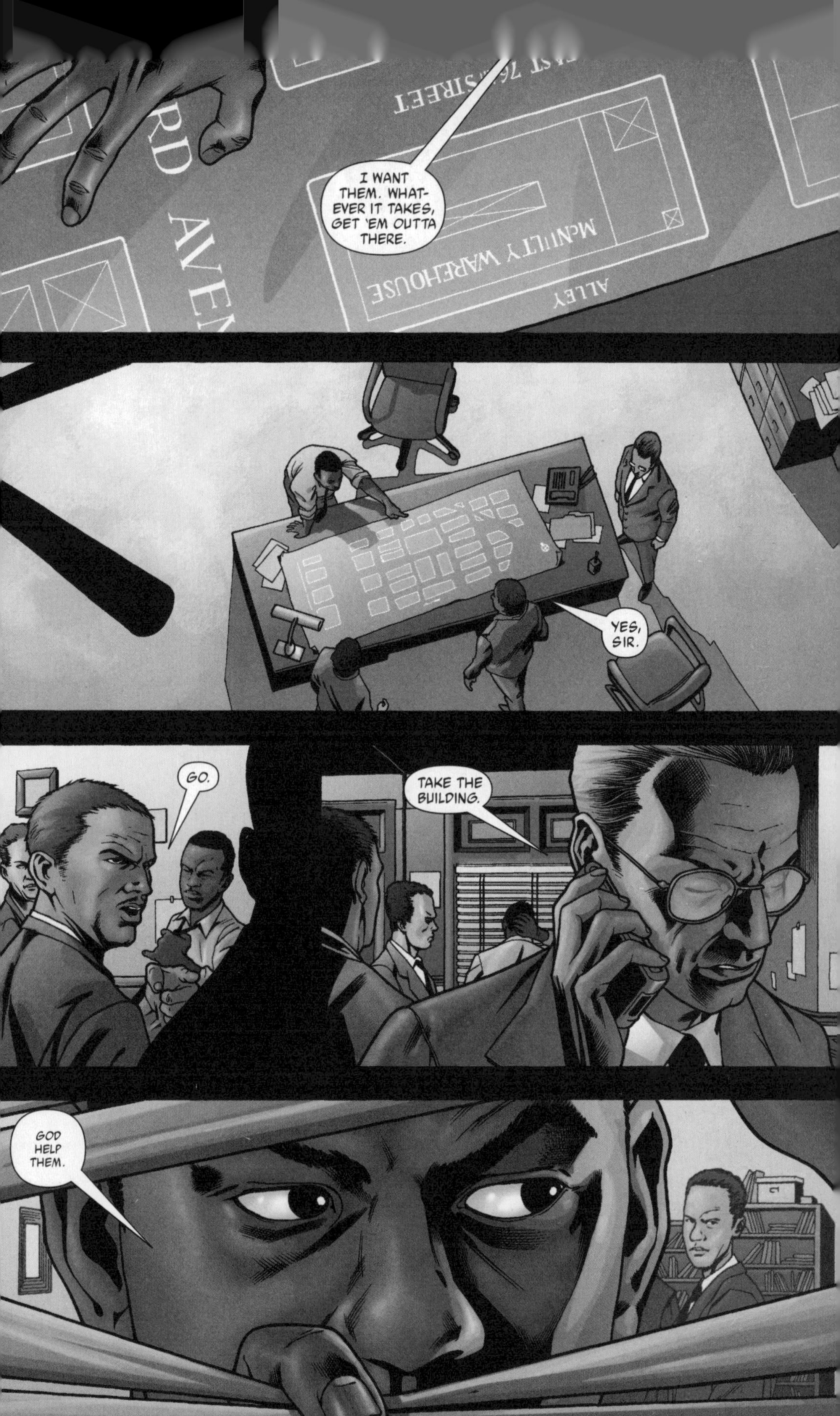
I WANT THEM. WHAT-EVER IT TAKES, GET 'EM OUTTA THERE.
McNULTY WAREHOUSE
ALLEY
YES, SIR.
GO.
TAKE THE BUILDING.
GOD HELP THEM.

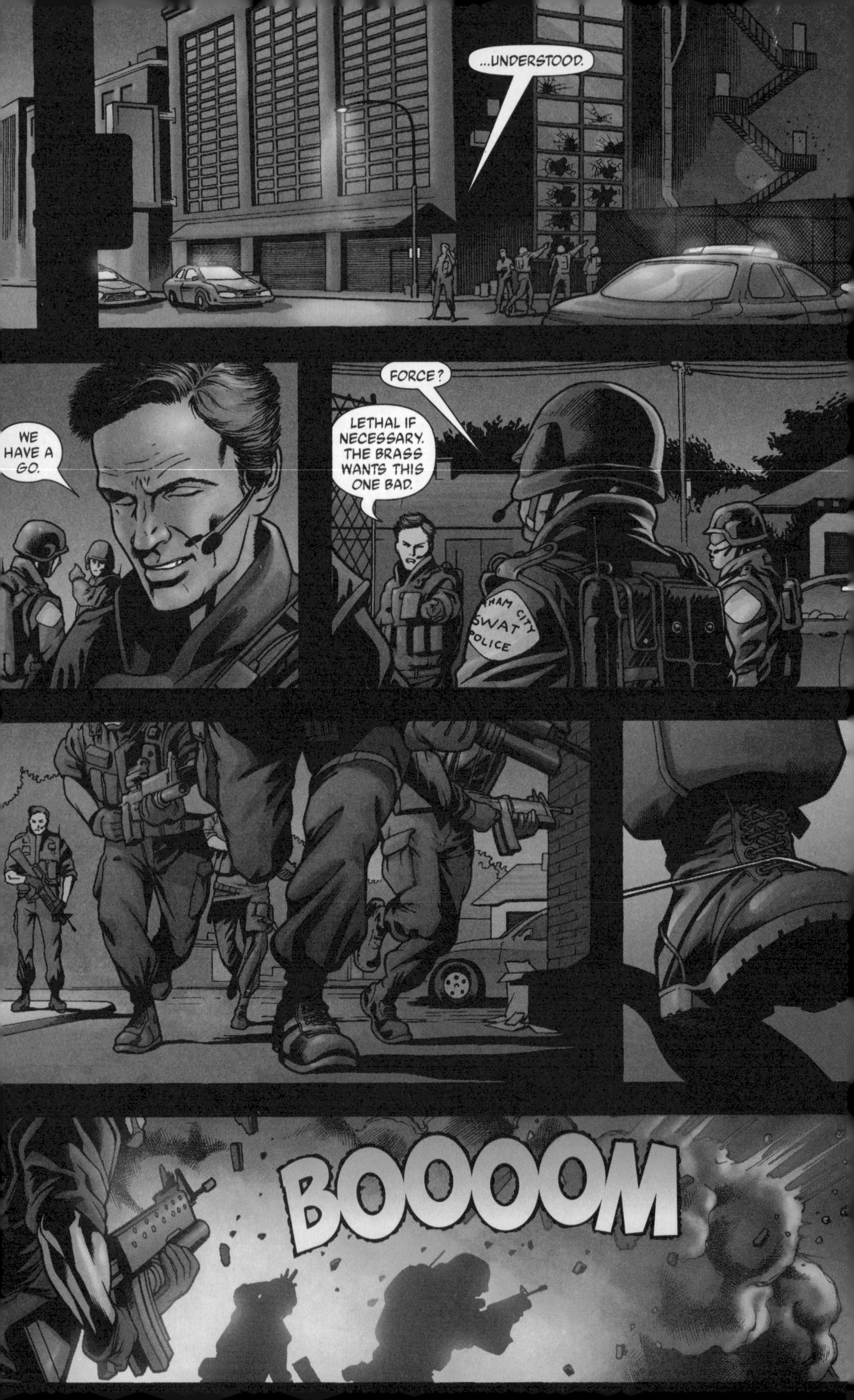

...UNDERSTOOD.
WE HAVE A GO.
FORCE?
LETHAL IF NECESSARY. THE BRASS WANTS THIS ONE BAD.
SWAT
POLICE
BOOOOOM

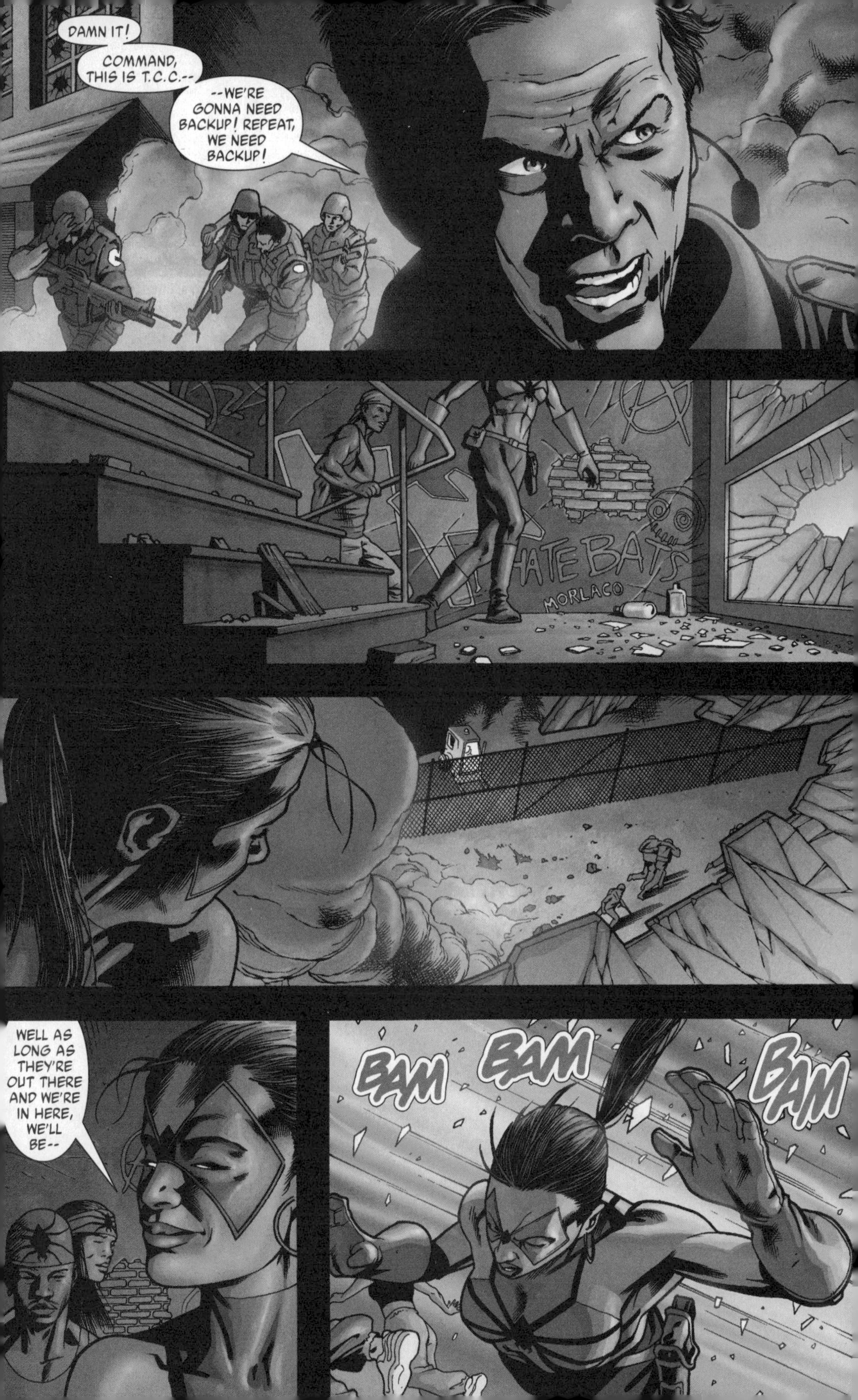
DAMN IT!
COMMAND, THIS IS T.C.C.--
--WE'RE GONNA NEED BACKUP! REPEAT, WE NEED BACKUP!
HATE BATS
MORLACO
WELL AS LONG AS THEY'RE OUT THERE AND WE'RE IN HERE, WE'LL BE--
BAM
BAM
BAM

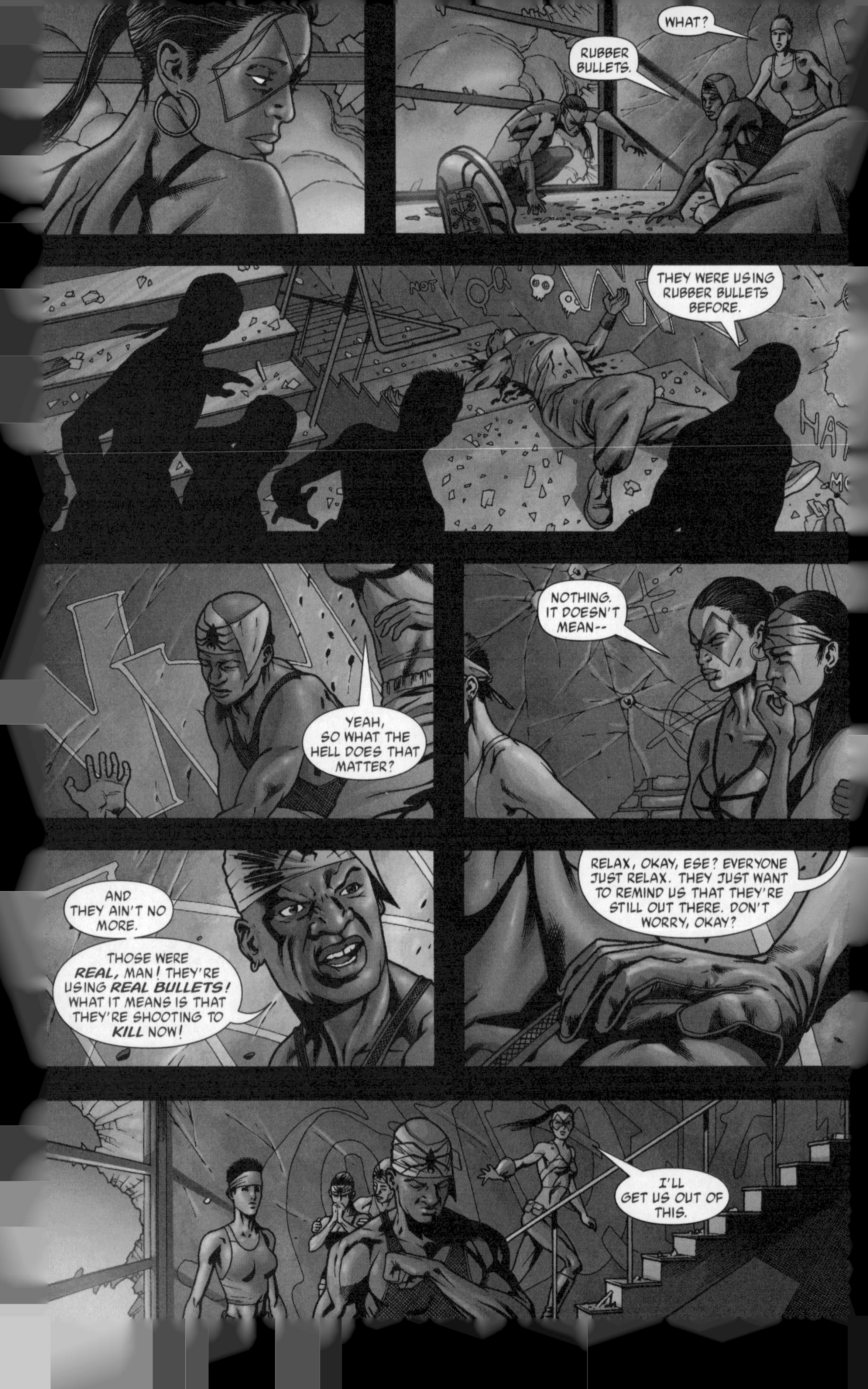
WHAT?
RUBBER BULLETS.
THEY WERE USING RUBBER BULLETS BEFORE.
YEAH, SO WHAT THE HELL DOES THAT MATTER?
NOTHING. IT DOESN'T MEAN--
AND THEY AIN'T NO MORE.
THOSE WERE REAL, MAN! THEY'RE USING REAL BULLETS! WHAT IT MEANS IS THAT THEY'RE SHOOTING TO KILL NOW!
RELAX, OKAY, ESE? EVERYONE JUST RELAX. THEY JUST WANT TO REMIND US THAT THEY'RE STILL OUT THERE. DON'T WORRY, OKAY?
I'LL GET US OUT OF THIS.

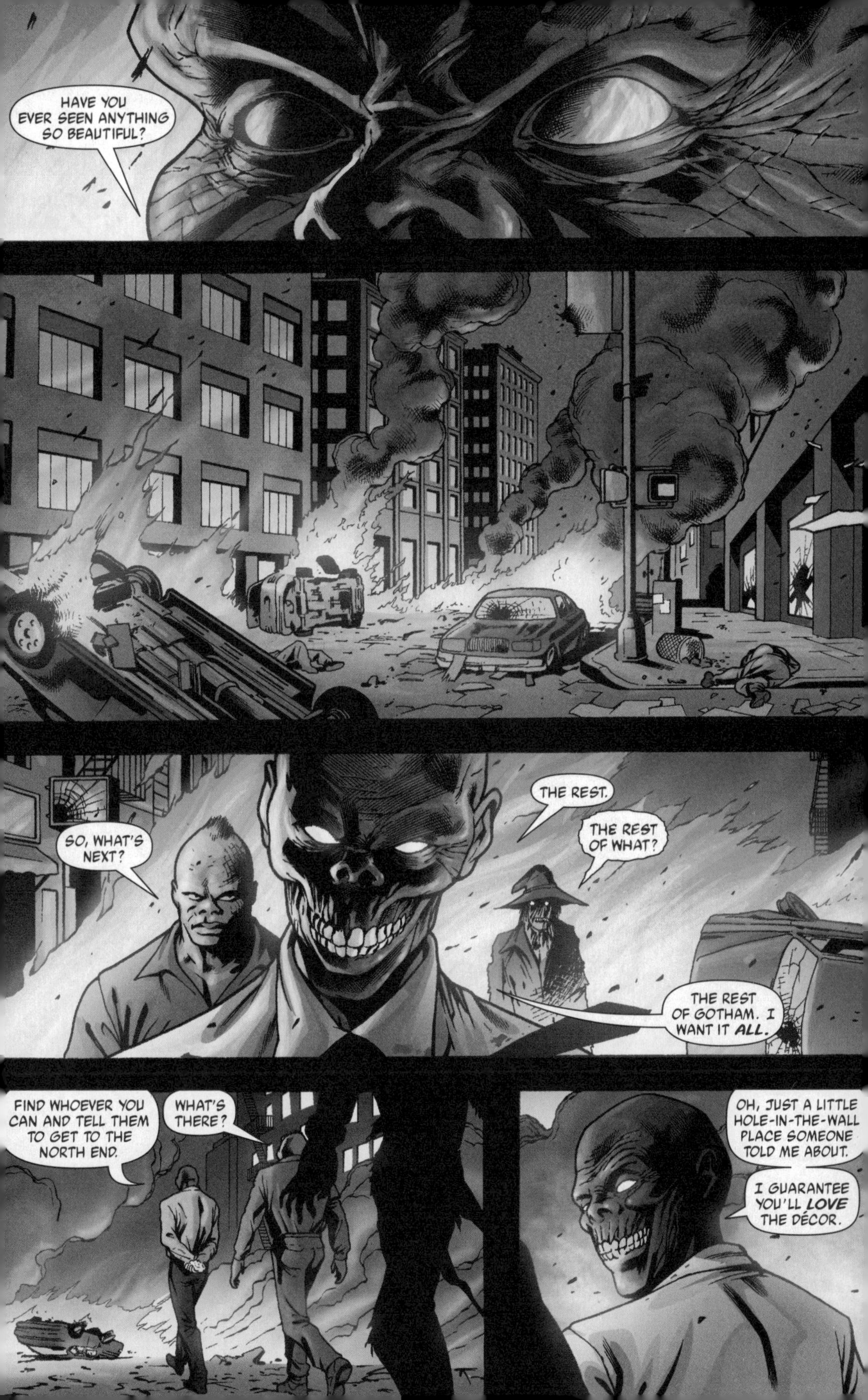
HAVE YOU EVER SEEN ANYTHING SO BEAUTIFUL?
SO, WHAT'S NEXT?
THE REST.
THE REST OF WHAT?
THE REST OF GOTHAM. I WANT IT ALL.
FIND WHOEVER YOU CAN AND TELL THEM TO GET TO THE NORTH END.
WHAT'S THERE?
OH, JUST A LITTLE HOLE-IN-THE-WALL PLACE SOMEONE TOLD ME ABOUT.
I GUARANTEE YOU'LL LOVE THE DÉCOR.

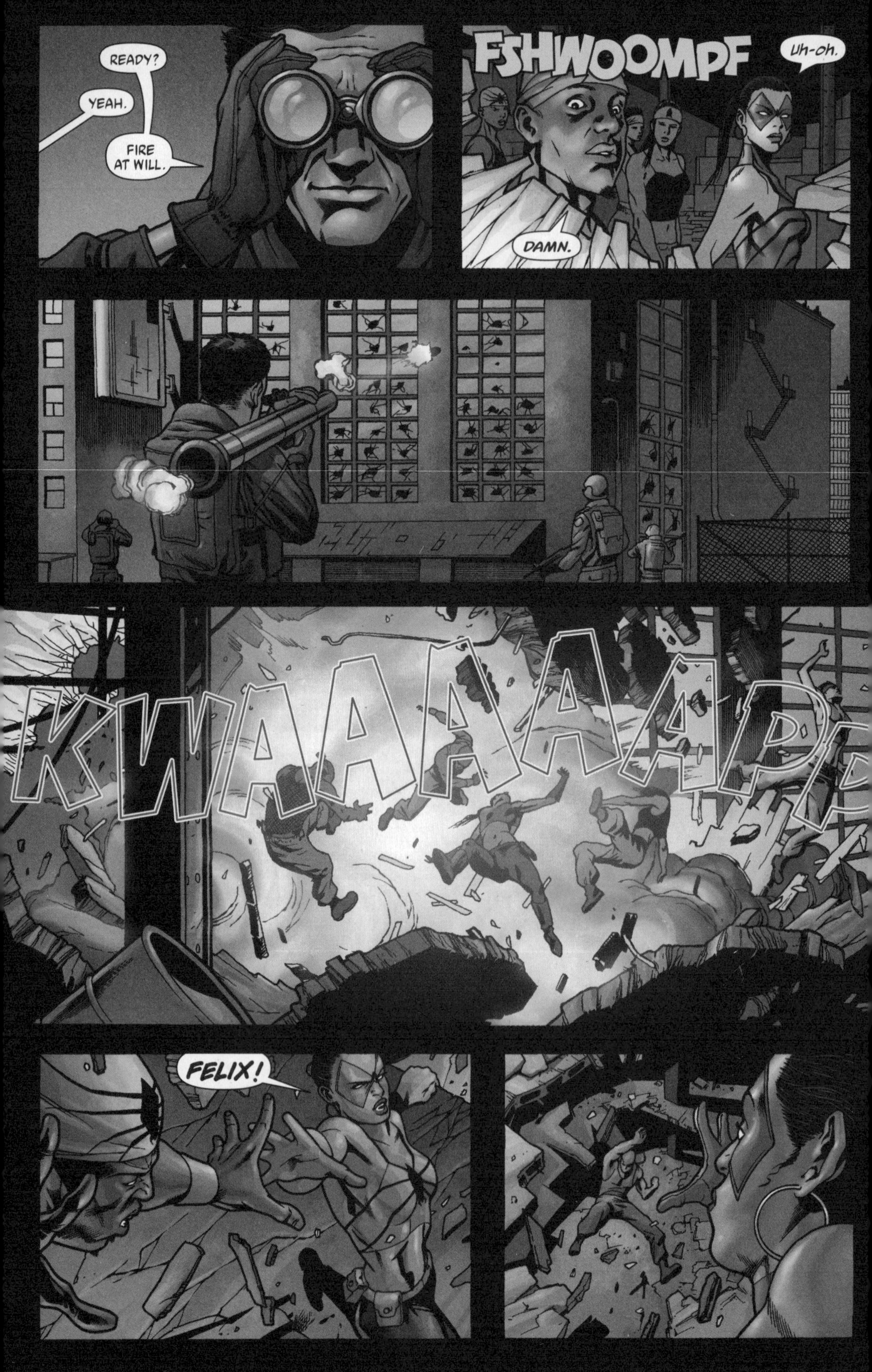
READY?
YEAH.
FIRE AT WILL.
FSHWOOMPF
Uh-oh.
DAMN.
KWAAAAAPP
FELIX!

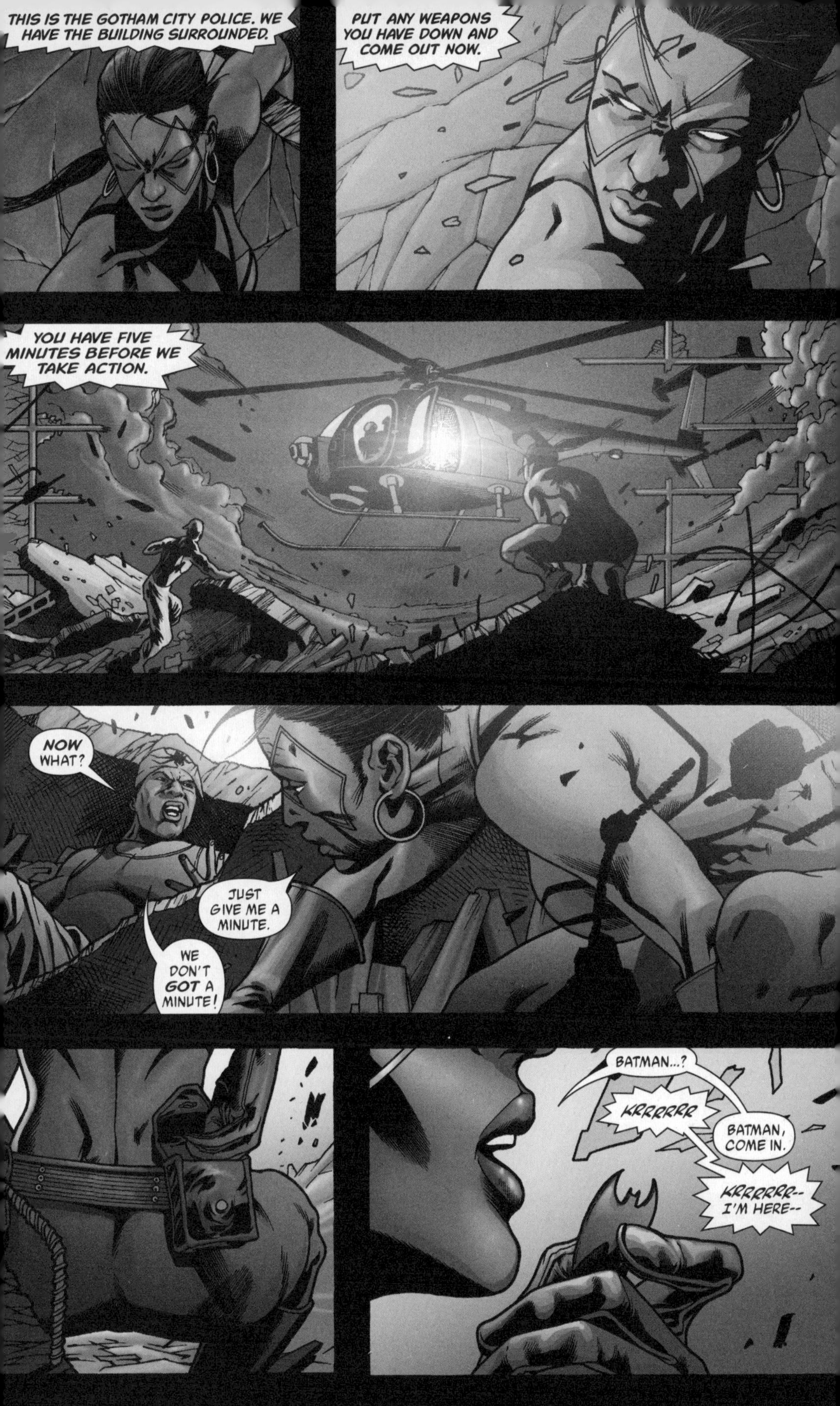
THIS IS THE GOTHAM CITY POLICE. WE HAVE THE BUILDING SURROUNDED.
PUT ANY WEAPONS YOU HAVE DOWN AND COME OUT NOW.
YOU HAVE FIVE MINUTES BEFORE WE TAKE ACTION.
NOW WHAT?
JUST GIVE ME A MINUTE.
WE DON'T GOT A MINUTE!
BATMAN...?
KRRRRRR
BATMAN, COME IN.
KRRRRRR-- I'M HERE--

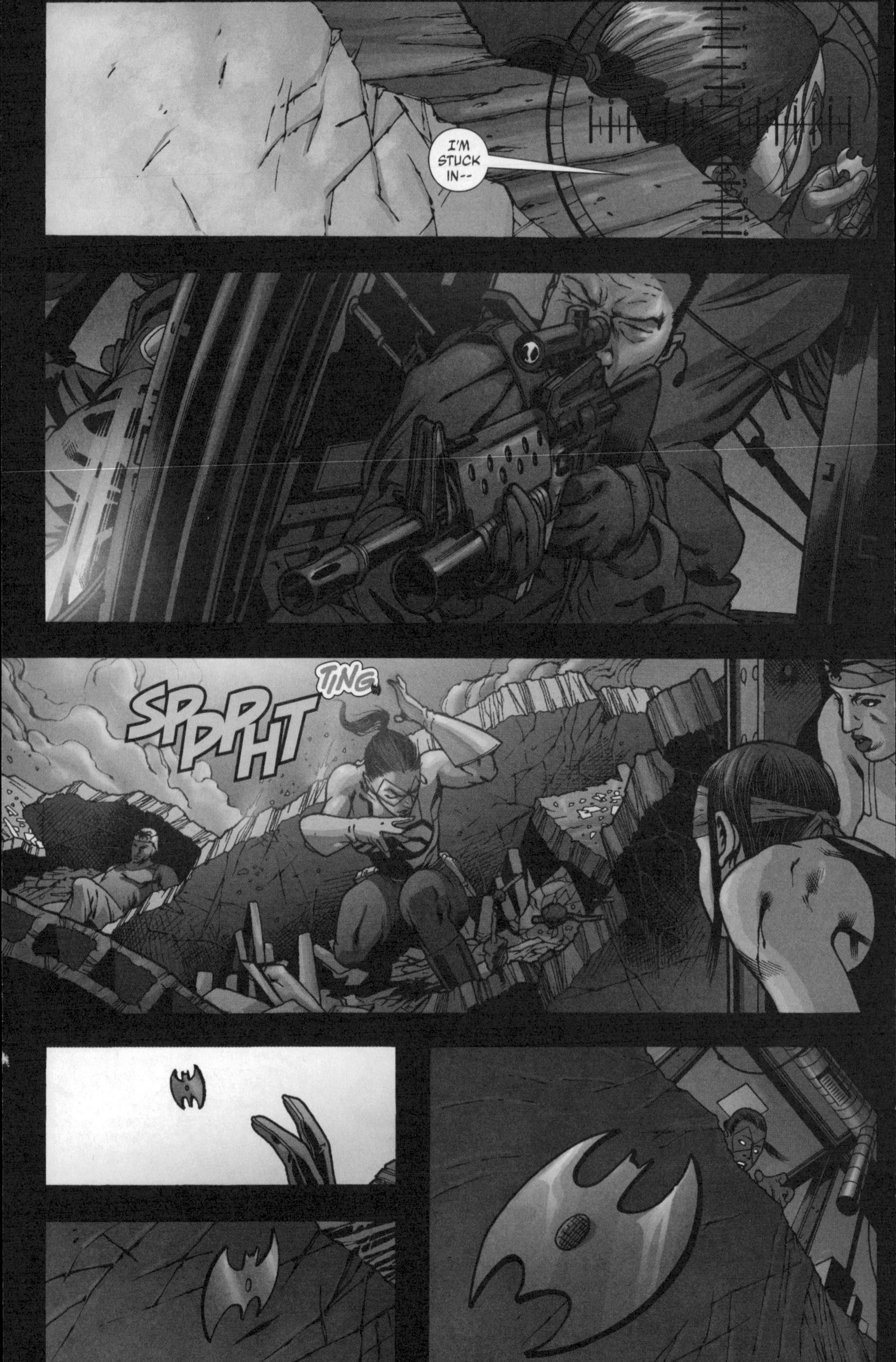
I'M STUCK IN--
SPDPHT
TING

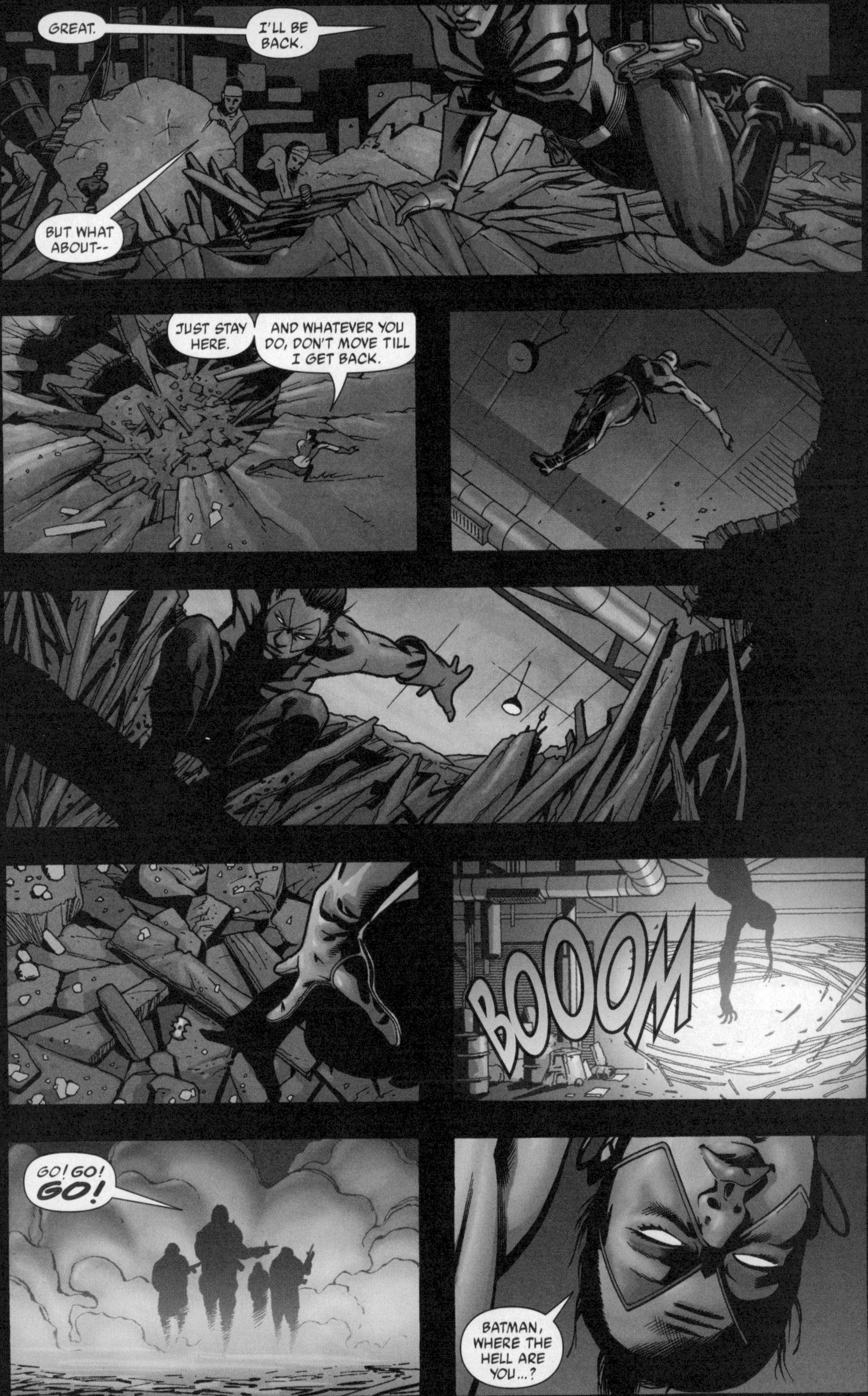

GREAT.
I'LL BE BACK.
BUT WHAT ABOUT--
JUST STAY HERE.
AND WHATEVER YOU DO, DON'T MOVE TILL I GET BACK.
BOOOM
GO! GO! GO!
BATMAN, WHERE THE HELL ARE YOU...?

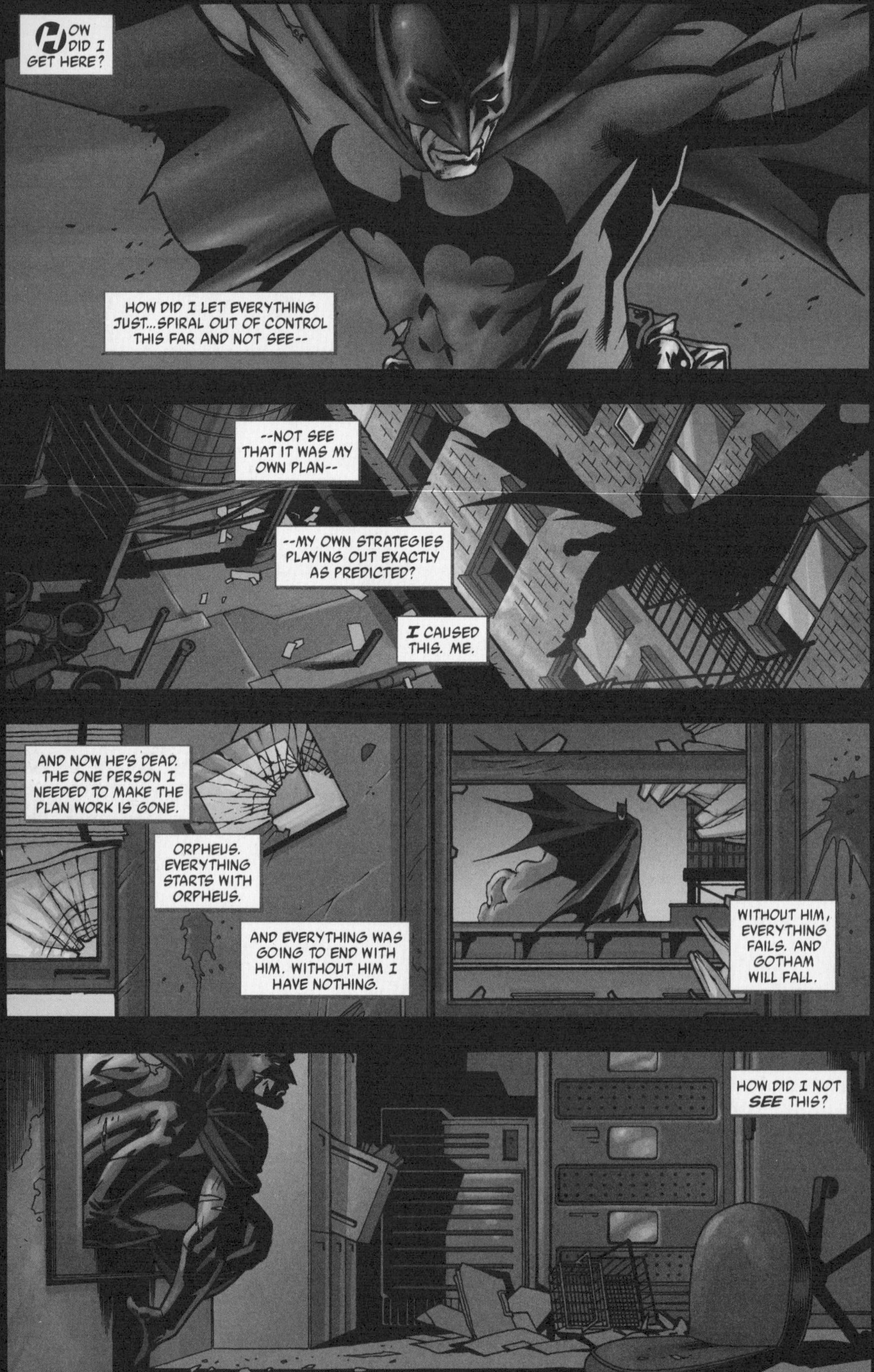
HOW DID I GET HERE?
HOW DID I LET EVERYTHING JUST...SPIRAL OUT OF CONTROL THIS FAR AND NOT SEE--
--NOT SEE THAT IT WAS MY OWN PLAN--
--MY OWN STRATEGIES PLAYING OUT EXACTLY AS PREDICTED?
I CAUSED THIS. ME.
AND NOW HE'S DEAD. THE ONE PERSON I NEEDED TO MAKE THE PLAN WORK IS GONE.
ORPHEUS. EVERYTHING STARTS WITH ORPHEUS.
AND EVERYTHING WAS GOING TO END WITH HIM. WITHOUT HIM I HAVE NOTHING.
WITHOUT HIM, EVERYTHING FAILS. AND GOTHAM WILL FALL.
HOW DID I NOT SEE THIS?

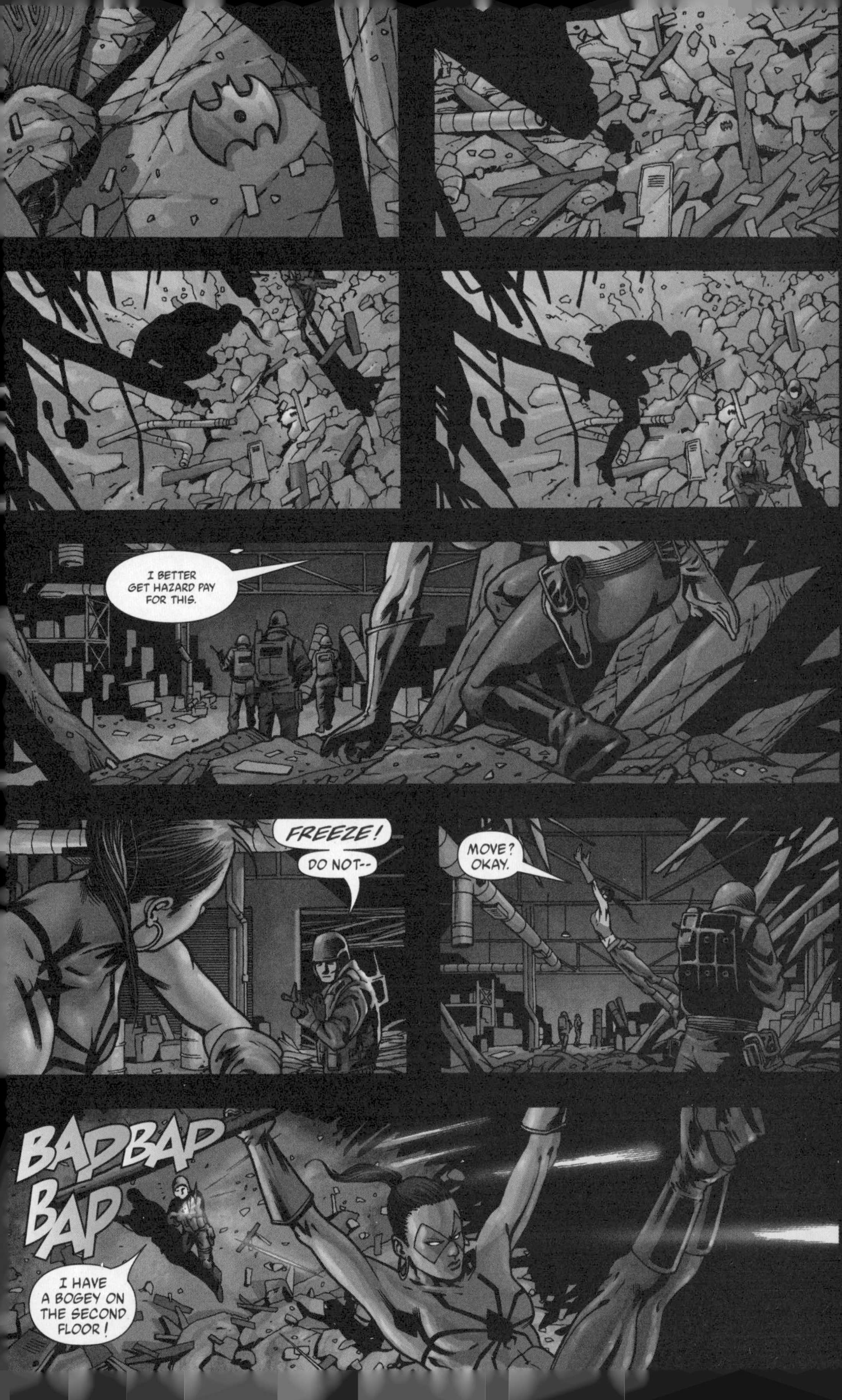
I BETTER GET HAZARD PAY FOR THIS.
FREEZE!
DO NOT--
MOVE? OKAY.
BADBAP BAP
I HAVE A BOGEY ON THE SECOND FLOOR!

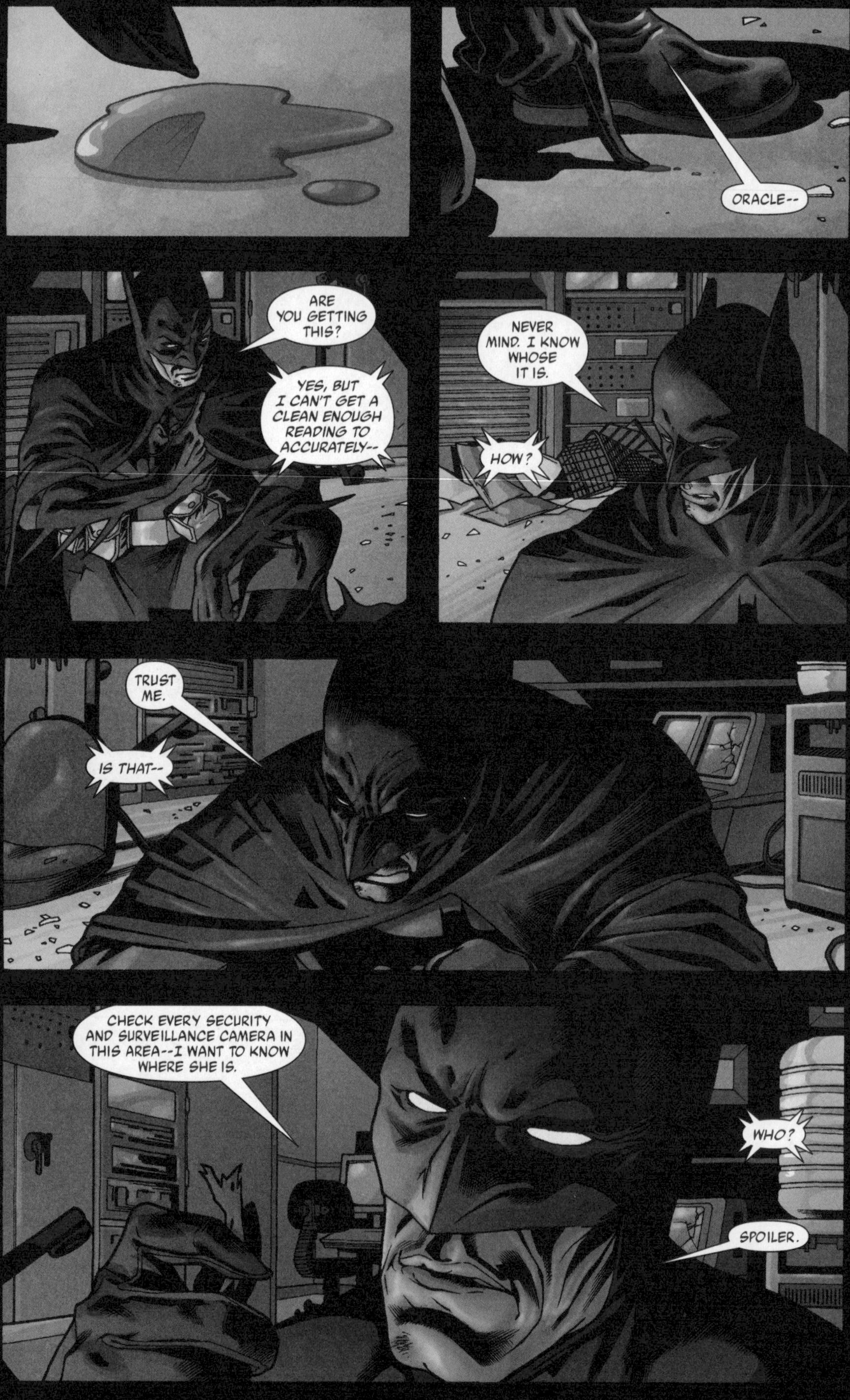
ORACLE--
ARE YOU GETTING THIS?
YES, BUT I CAN'T GET A CLEAN ENOUGH READING TO ACCURATELY--
NEVER MIND. I KNOW WHOSE IT IS.
HOW?
TRUST ME.
IS THAT--
CHECK EVERY SECURITY AND SURVEILLANCE CAMERA IN THIS AREA--I WANT TO KNOW WHERE SHE IS.
WHO?
SPOILER.

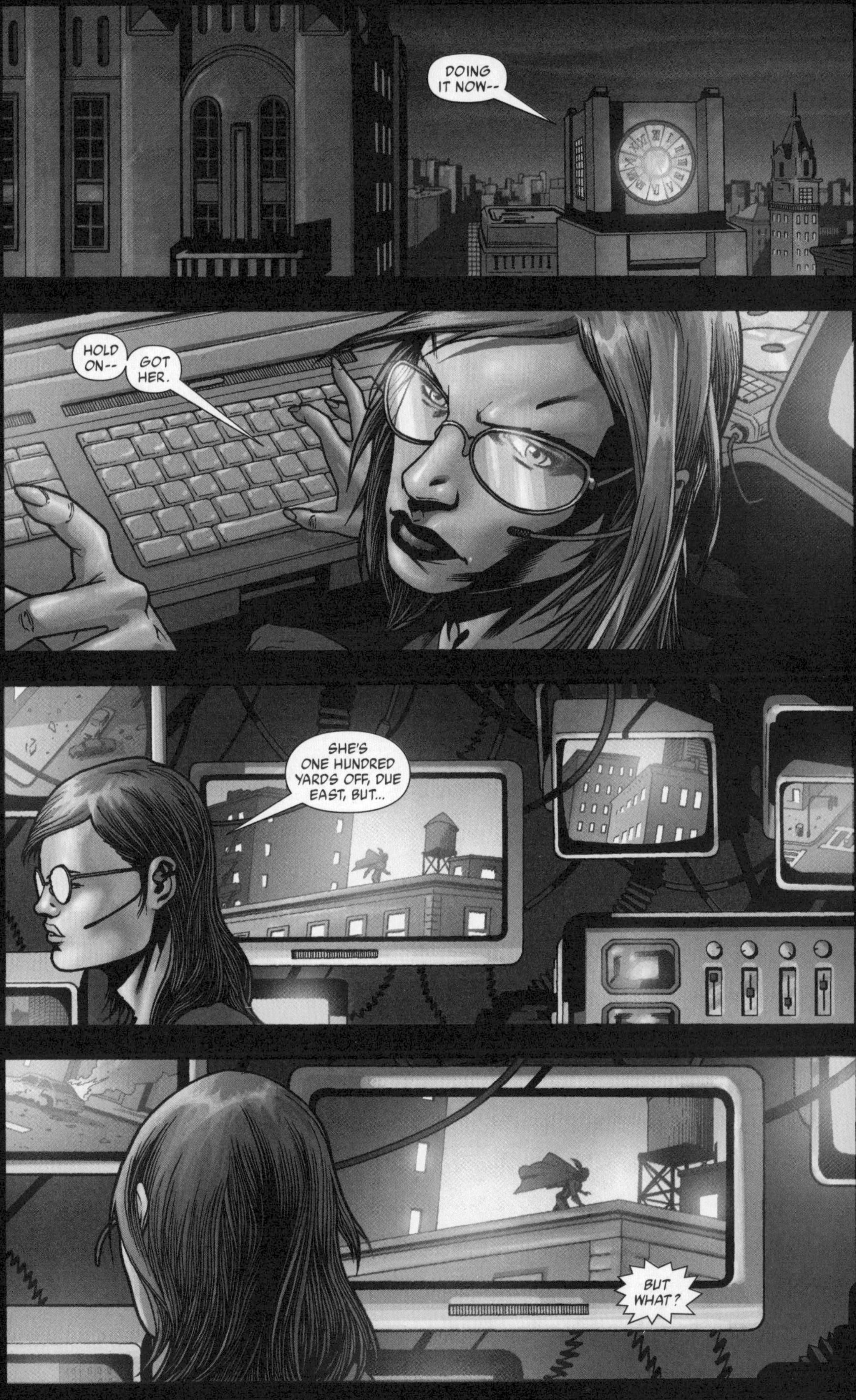
DOING IT NOW--
HOLD ON--
GOT HER.
SHE'S ONE HUNDRED YARDS OFF, DUE EAST, BUT...
BUT WHAT?

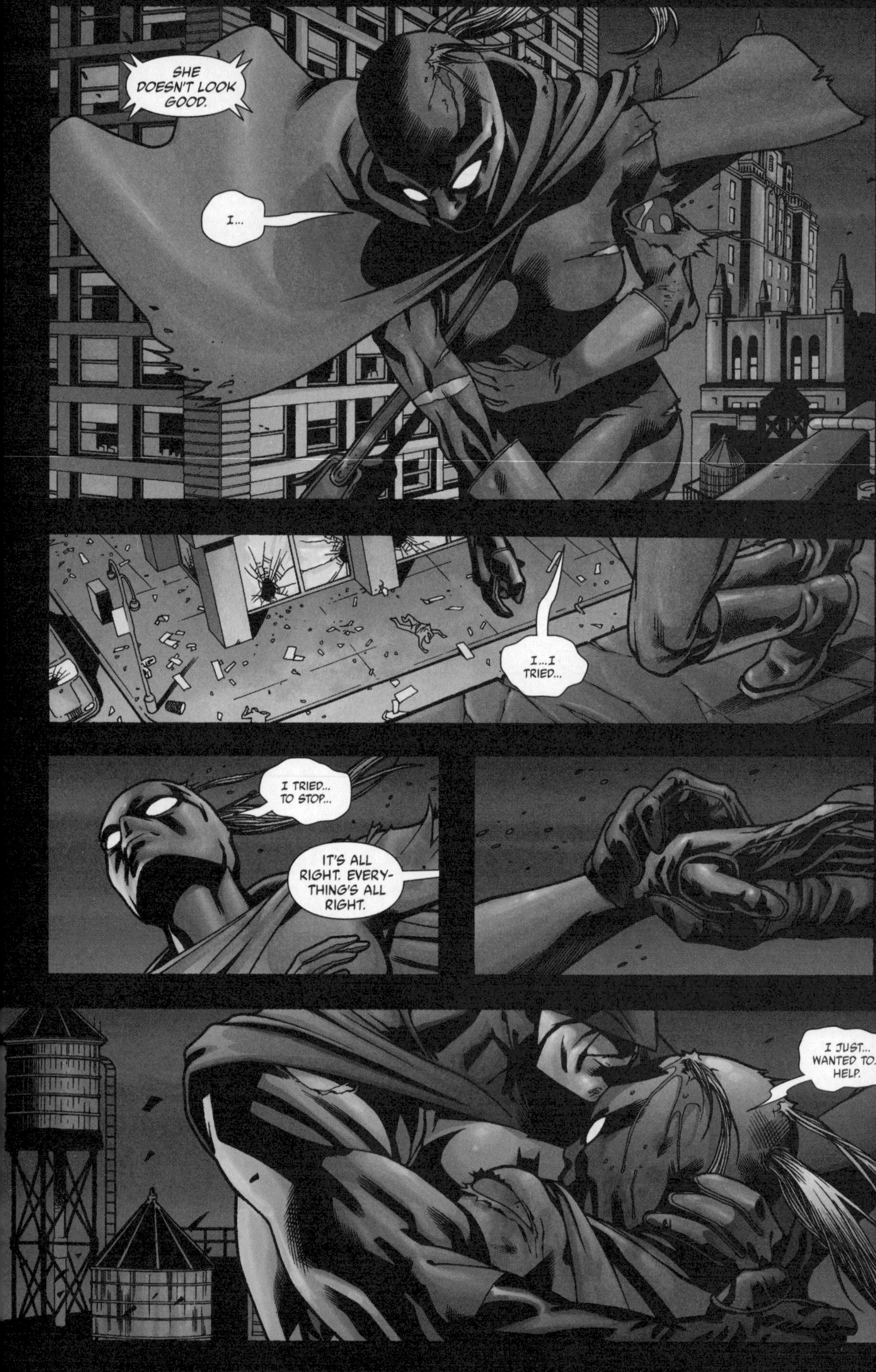
SHE DOESN'T LOOK GOOD.
I...
I...I TRIED...
I TRIED... TO STOP...
IT'S ALL RIGHT. EVERY-THING'S ALL RIGHT.
I JUST... WANTED TO... HELP.

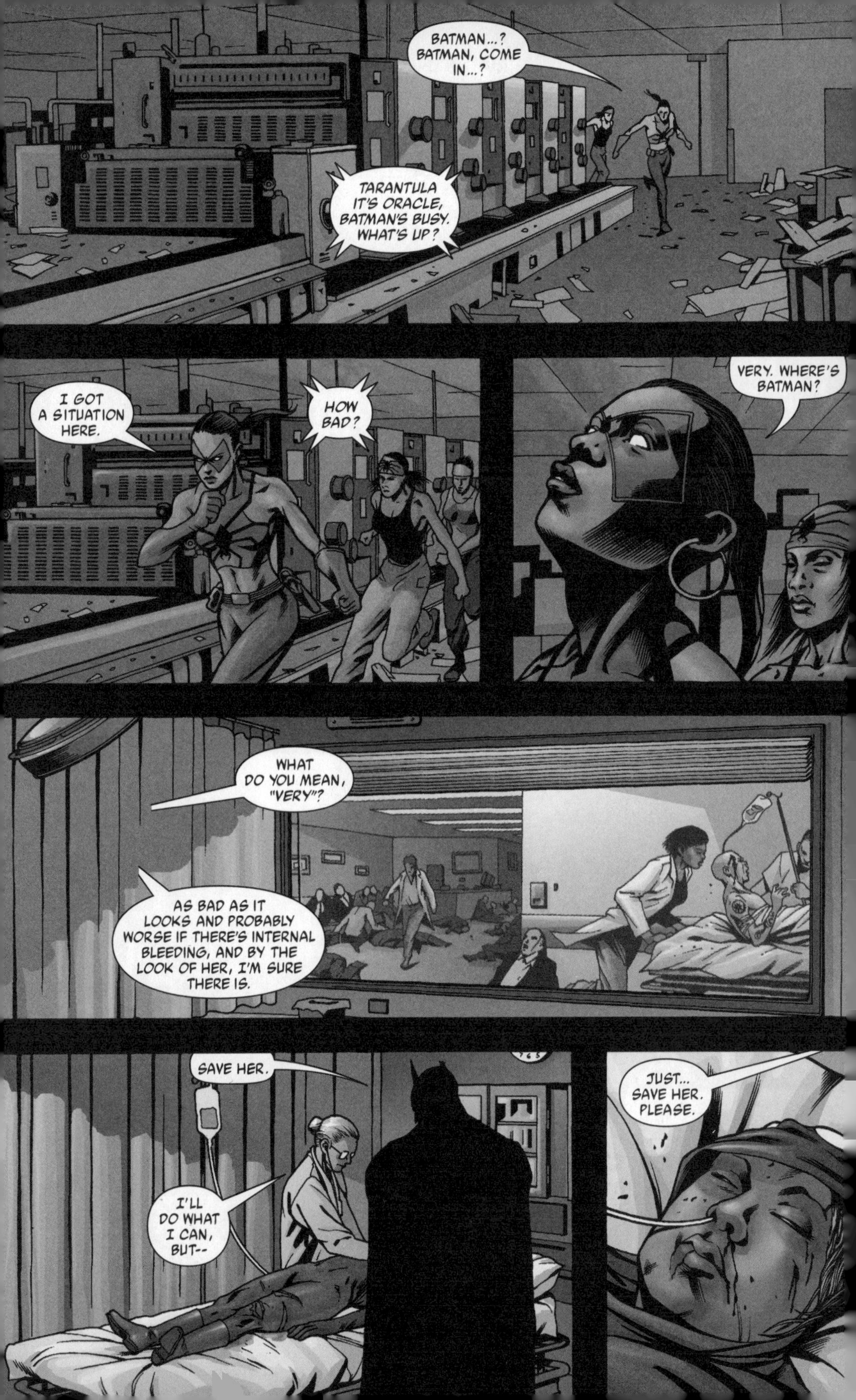
BATMAN...? BATMAN, COME IN...?
TARANTULA IT'S ORACLE, BATMAN'S BUSY. WHAT'S UP?
I GOT A SITUATION HERE.
HOW BAD?
VERY. WHERE'S BATMAN?
WHAT DO YOU MEAN, "VERY"?
AS BAD AS IT LOOKS AND PROBABLY WORSE IF THERE'S INTERNAL BLEEDING, AND BY THE LOOK OF HER, I'M SURE THERE IS.
SAVE HER.
I'LL DO WHAT I CAN, BUT--
JUST... SAVE HER. PLEASE.

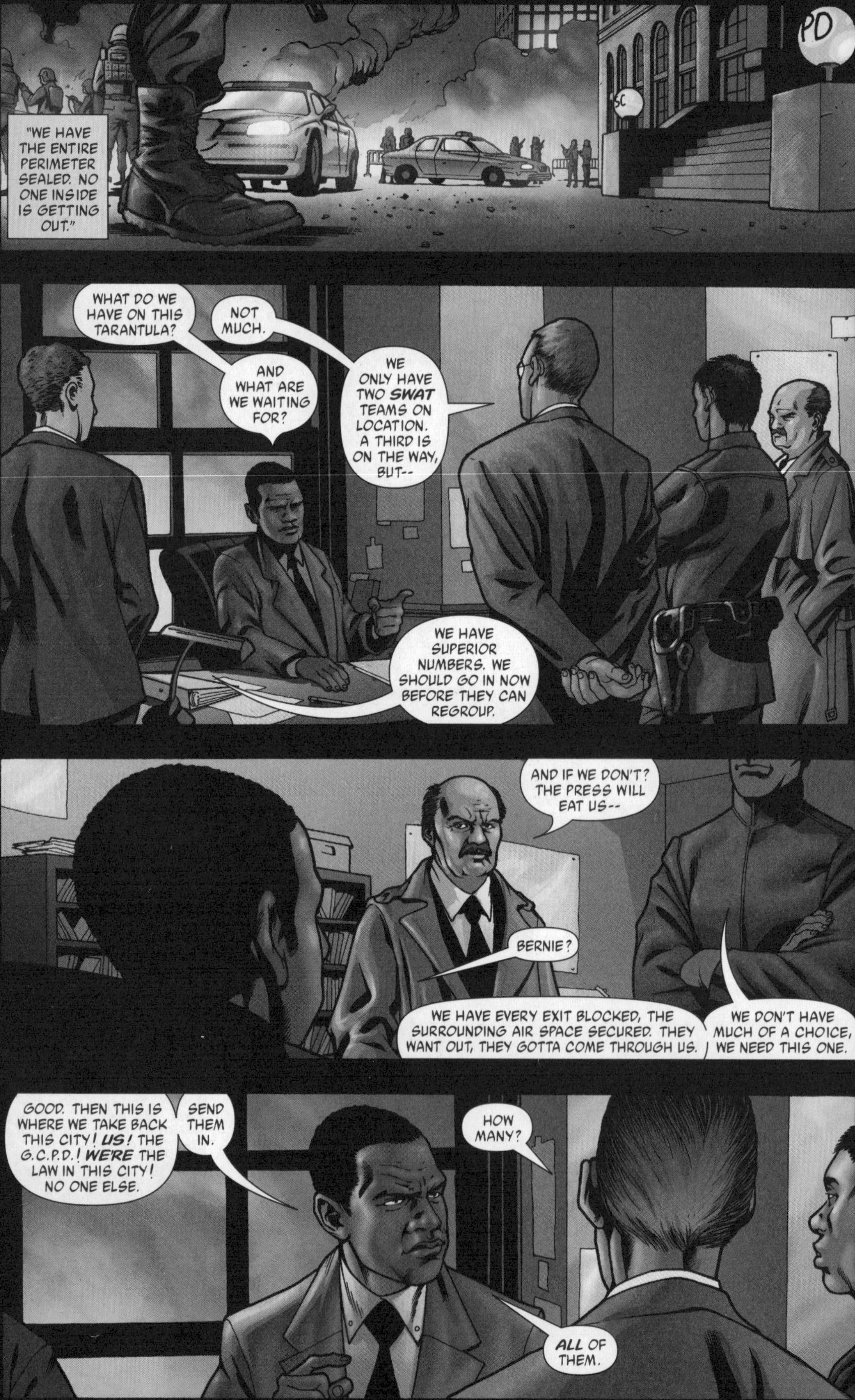

"WE HAVE THE ENTIRE PERIMETER SEALED. NO ONE INSIDE IS GETTING OUT."
PD
WHAT DO WE HAVE ON THIS TARANTULA?
NOT MUCH.
AND WHAT ARE WE WAITING FOR?
WE ONLY HAVE TWO SWAT TEAMS ON LOCATION. A THIRD IS ON THE WAY, BUT--
WE HAVE SUPERIOR NUMBERS. WE SHOULD GO IN NOW BEFORE THEY CAN REGROUP.
AND IF WE DON'T? THE PRESS WILL EAT US--
BERNIE?
WE HAVE EVERY EXIT BLOCKED, THE SURROUNDING AIR SPACE SECURED. THEY WANT OUT, THEY GOTTA COME THROUGH US.
WE DON'T HAVE MUCH OF A CHOICE, WE NEED THIS ONE.
GOOD. THEN THIS IS WHERE WE TAKE BACK THIS CITY! US! THE G.C.P.D.! WE'RE THE LAW IN THIS CITY! NO ONE ELSE.
SEND THEM IN.
HOW MANY?
ALL OF THEM.

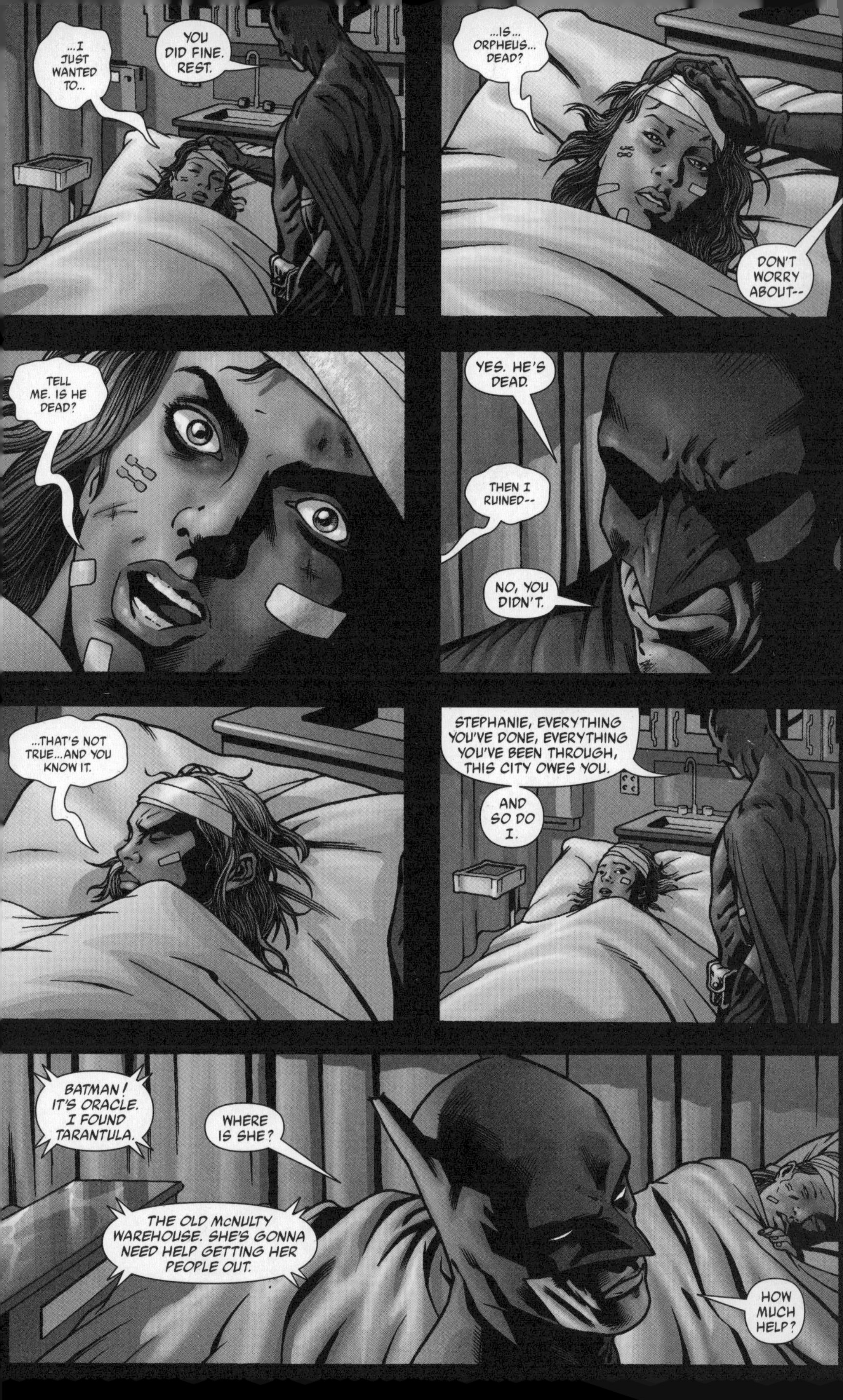
...I JUST WANTED TO...
YOU DID FINE. REST.
...IS... ORPHEUS... DEAD?
DON'T WORRY ABOUT--
TELL ME. IS HE DEAD?
YES. HE'S DEAD.
THEN I RUINED--
NO, YOU DIDN'T.
...THAT'S NOT TRUE...AND YOU KNOW IT.
STEPHANIE, EVERYTHING YOU'VE DONE, EVERYTHING YOU'VE BEEN THROUGH, THIS CITY OWES YOU.
AND SO DO I.
BATMAN! IT'S ORACLE. I FOUND TARANTULA.
WHERE IS SHE?
THE OLD McNULTY WAREHOUSE. SHE'S GONNA NEED HELP GETTING HER PEOPLE OUT.
HOW MUCH HELP?

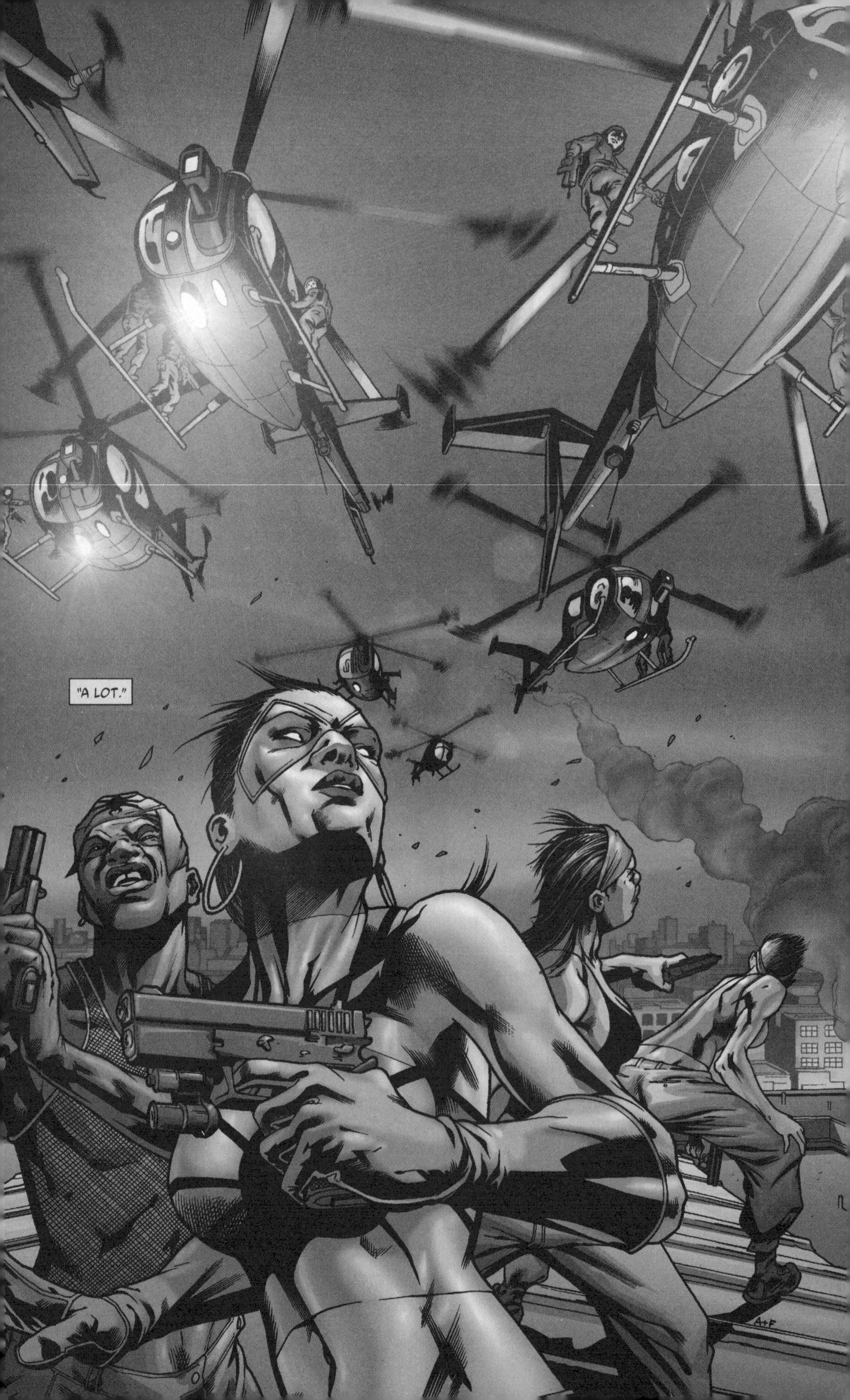
"A LOT."
A+F

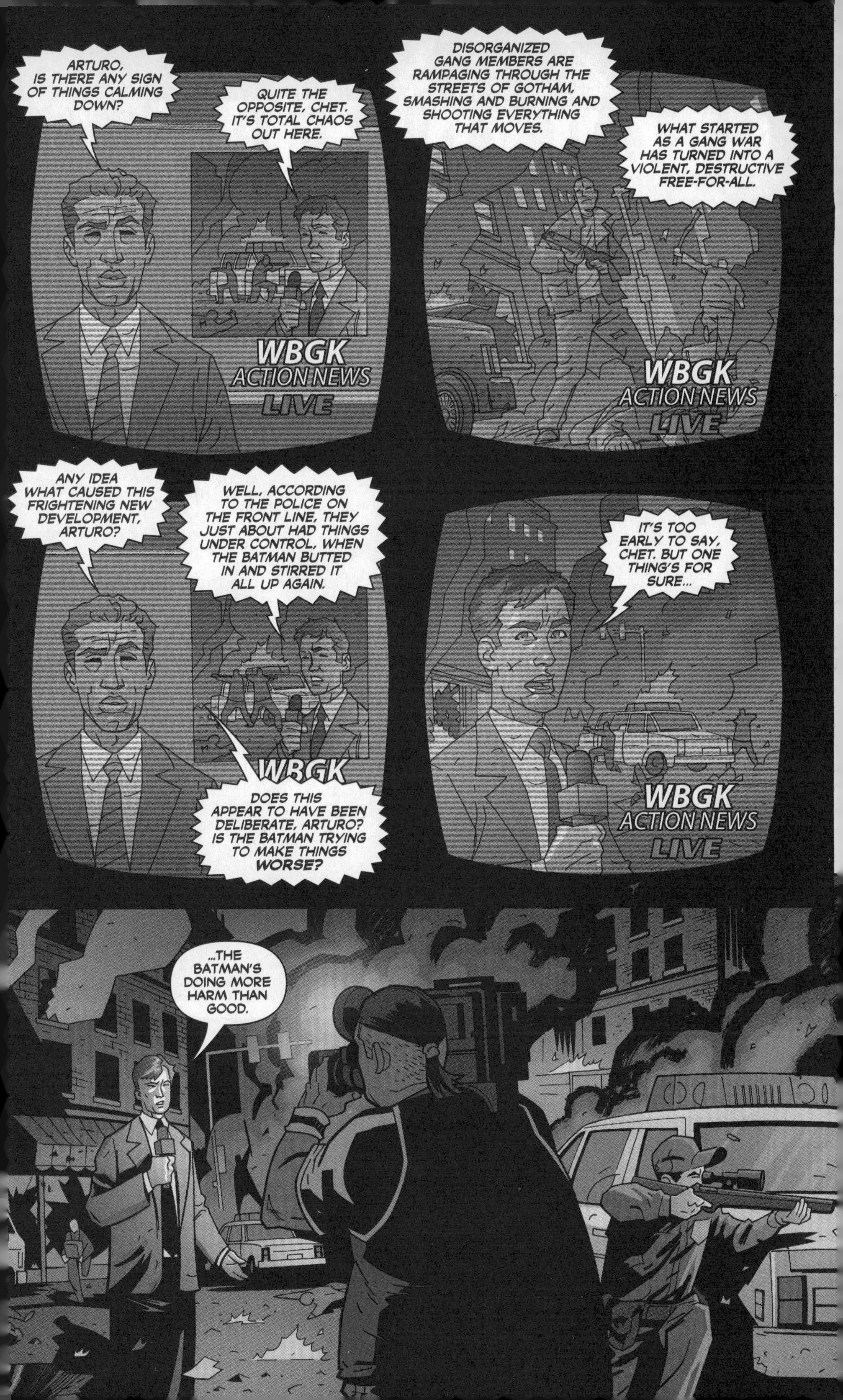
ARTURO, IS THERE ANY SIGN OF THINGS CALMING DOWN?
QUITE THE OPPOSITE, CHET. IT'S TOTAL CHAOS OUT HERE.
WBGK ACTION NEWS LIVE
DISORGANIZED GANG MEMBERS ARE RAMPAGING THROUGH THE STREETS OF GOTHAM, SMASHING AND BURNING AND SHOOTING EVERYTHING THAT MOVES.
WHAT STARTED AS A GANG WAR HAS TURNED INTO A VIOLENT, DESTRUCTIVE FREE-FOR-ALL.
WBGK ACTION NEWS LIVE
ANY IDEA WHAT CAUSED THIS FRIGHTENING NEW DEVELOPMENT, ARTURO?
WELL, ACCORDING TO THE POLICE ON THE FRONT LINE, THEY JUST ABOUT HAD THINGS UNDER CONTROL, WHEN THE BATMAN BUTTED IN AND STIRRED IT ALL UP AGAIN.
DOES THIS APPEAR TO HAVE BEEN DELIBERATE, ARTURO? IS THE BATMAN TRYING TO MAKE THINGS WORSE?
IT'S TOO EARLY TO SAY, CHET. BUT ONE THING'S FOR SURE...
WBGK ACTION NEWS LIVE
...THE BATMAN'S DOING MORE HARM THAN GOOD.

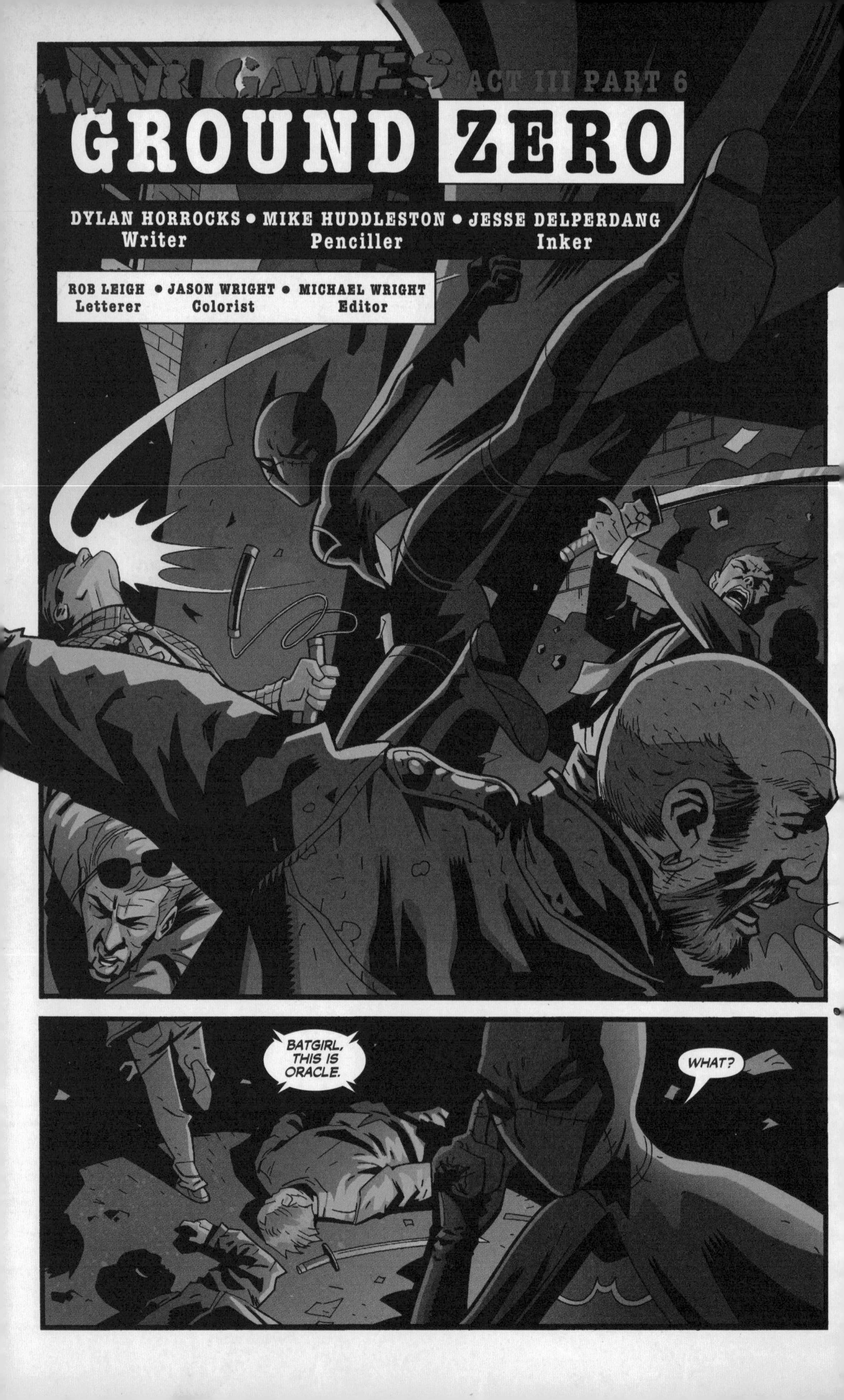
WAR GAMES
ACT III PART 6
GROUND ZERO
DYLAN HORROCKS • MIKE HUDDLESTON • JESSE DELPERDANG
Writer Penciller Inker
ROB LEIGH • JASON WRIGHT • MICHAEL WRIGHT
Letterer Colorist Editor
BATGIRL, THIS IS ORACLE.
WHAT?

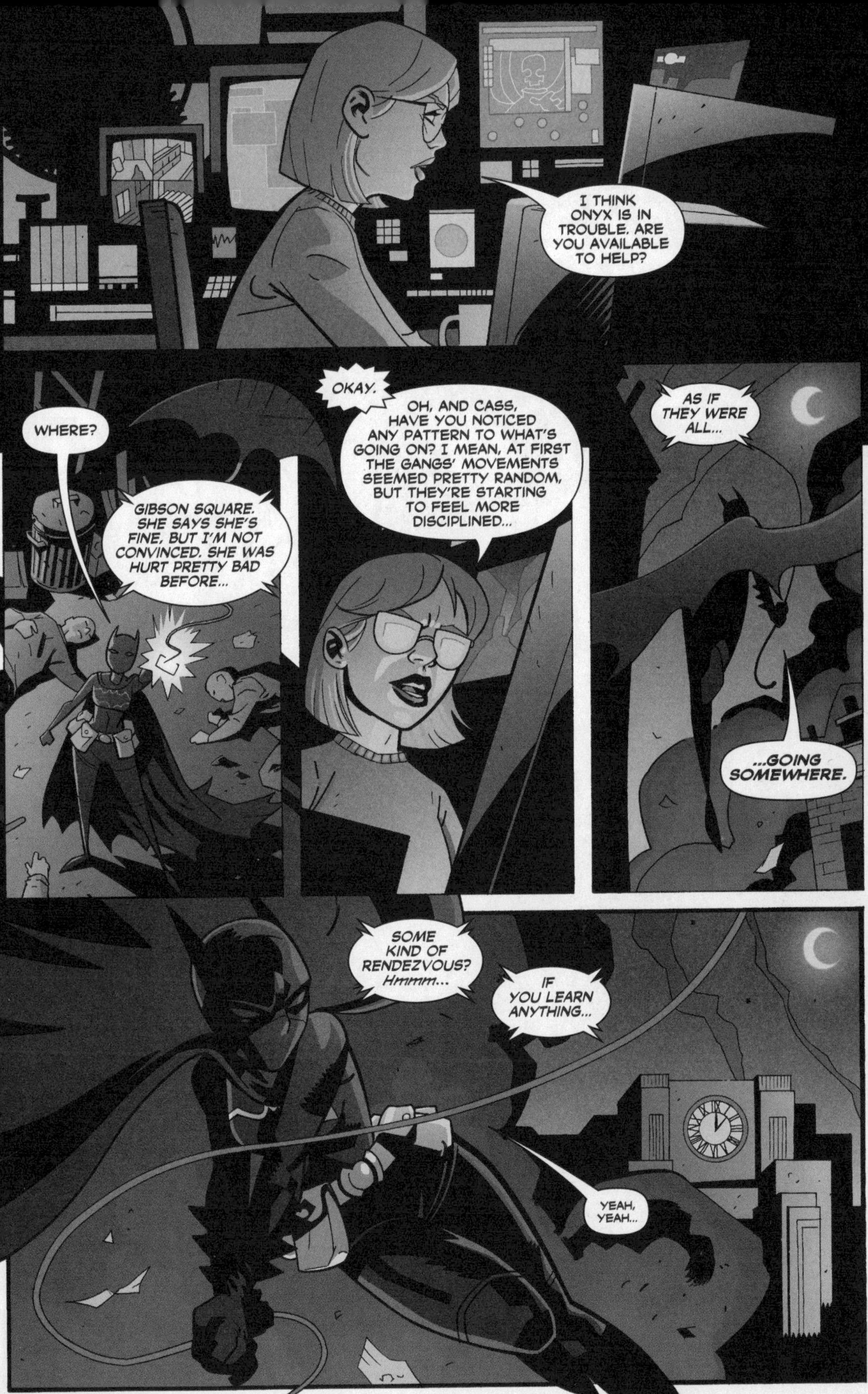
I THINK ONYX IS IN TROUBLE. ARE YOU AVAILABLE TO HELP?
WHERE?
GIBSON SQUARE. SHE SAYS SHE'S FINE, BUT I'M NOT CONVINCED. SHE WAS HURT PRETTY BAD BEFORE...
OKAY.
OH, AND CASS, HAVE YOU NOTICED ANY PATTERN TO WHAT'S GOING ON? I MEAN, AT FIRST THE GANGS' MOVEMENTS SEEMED PRETTY RANDOM, BUT THEY'RE STARTING TO FEEL MORE DISCIPLINED...
AS IF THEY WERE ALL...
...GOING SOMEWHERE.
SOME KIND OF RENDEZVOUS? Hmmm...
IF YOU LEARN ANYTHING...
YEAH, YEAH...

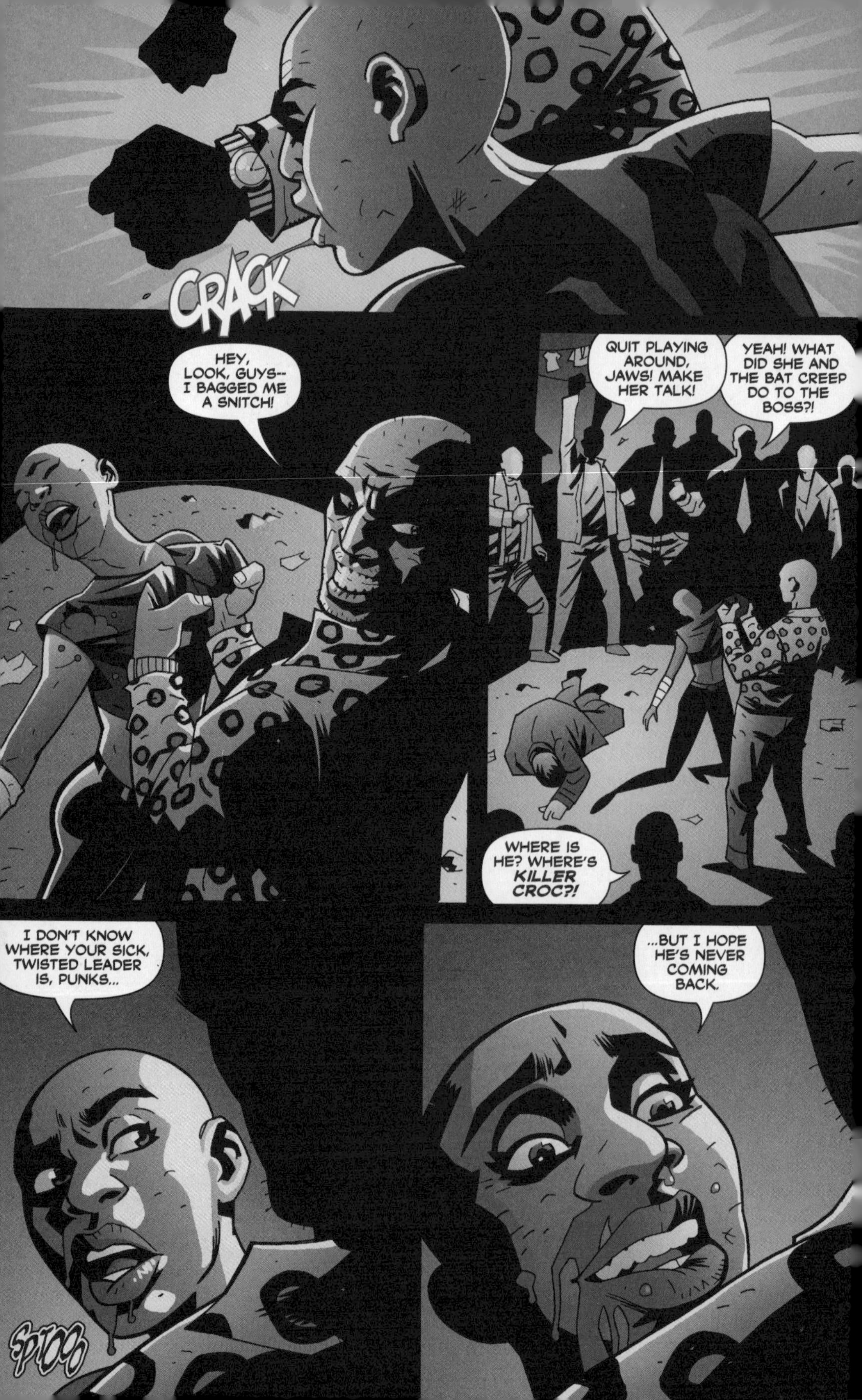
CRACK
HEY, LOOK, GUYS-- I BAGGED ME A SNITCH!
QUIT PLAYING AROUND, JAWS! MAKE HER TALK!
YEAH! WHAT DID SHE AND THE BAT CREEP DO TO THE BOSS?!
WHERE IS HE? WHERE'S KILLER CROC?!
I DON'T KNOW WHERE YOUR SICK, TWISTED LEADER IS, PUNKS...
SPTOOO
...BUT I HOPE HE'S NEVER COMING BACK.

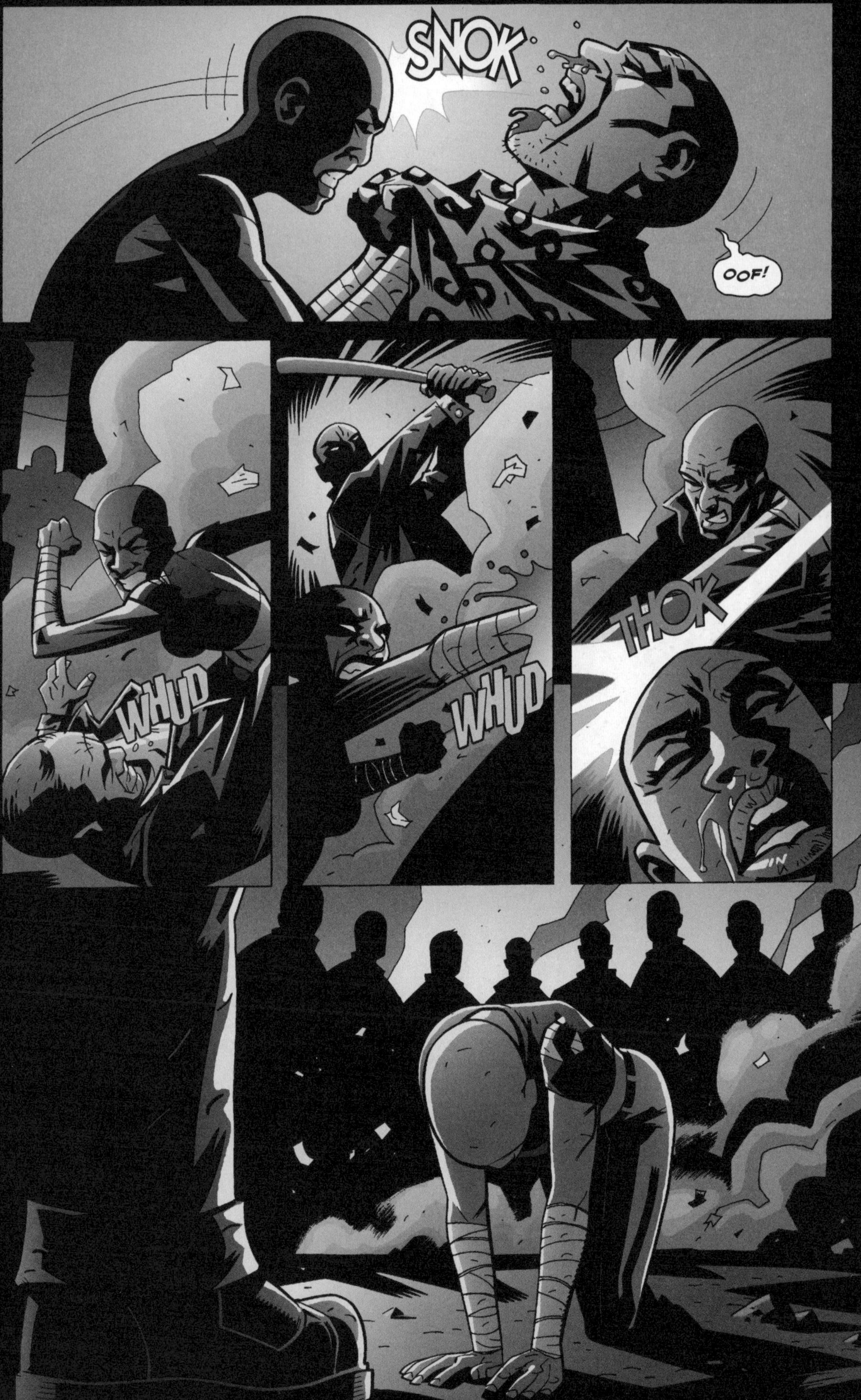
SNOK
OOF!
WHUD
WHUD
THOK

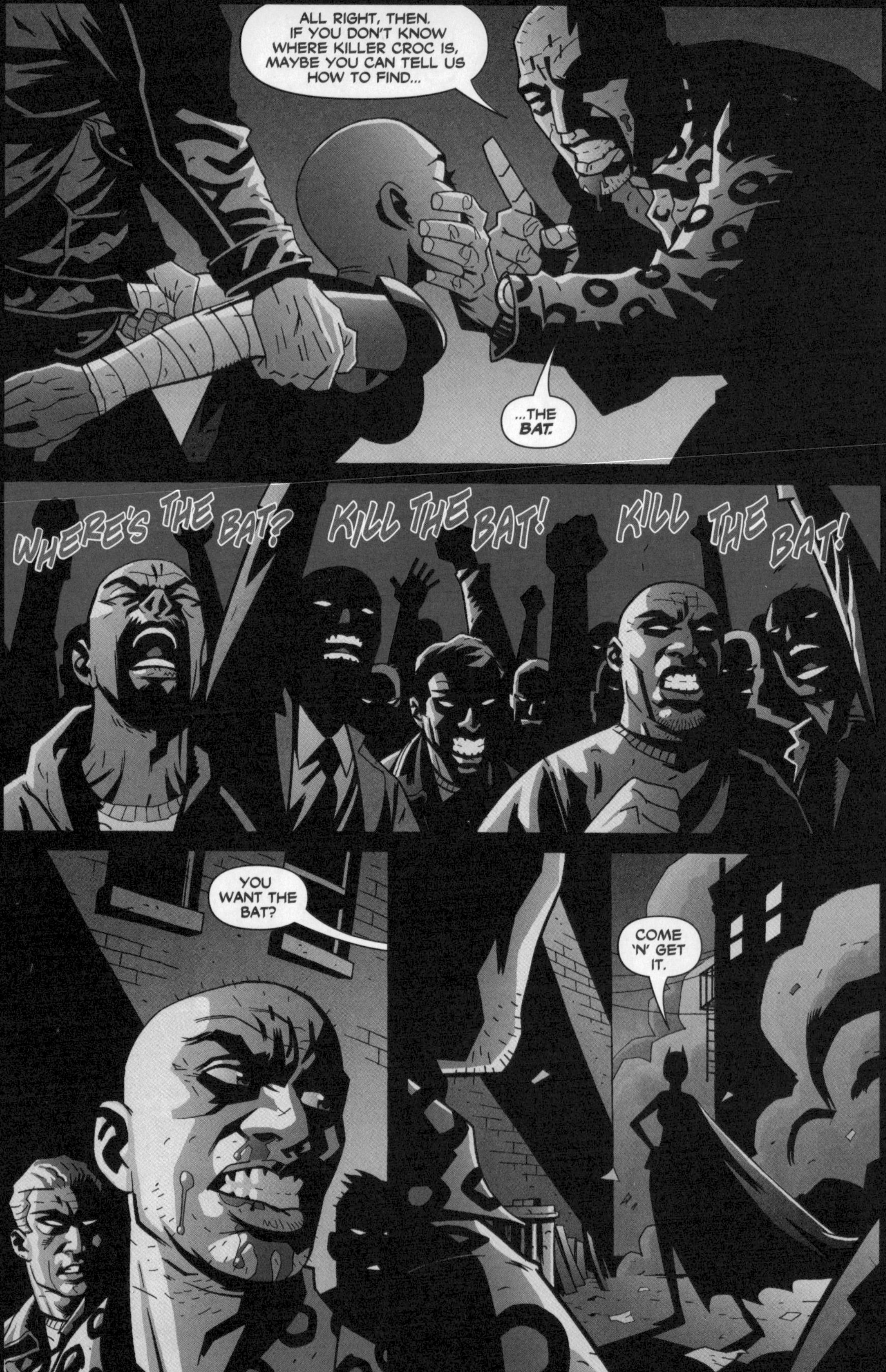
ALL RIGHT, THEN. IF YOU DON'T KNOW WHERE KILLER CROC IS, MAYBE YOU CAN TELL US HOW TO FIND...
...THE BAT.
WHERE'S THE BAT?
KILL THE BAT!
KILL THE BAT!
YOU WANT THE BAT?
COME 'N' GET IT.

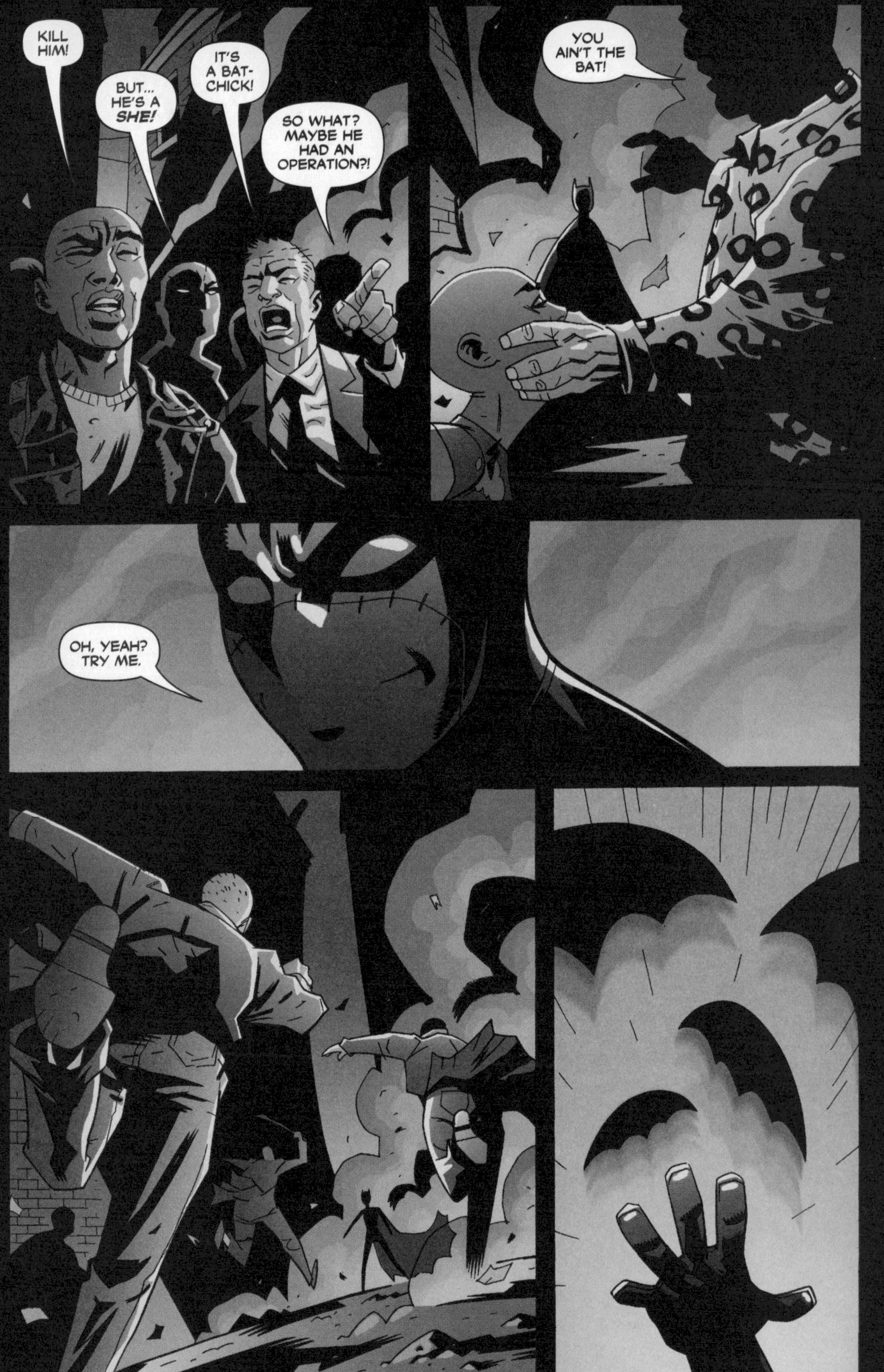

KILL HIM!
BUT... HE'S A SHE!
IT'S A BAT-CHICK!
SO WHAT? MAYBE HE HAD AN OPERATION?!
YOU AIN'T THE BAT!
OH, YEAH? TRY ME.

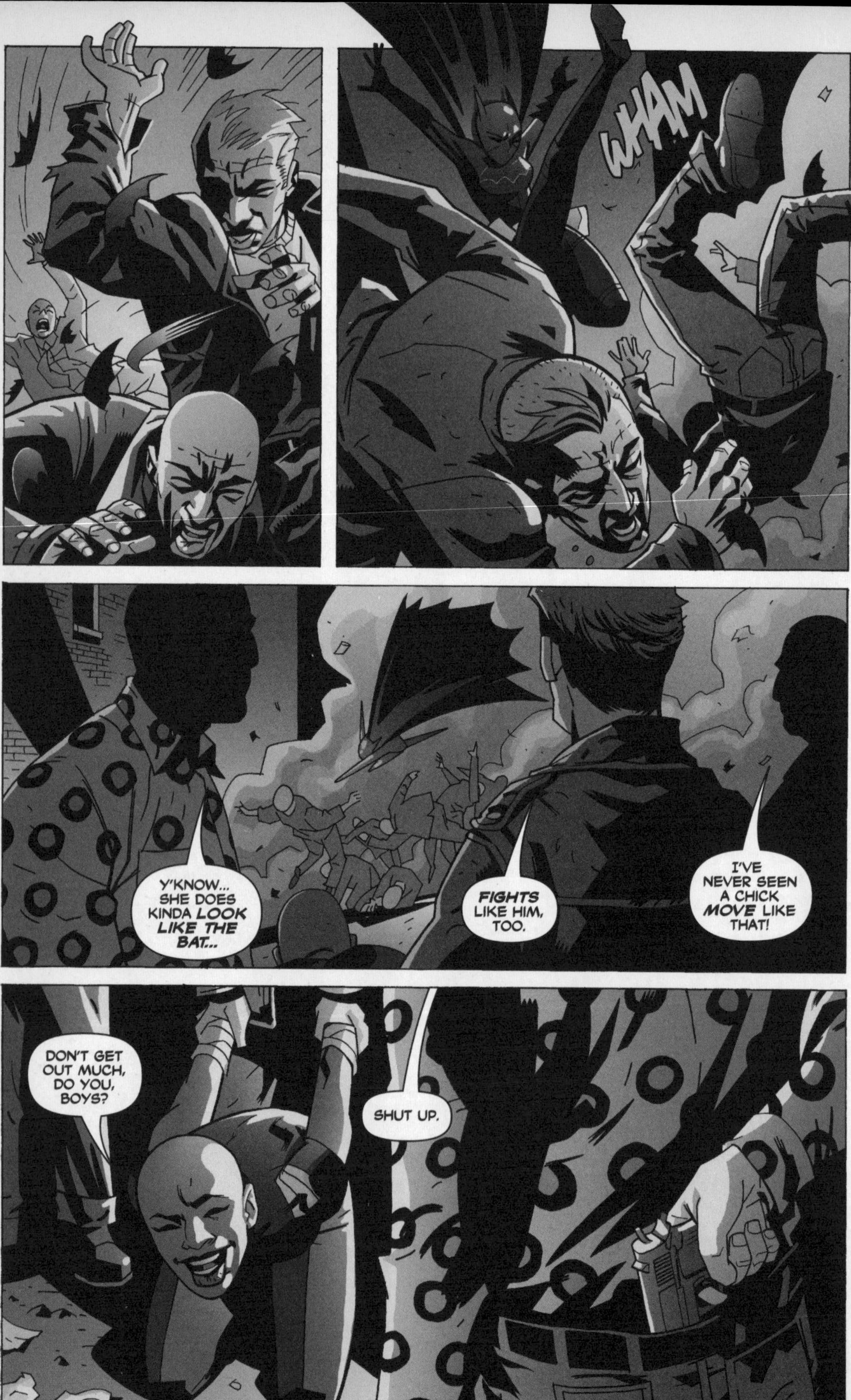
WHAM
Y'KNOW... SHE DOES KINDA LOOK LIKE THE BAT...
FIGHTS LIKE HIM, TOO.
I'VE NEVER SEEN A CHICK MOVE LIKE THAT!
DON'T GET OUT MUCH, DO YOU, BOYS?
SHUT UP.

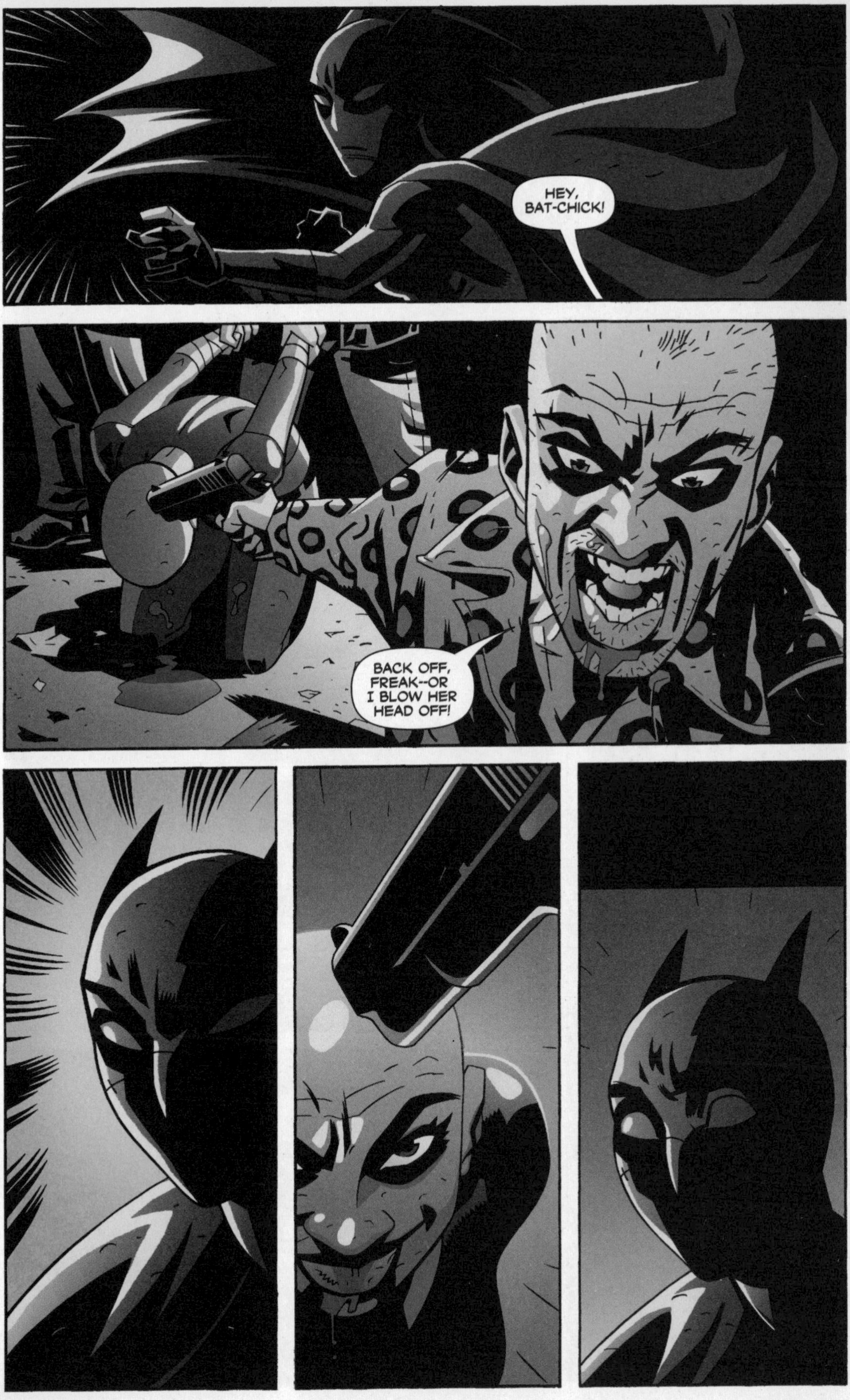
HEY, BAT-CHICK!
BACK OFF, FREAK--OR I BLOW HER HEAD OFF!

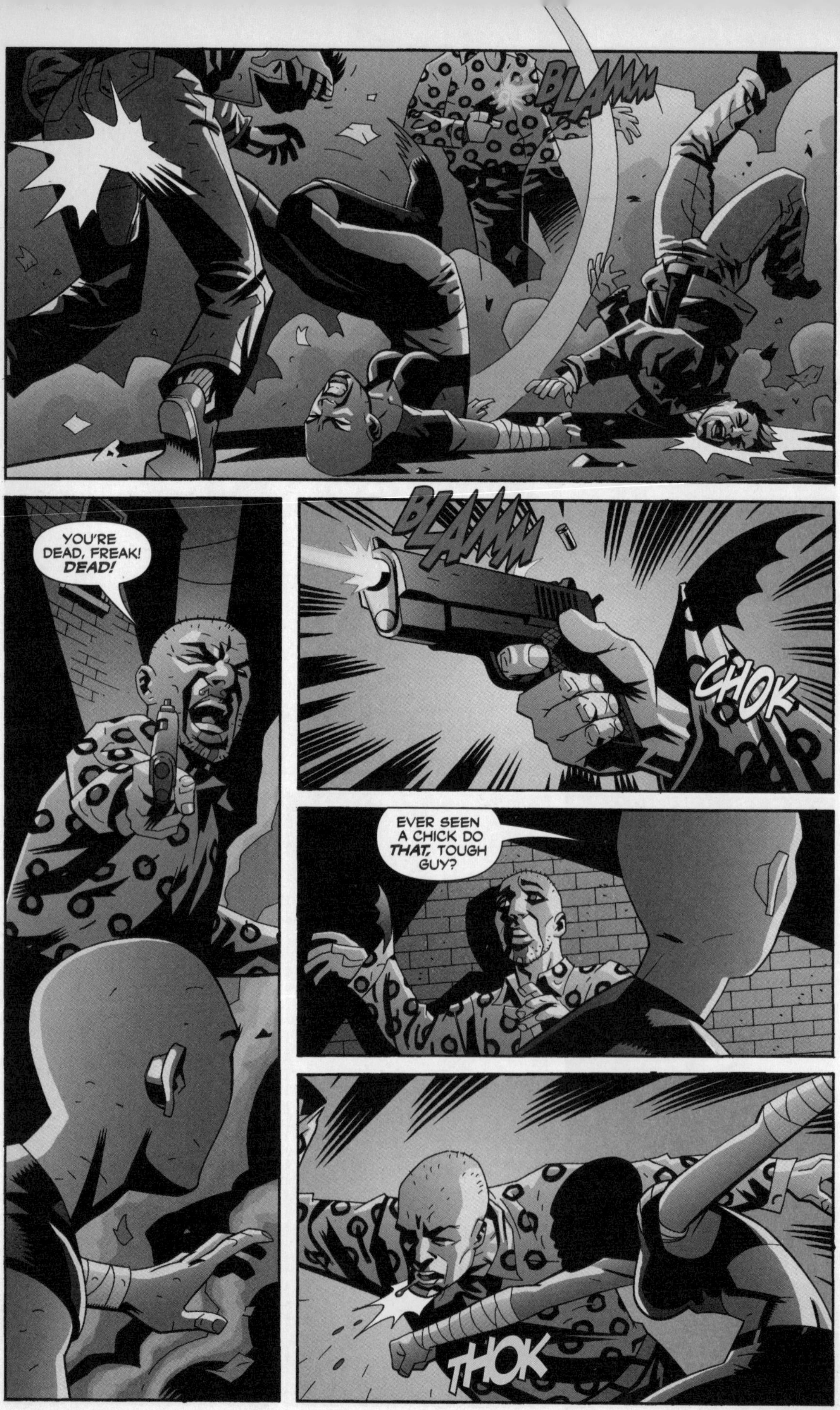
BLAMM
YOU'RE DEAD, FREAK! *DEAD!*
BLAMM
CHOK
EVER SEEN A CHICK DO *THAT,* TOUGH GUY?
THOK

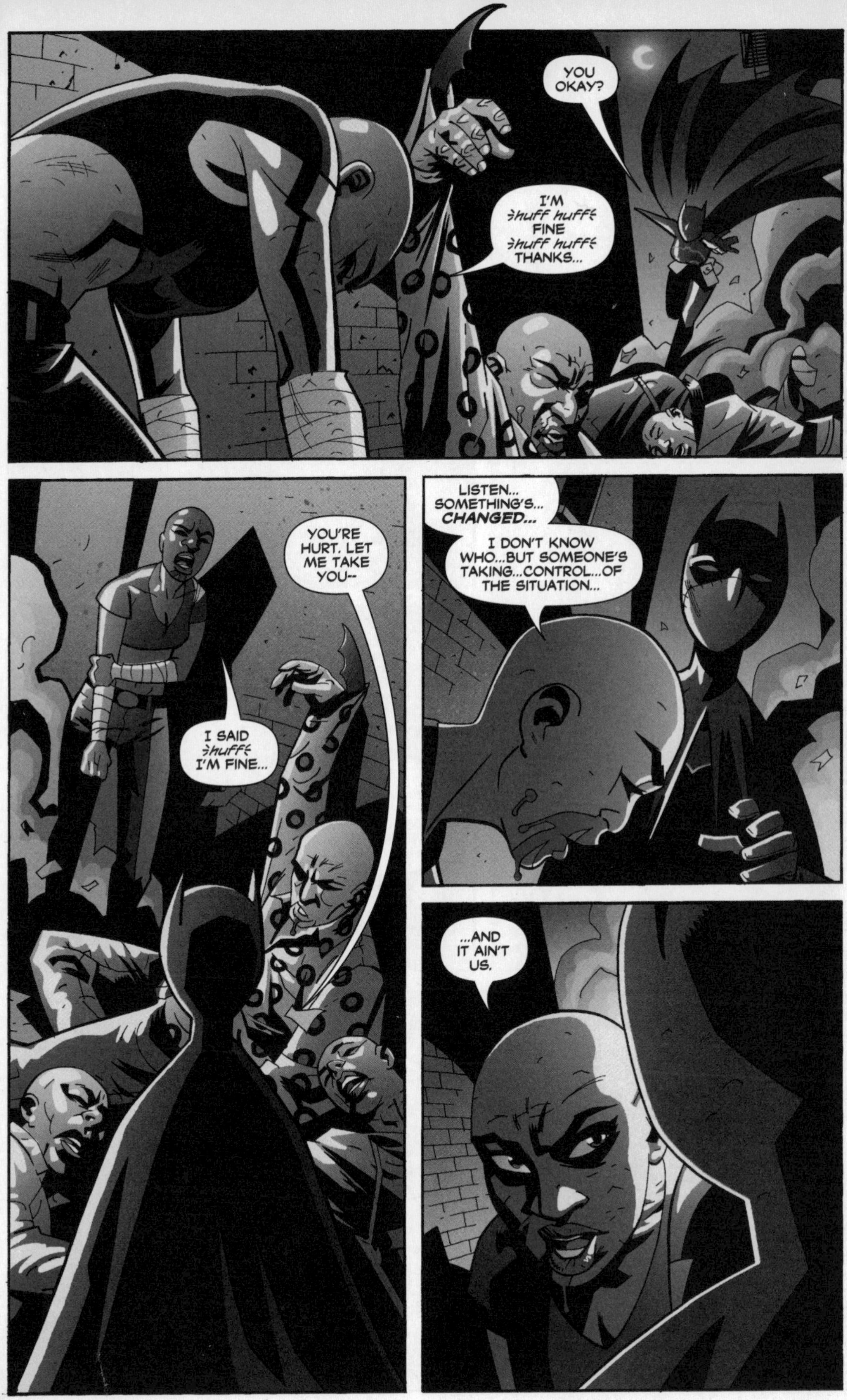
YOU OKAY?
I'M ≯huff huff≮ FINE ≯huff huff≮ THANKS...
YOU'RE HURT. LET ME TAKE YOU--
I SAID ≯huff≮ I'M FINE...
LISTEN... SOMETHING'S... CHANGED...
I DON'T KNOW WHO...BUT SOMEONE'S TAKING...CONTROL...OF THE SITUATION...
...AND IT AIN'T US.

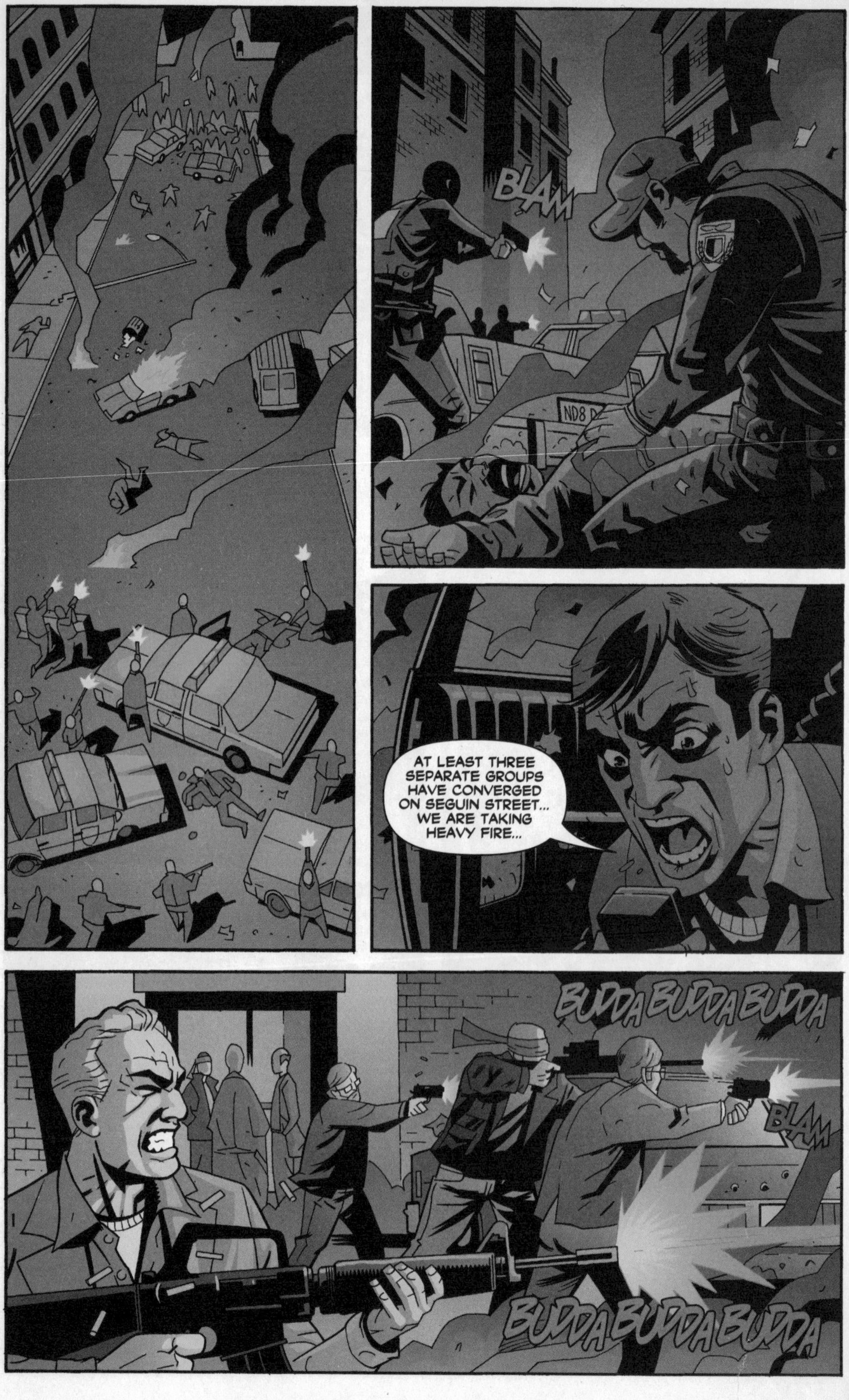
BLAM
AT LEAST THREE SEPARATE GROUPS HAVE CONVERGED ON SEGUIN STREET... WE ARE TAKING HEAVY FIRE...
BUDDA BUDDA BUDDA
BLAM
BUDDA BUDDA BUDDA

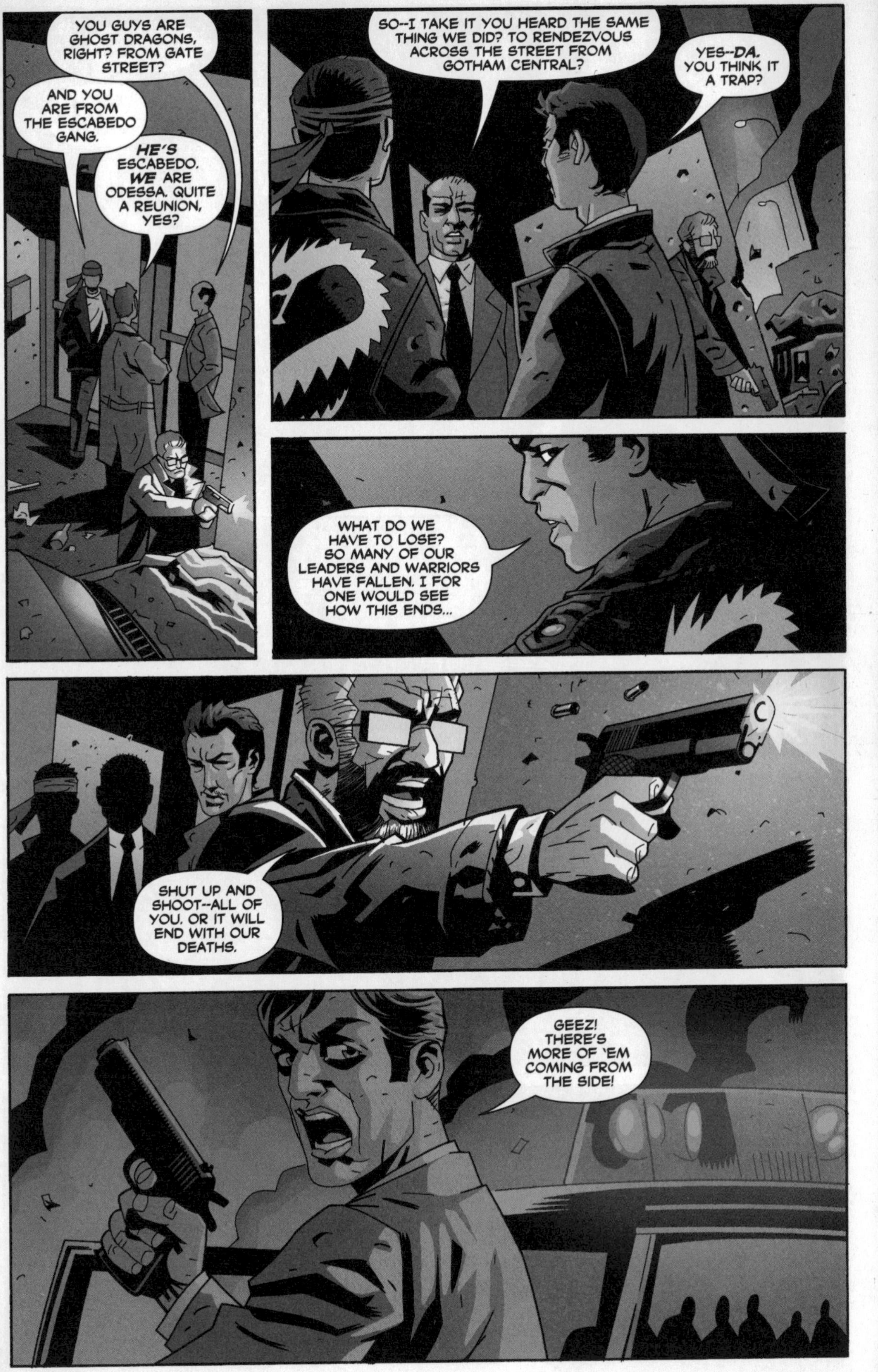
YOU GUYS ARE GHOST DRAGONS, RIGHT? FROM GATE STREET?
AND YOU ARE FROM THE ESCABEDO GANG.
HE'S ESCABEDO. WE ARE ODESSA. QUITE A REUNION, YES?
SO--I TAKE IT YOU HEARD THE SAME THING WE DID? TO RENDEZVOUS ACROSS THE STREET FROM GOTHAM CENTRAL?
YES--DA. YOU THINK IT A TRAP?
WHAT DO WE HAVE TO LOSE? SO MANY OF OUR LEADERS AND WARRIORS HAVE FALLEN. I FOR ONE WOULD SEE HOW THIS ENDS...
SHUT UP AND SHOOT--ALL OF YOU, OR IT WILL END WITH OUR DEATHS.
GEEZ! THERE'S MORE OF 'EM COMING FROM THE SIDE!

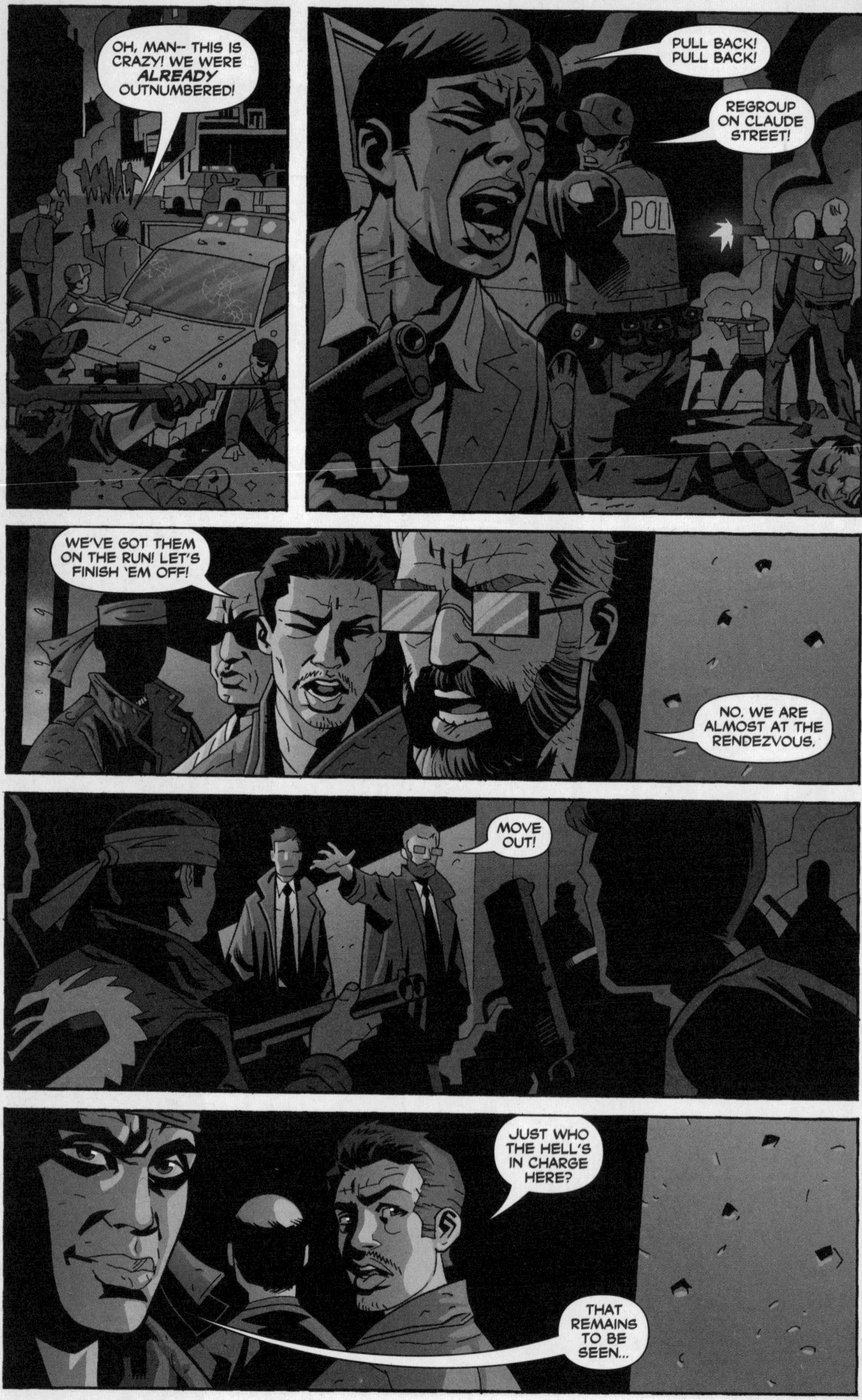
OH, MAN-- THIS IS CRAZY! WE WERE ALREADY OUTNUMBERED!
PULL BACK! PULL BACK!
REGROUP ON CLAUDE STREET!
POLI
WE'VE GOT THEM ON THE RUN! LET'S FINISH 'EM OFF!
NO. WE ARE ALMOST AT THE RENDEZVOUS.
MOVE OUT!
JUST WHO THE HELL'S IN CHARGE HERE?
THAT REMAINS TO BE SEEN...

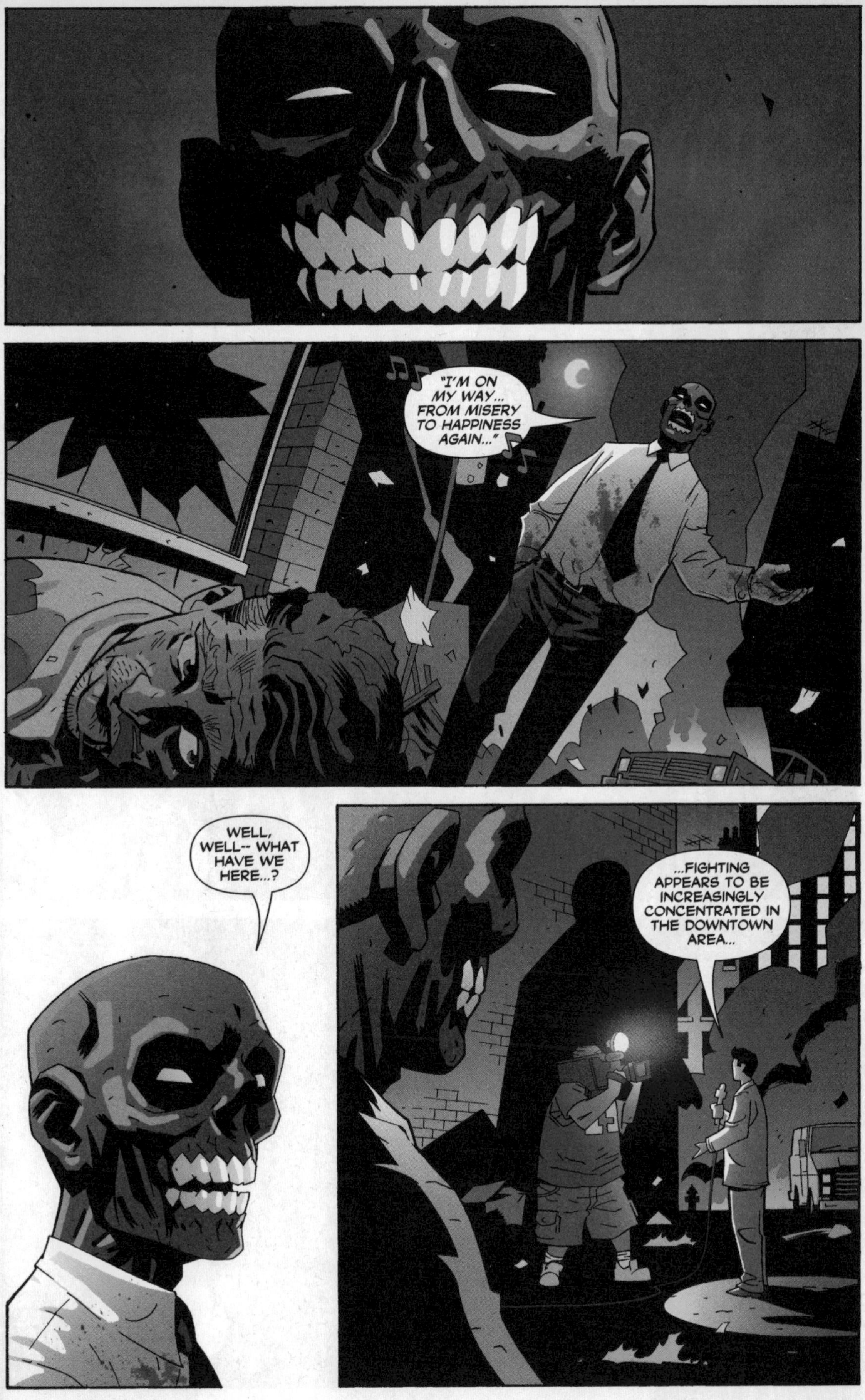
"I'M ON MY WAY... FROM MISERY TO HAPPINESS AGAIN..."
WELL, WELL-- WHAT HAVE WE HERE...?
...FIGHTING APPEARS TO BE INCREASINGLY CONCENTRATED IN THE DOWNTOWN AREA...

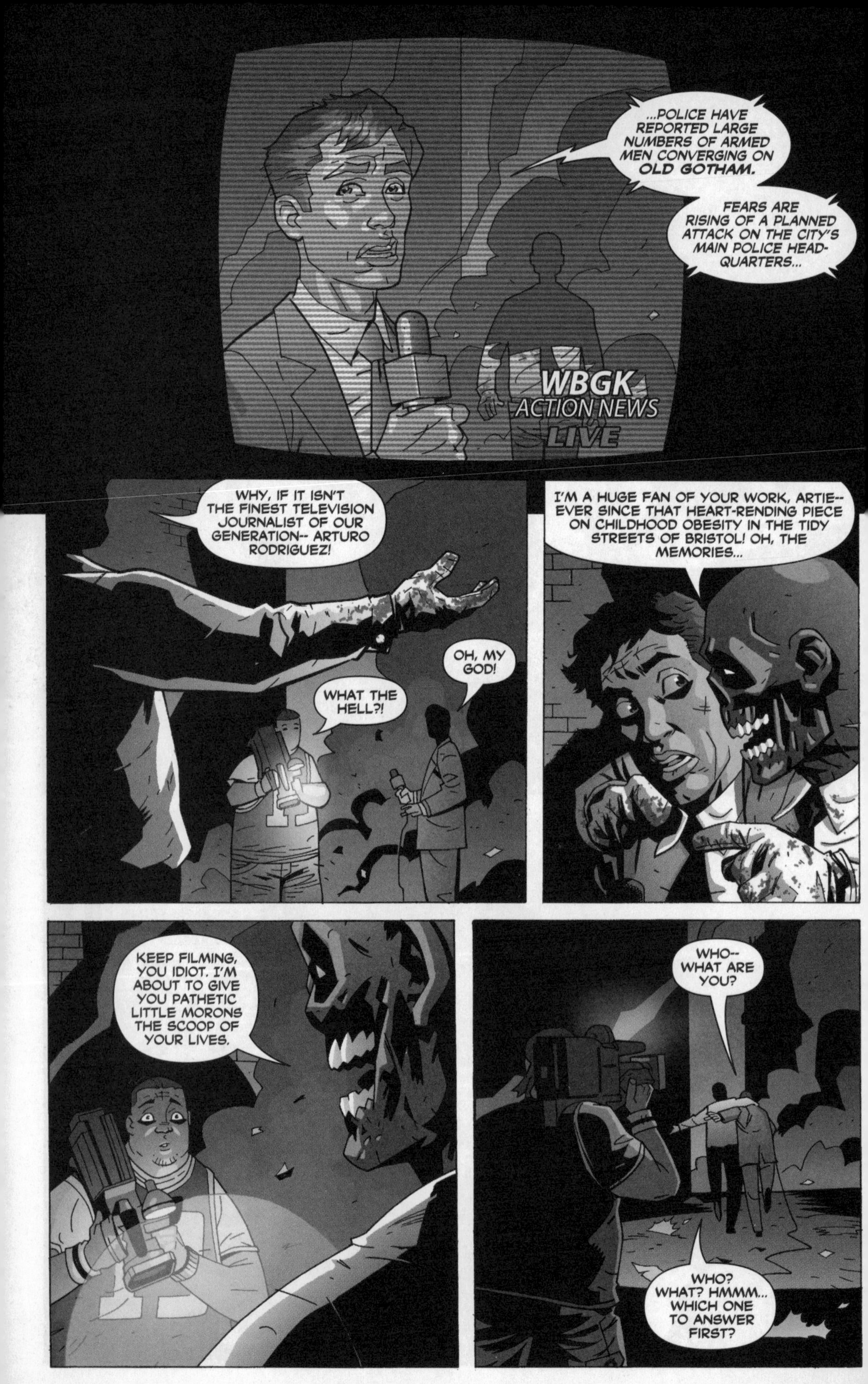
...POLICE HAVE REPORTED LARGE NUMBERS OF ARMED MEN CONVERGING ON OLD GOTHAM.
FEARS ARE RISING OF A PLANNED ATTACK ON THE CITY'S MAIN POLICE HEAD-QUARTERS...
WBGK ACTION NEWS LIVE
WHY, IF IT ISN'T THE FINEST TELEVISION JOURNALIST OF OUR GENERATION-- ARTURO RODRIGUEZ!
WHAT THE HELL?!
OH, MY GOD!
I'M A HUGE FAN OF YOUR WORK, ARTIE-- EVER SINCE THAT HEART-RENDING PIECE ON CHILDHOOD OBESITY IN THE TIDY STREETS OF BRISTOL! OH, THE MEMORIES...
KEEP FILMING, YOU IDIOT. I'M ABOUT TO GIVE YOU PATHETIC LITTLE MORONS THE SCOOP OF YOUR LIVES.
WHO-- WHAT ARE YOU?
WHO? WHAT? HMMM... WHICH ONE TO ANSWER FIRST?

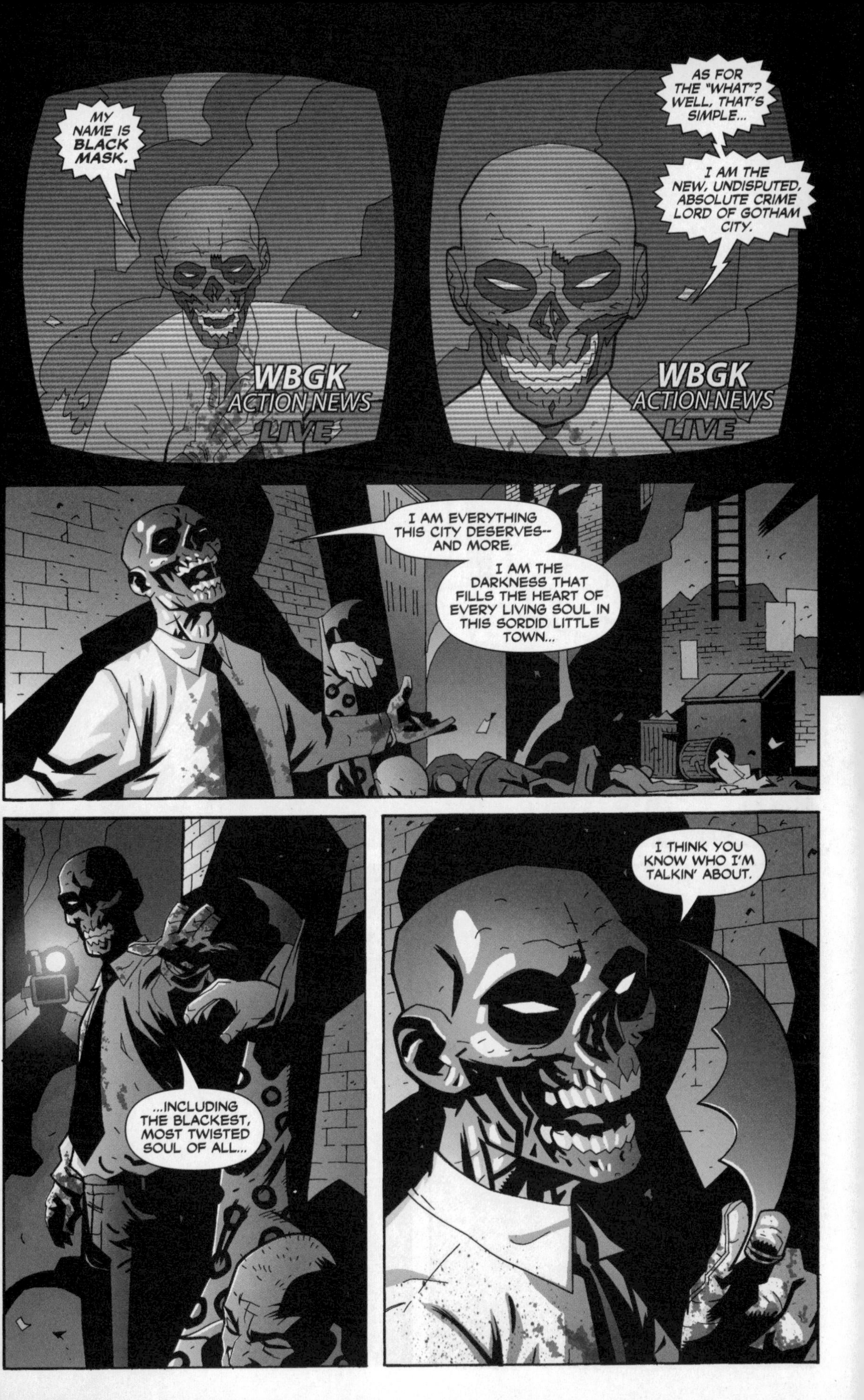
MY NAME IS BLACK MASK.
WBGK ACTION NEWS LIVE
AS FOR THE "WHAT"? WELL, THAT'S SIMPLE...
I AM THE NEW, UNDISPUTED, ABSOLUTE CRIME LORD OF GOTHAM CITY.
WBGK ACTION NEWS LIVE
I AM EVERYTHING THIS CITY DESERVES-- AND MORE.
I AM THE DARKNESS THAT FILLS THE HEART OF EVERY LIVING SOUL IN THIS SORDID LITTLE TOWN...
...INCLUDING THE BLACKEST, MOST TWISTED SOUL OF ALL...
I THINK YOU KNOW WHO I'M TALKIN' ABOUT.

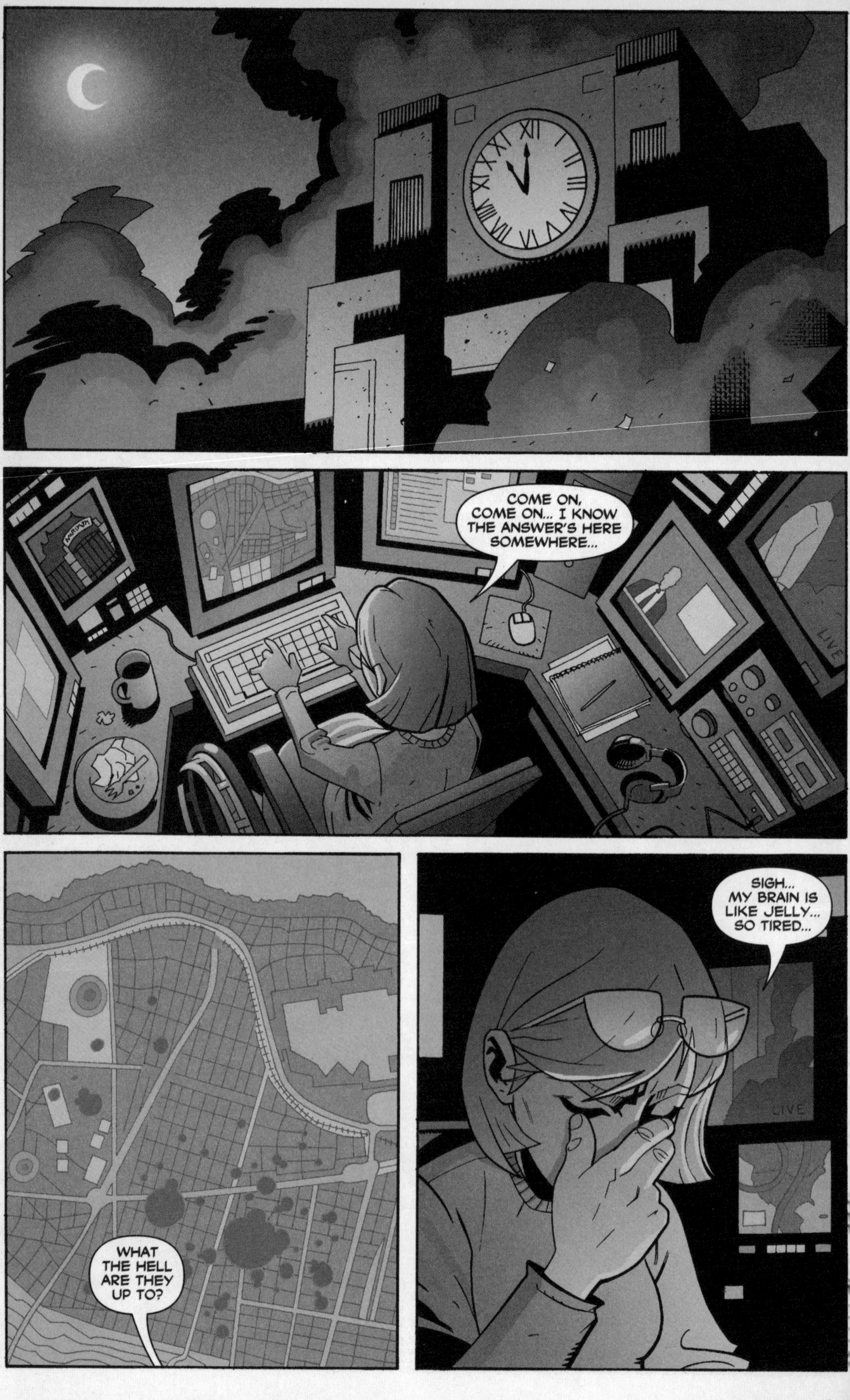
COME ON, COME ON... I KNOW THE ANSWER'S HERE SOMEWHERE...
WHAT THE HELL ARE THEY UP TO?
SIGH... MY BRAIN IS LIKE JELLY... SO TIRED...

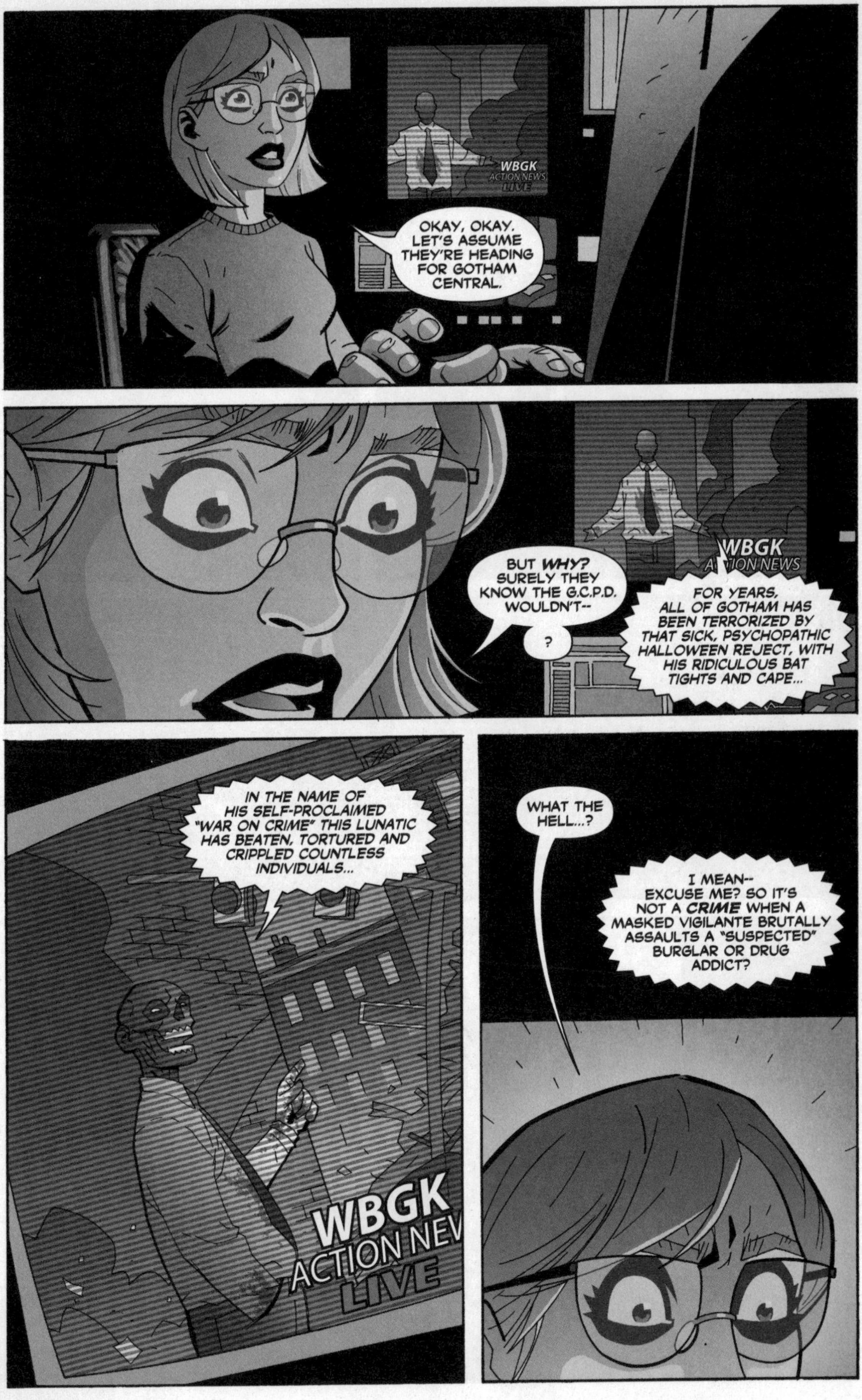
WBGK
ACTION NEWS
LIVE
OKAY, OKAY. LET'S ASSUME THEY'RE HEADING FOR GOTHAM CENTRAL.
WBGK
ACTION NEWS
BUT WHY? SURELY THEY KNOW THE G.C.P.D. WOULDN'T--
?
FOR YEARS, ALL OF GOTHAM HAS BEEN TERRORIZED BY THAT SICK, PSYCHOPATHIC HALLOWEEN REJECT, WITH HIS RIDICULOUS BAT TIGHTS AND CAPE...
IN THE NAME OF HIS SELF-PROCLAIMED "WAR ON CRIME" THIS LUNATIC HAS BEATEN, TORTURED AND CRIPPLED COUNTLESS INDIVIDUALS...
WBGK
LIVE
WHAT THE HELL...?
I MEAN-- EXCUSE ME? SO IT'S NOT A CRIME WHEN A MASKED VIGILANTE BRUTALLY ASSAULTS A "SUSPECTED" BURGLAR OR DRUG ADDICT?

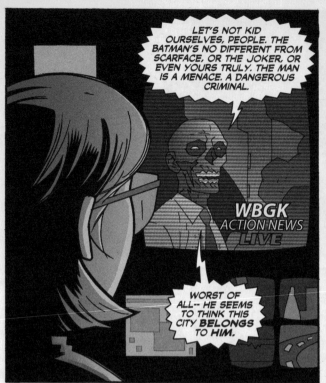

LET'S NOT KID OURSELVES, PEOPLE. THE BATMAN'S NO DIFFERENT FROM SCARFACE, OR THE JOKER, OR EVEN YOURS TRULY. THE MAN IS A MENACE. A DANGEROUS CRIMINAL.

WBGK ACTION NEWS LIVE

WORST OF ALL-- HE SEEMS TO THINK THIS CITY BELONGS TO HIM.

WELL, I'M HERE TO TELL YOU, BATMAN-- GOTHAM IS NO LONGER YOURS.

FROM TONIGHT AND FOREVER MORE...

...THIS CITY IS MINE.

I HAVE SUMMONED THE ENTIRE CRIMINAL POPULATION OF GOTHAM-- FOLLOWED, NO DOUBT, BY THOSE FINE BOYS IN BLUE-- HERE...

...TO WITNESS THE END OF AN ERA...

...AND THE RISE OF A NEW POWER IN GOTHAM CITY.

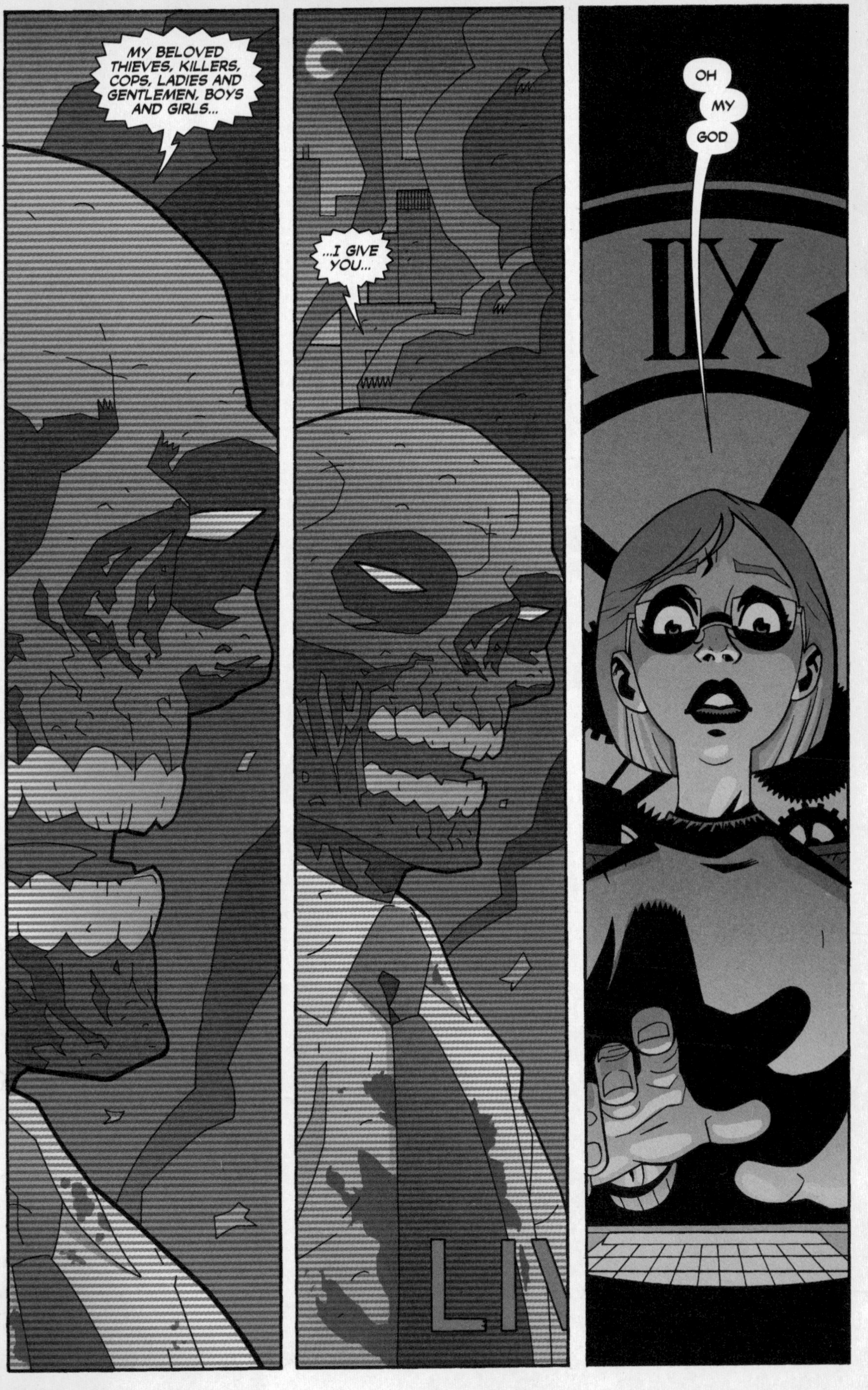
MY BELOVED THIEVES, KILLERS, COPS, LADIES AND GENTLEMEN, BOYS AND GIRLS...
...I GIVE YOU...
OH
MY
GOD

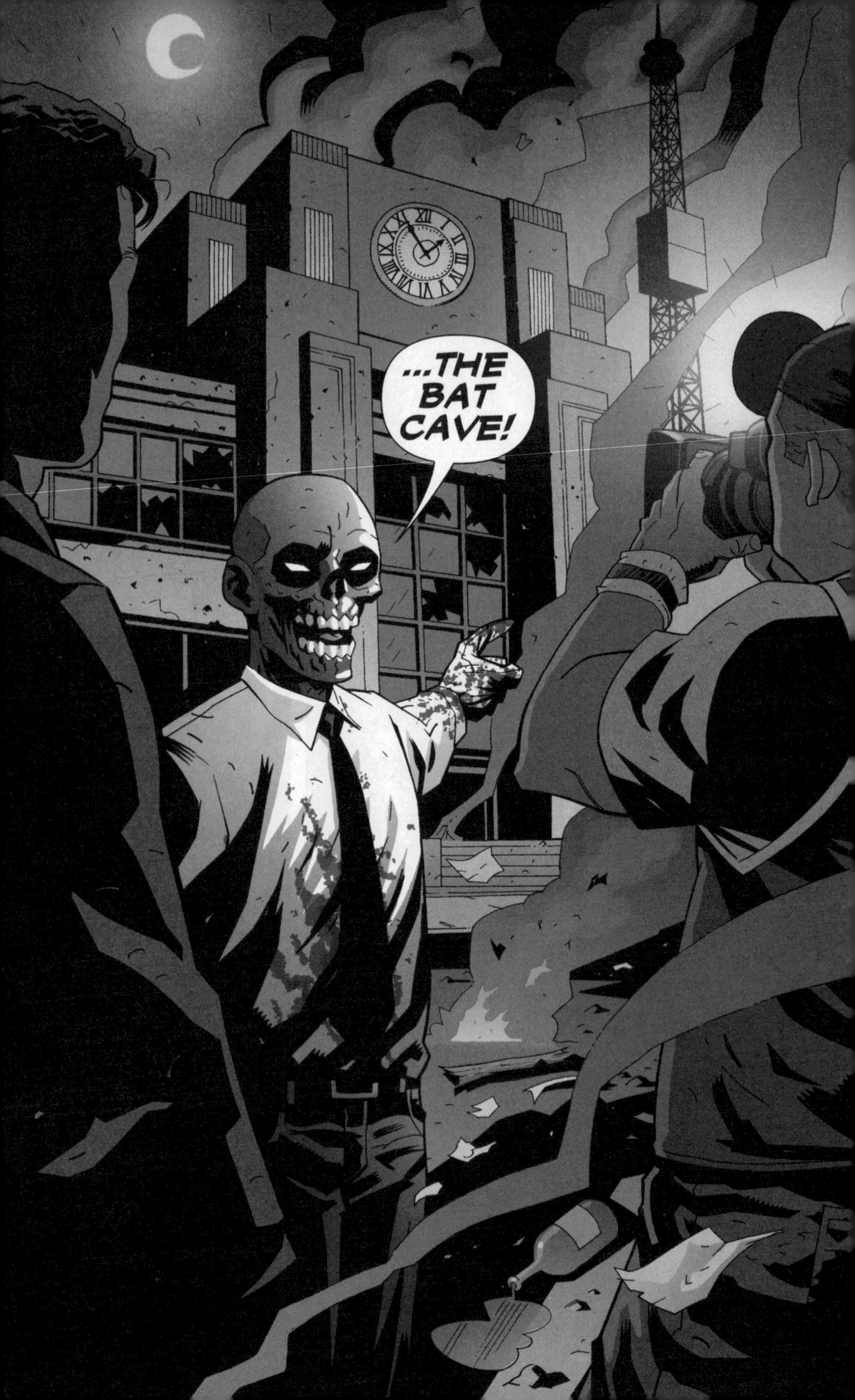
...THE BAT CAVE!

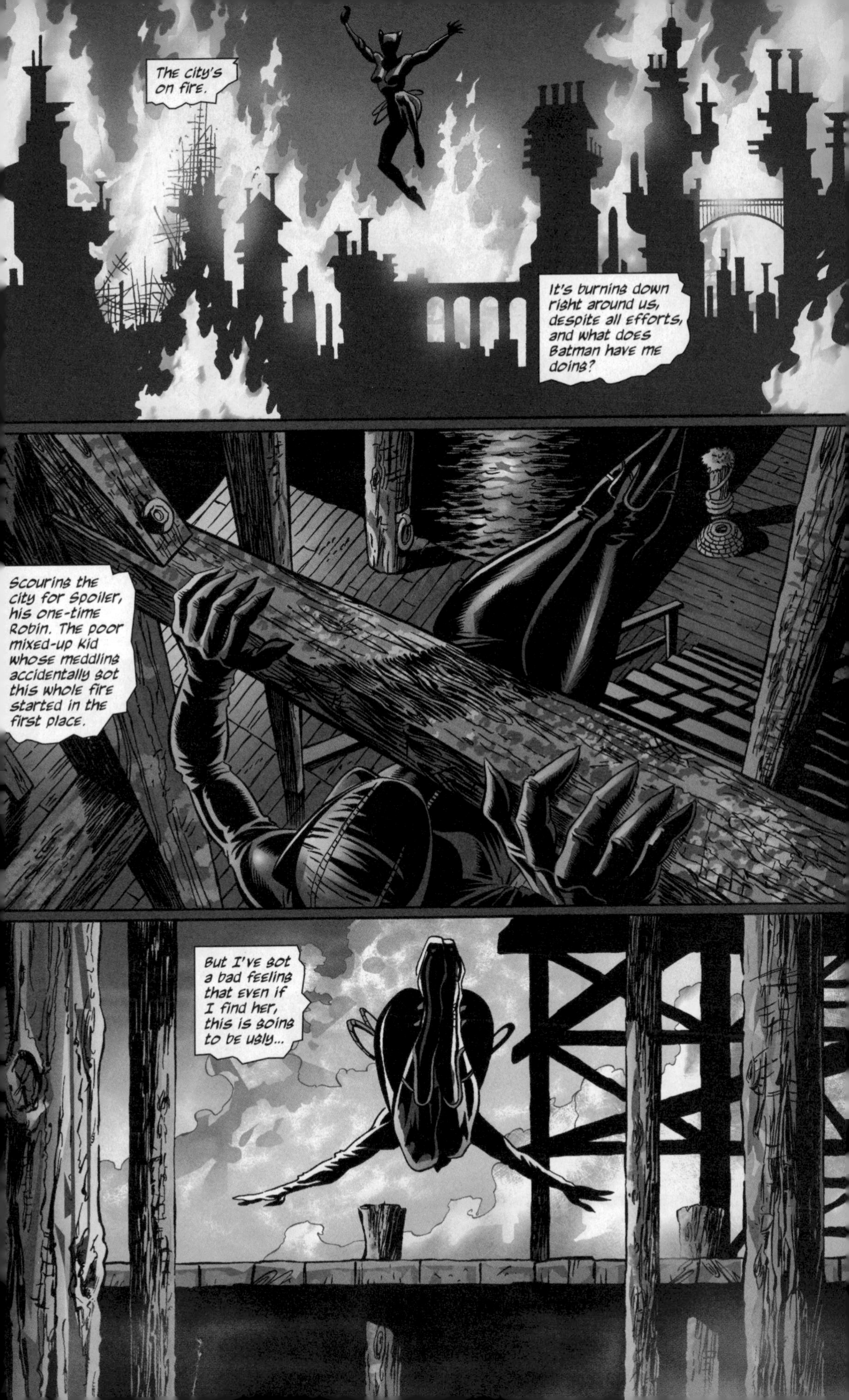

The city's on fire.
It's burning down right around us, despite all efforts, and what does Batman have me doing?
Scouring the city for Spoiler, his one-time Robin. The poor mixed-up kid whose meddling accidentally got this whole fire started in the first place.
But I've got a bad feeling that even if I find her, this is going to be ugly...

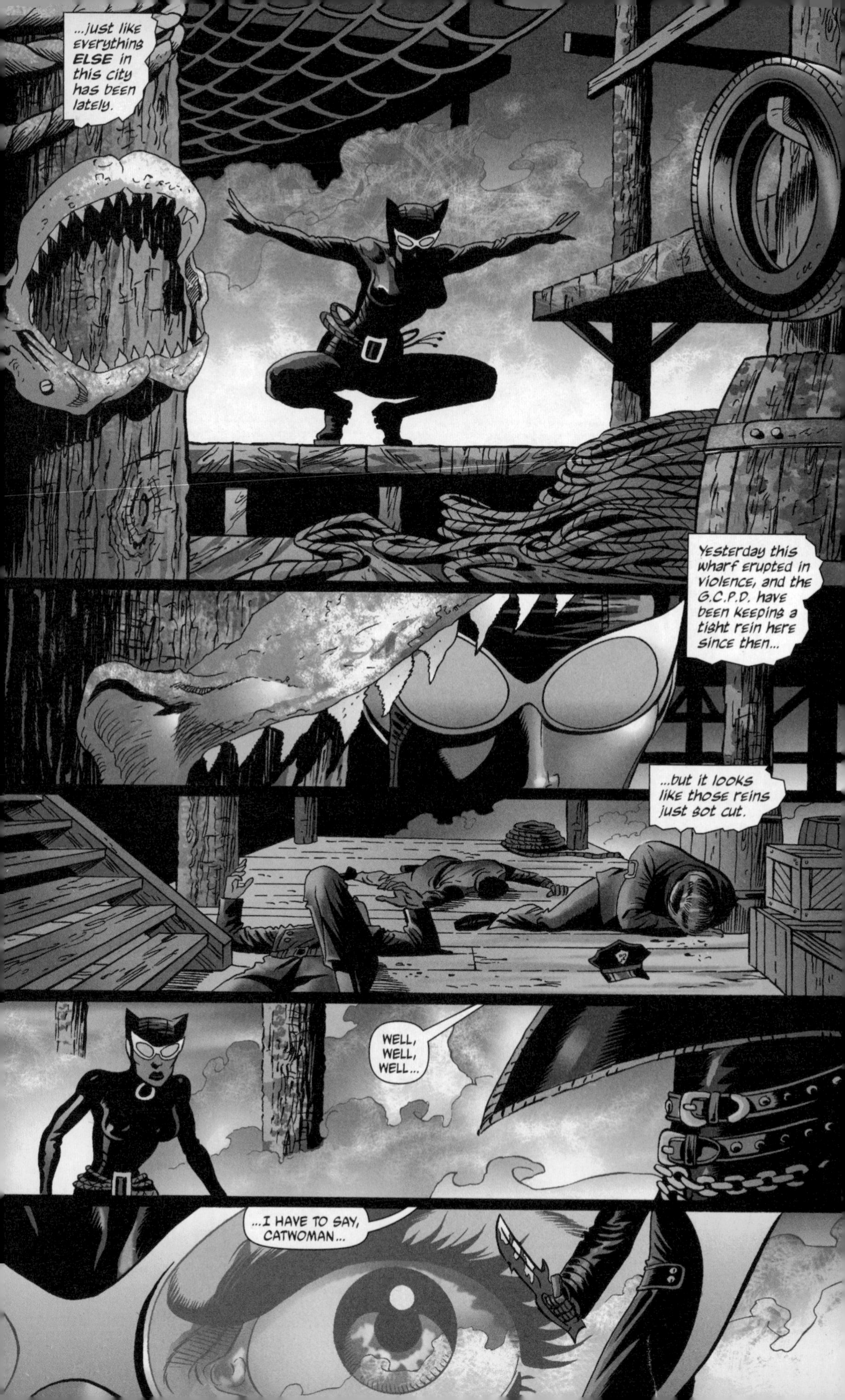
...just like everything ELSE in this city has been lately.
Yesterday this wharf erupted in violence, and the G.C.P.D. have been keeping a tight rein here since then...
...but it looks like those reins just got cut.
WELL, WELL, WELL...
...I HAVE TO SAY, CATWOMAN...

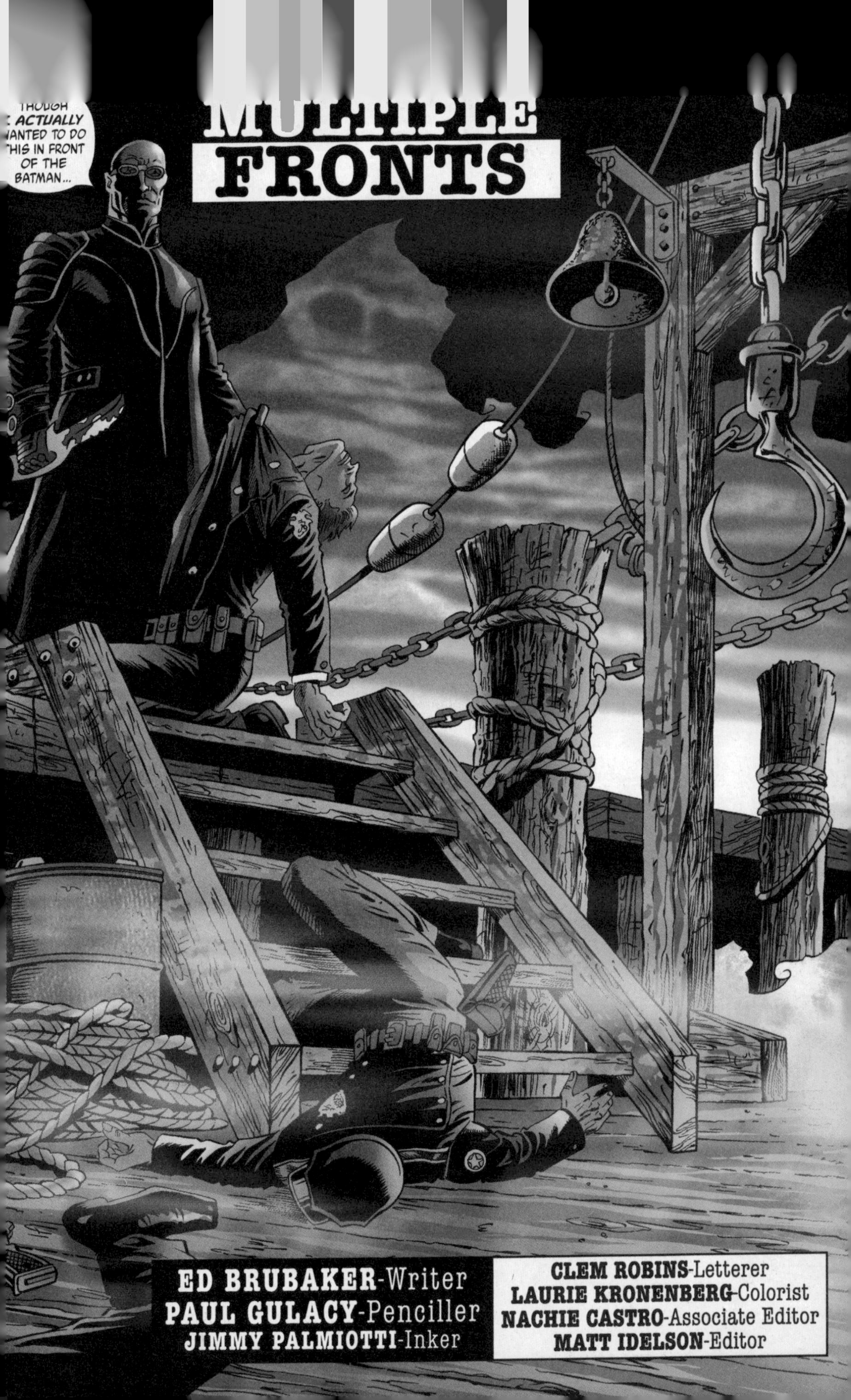

THOUGH ACTUALLY ANTED TO DO THIS IN FRONT OF THE BATMAN...
MULTIPLE FRONTS
ED BRUBAKER-Writer
PAUL GULACY-Penciller
JIMMY PALMIOTTI-Inker
CLEM ROBINS-Letterer
LAURIE KRONENBERG-Colorist
NACHIE CASTRO-Associate Editor
MATT IDELSON-Editor

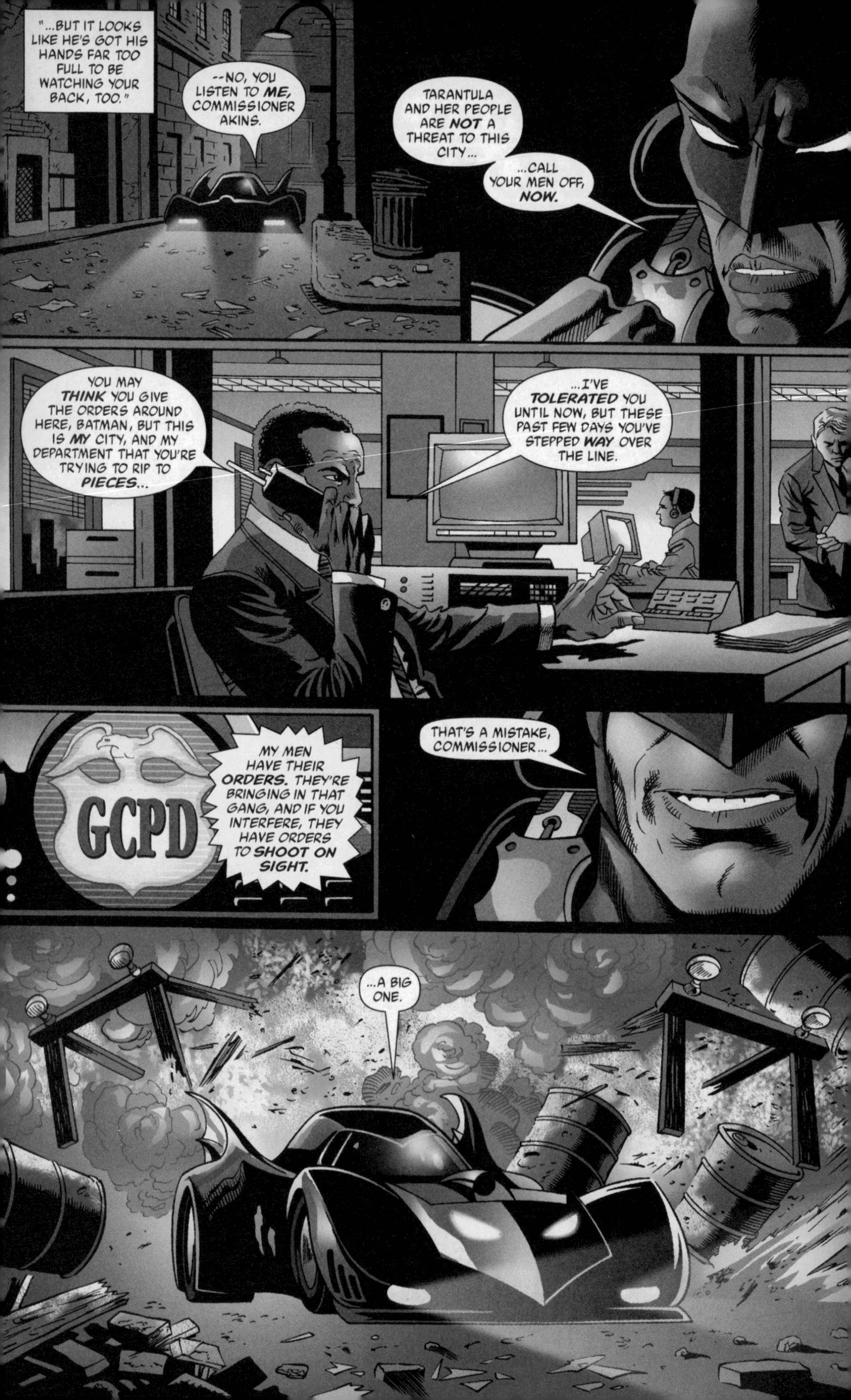
"...BUT IT LOOKS LIKE HE'S GOT HIS HANDS FAR TOO FULL TO BE WATCHING YOUR BACK, TOO."
--NO, YOU LISTEN TO ME, COMMISSIONER AKINS.
TARANTULA AND HER PEOPLE ARE NOT A THREAT TO THIS CITY...
...CALL YOUR MEN OFF, NOW.
YOU MAY THINK YOU GIVE THE ORDERS AROUND HERE, BATMAN, BUT THIS IS MY CITY, AND MY DEPARTMENT THAT YOU'RE TRYING TO RIP TO PIECES...
...I'VE TOLERATED YOU UNTIL NOW, BUT THESE PAST FEW DAYS YOU'VE STEPPED WAY OVER THE LINE.
GCPD
MY MEN HAVE THEIR ORDERS. THEY'RE BRINGING IN THAT GANG, AND IF YOU INTERFERE, THEY HAVE ORDERS TO SHOOT ON SIGHT.
THAT'S A MISTAKE, COMMISSIONER...
...A BIG ONE.

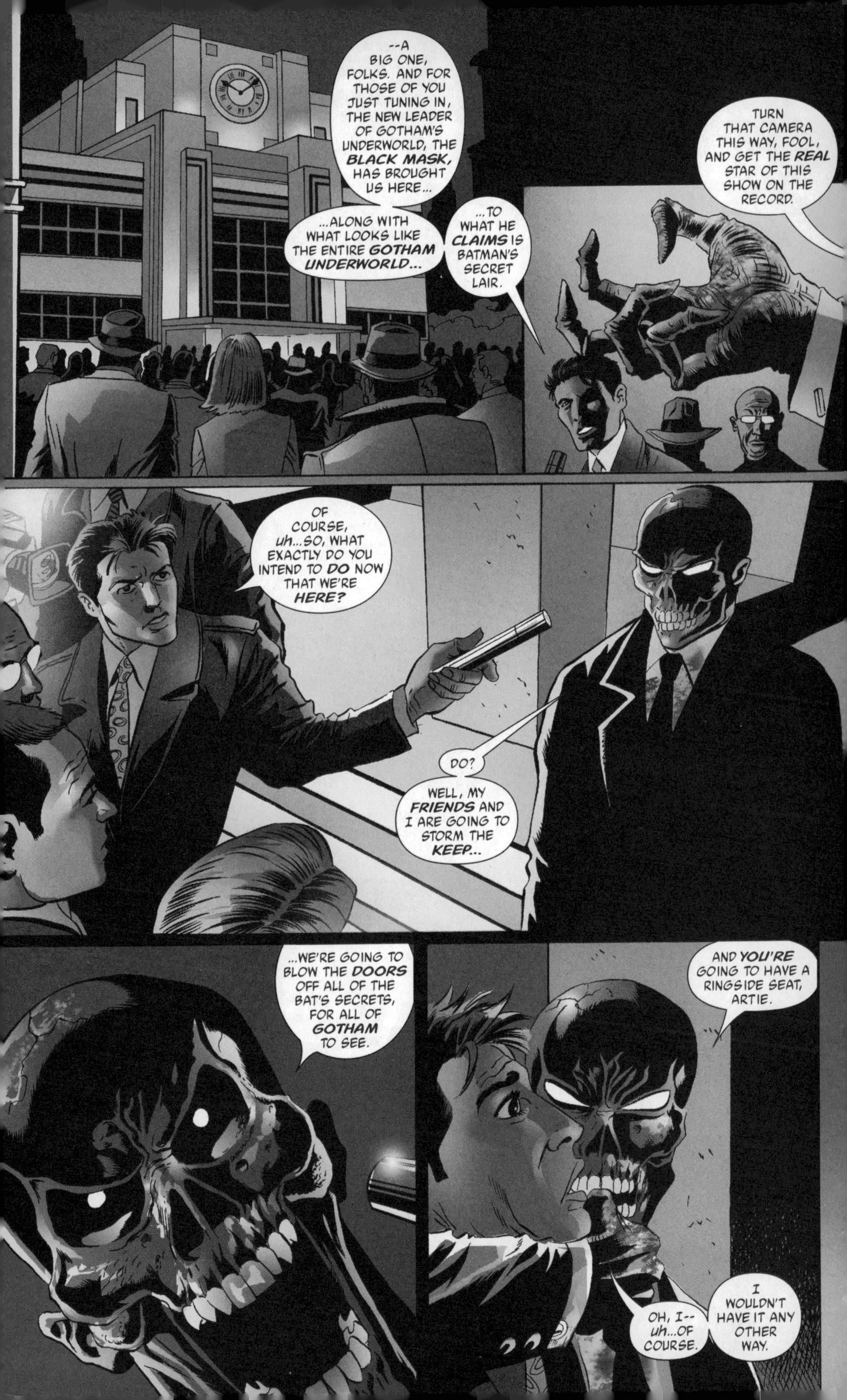
--A BIG ONE, FOLKS. AND FOR THOSE OF YOU JUST TUNING IN, THE NEW LEADER OF GOTHAM'S UNDERWORLD, THE BLACK MASK, HAS BROUGHT US HERE...
...ALONG WITH WHAT LOOKS LIKE THE ENTIRE GOTHAM UNDERWORLD...
...TO WHAT HE CLAIMS IS BATMAN'S SECRET LAIR.
TURN THAT CAMERA THIS WAY, FOOL, AND GET THE REAL STAR OF THIS SHOW ON THE RECORD.
OF COURSE, uh...SO, WHAT EXACTLY DO YOU INTEND TO DO NOW THAT WE'RE HERE?
DO?
WELL, MY FRIENDS AND I ARE GOING TO STORM THE KEEP...
...WE'RE GOING TO BLOW THE DOORS OFF ALL OF THE BAT'S SECRETS, FOR ALL OF GOTHAM TO SEE.
AND YOU'RE GOING TO HAVE A RINGSIDE SEAT, ARTIE.
OH, I-- uh...OF COURSE.
I WOULDN'T HAVE IT ANY OTHER WAY.

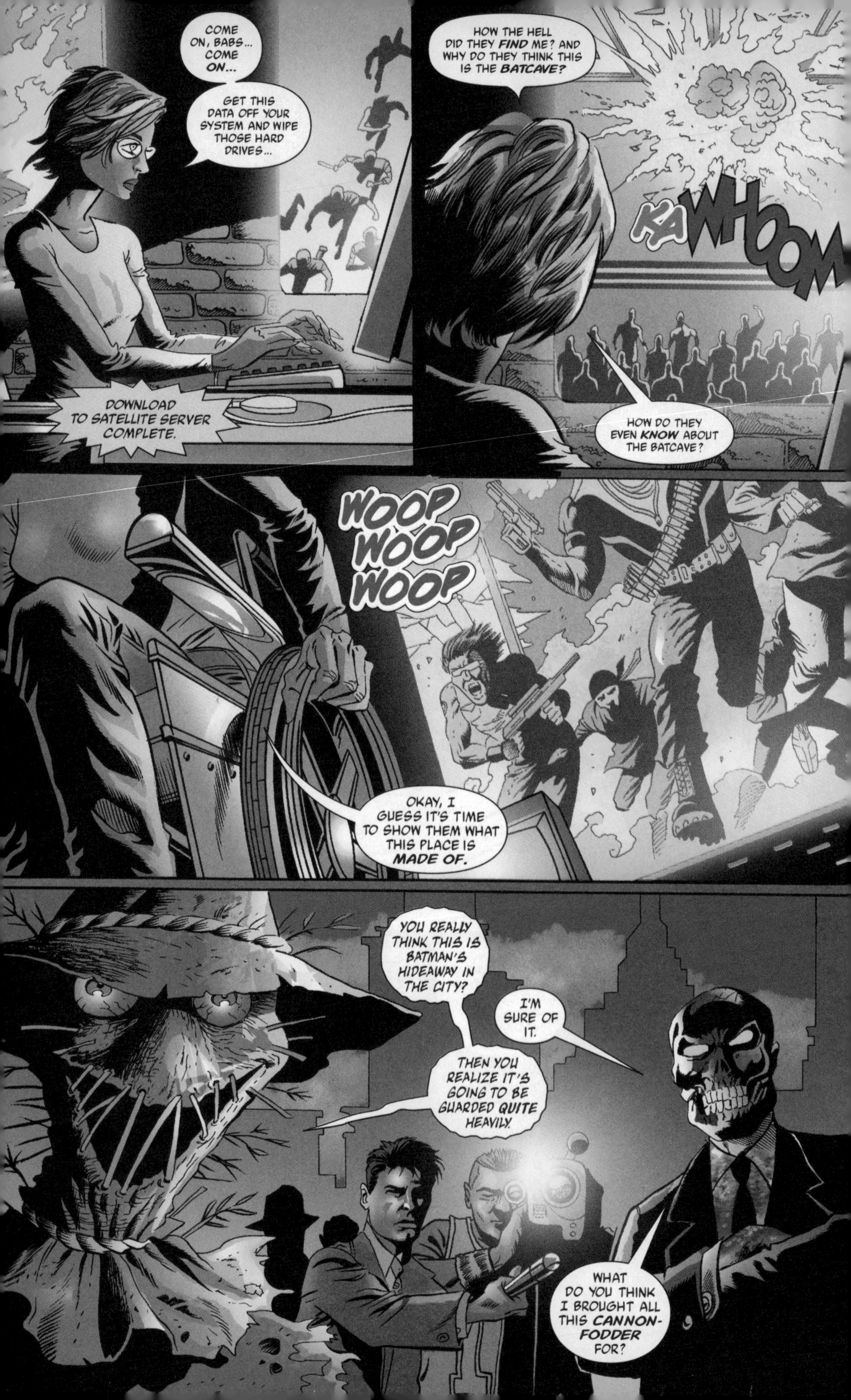

COME ON, BABS... COME ON...
GET THIS DATA OFF YOUR SYSTEM AND WIPE THOSE HARD DRIVES...
DOWNLOAD TO SATELLITE SERVER COMPLETE.
HOW THE HELL DID THEY FIND ME? AND WHY DO THEY THINK THIS IS THE BATCAVE?
KAWHOOM
HOW DO THEY EVEN KNOW ABOUT THE BATCAVE?
WOOP WOOP WOOP
OKAY, I GUESS IT'S TIME TO SHOW THEM WHAT THIS PLACE IS MADE OF.
YOU REALLY THINK THIS IS BATMAN'S HIDEAWAY IN THE CITY?
I'M SURE OF IT.
THEN YOU REALIZE IT'S GOING TO BE GUARDED QUITE HEAVILY.
WHAT DO YOU THINK I BROUGHT ALL THIS CANNON-FODDER FOR?

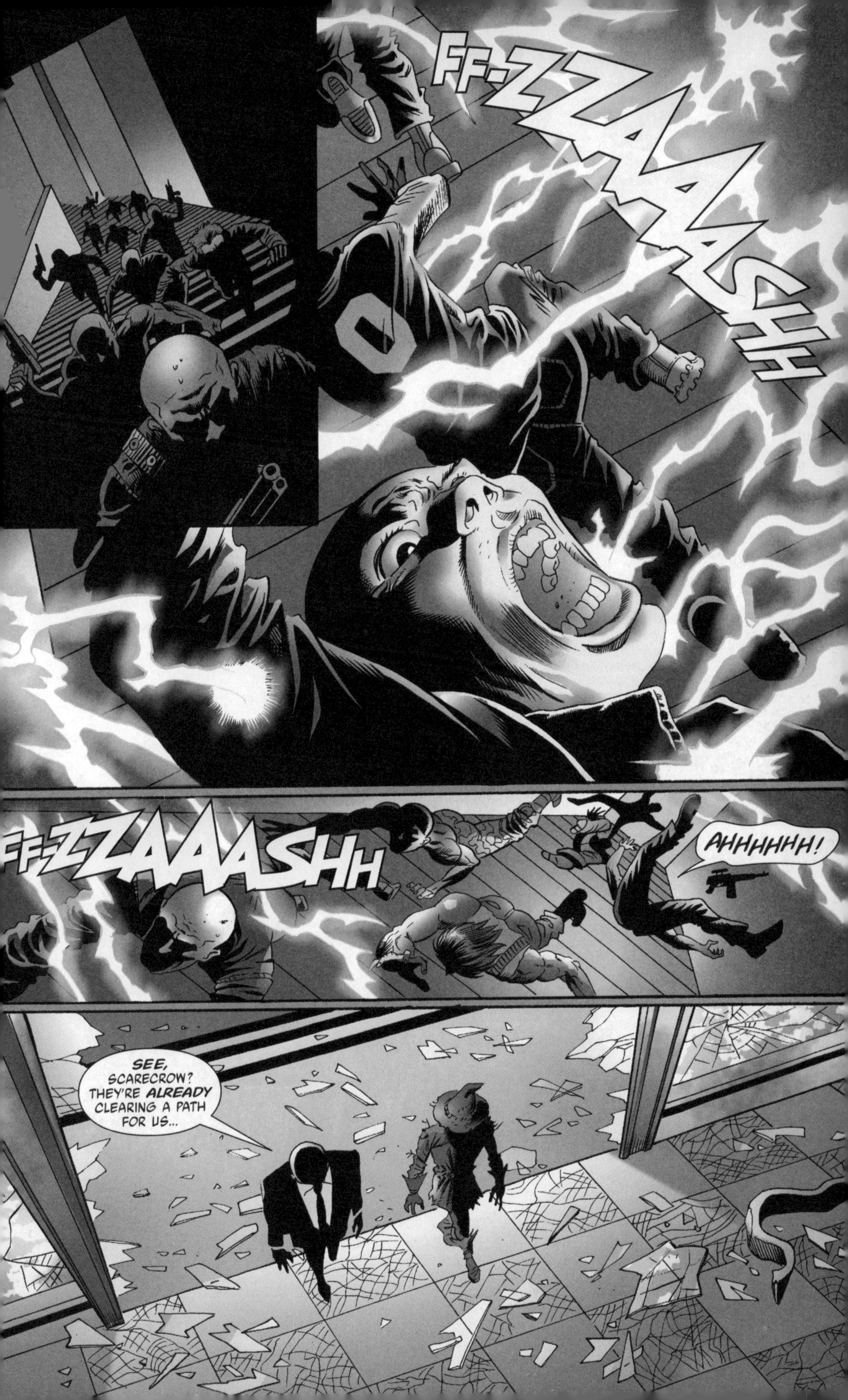
FF-ZZAAASHH
FF-ZZAAASHH
AHHHHHH!
SEE, SCARECROW? THEY'RE ALREADY CLEARING A PATH FOR US...

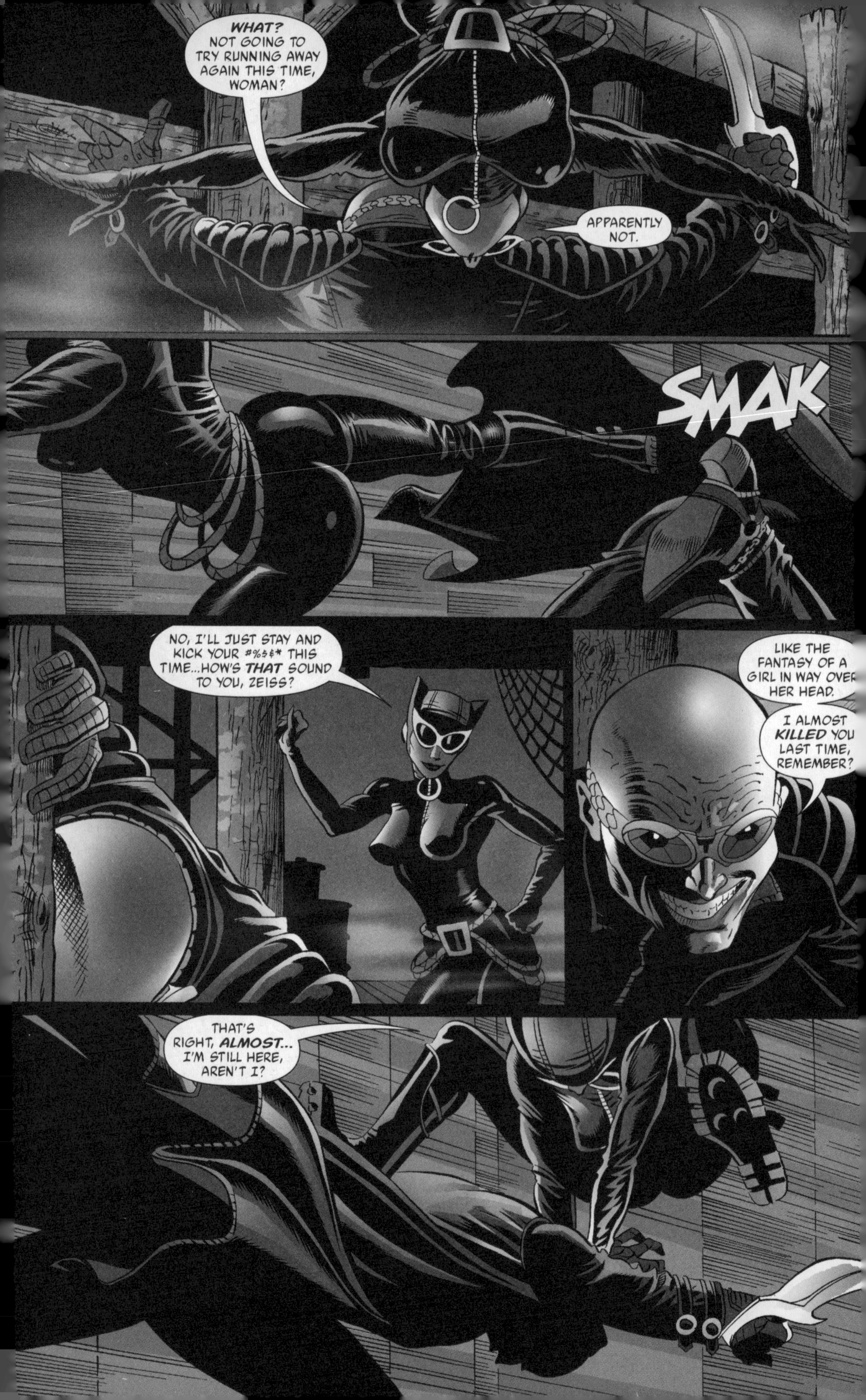
WHAT? NOT GOING TO TRY RUNNING AWAY AGAIN THIS TIME, WOMAN?
APPARENTLY NOT.
SMAK
NO, I'LL JUST STAY AND KICK YOUR #%$&* THIS TIME...HOW'S THAT SOUND TO YOU, ZEISS?
LIKE THE FANTASY OF A GIRL IN WAY OVER HER HEAD.
I ALMOST KILLED YOU LAST TIME, REMEMBER?
THAT'S RIGHT, ALMOST... I'M STILL HERE, AREN'T I?

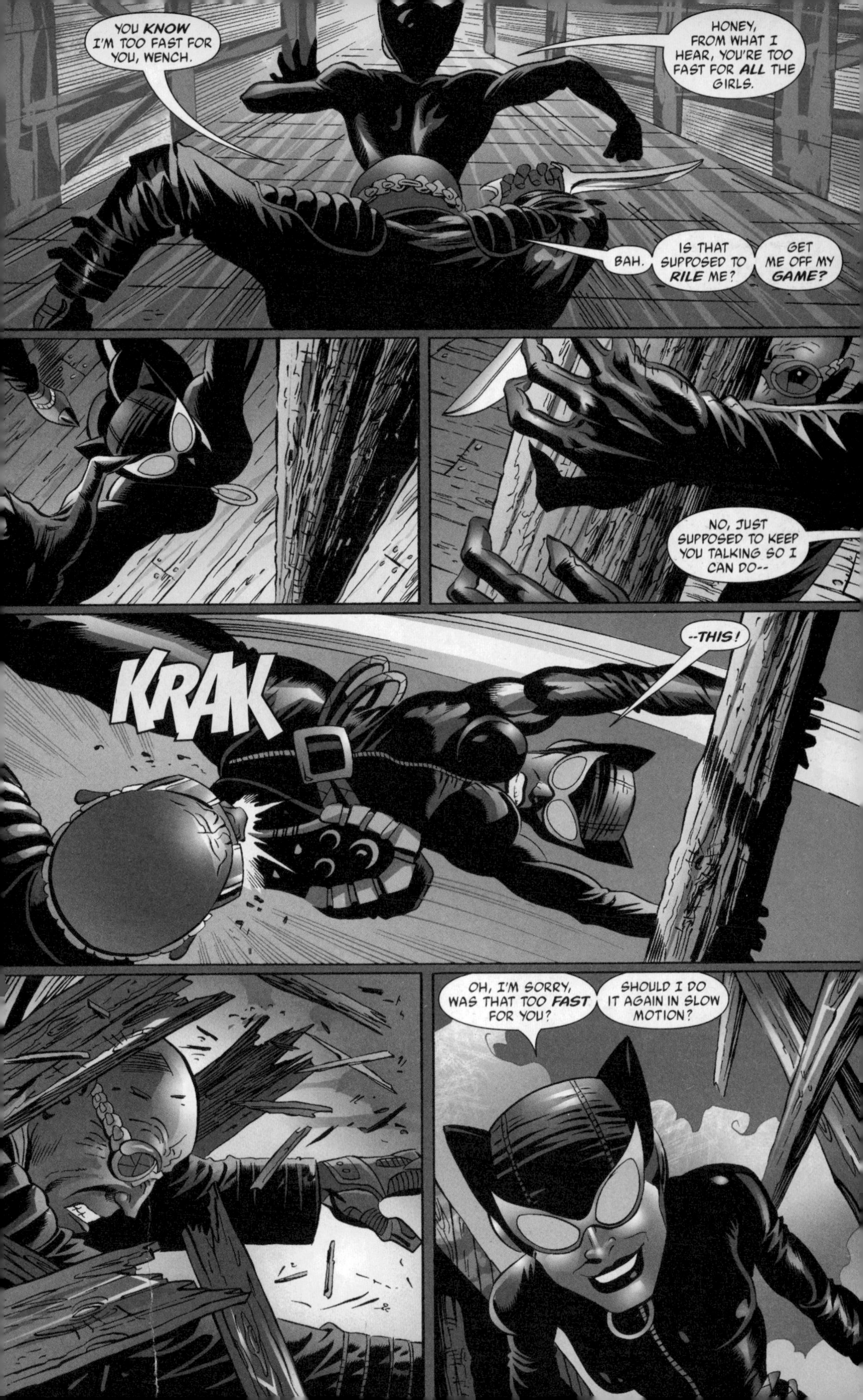
YOU KNOW I'M TOO FAST FOR YOU, WENCH.
HONEY, FROM WHAT I HEAR, YOU'RE TOO FAST FOR ALL THE GIRLS.
BAH.
IS THAT SUPPOSED TO RILE ME?
GET ME OFF MY GAME?
NO, JUST SUPPOSED TO KEEP YOU TALKING SO I CAN DO--
KRAK
--THIS!
OH, I'M SORRY, WAS THAT TOO FAST FOR YOU?
SHOULD I DO IT AGAIN IN SLOW MOTION?

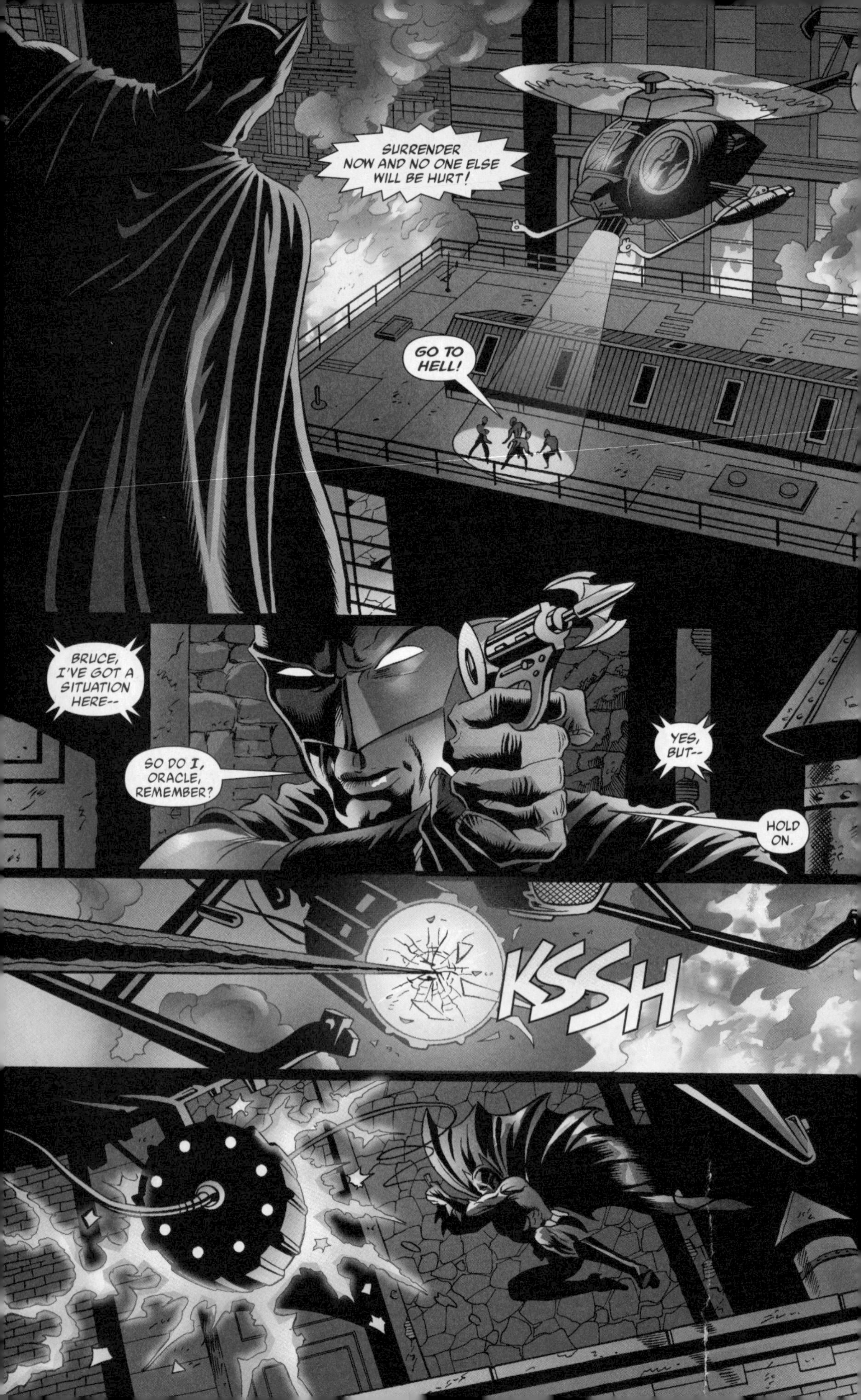
SURRENDER NOW AND NO ONE ELSE WILL BE HURT!
GO TO HELL!
BRUCE, I'VE GOT A SITUATION HERE--
SO DO I, ORACLE, REMEMBER?
YES, BUT--
HOLD ON.
KSSH

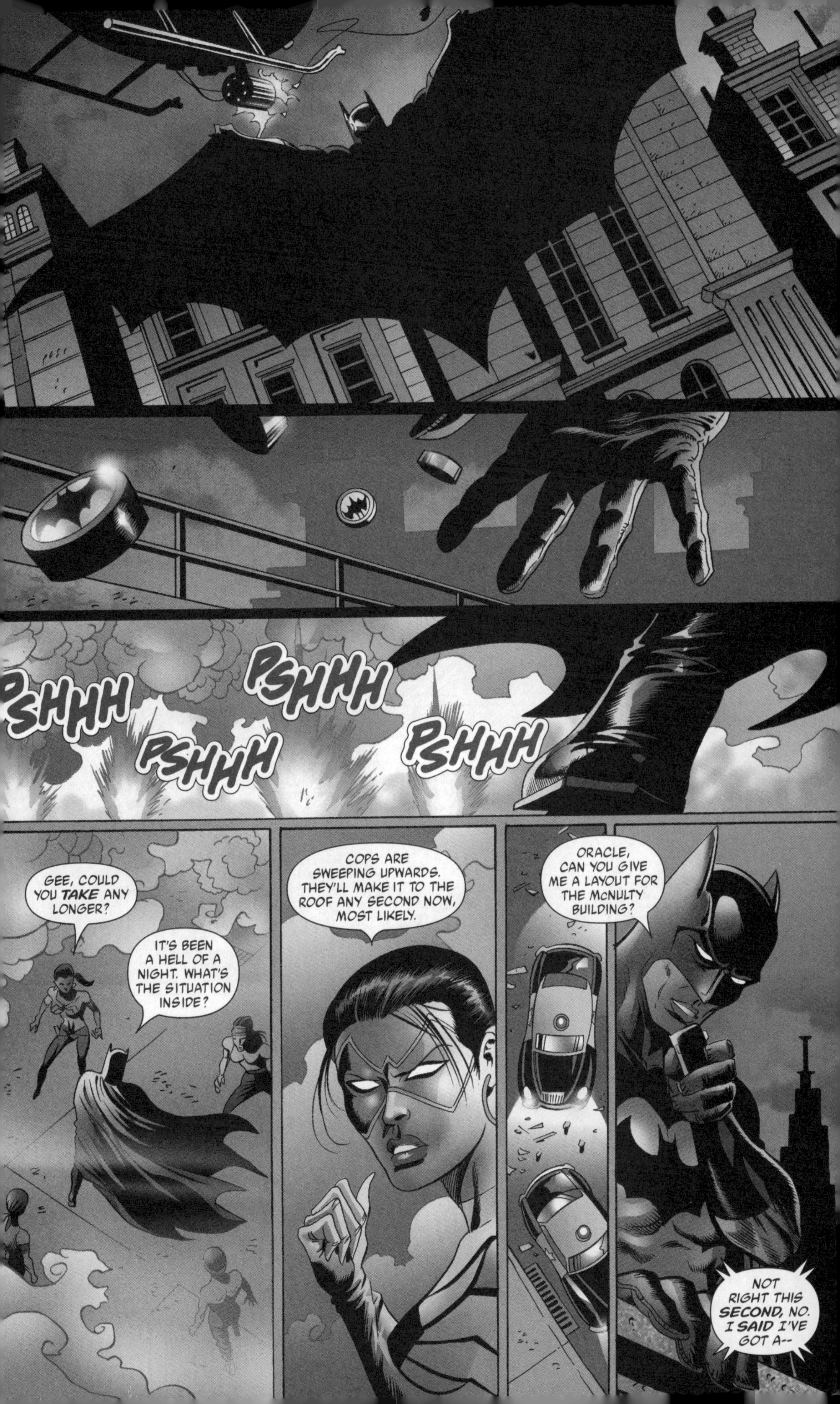
PSHHH
PSHHH
PSHHH
PSHHH
GEE, COULD YOU TAKE ANY LONGER?
IT'S BEEN A HELL OF A NIGHT. WHAT'S THE SITUATION INSIDE?
COPS ARE SWEEPING UPWARDS. THEY'LL MAKE IT TO THE ROOF ANY SECOND NOW, MOST LIKELY.
ORACLE, CAN YOU GIVE ME A LAYOUT FOR THE McNULTY BUILDING?
NOT RIGHT THIS SECOND, NO. I SAID I'VE GOT A--

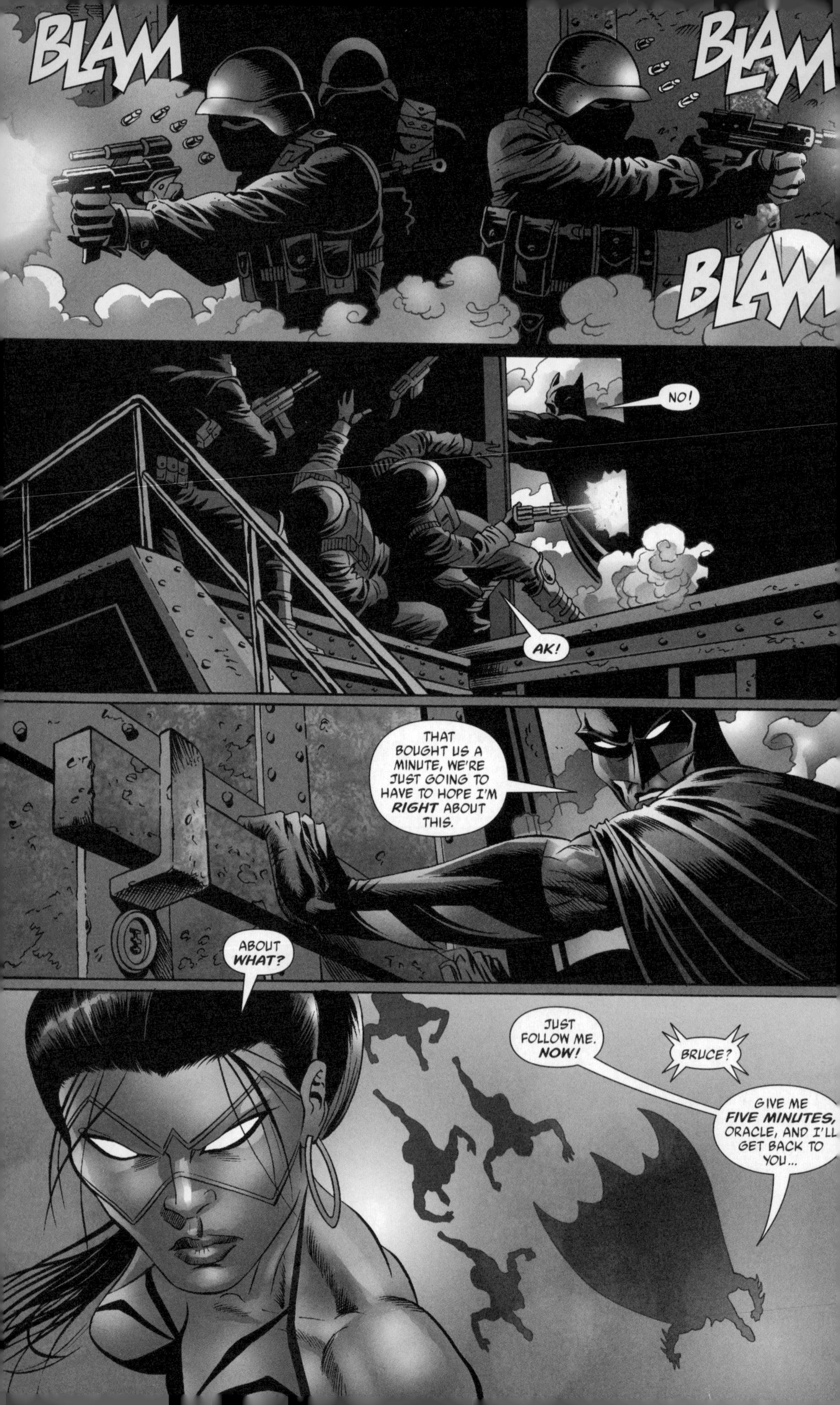
BLAM
BLAM
BLAM
NO!
AK!
THAT BOUGHT US A MINUTE, WE'RE JUST GOING TO HAVE TO HOPE I'M **RIGHT** ABOUT THIS.
ABOUT **WHAT?**
JUST FOLLOW ME. **NOW!**
BRUCE?
GIVE ME **FIVE MINUTES,** ORACLE, AND I'LL GET BACK TO YOU...

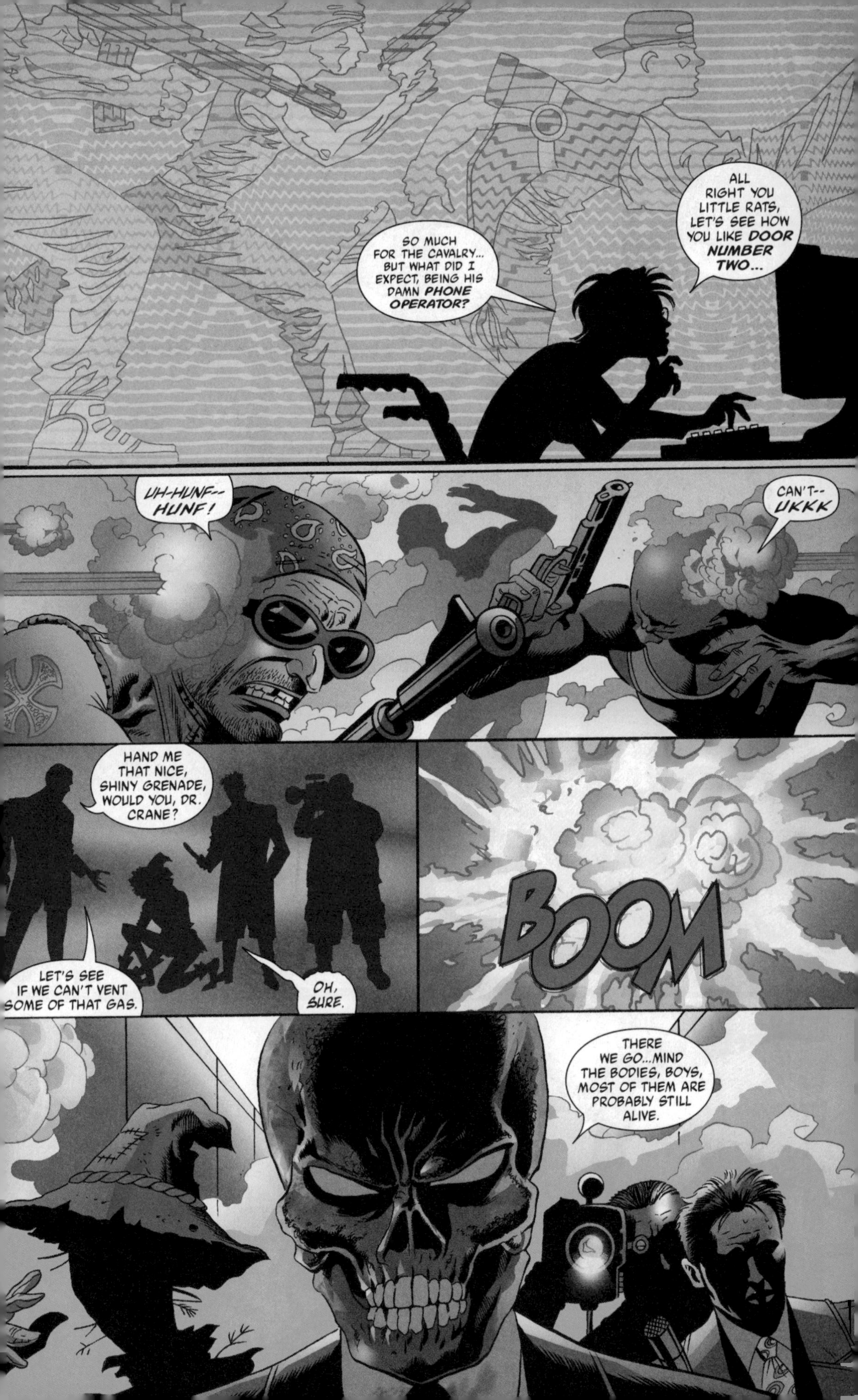
SO MUCH FOR THE CAVALRY... BUT WHAT DID I EXPECT, BEING HIS DAMN PHONE OPERATOR?
ALL RIGHT YOU LITTLE RATS, LET'S SEE HOW YOU LIKE DOOR NUMBER TWO...
UH-HUNF-- HUNF!
CAN'T-- UKKK
HAND ME THAT NICE, SHINY GRENADE, WOULD YOU, DR. CRANE?
LET'S SEE IF WE CAN'T VENT SOME OF THAT GAS.
OH, SURE.
BOOM
THERE WE GO...MIND THE BODIES, BOYS, MOST OF THEM ARE PROBABLY STILL ALIVE.

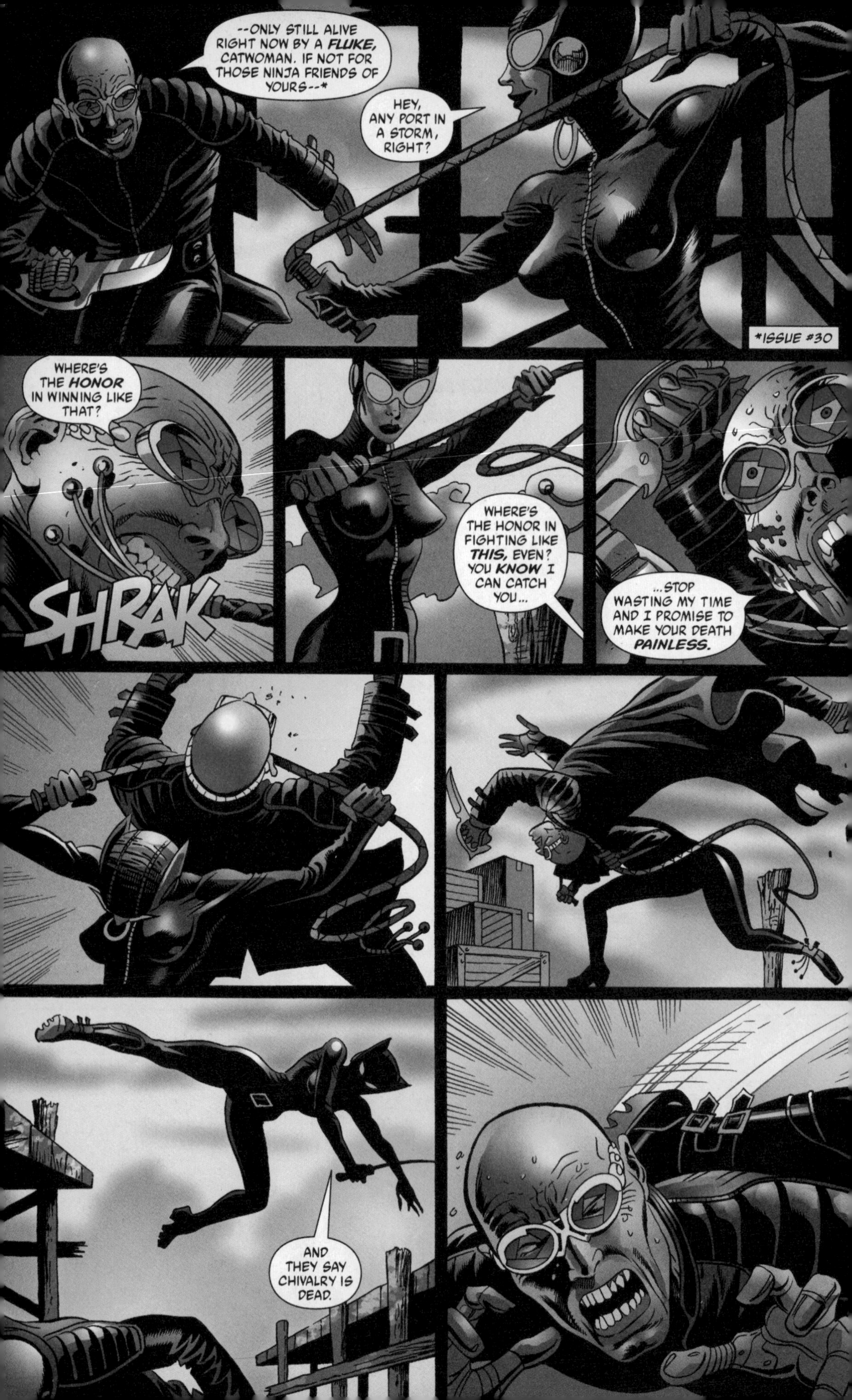
--ONLY STILL ALIVE RIGHT NOW BY A FLUKE, CATWOMAN. IF NOT FOR THOSE NINJA FRIENDS OF YOURS--*
HEY, ANY PORT IN A STORM, RIGHT?
*ISSUE #30
WHERE'S THE HONOR IN WINNING LIKE THAT?
SHRAK
WHERE'S THE HONOR IN FIGHTING LIKE THIS, EVEN? YOU KNOW I CAN CATCH YOU...
...STOP WASTING MY TIME AND I PROMISE TO MAKE YOUR DEATH PAINLESS.
AND THEY SAY CHIVALRY IS DEAD.

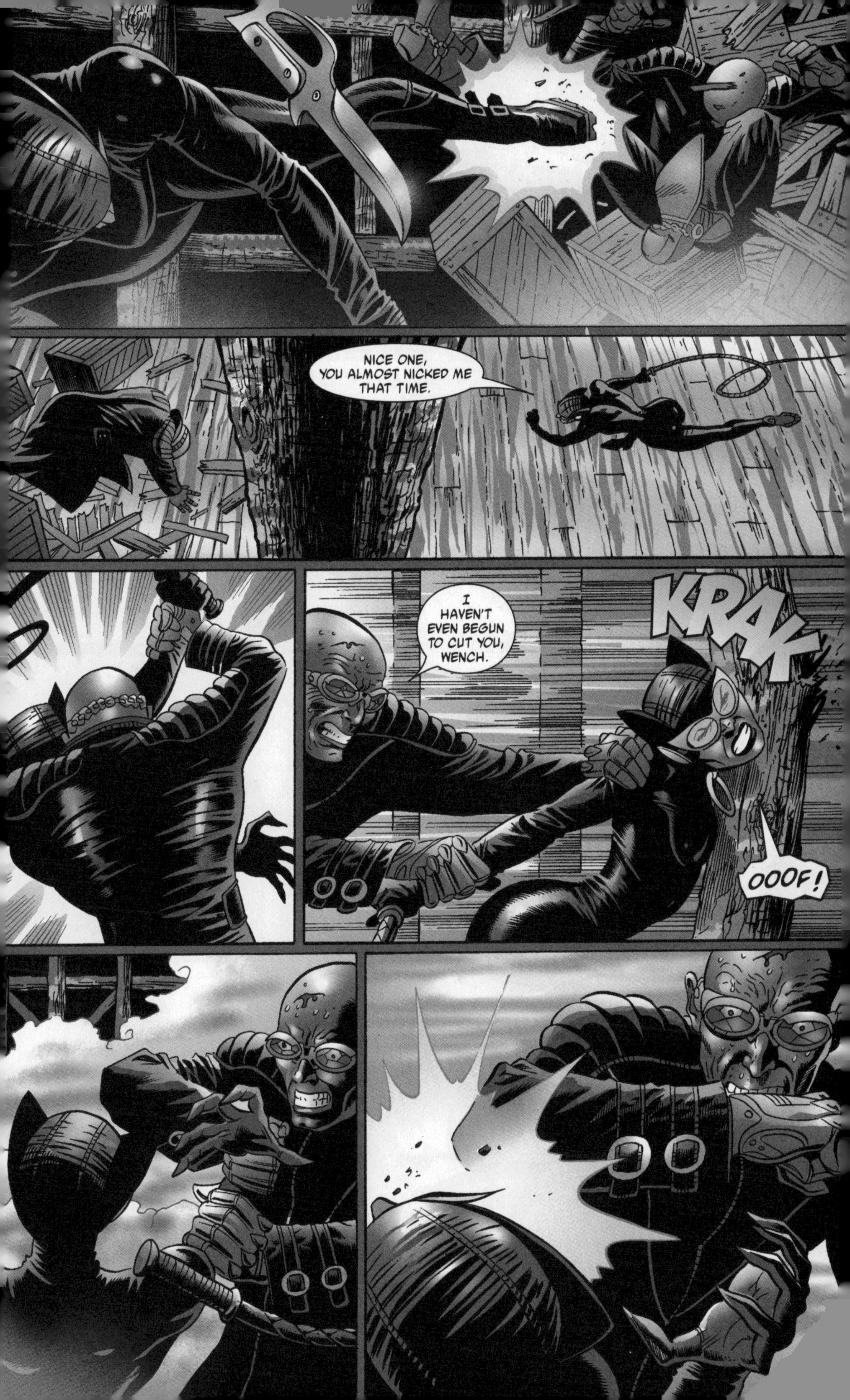

NICE ONE, YOU ALMOST NICKED ME THAT TIME.
I HAVEN'T EVEN BEGUN TO CUT YOU, WENCH.
KRAK
OOOF!

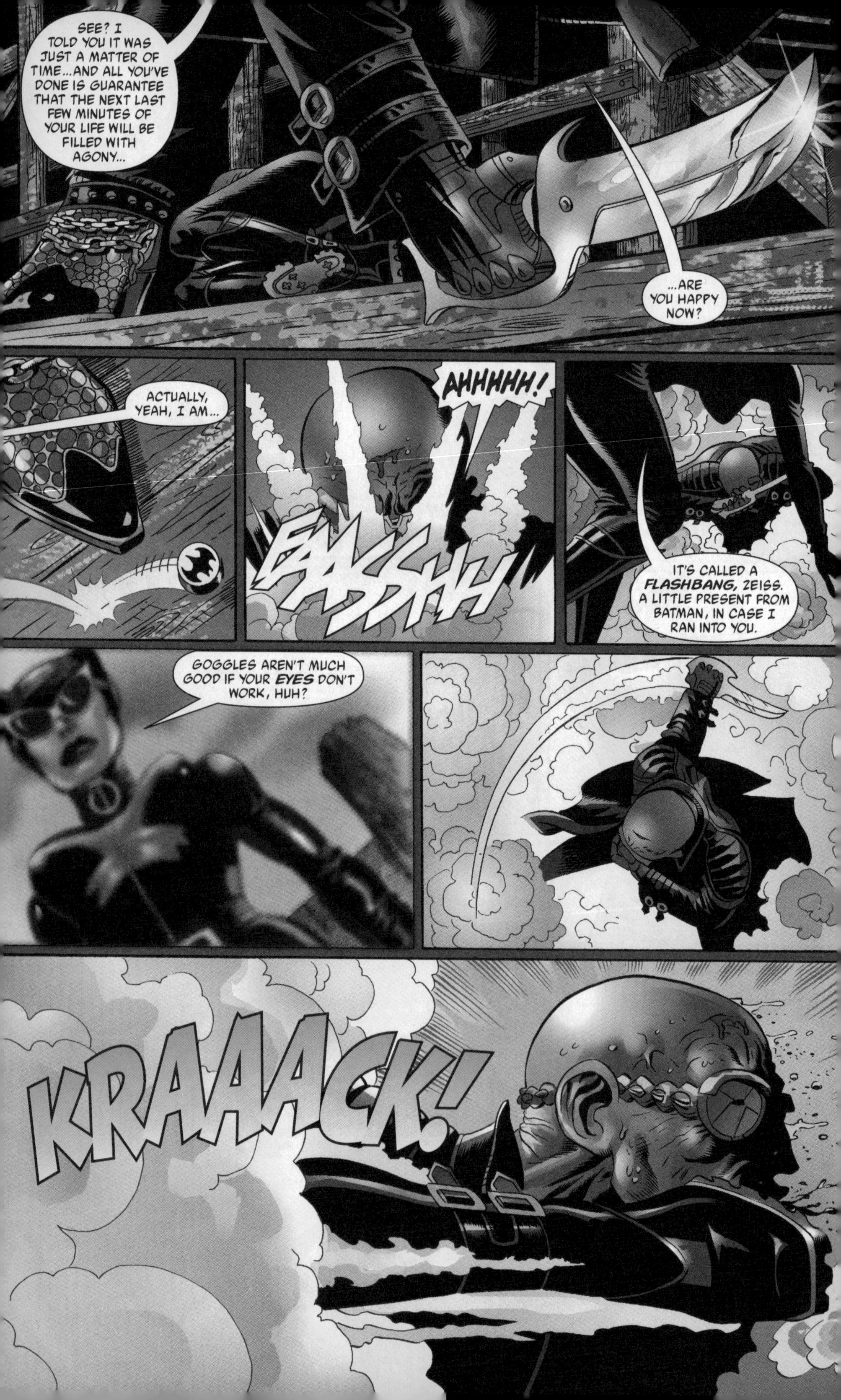
SEE? I TOLD YOU IT WAS JUST A MATTER OF TIME...AND ALL YOU'VE DONE IS GUARANTEE THAT THE NEXT LAST FEW MINUTES OF YOUR LIFE WILL BE FILLED WITH AGONY...
...ARE YOU HAPPY NOW?
ACTUALLY, YEAH, I AM...
AHHHHH!
FASSHH
IT'S CALLED A FLASHBANG, ZEISS. A LITTLE PRESENT FROM BATMAN, IN CASE I RAN INTO YOU.
GOGGLES AREN'T MUCH GOOD IF YOUR EYES DON'T WORK, HUH?
KRAAACK!

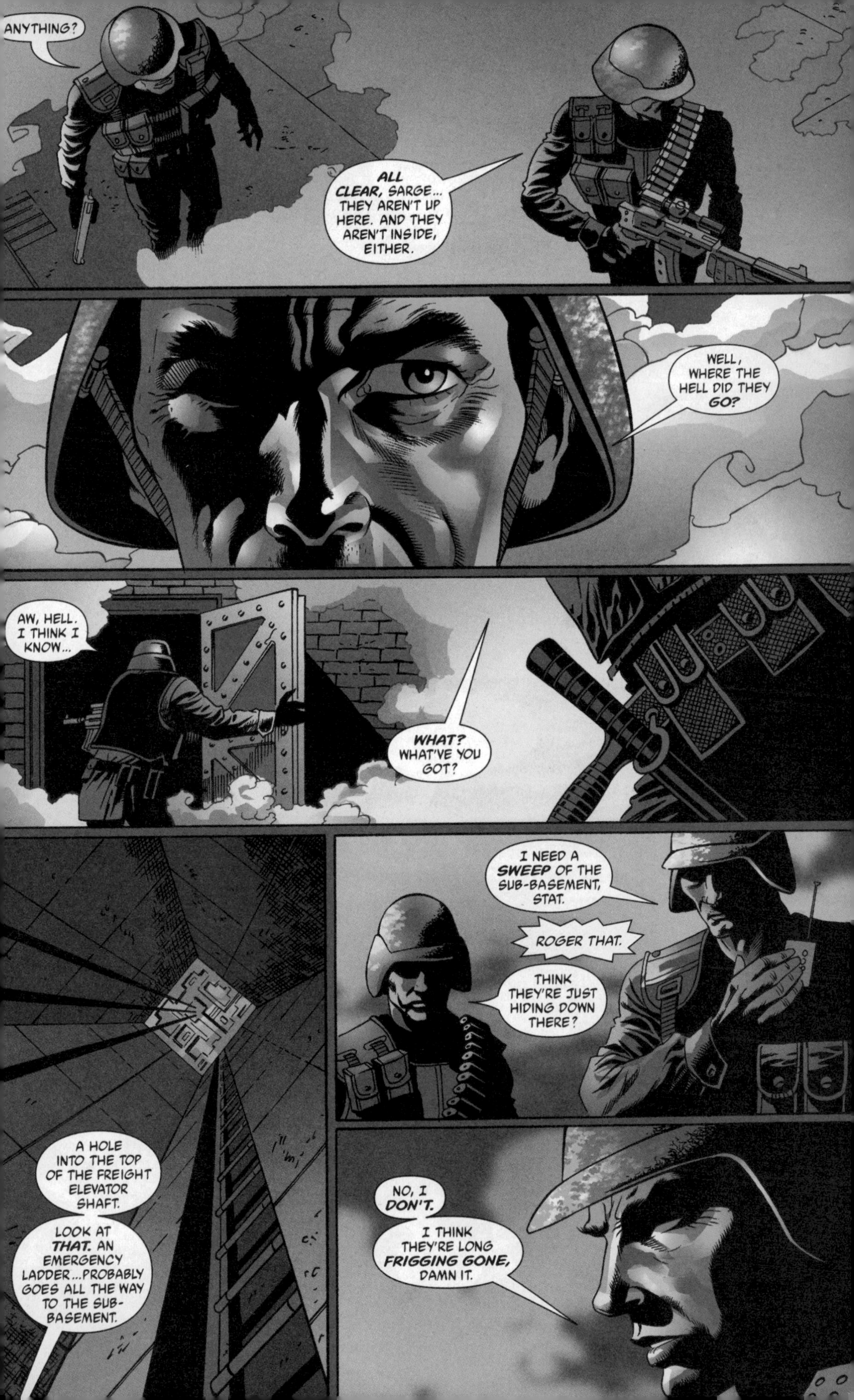
ANYTHING?
ALL CLEAR, SARGE... THEY AREN'T UP HERE. AND THEY AREN'T INSIDE, EITHER.
WELL, WHERE THE HELL DID THEY GO?
AW, HELL. I THINK I KNOW...
WHAT? WHAT'VE YOU GOT?
A HOLE INTO THE TOP OF THE FREIGHT ELEVATOR SHAFT.
LOOK AT THAT. AN EMERGENCY LADDER...PROBABLY GOES ALL THE WAY TO THE SUB-BASEMENT.
I NEED A SWEEP OF THE SUB-BASEMENT, STAT.
ROGER THAT.
THINK THEY'RE JUST HIDING DOWN THERE?
NO, I DON'T.
I THINK THEY'RE LONG FRIGGING GONE, DAMN IT.

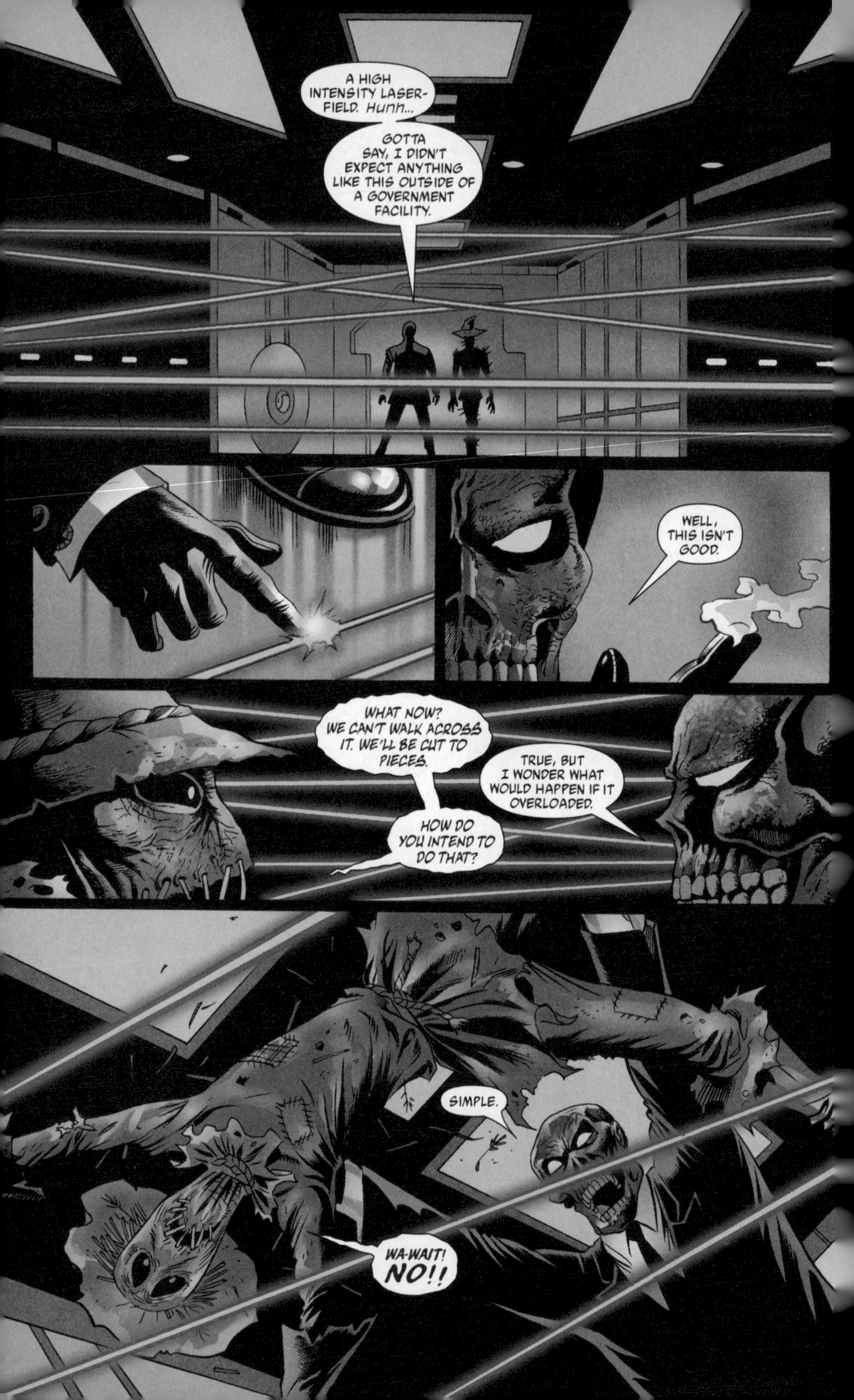
A HIGH INTENSITY LASER-FIELD. Hunh...
GOTTA SAY, I DIDN'T EXPECT ANYTHING LIKE THIS OUTSIDE OF A GOVERNMENT FACILITY.
WELL, THIS ISN'T GOOD.
WHAT NOW? WE CAN'T WALK ACROSS IT. WE'LL BE CUT TO PIECES.
TRUE, BUT I WONDER WHAT WOULD HAPPEN IF IT OVERLOADED.
HOW DO YOU INTEND TO DO THAT?
SIMPLE.
WA-WAIT! NO!!

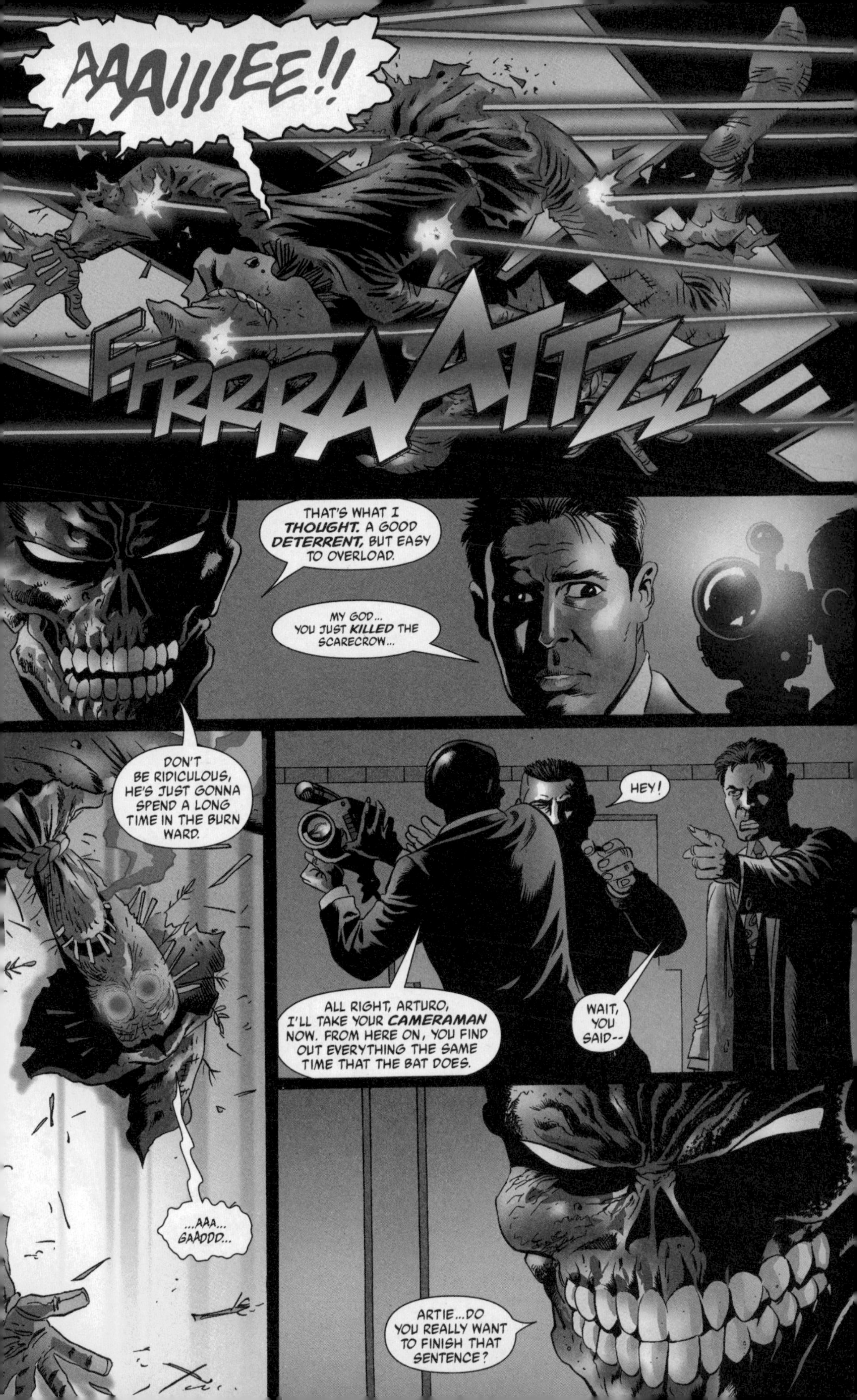
AAAIIIIEE!!
FFRRRRAAATTZZ
THAT'S WHAT I THOUGHT. A GOOD DETERRENT, BUT EASY TO OVERLOAD.
MY GOD... YOU JUST KILLED THE SCARECROW...
DON'T BE RIDICULOUS, HE'S JUST GONNA SPEND A LONG TIME IN THE BURN WARD.
HEY!
ALL RIGHT, ARTURO, I'LL TAKE YOUR CAMERAMAN NOW. FROM HERE ON, YOU FIND OUT EVERYTHING THE SAME TIME THAT THE BAT DOES.
WAIT, YOU SAID--
...AAA... GAADDD...
ARTIE...DO YOU REALLY WANT TO FINISH THAT SENTENCE?

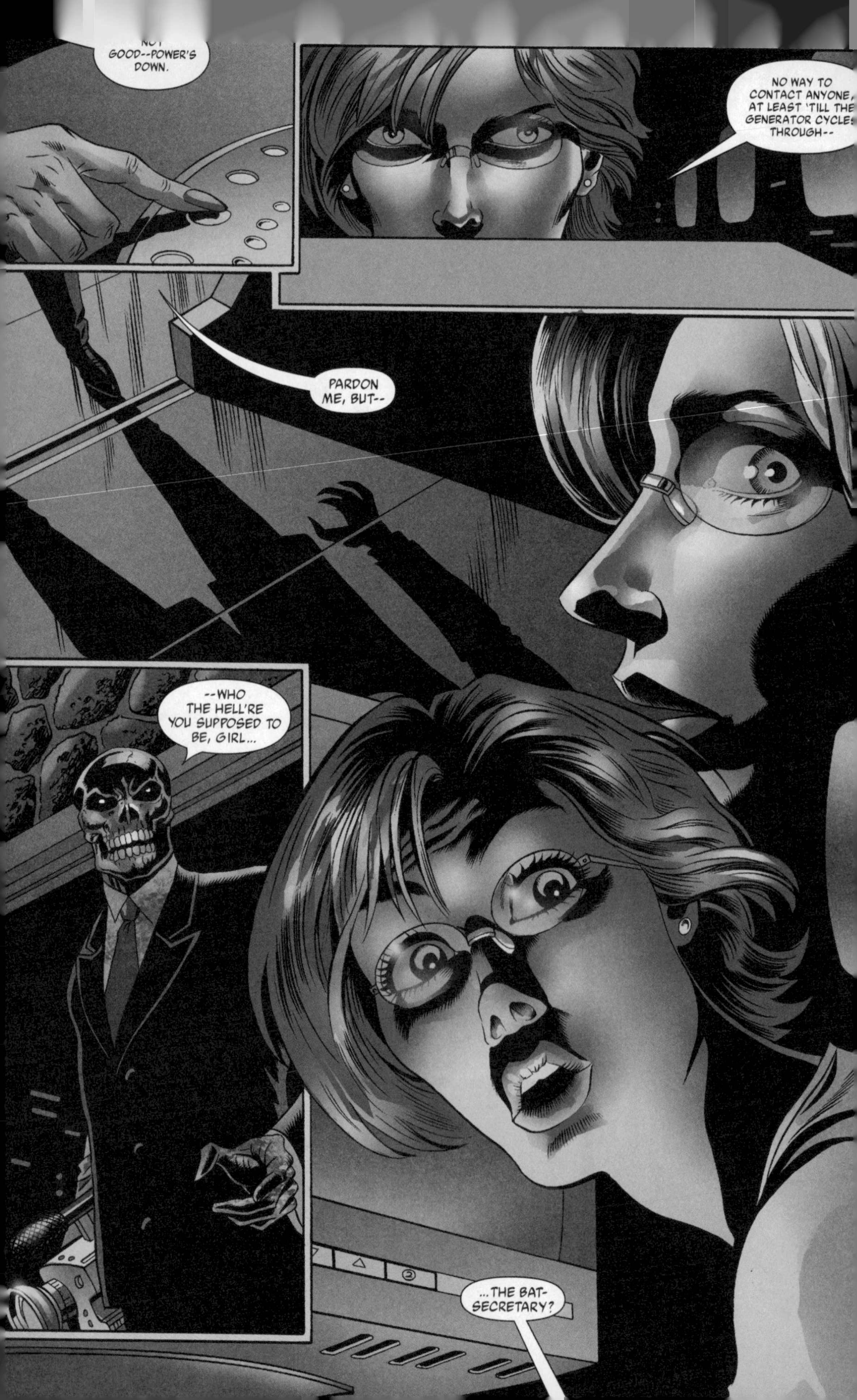
GOOD--POWER'S DOWN.
NO WAY TO CONTACT ANYONE, AT LEAST 'TILL THE GENERATOR CYCLES THROUGH--
PARDON ME, BUT--
--WHO THE HELL'RE YOU SUPPOSED TO BE, GIRL...
...THE BAT-SECRETARY?

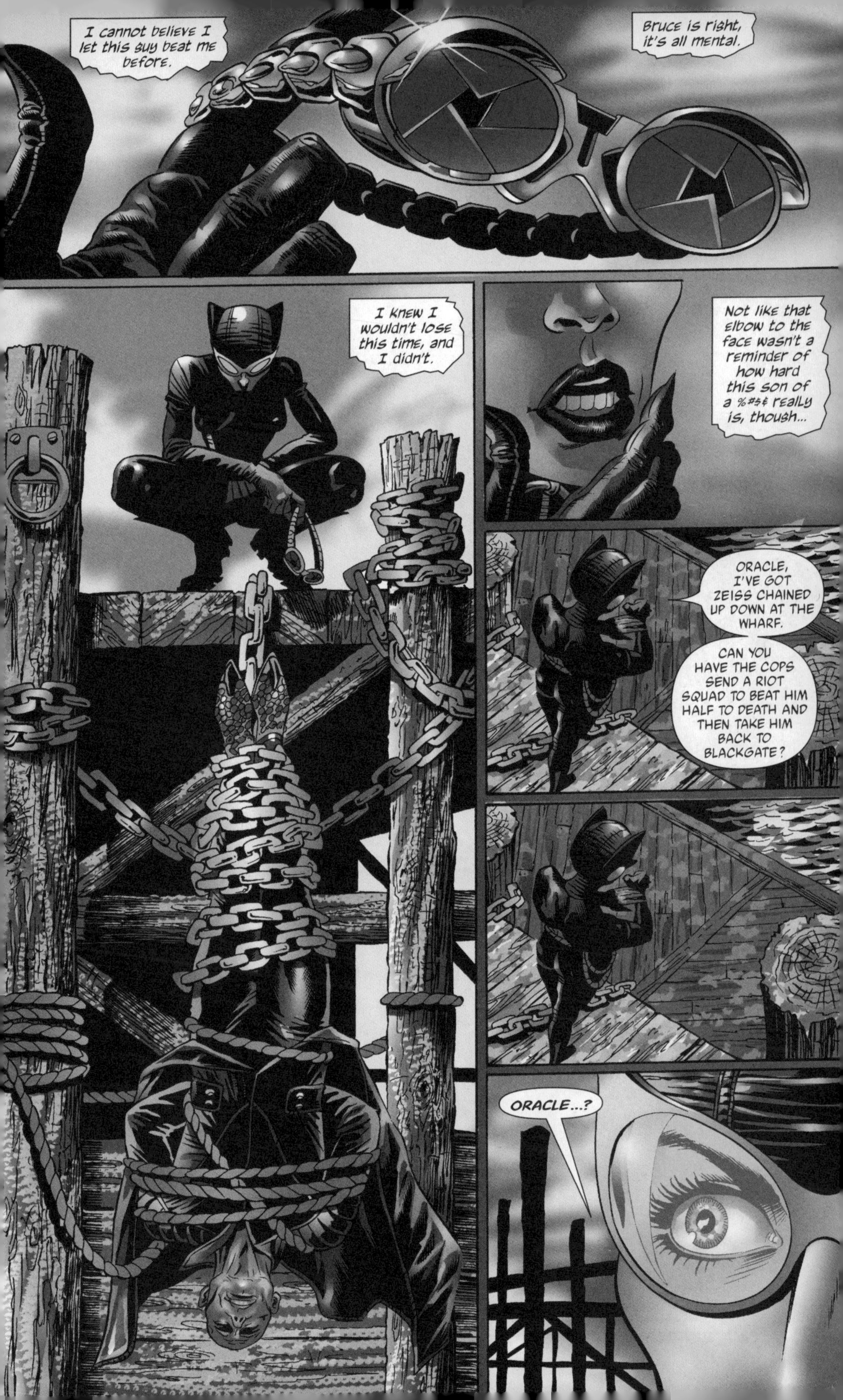

I cannot believe I let this guy beat me before.
Bruce is right, it's all mental.
I knew I wouldn't lose this time, and I didn't.
Not like that elbow to the face wasn't a reminder of how hard this son of a %#$¢ really is, though...
ORACLE, I'VE GOT ZEISS CHAINED UP DOWN AT THE WHARF.
CAN YOU HAVE THE COPS SEND A RIOT SQUAD TO BEAT HIM HALF TO DEATH AND THEN TAKE HIM BACK TO BLACKGATE?
ORACLE...?

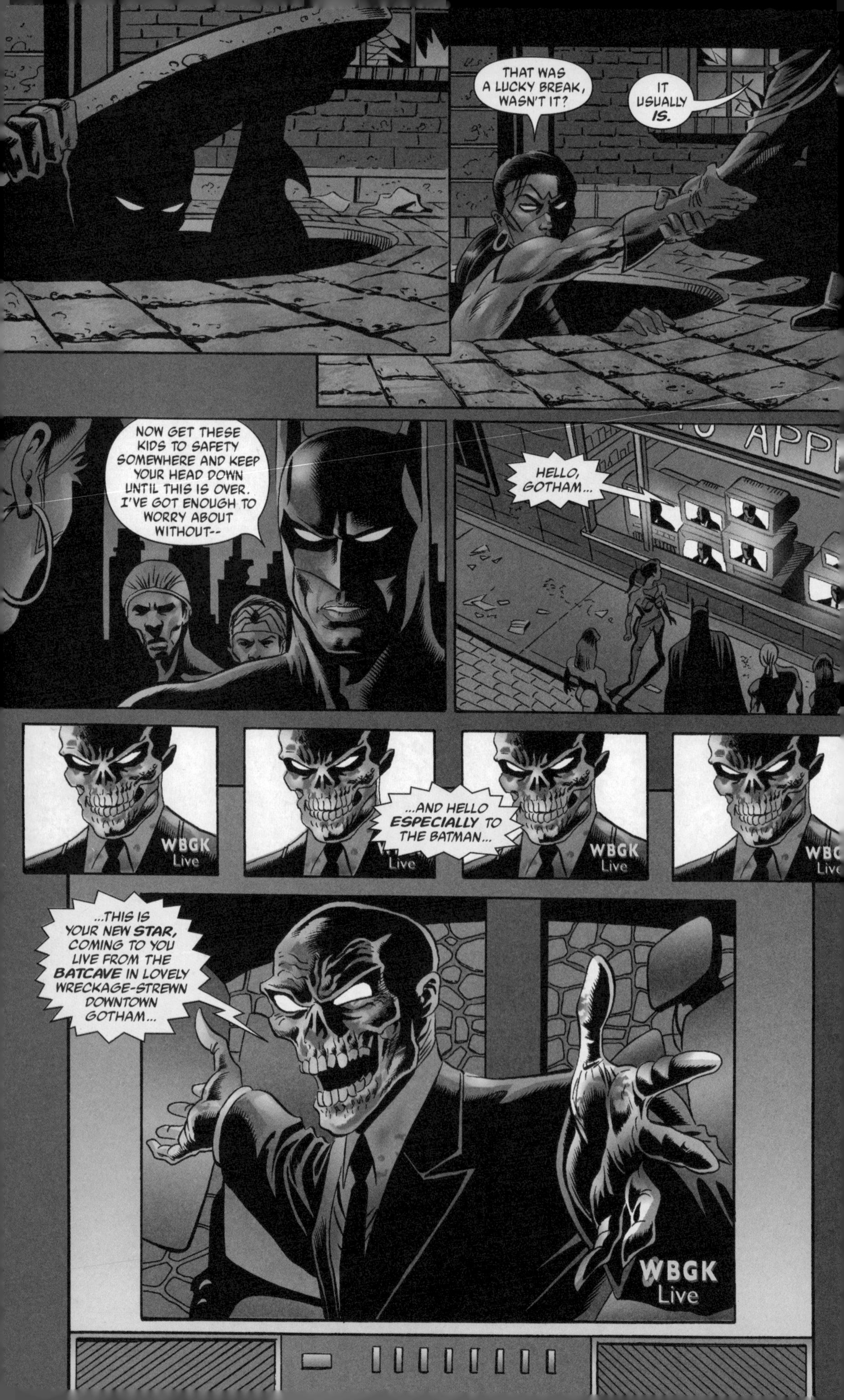
THAT WAS A LUCKY BREAK, WASN'T IT?
IT USUALLY IS.
NOW GET THESE KIDS TO SAFETY SOMEWHERE AND KEEP YOUR HEAD DOWN UNTIL THIS IS OVER. I'VE GOT ENOUGH TO WORRY ABOUT WITHOUT--
HELLO, GOTHAM...
WBGK Live
...AND HELLO ESPECIALLY TO THE BATMAN...
WBGK Live
...THIS IS YOUR NEW STAR, COMING TO YOU LIVE FROM THE BATCAVE IN LOVELY WRECKAGE-STREWN DOWNTOWN GOTHAM...
WBGK Live

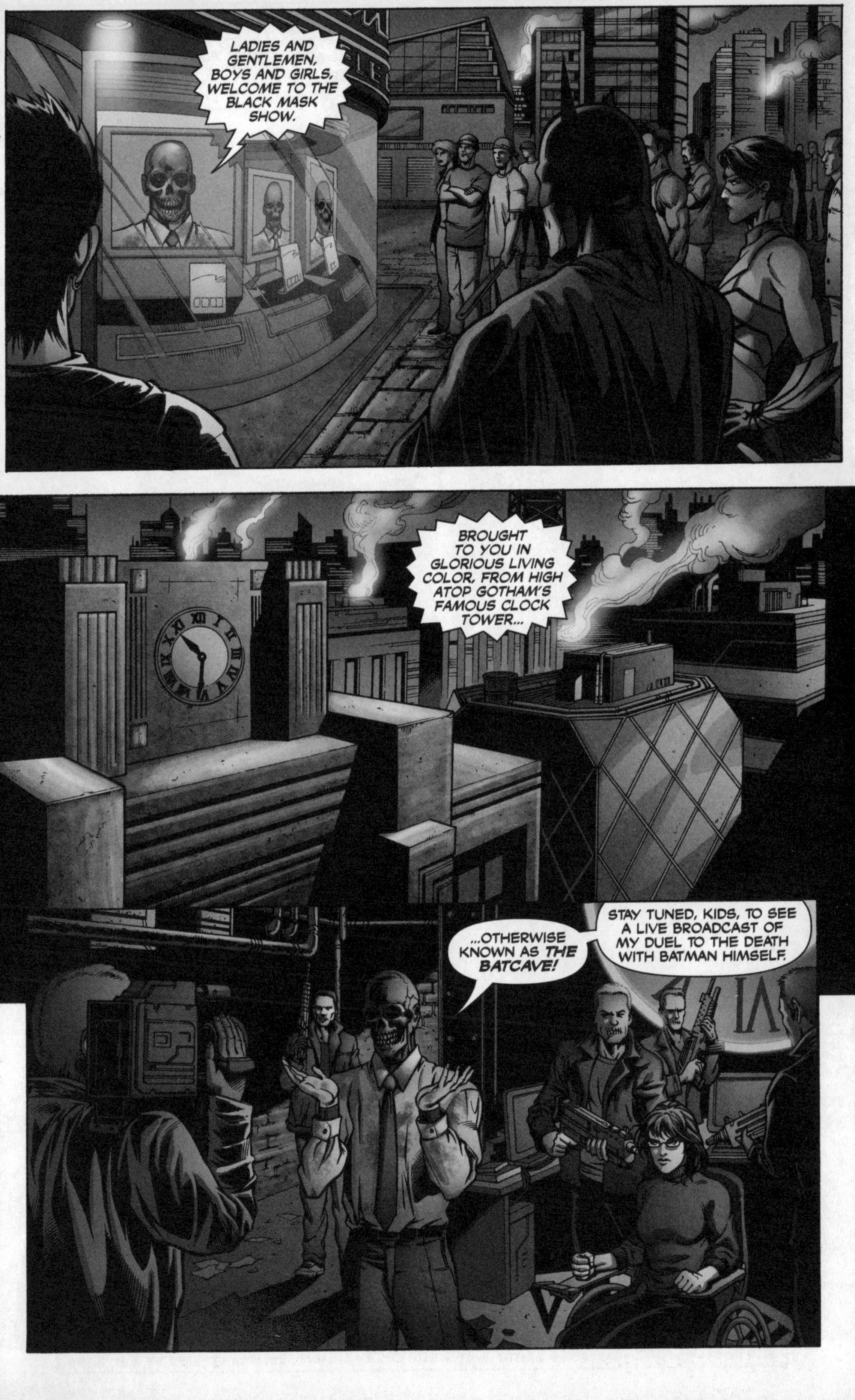
LADIES AND GENTLEMEN, BOYS AND GIRLS, WELCOME TO THE BLACK MASK SHOW.
BROUGHT TO YOU IN GLORIOUS LIVING COLOR, FROM HIGH ATOP GOTHAM'S FAMOUS CLOCK TOWER...
...OTHERWISE KNOWN AS *THE BATCAVE!*
STAY TUNED, KIDS, TO SEE A LIVE BROADCAST OF MY DUEL TO THE DEATH WITH BATMAN HIMSELF.

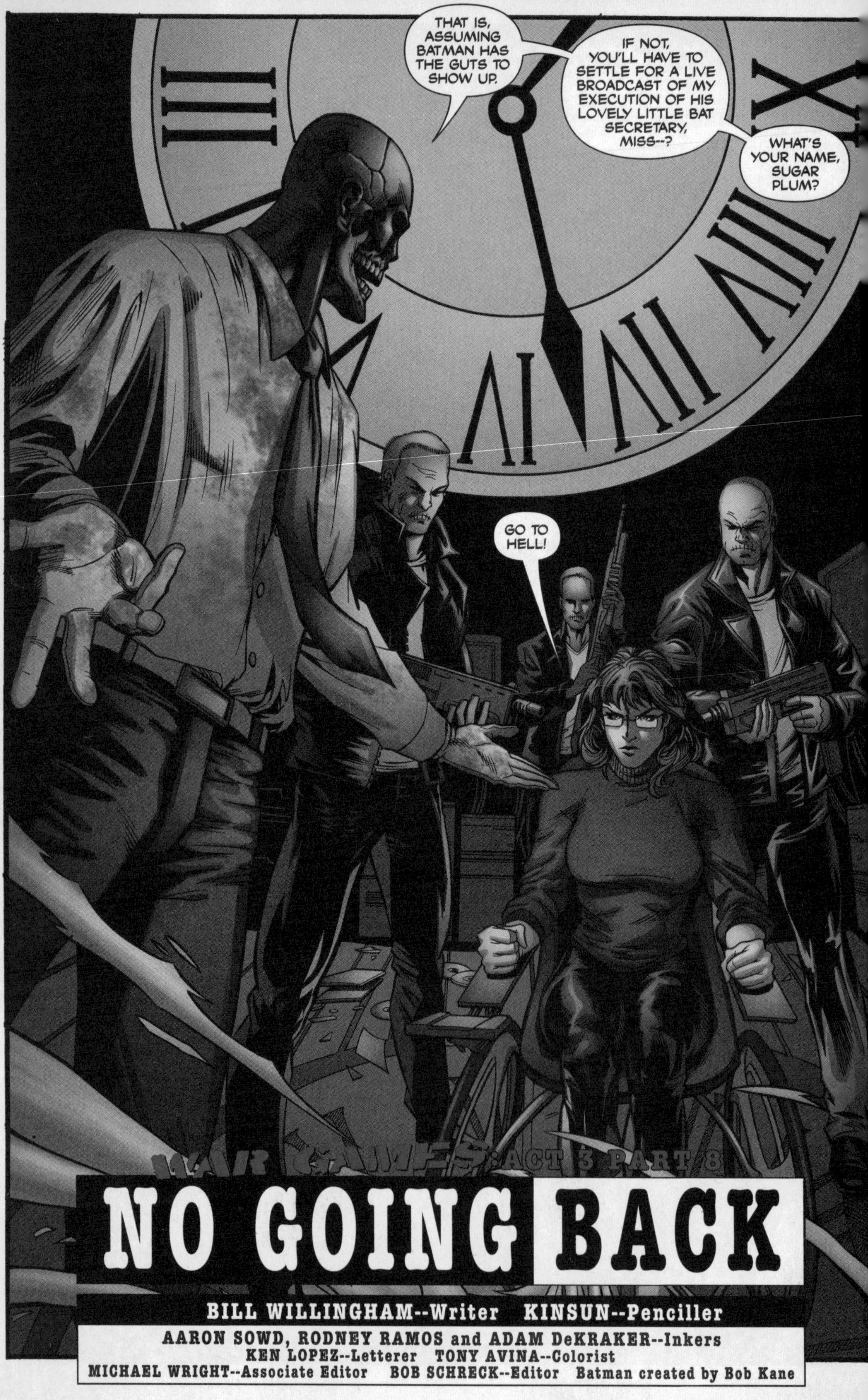
THAT IS, ASSUMING BATMAN HAS THE GUTS TO SHOW UP.
IF NOT, YOU'LL HAVE TO SETTLE FOR A LIVE BROADCAST OF MY EXECUTION OF HIS LOVELY LITTLE BAT SECRETARY, MISS--?
WHAT'S YOUR NAME, SUGAR PLUM?
GO TO HELL!
WAR GAMES: ACT 3 PART 8
NO GOING BACK
BILL WILLINGHAM--Writer KINSUN--Penciller
AARON SOWD, RODNEY RAMOS and ADAM DeKRAKER--Inkers
KEN LOPEZ--Letterer TONY AVINA--Colorist
MICHAEL WRIGHT--Associate Editor BOB SCHRECK--Editor Batman created by Bob Kane

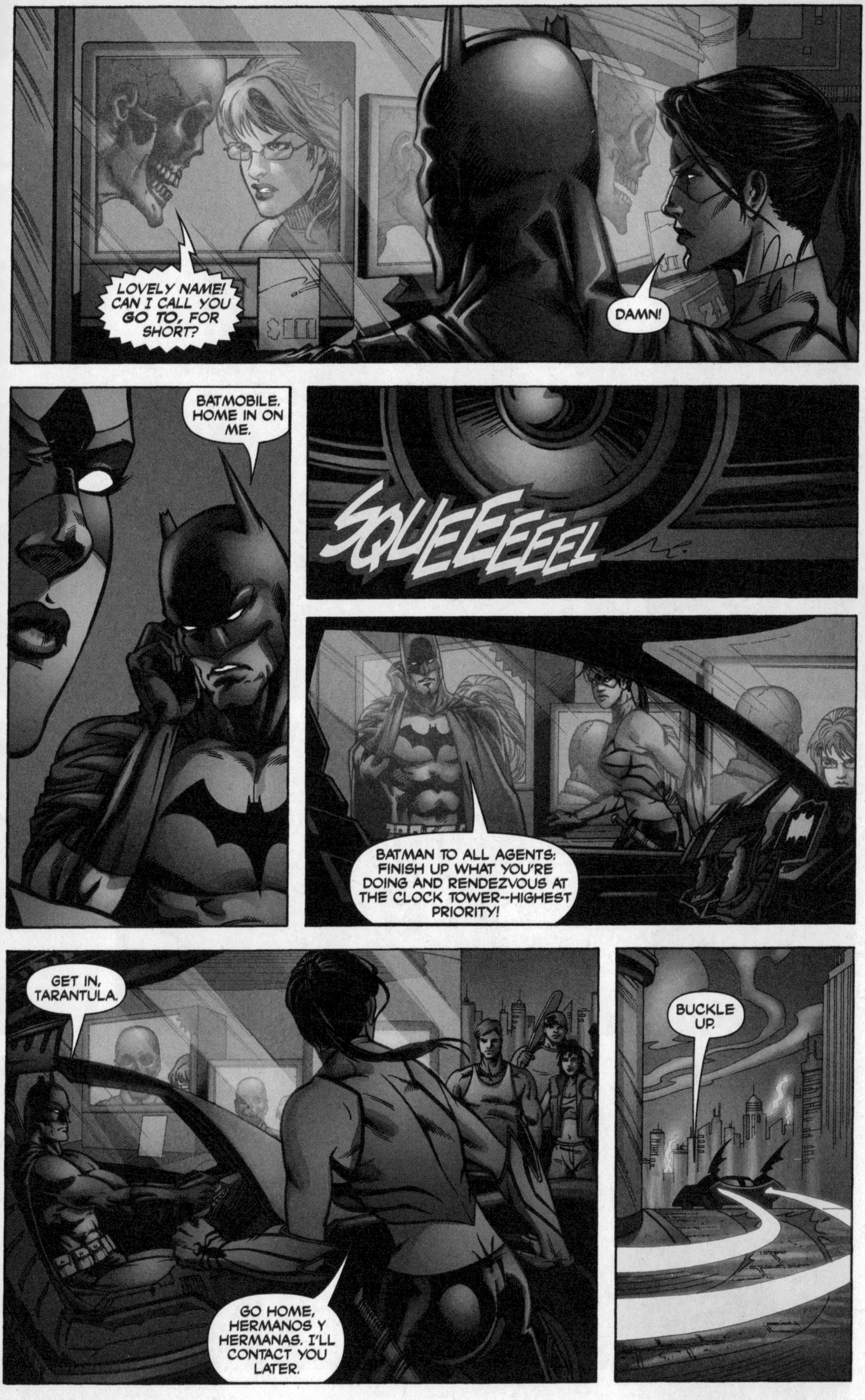
LOVELY NAME! CAN I CALL YOU GO TO, FOR SHORT?
DAMN!
BATMOBILE. HOME IN ON ME.
SQUEEEEEL
BATMAN TO ALL AGENTS: FINISH UP WHAT YOU'RE DOING AND RENDEZVOUS AT THE CLOCK TOWER--HIGHEST PRIORITY!
GET IN, TARANTULA.
GO HOME, HERMANOS Y HERMANAS. I'LL CONTACT YOU LATER.
BUCKLE UP.

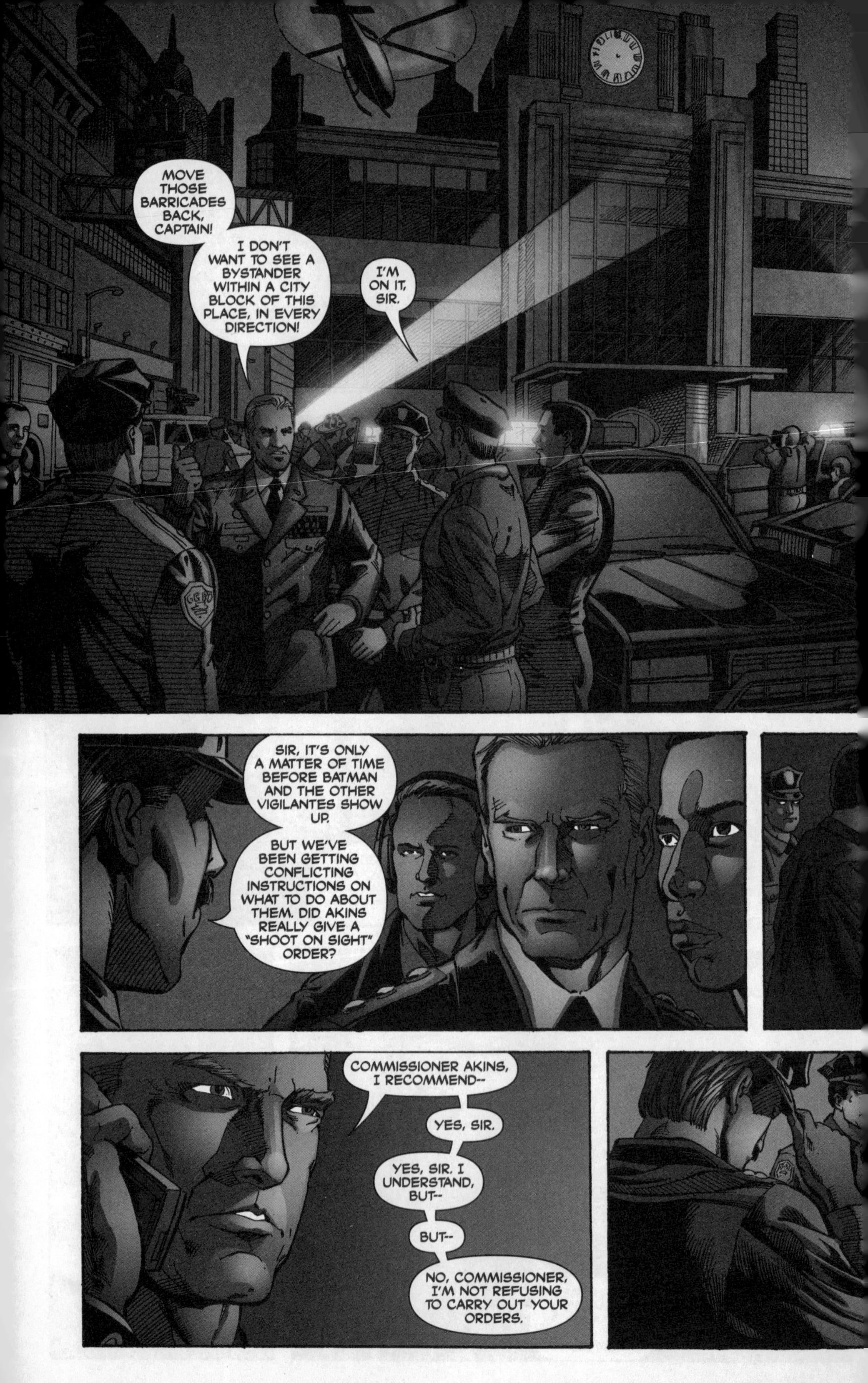
MOVE THOSE BARRICADES BACK, CAPTAIN!
I DON'T WANT TO SEE A BYSTANDER WITHIN A CITY BLOCK OF THIS PLACE, IN EVERY DIRECTION!
I'M ON IT, SIR.
SIR, IT'S ONLY A MATTER OF TIME BEFORE BATMAN AND THE OTHER VIGILANTES SHOW UP.
BUT WE'VE BEEN GETTING CONFLICTING INSTRUCTIONS ON WHAT TO DO ABOUT THEM. DID AKINS REALLY GIVE A "SHOOT ON SIGHT" ORDER?
COMMISSIONER AKINS, I RECOMMEND--
YES, SIR.
YES, SIR. I UNDERSTAND, BUT--
BUT--
NO, COMMISSIONER, I'M NOT REFUSING TO CARRY OUT YOUR ORDERS.

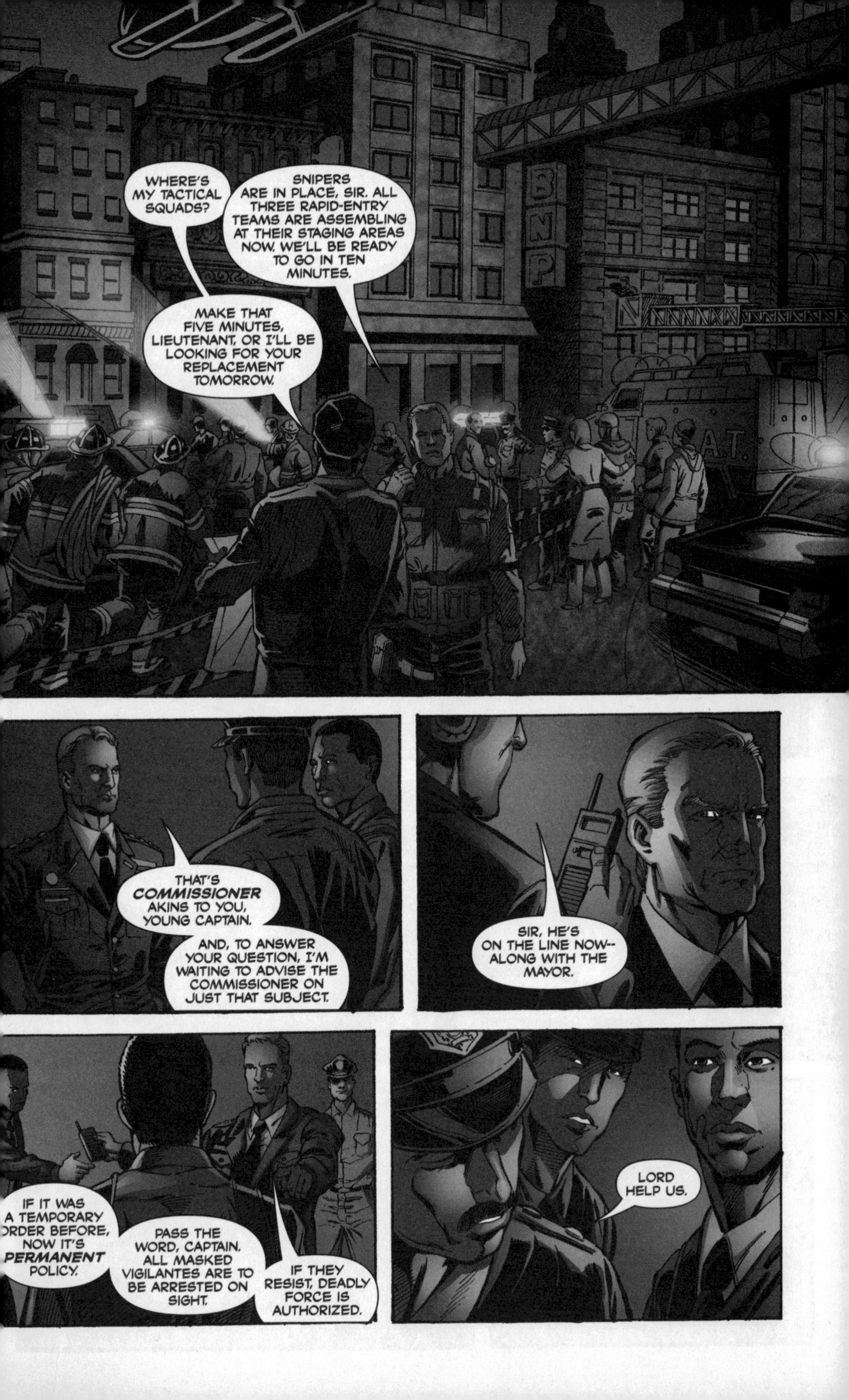
WHERE'S MY TACTICAL SQUADS?
SNIPERS ARE IN PLACE, SIR. ALL THREE RAPID-ENTRY TEAMS ARE ASSEMBLING AT THEIR STAGING AREAS NOW. WE'LL BE READY TO GO IN TEN MINUTES.
MAKE THAT FIVE MINUTES, LIEUTENANT, OR I'LL BE LOOKING FOR YOUR REPLACEMENT TOMORROW.
BNP
THAT'S *COMMISSIONER* AKINS TO YOU, YOUNG CAPTAIN.
AND, TO ANSWER YOUR QUESTION, I'M WAITING TO ADVISE THE COMMISSIONER ON JUST THAT SUBJECT.
SIR, HE'S ON THE LINE NOW-- ALONG WITH THE MAYOR.
IF IT WAS A TEMPORARY ORDER BEFORE, NOW IT'S *PERMANENT* POLICY.
PASS THE WORD, CAPTAIN. ALL MASKED VIGILANTES ARE TO BE ARRESTED ON SIGHT.
IF THEY RESIST, DEADLY FORCE IS AUTHORIZED.
LORD HELP US.

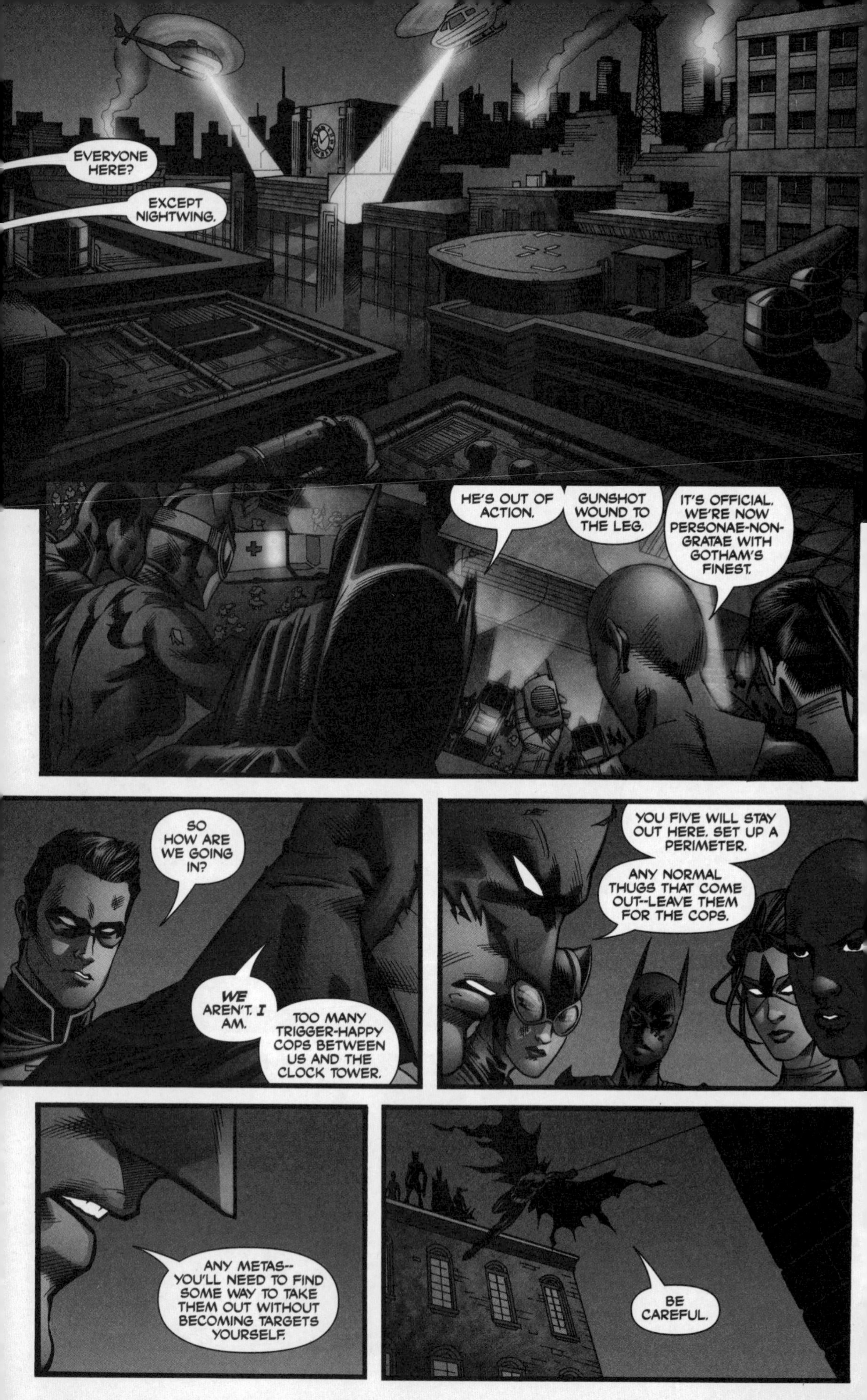
EVERYONE HERE?
EXCEPT NIGHTWING.
HE'S OUT OF ACTION.
GUNSHOT WOUND TO THE LEG.
IT'S OFFICIAL. WE'RE NOW PERSONAE-NON-GRATAE WITH GOTHAM'S FINEST.
SO HOW ARE WE GOING IN?
WE AREN'T. I AM.
TOO MANY TRIGGER-HAPPY COPS BETWEEN US AND THE CLOCK TOWER.
YOU FIVE WILL STAY OUT HERE. SET UP A PERIMETER.
ANY NORMAL THUGS THAT COME OUT--LEAVE THEM FOR THE COPS.
ANY METAS--YOU'LL NEED TO FIND SOME WAY TO TAKE THEM OUT WITHOUT BECOMING TARGETS YOURSELF.
BE CAREFUL.

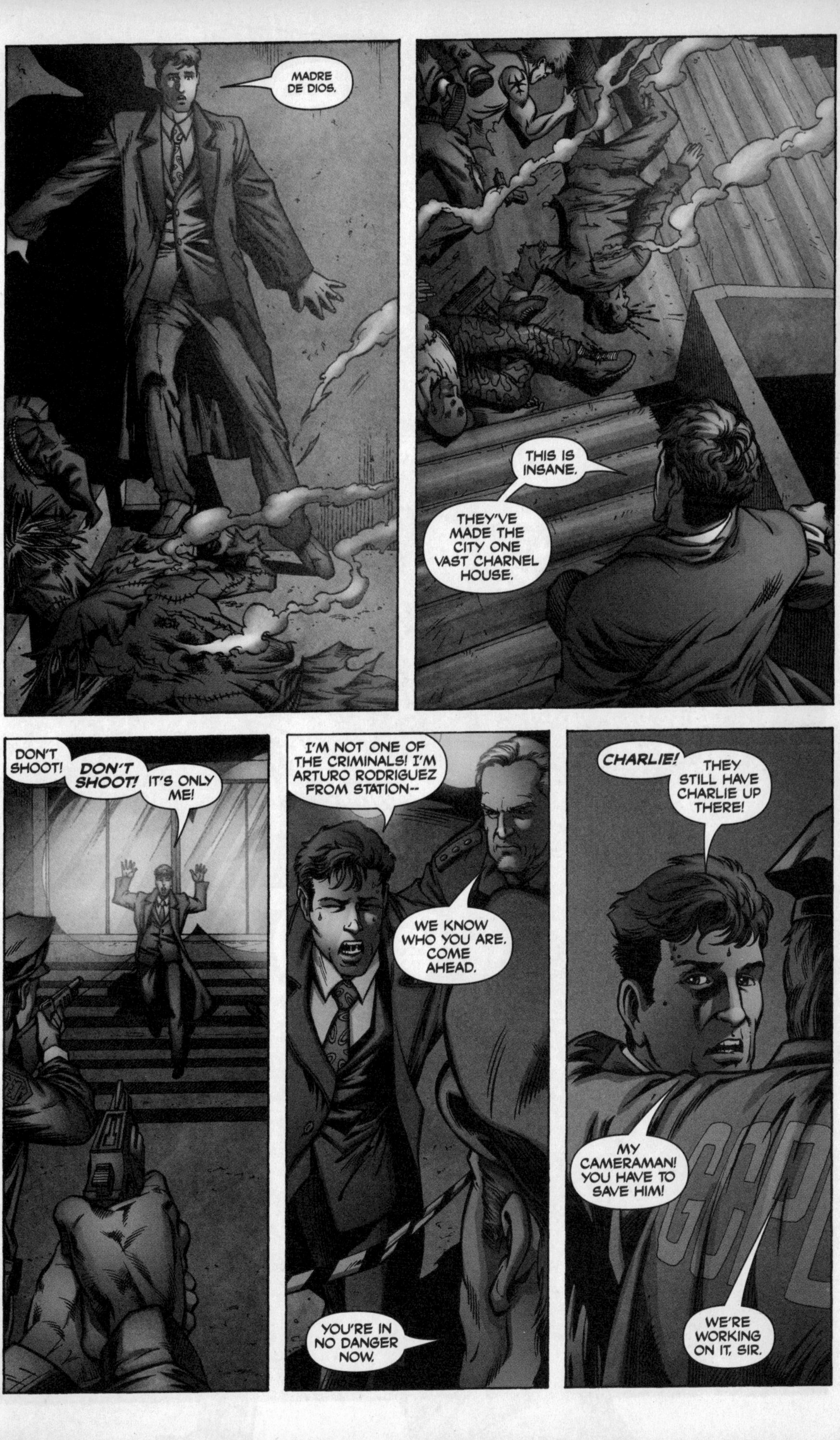
MADRE DE DIOS.
THIS IS INSANE.
THEY'VE MADE THE CITY ONE VAST CHARNEL HOUSE.
DON'T SHOOT!
DON'T SHOOT!
IT'S ONLY ME!
I'M NOT ONE OF THE CRIMINALS! I'M ARTURO RODRIGUEZ FROM STATION--
WE KNOW WHO YOU ARE. COME AHEAD.
YOU'RE IN NO DANGER NOW.
CHARLIE!
THEY STILL HAVE CHARLIE UP THERE!
MY CAMERAMAN! YOU HAVE TO SAVE HIM!
WE'RE WORKING ON IT, SIR.

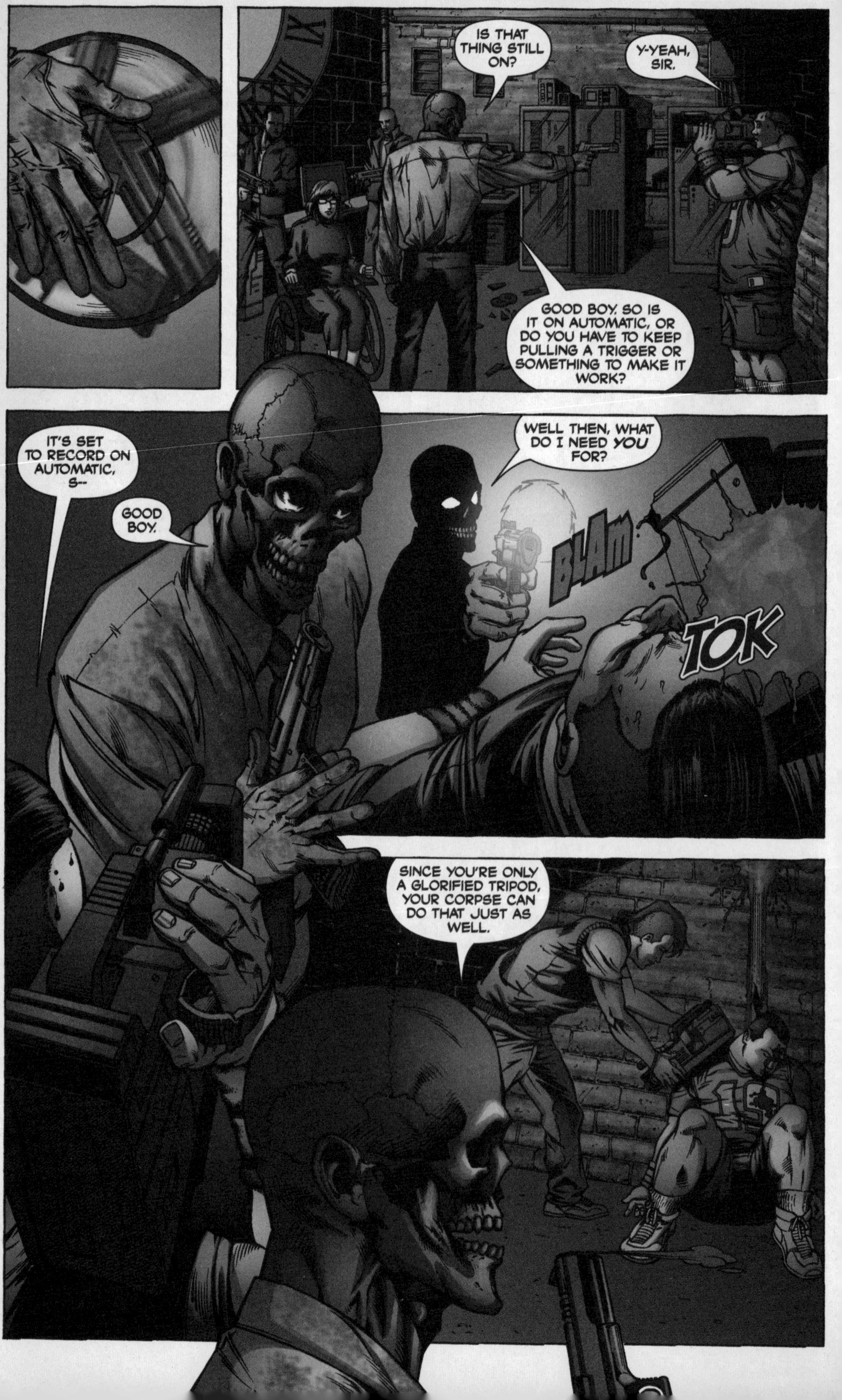
IS THAT THING STILL ON?
Y-YEAH, SIR.
GOOD BOY. SO IS IT ON AUTOMATIC, OR DO YOU HAVE TO KEEP PULLING A TRIGGER OR SOMETHING TO MAKE IT WORK?
IT'S SET TO RECORD ON AUTOMATIC, S--
GOOD BOY.
WELL THEN, WHAT DO I NEED YOU FOR?
BLAM
TOK
SINCE YOU'RE ONLY A GLORIFIED TRIPOD, YOUR CORPSE CAN DO THAT JUST AS WELL.

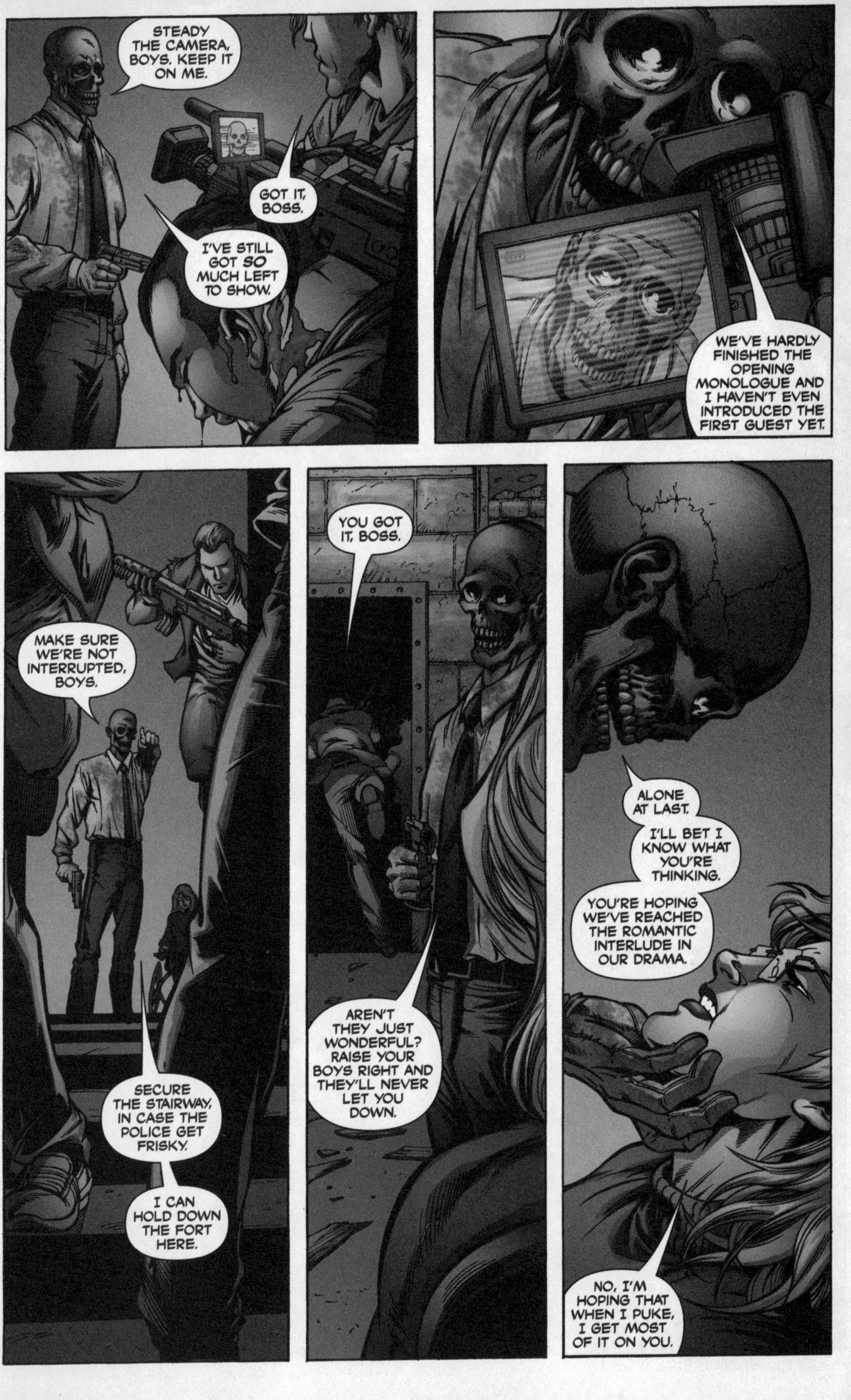
STEADY THE CAMERA, BOYS. KEEP IT ON ME.
GOT IT, BOSS.
I'VE STILL GOT SO MUCH LEFT TO SHOW.
WE'VE HARDLY FINISHED THE OPENING MONOLOGUE AND I HAVEN'T EVEN INTRODUCED THE FIRST GUEST YET.
MAKE SURE WE'RE NOT INTERRUPTED, BOYS.
SECURE THE STAIRWAY, IN CASE THE POLICE GET FRISKY.
I CAN HOLD DOWN THE FORT HERE.
YOU GOT IT, BOSS.
AREN'T THEY JUST WONDERFUL? RAISE YOUR BOYS RIGHT AND THEY'LL NEVER LET YOU DOWN.
ALONE AT LAST.
I'LL BET I KNOW WHAT YOU'RE THINKING.
YOU'RE HOPING WE'VE REACHED THE ROMANTIC INTERLUDE IN OUR DRAMA.
NO, I'M HOPING THAT WHEN I PUKE, I GET MOST OF IT ON YOU.

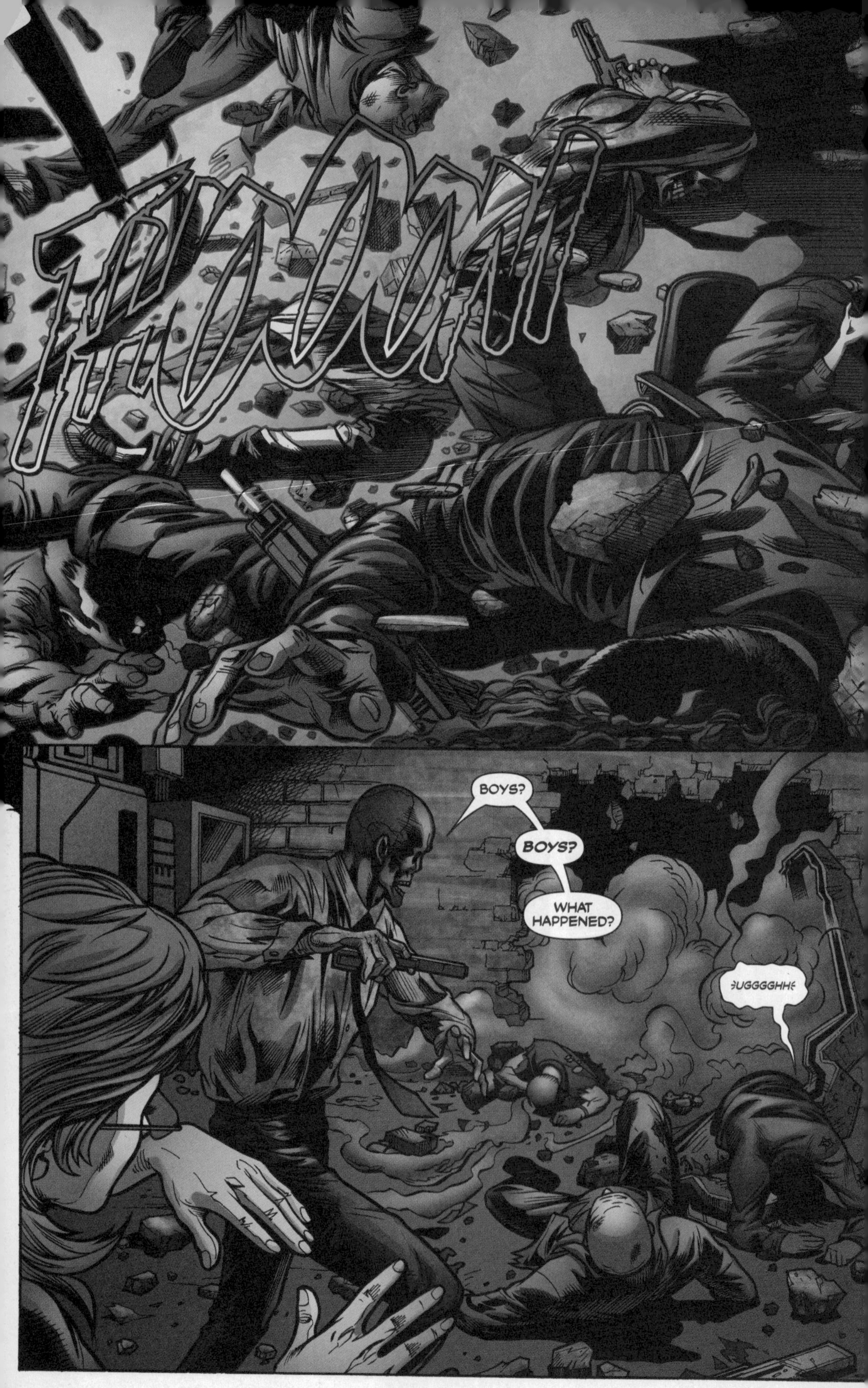
BOYS?
BOYS?
WHAT HAPPENED?
UGGGGHH

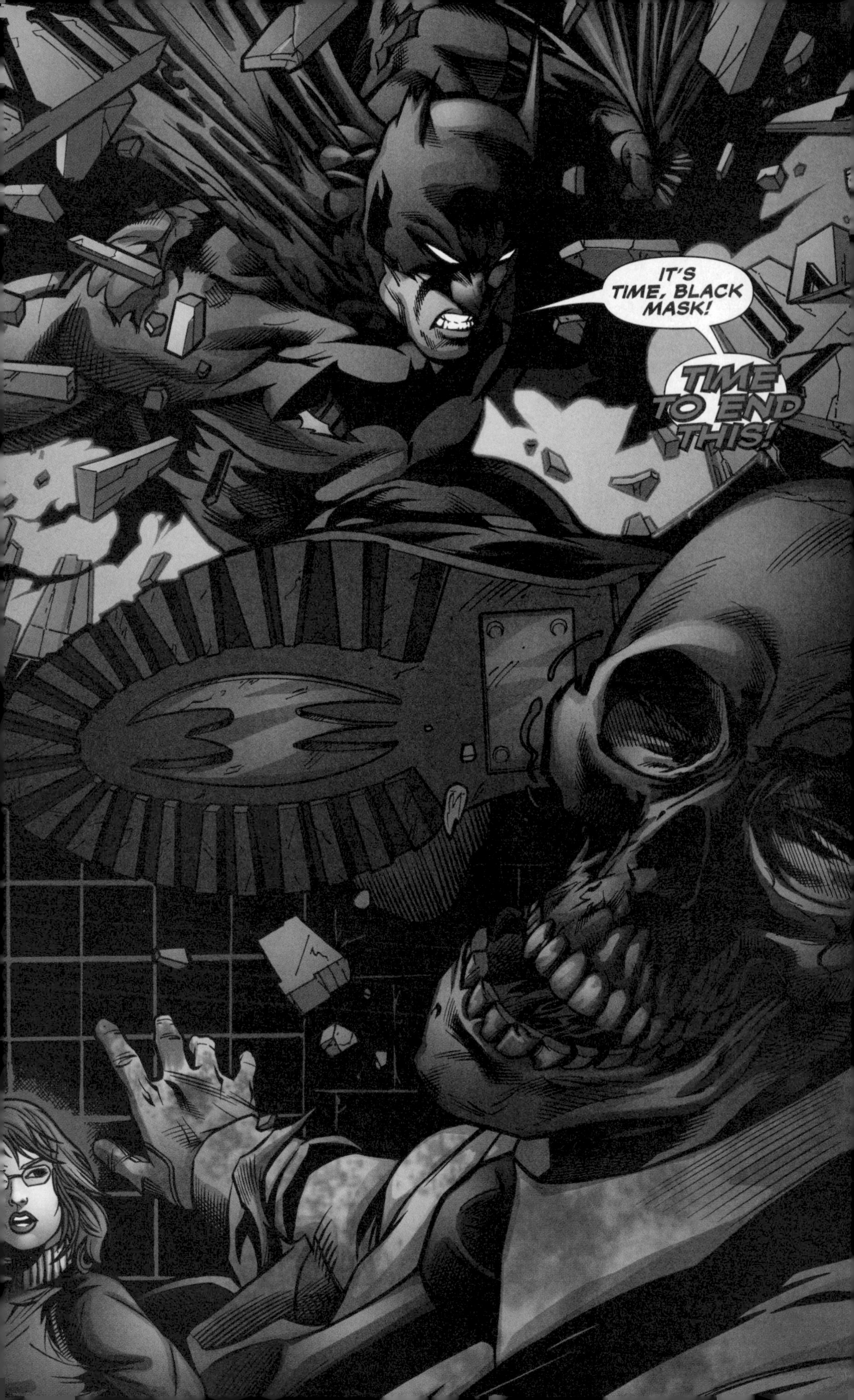
IT'S TIME, BLACK MASK!
TIME TO END THIS!

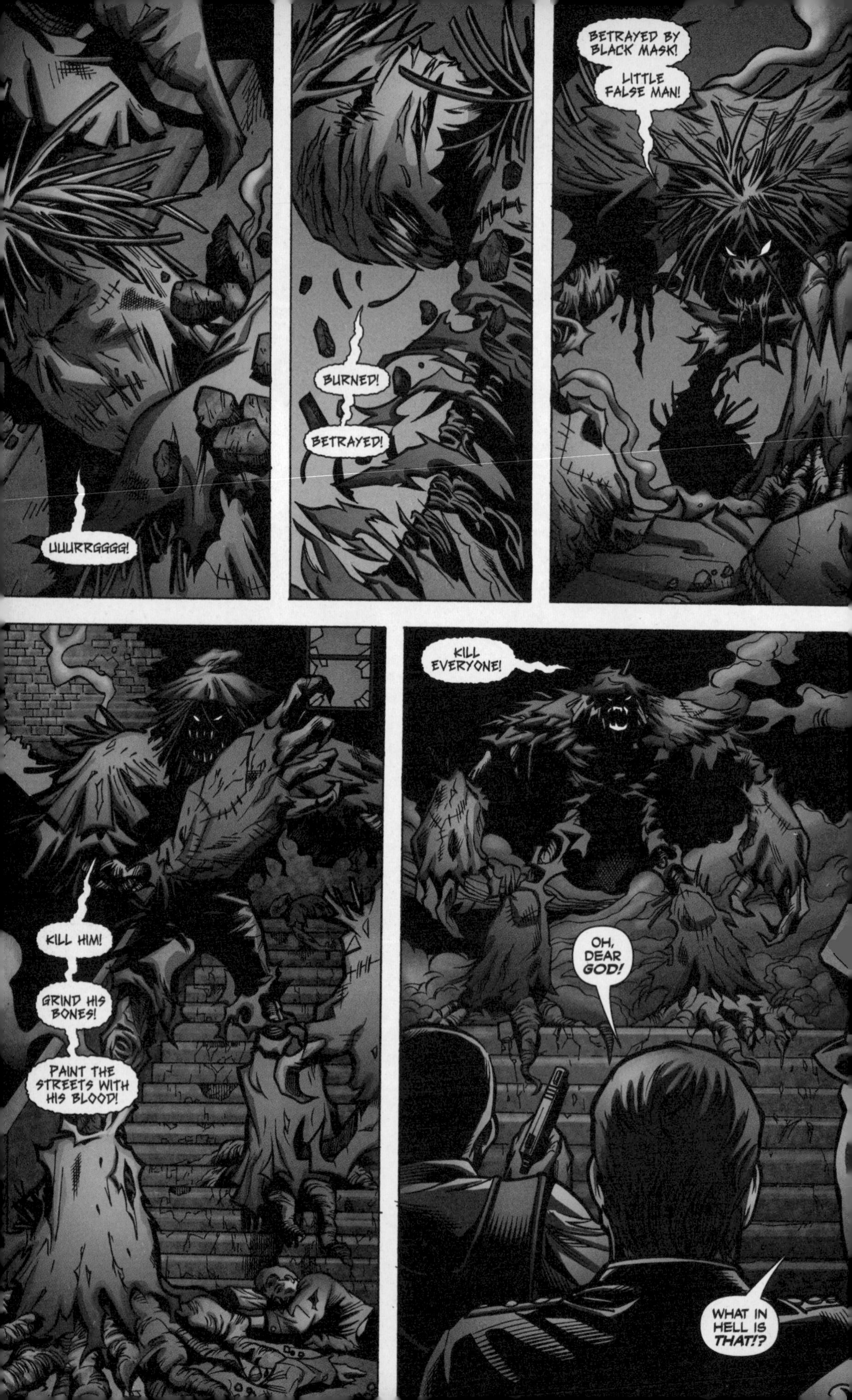
UUURRGGGG!
BURNED!
BETRAYED!
BETRAYED BY BLACK MASK!
LITTLE FALSE MAN!
KILL HIM!
GRIND HIS BONES!
PAINT THE STREETS WITH HIS BLOOD!
KILL EVERYONE!
OH, DEAR GOD!
WHAT IN HELL IS THAT!?

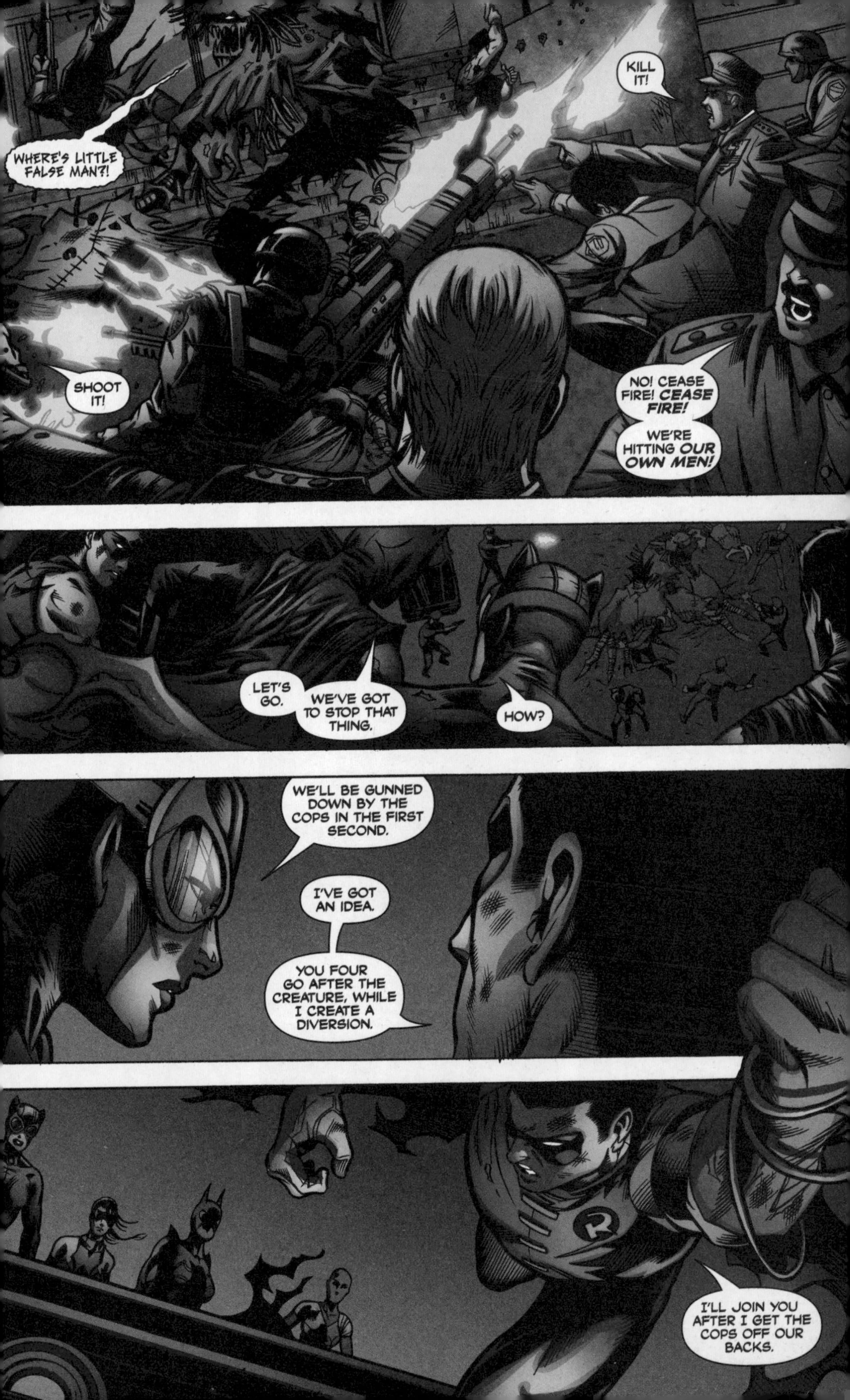
WHERE'S LITTLE FALSE MAN?!
KILL IT!
SHOOT IT!
NO! CEASE FIRE! CEASE FIRE!
WE'RE HITTING OUR OWN MEN!
LET'S GO.
WE'VE GOT TO STOP THAT THING.
HOW?
WE'LL BE GUNNED DOWN BY THE COPS IN THE FIRST SECOND.
I'VE GOT AN IDEA.
YOU FOUR GO AFTER THE CREATURE, WHILE I CREATE A DIVERSION.
I'LL JOIN YOU AFTER I GET THE COPS OFF OUR BACKS.

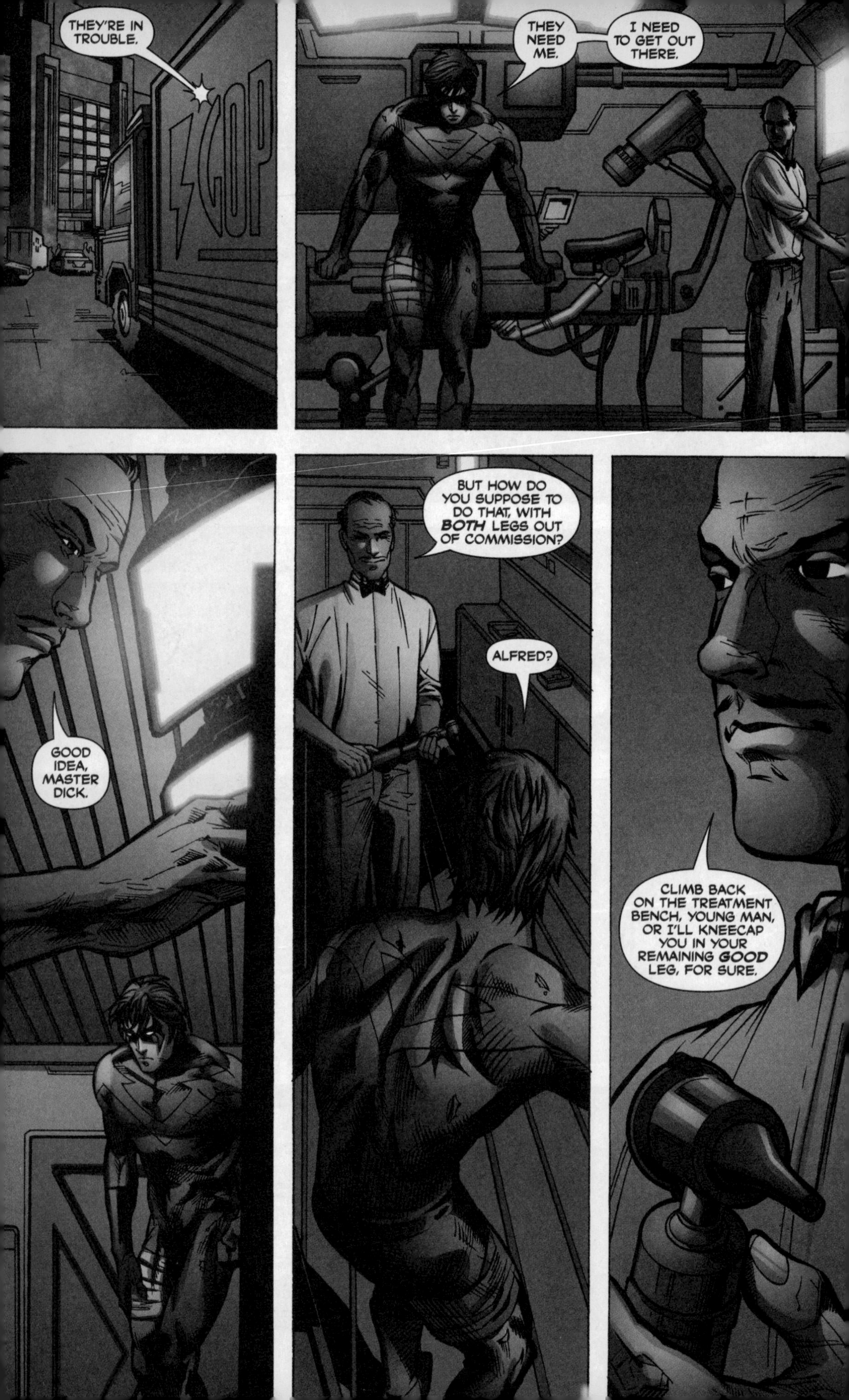
THEY'RE IN TROUBLE.
THEY NEED ME.
I NEED TO GET OUT THERE.
GOOD IDEA, MASTER DICK.
BUT HOW DO YOU SUPPOSE TO DO THAT, WITH BOTH LEGS OUT OF COMMISSION?
ALFRED?
CLIMB BACK ON THE TREATMENT BENCH, YOUNG MAN, OR I'LL KNEECAP YOU IN YOUR REMAINING GOOD LEG, FOR SURE.

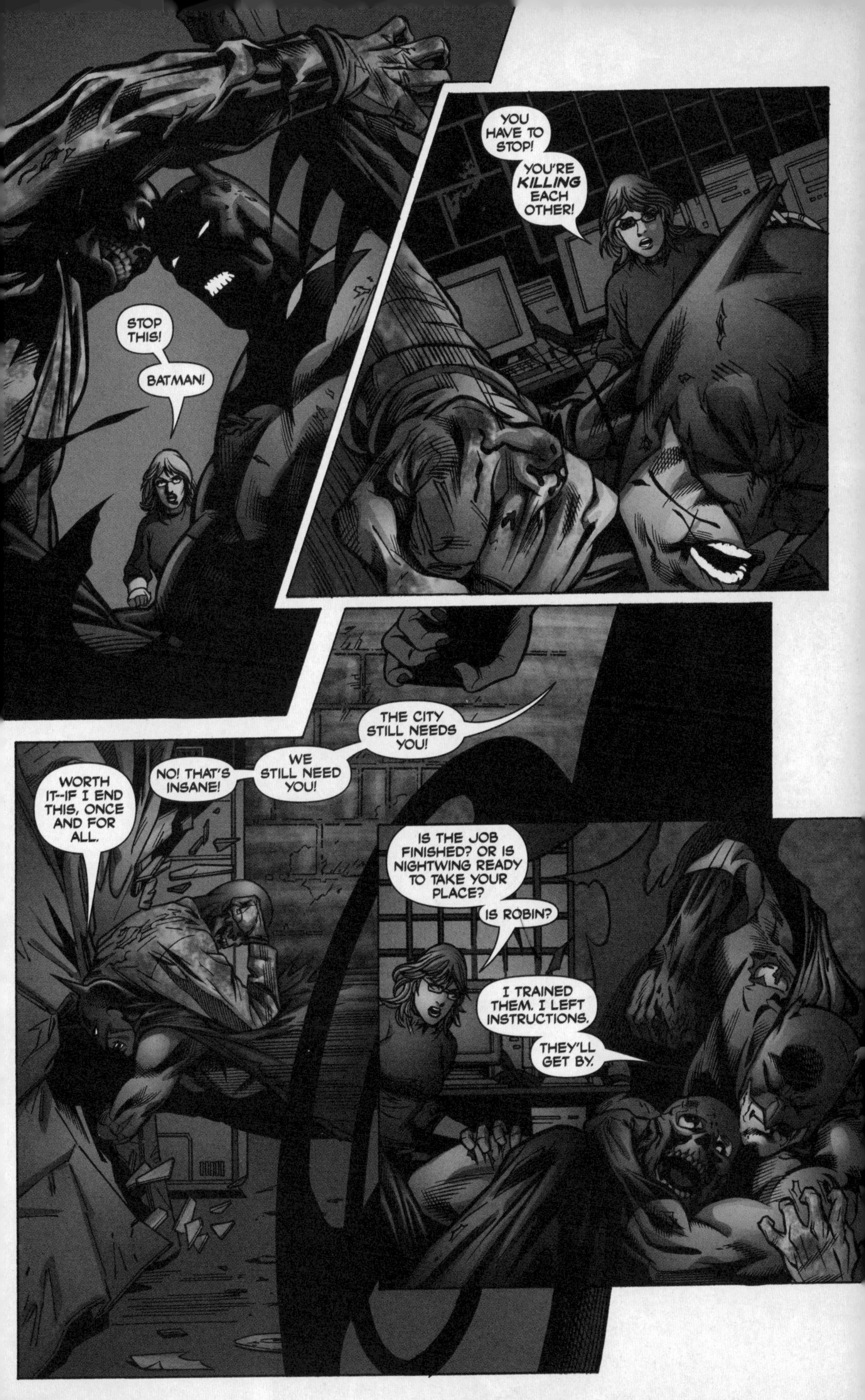

STOP THIS!
BATMAN!
YOU HAVE TO STOP!
YOU'RE KILLING EACH OTHER!
THE CITY STILL NEEDS YOU!
WE STILL NEED YOU!
NO! THAT'S INSANE!
WORTH IT--IF I END THIS, ONCE AND FOR ALL.
IS THE JOB FINISHED? OR IS NIGHTWING READY TO TAKE YOUR PLACE?
IS ROBIN?
I TRAINED THEM. I LEFT INSTRUCTIONS.
THEY'LL GET BY.

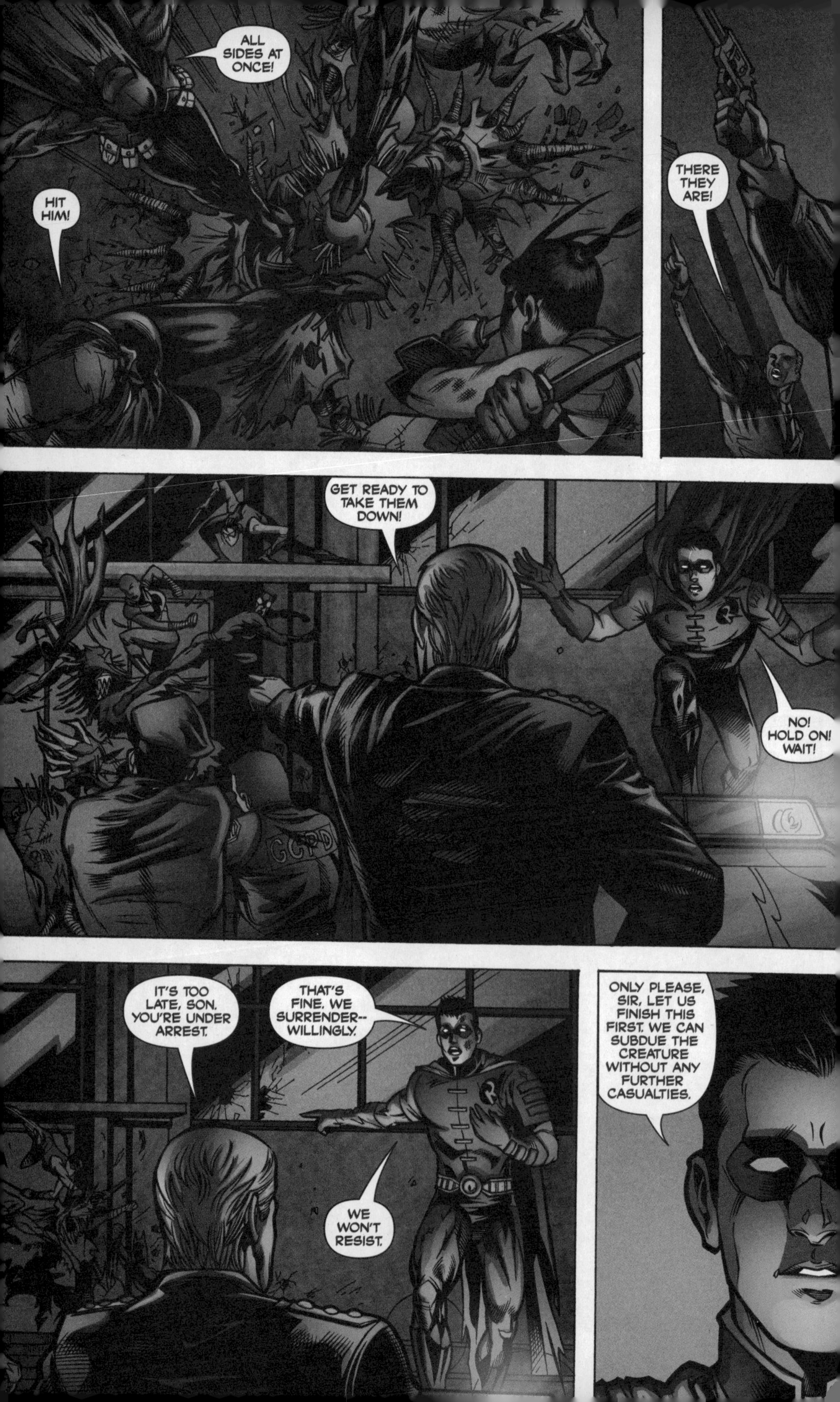
ALL SIDES AT ONCE!
HIT HIM!
THERE THEY ARE!
GET READY TO TAKE THEM DOWN!
NO! HOLD ON! WAIT!
GCPD
IT'S TOO LATE, SON. YOU'RE UNDER ARREST.
THAT'S FINE. WE SURRENDER-- WILLINGLY.
WE WON'T RESIST.
ONLY PLEASE, SIR, LET US FINISH THIS FIRST. WE CAN SUBDUE THE CREATURE WITHOUT ANY FURTHER CASUALTIES.

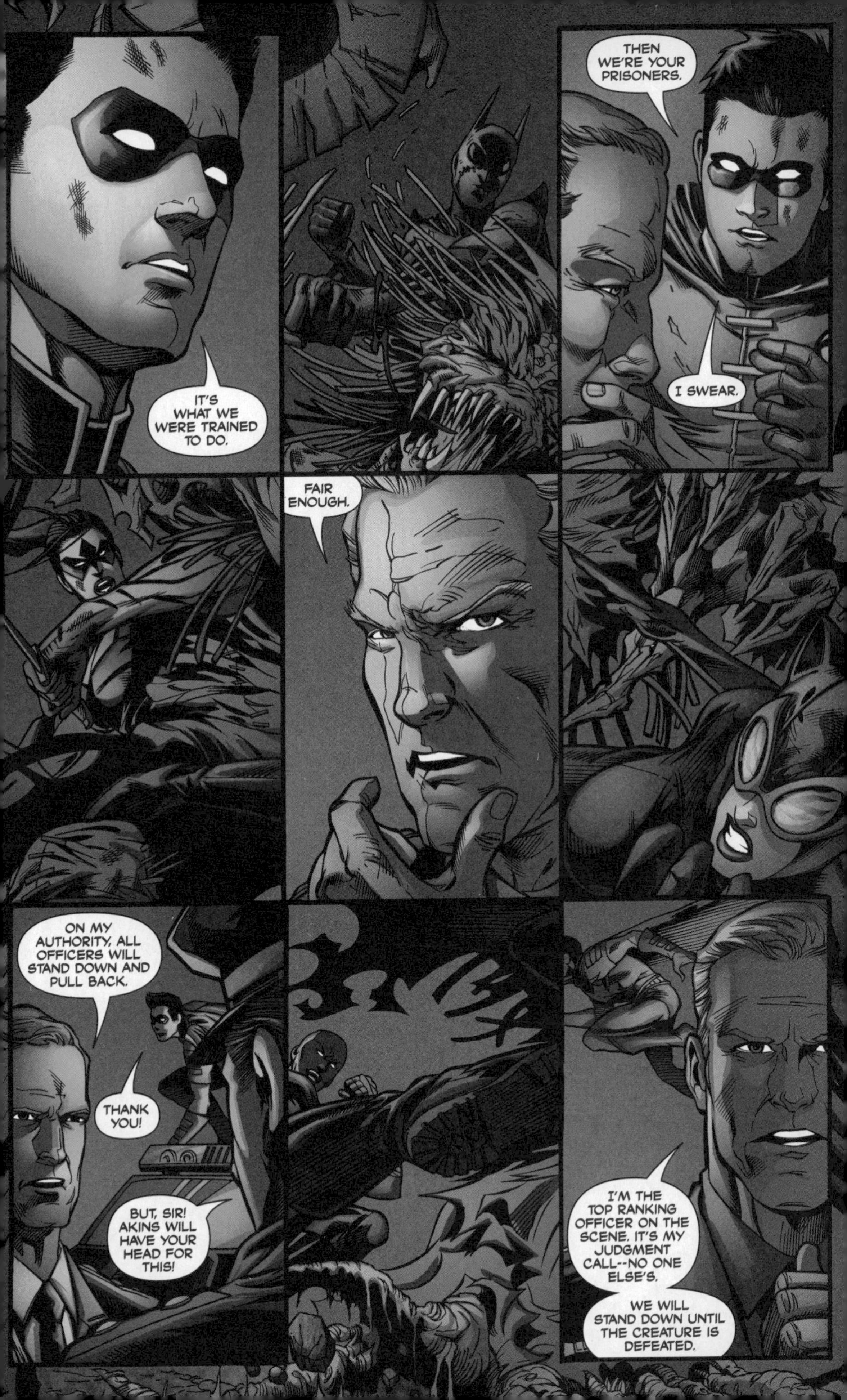
IT'S WHAT WE WERE TRAINED TO DO.
THEN WE'RE YOUR PRISONERS.
I SWEAR.
FAIR ENOUGH.
ON MY AUTHORITY, ALL OFFICERS WILL STAND DOWN AND PULL BACK.
THANK YOU!
BUT, SIR! AKINS WILL HAVE YOUR HEAD FOR THIS!
I'M THE TOP RANKING OFFICER ON THE SCENE. IT'S MY JUDGMENT CALL--NO ONE ELSE'S.
WE WILL STAND DOWN UNTIL THE CREATURE IS DEFEATED.

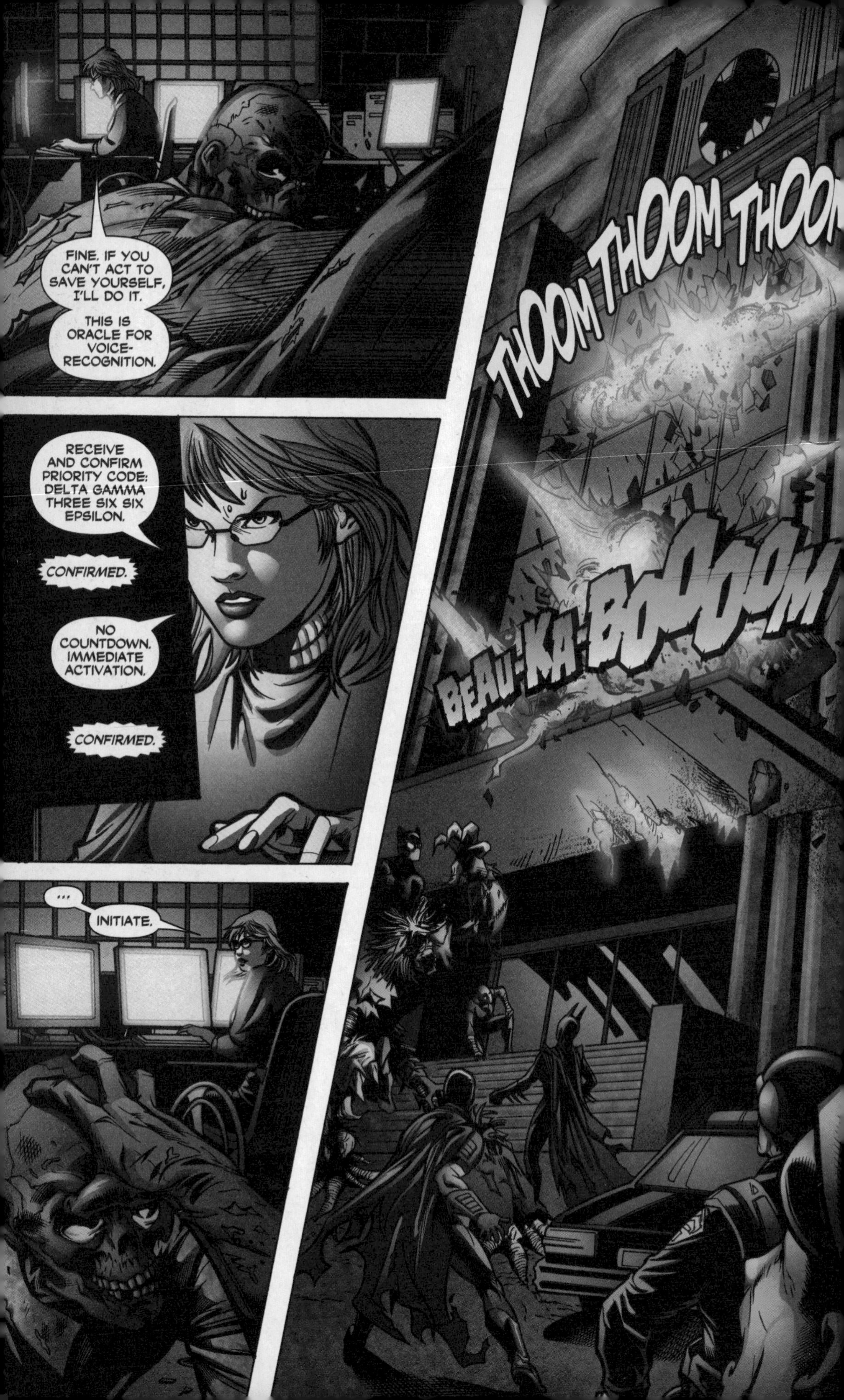
FINE. IF YOU CAN'T ACT TO SAVE YOURSELF, I'LL DO IT.
THIS IS ORACLE FOR VOICE-RECOGNITION.
RECEIVE AND CONFIRM PRIORITY CODE: DELTA GAMMA THREE SIX SIX EPSILON.
CONFIRMED.
NO COUNTDOWN. IMMEDIATE ACTIVATION.
CONFIRMED.
...
INITIATE.
THOOM THOOM THOOM
BEAU-KA-BOOOOM

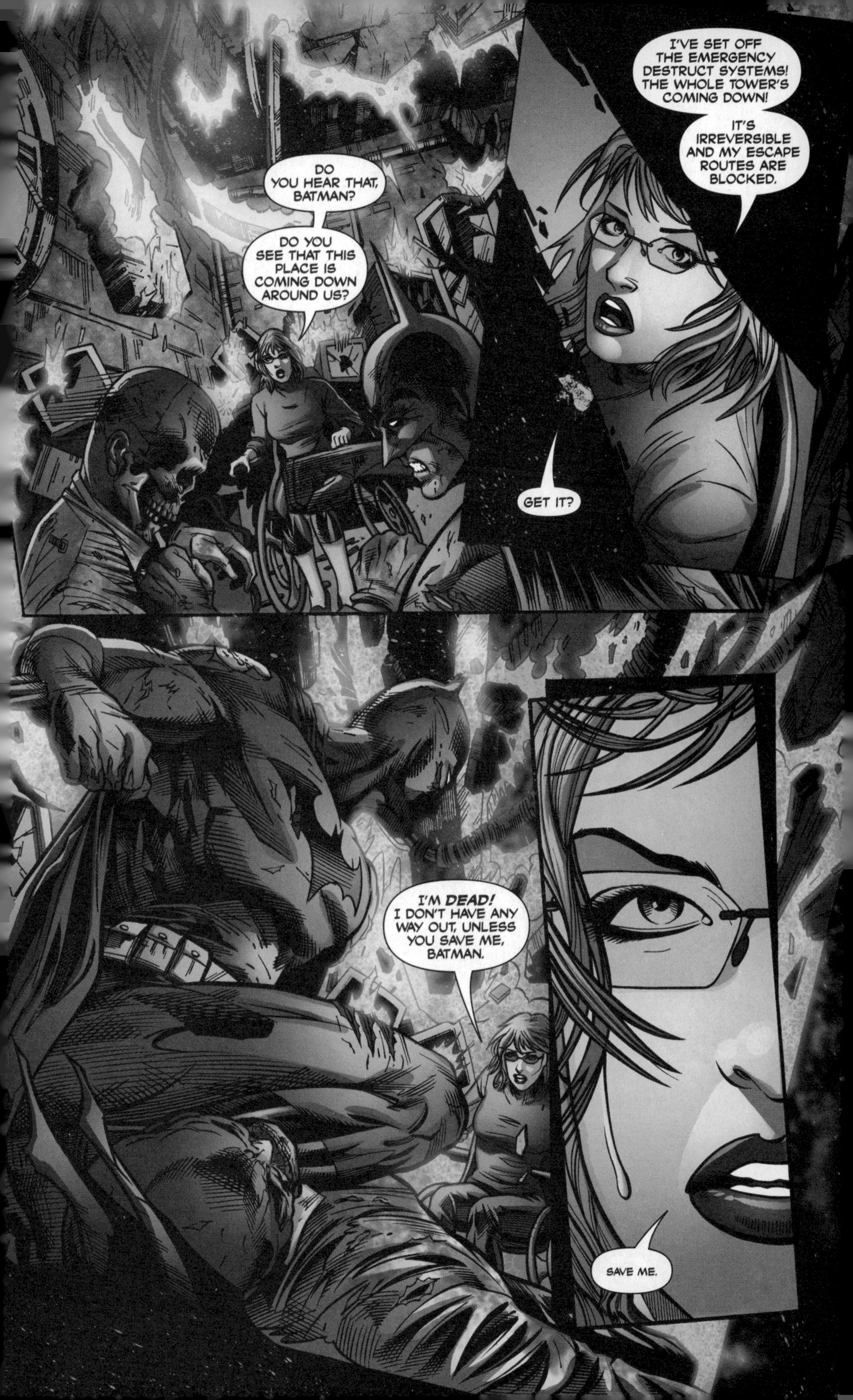
DO YOU HEAR THAT, BATMAN?
DO YOU SEE THAT THIS PLACE IS COMING DOWN AROUND US?
I'VE SET OFF THE EMERGENCY DESTRUCT SYSTEMS! THE WHOLE TOWER'S COMING DOWN!
IT'S IRREVERSIBLE AND MY ESCAPE ROUTES ARE BLOCKED.
GET IT?
I'M DEAD! I DON'T HAVE ANY WAY OUT, UNLESS YOU SAVE ME, BATMAN.
SAVE ME.

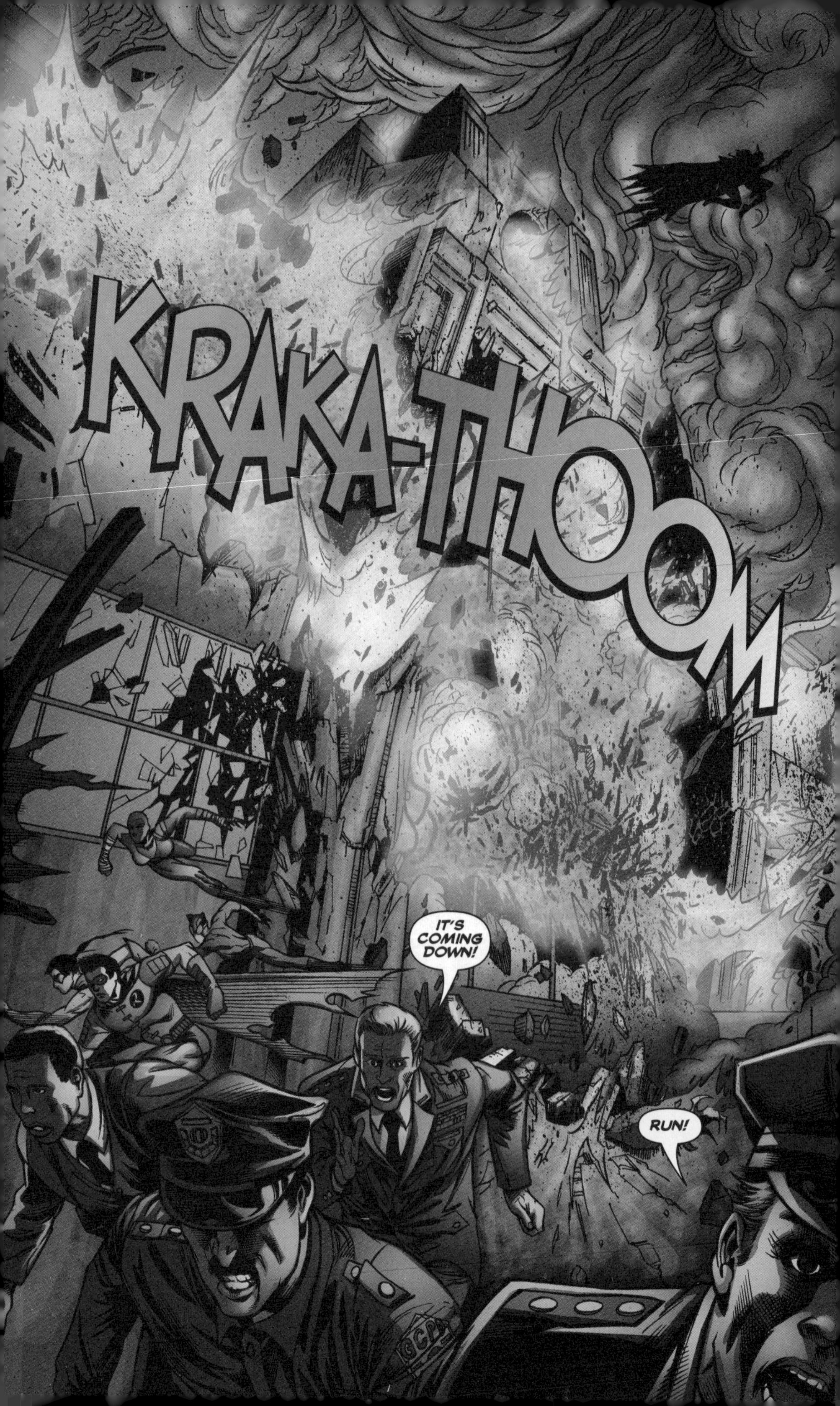
KRAKA-THOOOM
IT'S COMING DOWN!
RUN!

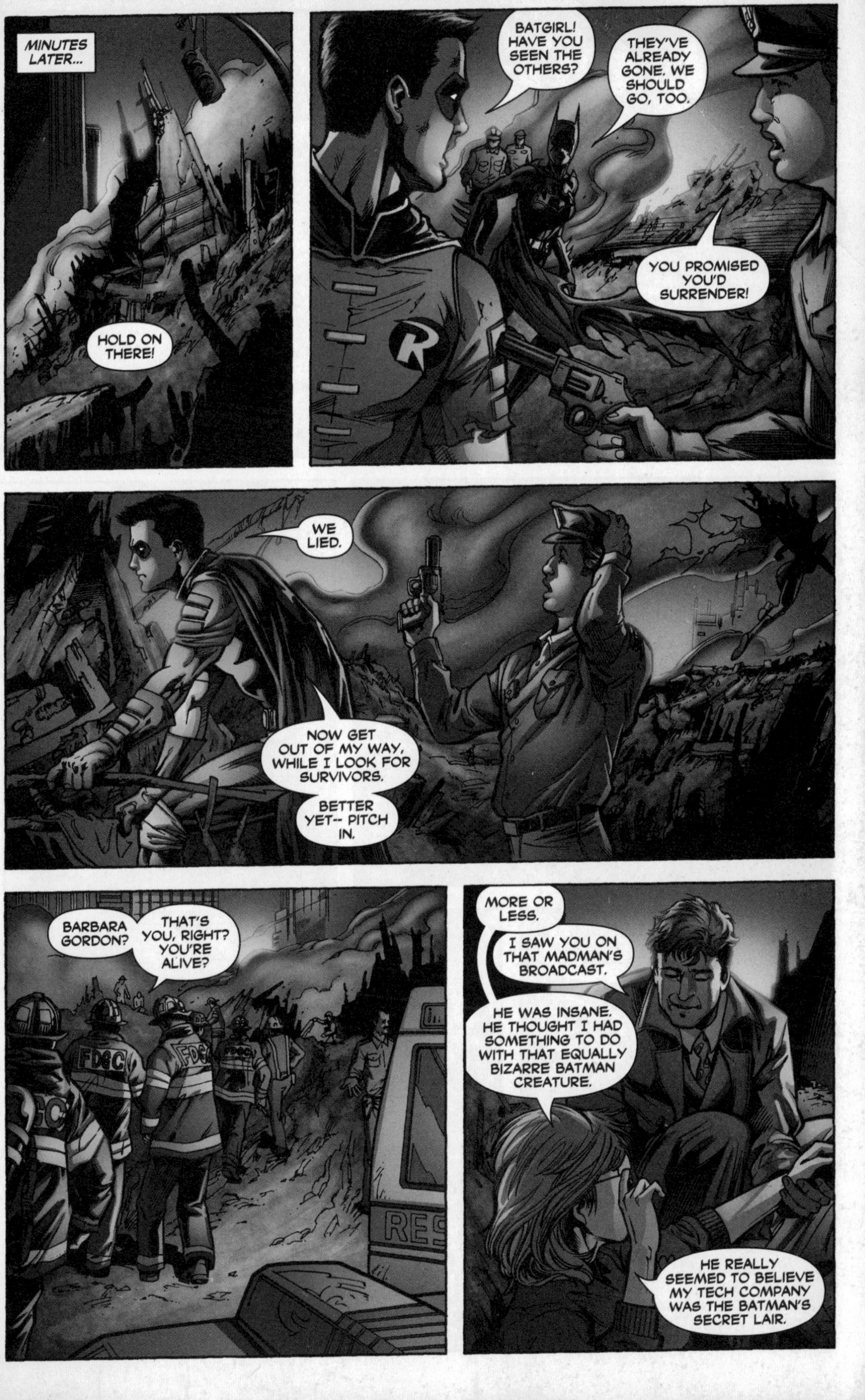
MINUTES LATER...
HOLD ON THERE!
BATGIRL! HAVE YOU SEEN THE OTHERS?
THEY'VE ALREADY GONE. WE SHOULD GO, TOO.
YOU PROMISED YOU'D SURRENDER!
WE LIED.
NOW GET OUT OF MY WAY, WHILE I LOOK FOR SURVIVORS.
BETTER YET-- PITCH IN.
BARBARA GORDON?
THAT'S YOU, RIGHT? YOU'RE ALIVE?
FDGC
MORE OR LESS.
I SAW YOU ON THAT MADMAN'S BROADCAST.
HE WAS INSANE. HE THOUGHT I HAD SOMETHING TO DO WITH THAT EQUALLY BIZARRE BATMAN CREATURE.
HE REALLY SEEMED TO BELIEVE MY TECH COMPANY WAS THE BATMAN'S SECRET LAIR.

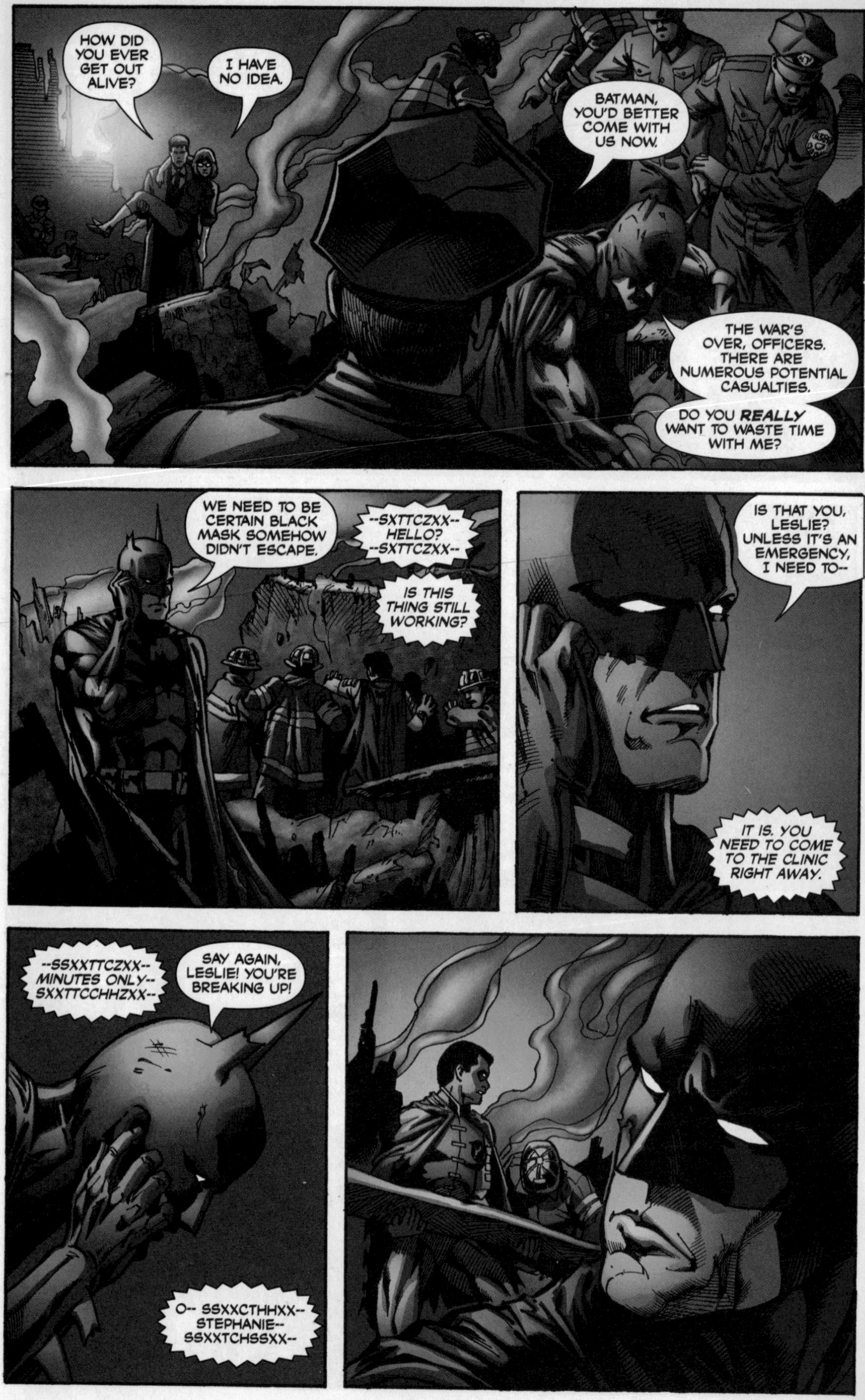
HOW DID YOU EVER GET OUT ALIVE?
I HAVE NO IDEA.
BATMAN, YOU'D BETTER COME WITH US NOW.
THE WAR'S OVER, OFFICERS. THERE ARE NUMEROUS POTENTIAL CASUALTIES.
DO YOU REALLY WANT TO WASTE TIME WITH ME?
WE NEED TO BE CERTAIN BLACK MASK SOMEHOW DIDN'T ESCAPE.
--SXTTCZXX-- HELLO? --SXTTCZXX--
IS THIS THING STILL WORKING?
IS THAT YOU, LESLIE? UNLESS IT'S AN EMERGENCY, I NEED TO--
IT IS. YOU NEED TO COME TO THE CLINIC RIGHT AWAY.
--SSXXTTCZXX-- MINUTES ONLY-- SXXTTCCHHZXX--
SAY AGAIN, LESLIE! YOU'RE BREAKING UP!
O-- SSXXCTHHXX-- STEPHANIE-- SSXXTCHSSXX--

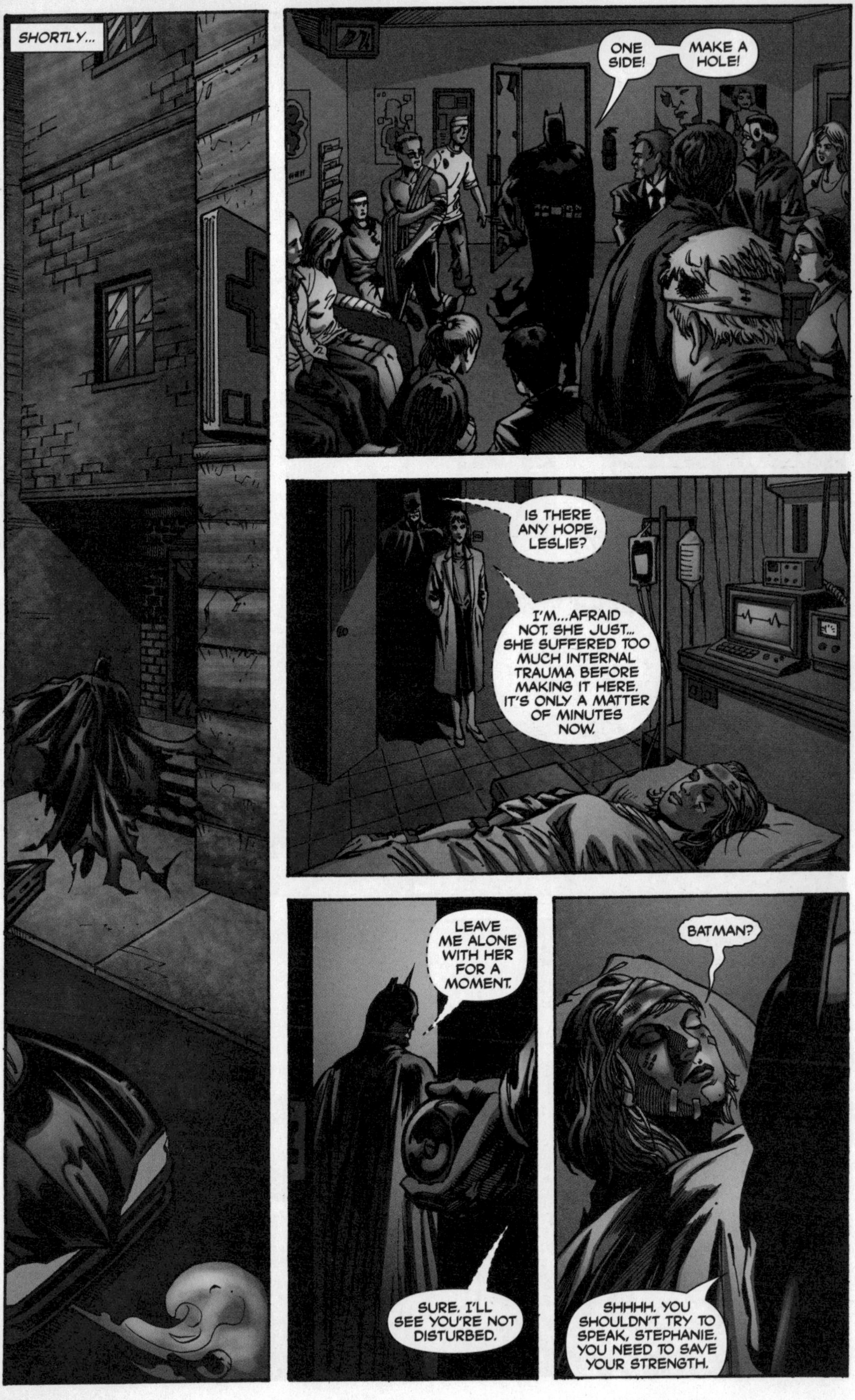
SHORTLY...
ONE SIDE!
MAKE A HOLE!
IS THERE ANY HOPE, LESLIE?
I'M...AFRAID NOT. SHE JUST... SHE SUFFERED TOO MUCH INTERNAL TRAUMA BEFORE MAKING IT HERE. IT'S ONLY A MATTER OF MINUTES NOW.
LEAVE ME ALONE WITH HER FOR A MOMENT.
SURE. I'LL SEE YOU'RE NOT DISTURBED.
BATMAN?
SHHHH. YOU SHOULDN'T TRY TO SPEAK, STEPHANIE. YOU NEED TO SAVE YOUR STRENGTH.

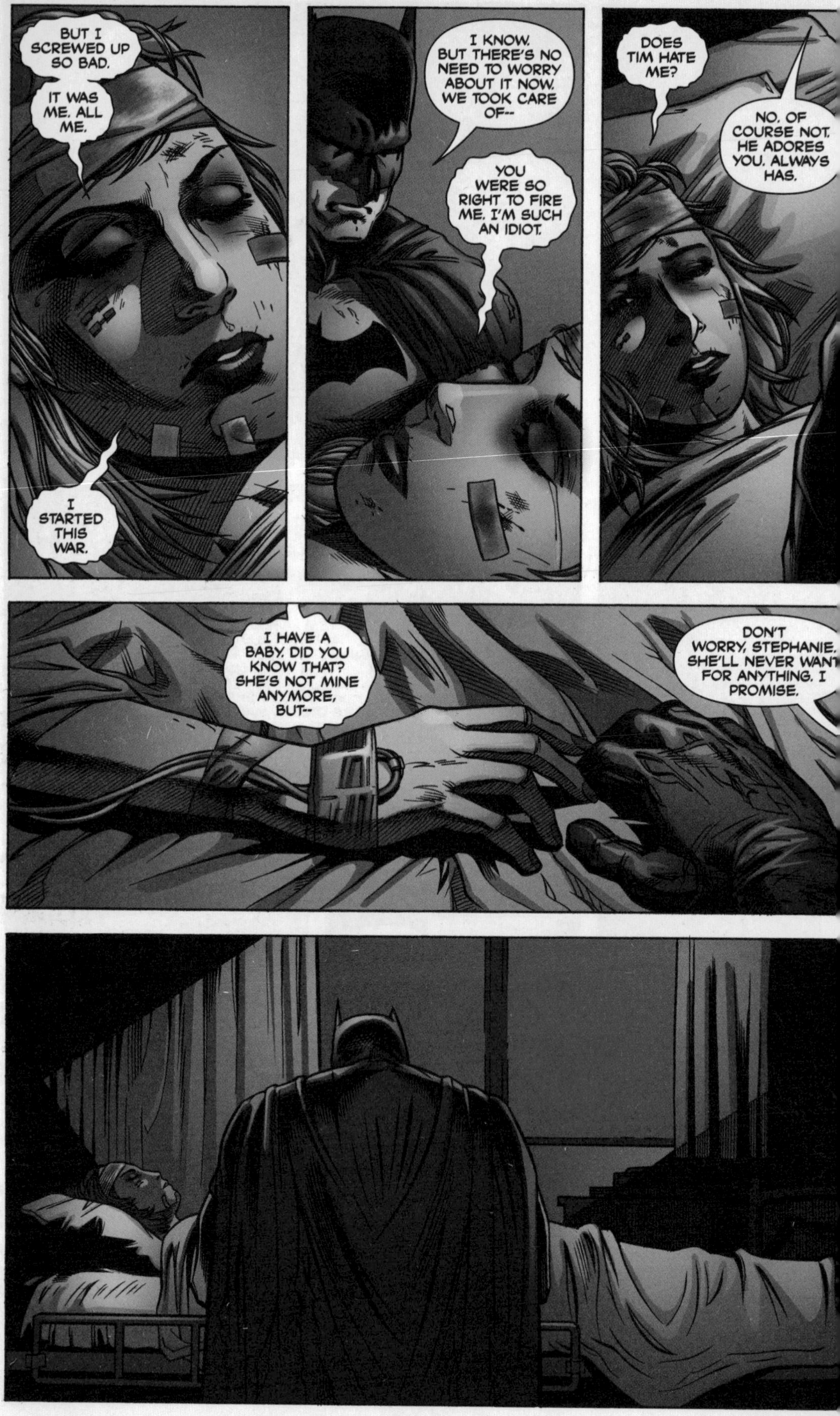
BUT I SCREWED UP SO BAD.
IT WAS ME. ALL ME.
I STARTED THIS WAR.
I KNOW. BUT THERE'S NO NEED TO WORRY ABOUT IT NOW. WE TOOK CARE OF--
YOU WERE SO RIGHT TO FIRE ME. I'M SUCH AN IDIOT.
DOES TIM HATE ME?
NO. OF COURSE NOT. HE ADORES YOU. ALWAYS HAS.
I HAVE A BABY. DID YOU KNOW THAT? SHE'S NOT MINE ANYMORE, BUT--
DON'T WORRY, STEPHANIE. SHE'LL NEVER WANT FOR ANYTHING. I PROMISE.

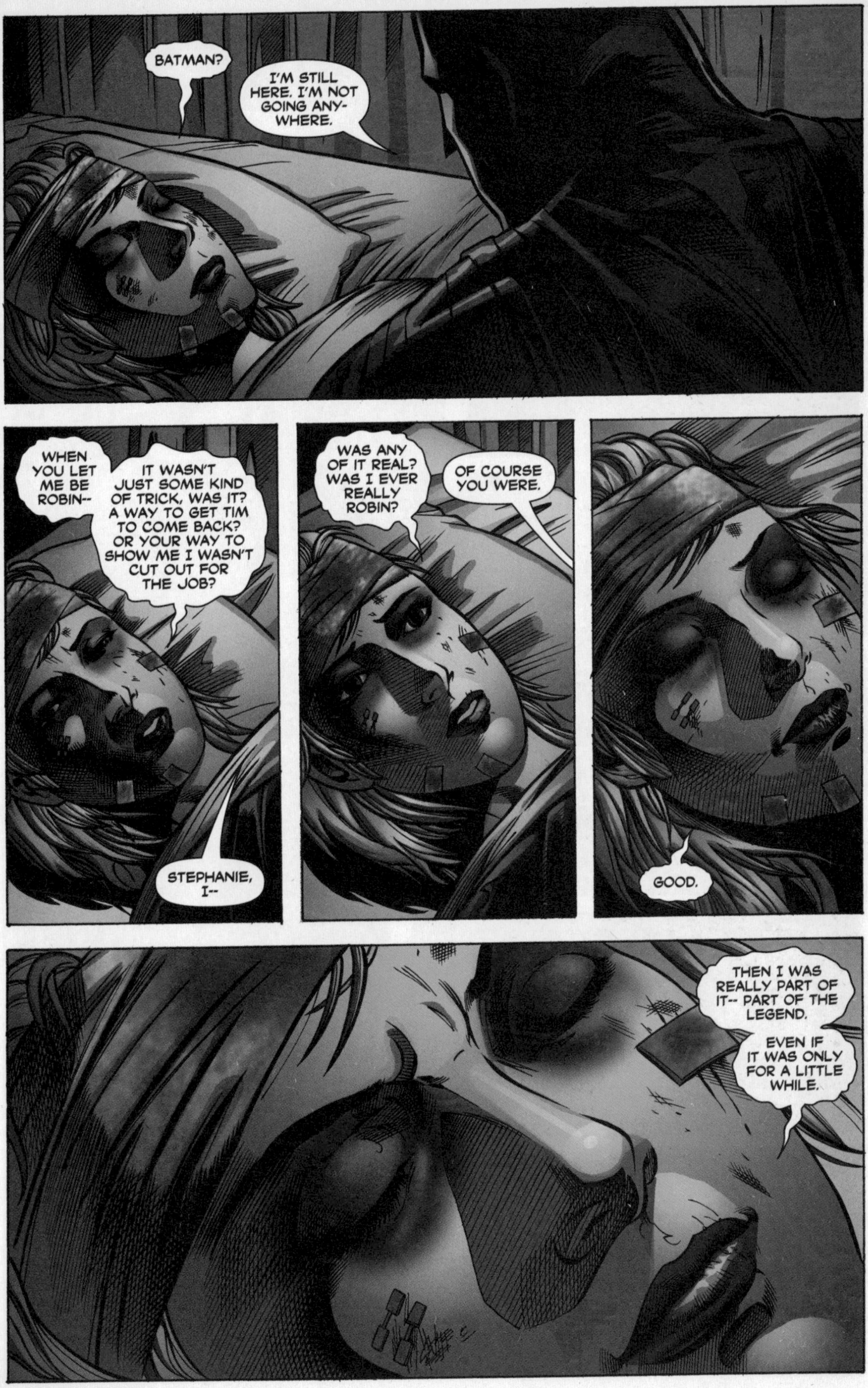
BATMAN?
I'M STILL HERE. I'M NOT GOING ANY-WHERE.
WHEN YOU LET ME BE ROBIN--
IT WASN'T JUST SOME KIND OF TRICK, WAS IT? A WAY TO GET TIM TO COME BACK? OR YOUR WAY TO SHOW ME I WASN'T CUT OUT FOR THE JOB?
STEPHANIE, I--
WAS ANY OF IT REAL? WAS I EVER REALLY ROBIN?
OF COURSE YOU WERE.
GOOD.
THEN I WAS REALLY PART OF IT-- PART OF THE LEGEND.
EVEN IF IT WAS ONLY FOR A LITTLE WHILE.

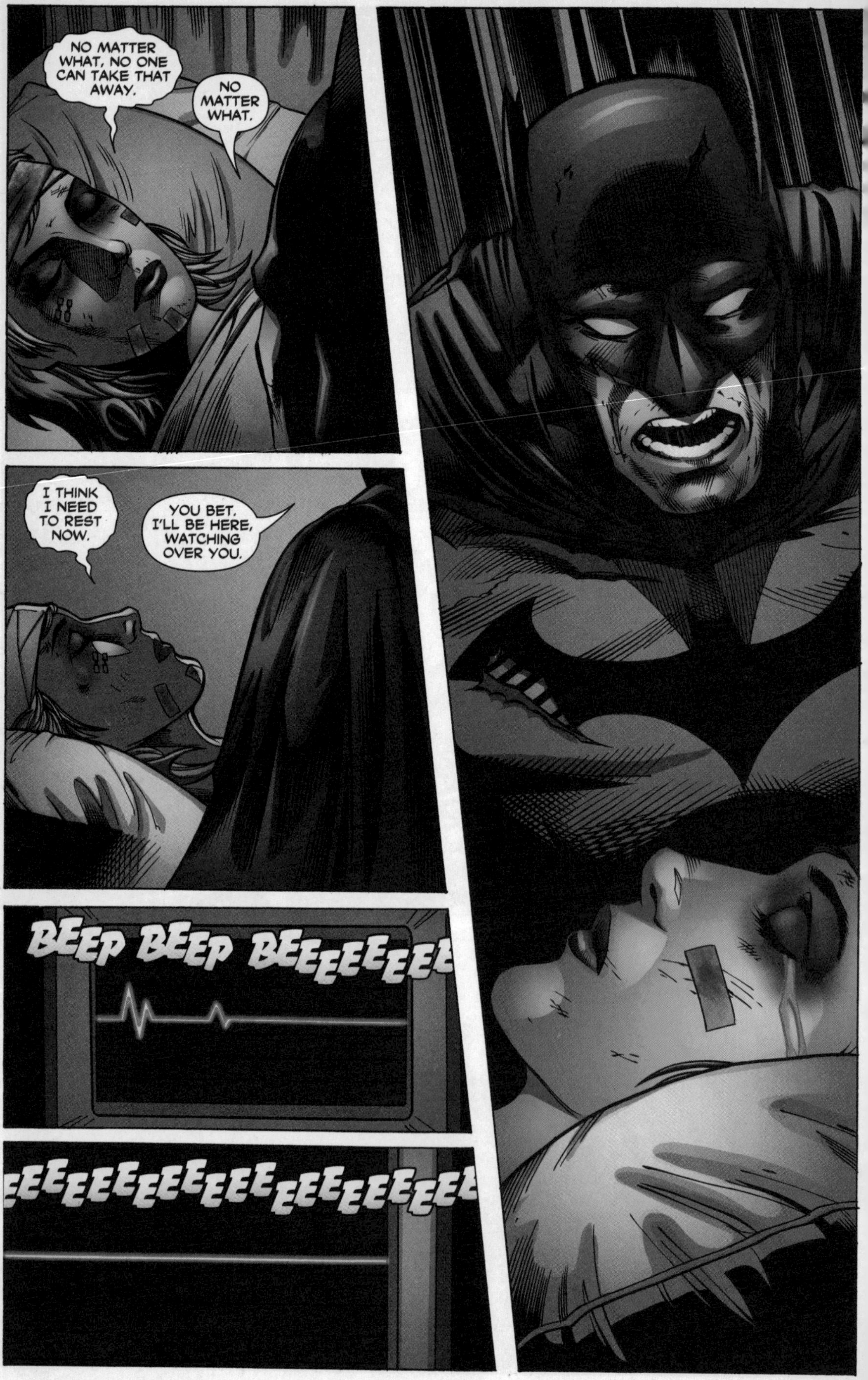
NO MATTER WHAT, NO ONE CAN TAKE THAT AWAY.
NO MATTER WHAT.
I THINK I NEED TO REST NOW.
YOU BET. I'LL BE HERE, WATCHING OVER YOU.
BEEP BEEP BEEEEEEEEE
EEEEEEEEEEEEEEEEEEEEEE

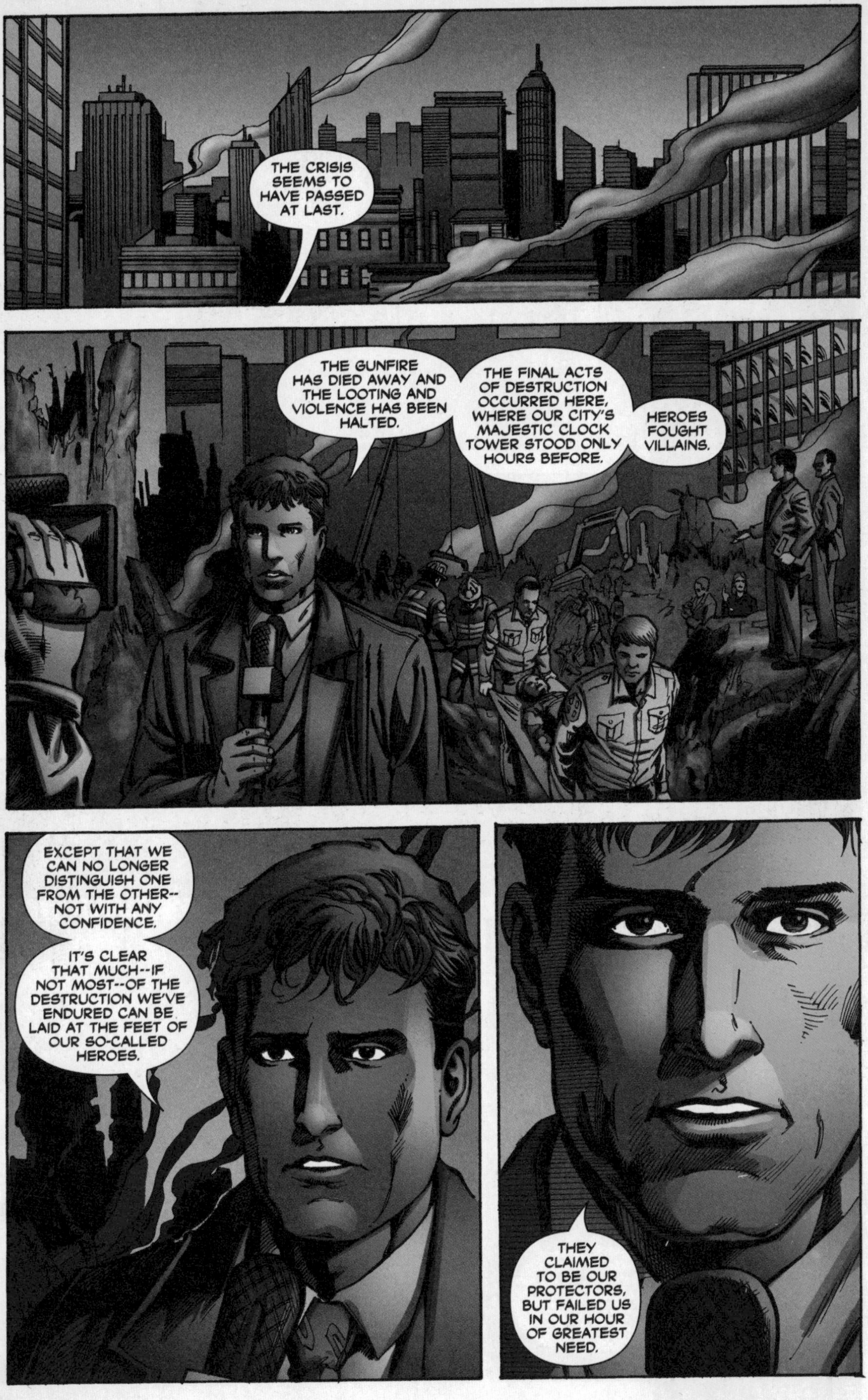
THE CRISIS SEEMS TO HAVE PASSED AT LAST.
THE GUNFIRE HAS DIED AWAY AND THE LOOTING AND VIOLENCE HAS BEEN HALTED.
THE FINAL ACTS OF DESTRUCTION OCCURRED HERE, WHERE OUR CITY'S MAJESTIC CLOCK TOWER STOOD ONLY HOURS BEFORE.
HEROES FOUGHT VILLAINS.
EXCEPT THAT WE CAN NO LONGER DISTINGUISH ONE FROM THE OTHER-- NOT WITH ANY CONFIDENCE.
IT'S CLEAR THAT MUCH--IF NOT MOST--OF THE DESTRUCTION WE'VE ENDURED CAN BE LAID AT THE FEET OF OUR SO-CALLED HEROES.
THEY CLAIMED TO BE OUR PROTECTORS, BUT FAILED US IN OUR HOUR OF GREATEST NEED.

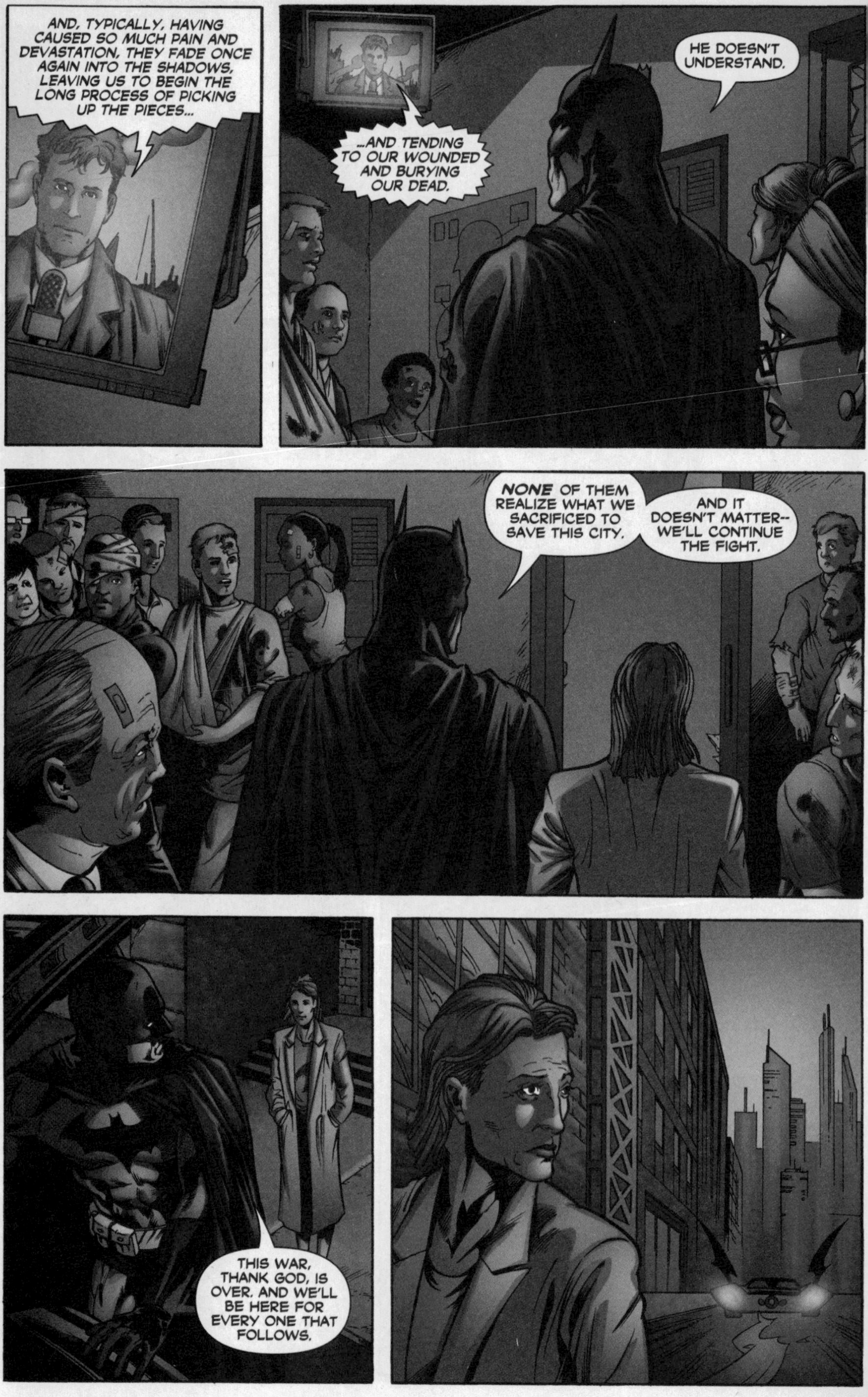
AND, TYPICALLY, HAVING CAUSED SO MUCH PAIN AND DEVASTATION, THEY FADE ONCE AGAIN INTO THE SHADOWS, LEAVING US TO BEGIN THE LONG PROCESS OF PICKING UP THE PIECES...
...AND TENDING TO OUR WOUNDED AND BURYING OUR DEAD.
HE DOESN'T UNDERSTAND.
NONE OF THEM REALIZE WHAT WE SACRIFICED TO SAVE THIS CITY.
AND IT DOESN'T MATTER-- WE'LL CONTINUE THE FIGHT.
THIS WAR, THANK GOD, IS OVER. AND WE'LL BE HERE FOR EVERY ONE THAT FOLLOWS.

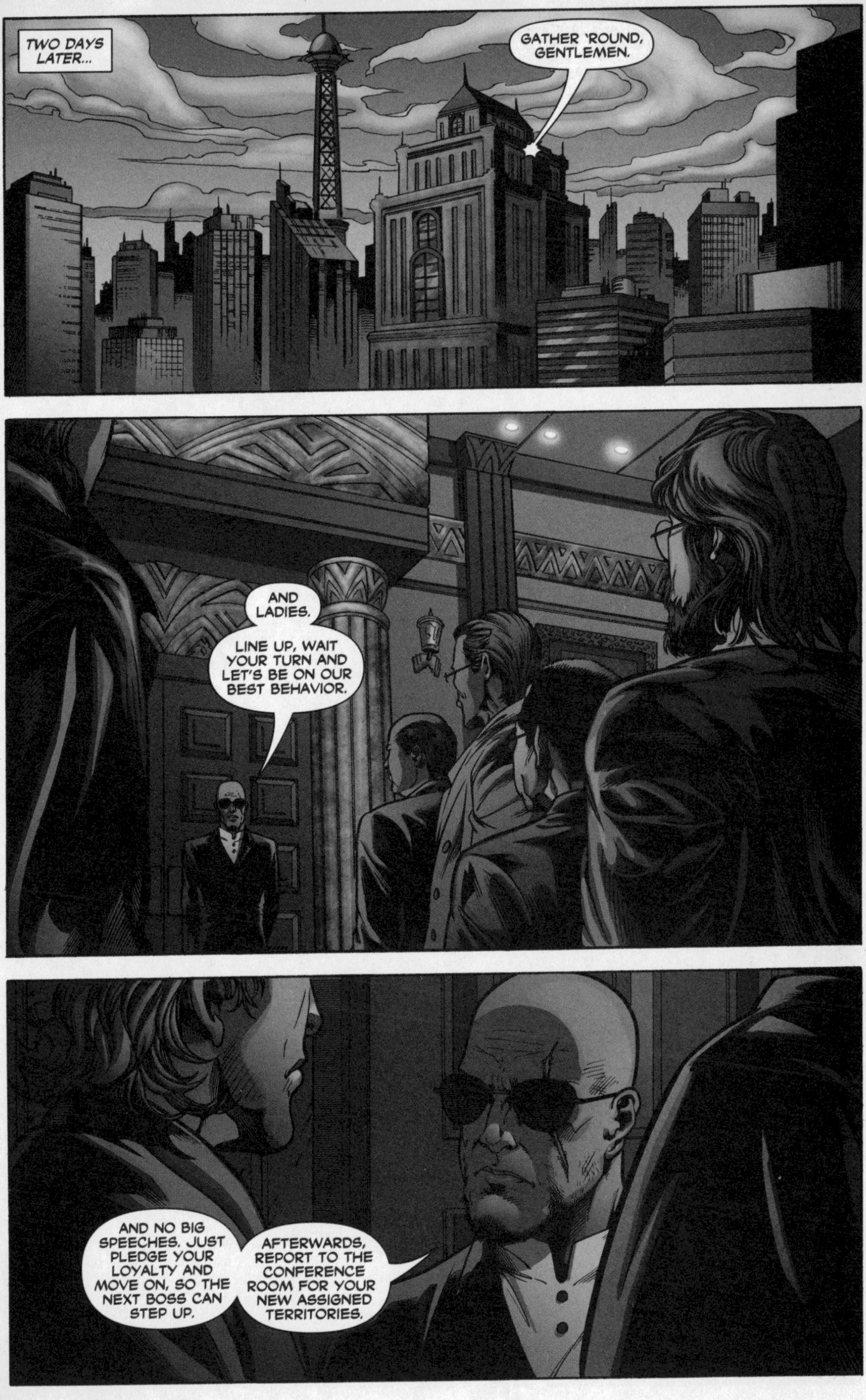

TWO DAYS LATER...
GATHER 'ROUND, GENTLEMEN.
AND LADIES.
LINE UP, WAIT YOUR TURN AND LET'S BE ON OUR BEST BEHAVIOR.
AND NO BIG SPEECHES. JUST PLEDGE YOUR LOYALTY AND MOVE ON, SO THE NEXT BOSS CAN STEP UP.
AFTERWARDS, REPORT TO THE CONFERENCE ROOM FOR YOUR NEW ASSIGNED TERRITORIES.

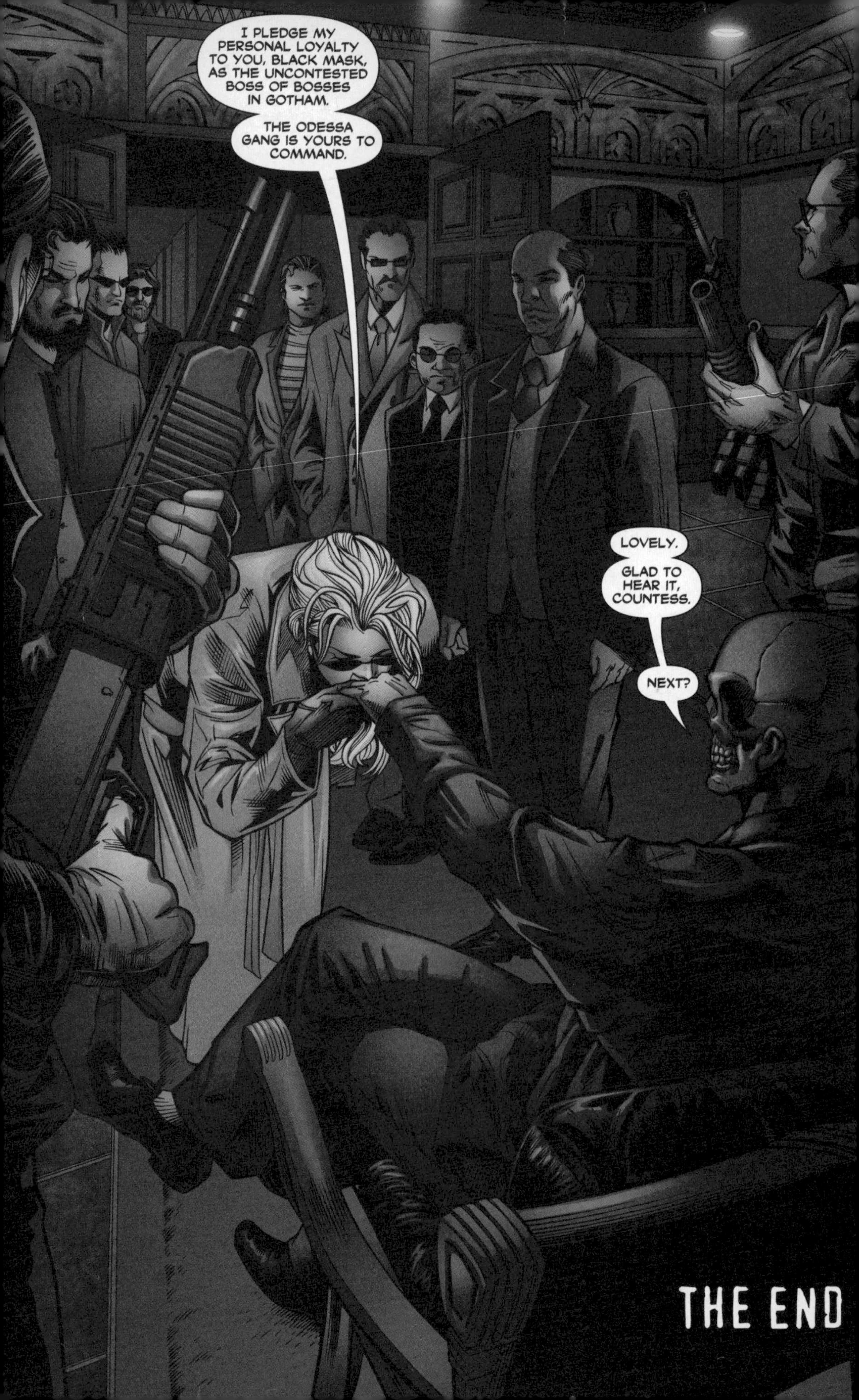
I PLEDGE MY PERSONAL LOYALTY TO YOU, BLACK MASK, AS THE UNCONTESTED BOSS OF BOSSES IN GOTHAM.
THE ODESSA GANG IS YOURS TO COMMAND.
LOVELY.
GLAD TO HEAR IT, COUNTESS.
NEXT?
THE END

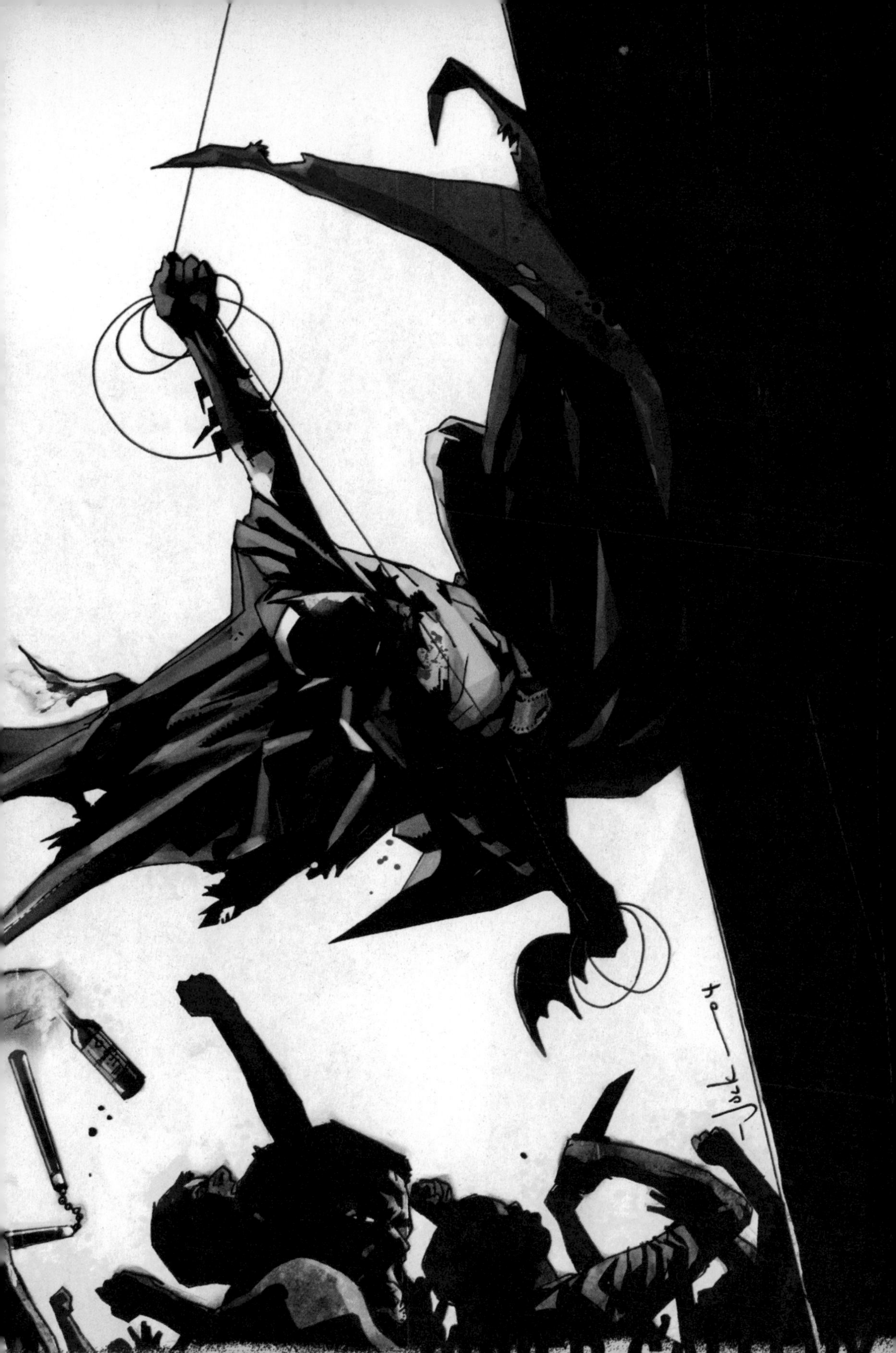

COVER GALLERY

DETECTIVE COMICS #799 Cover by Jock

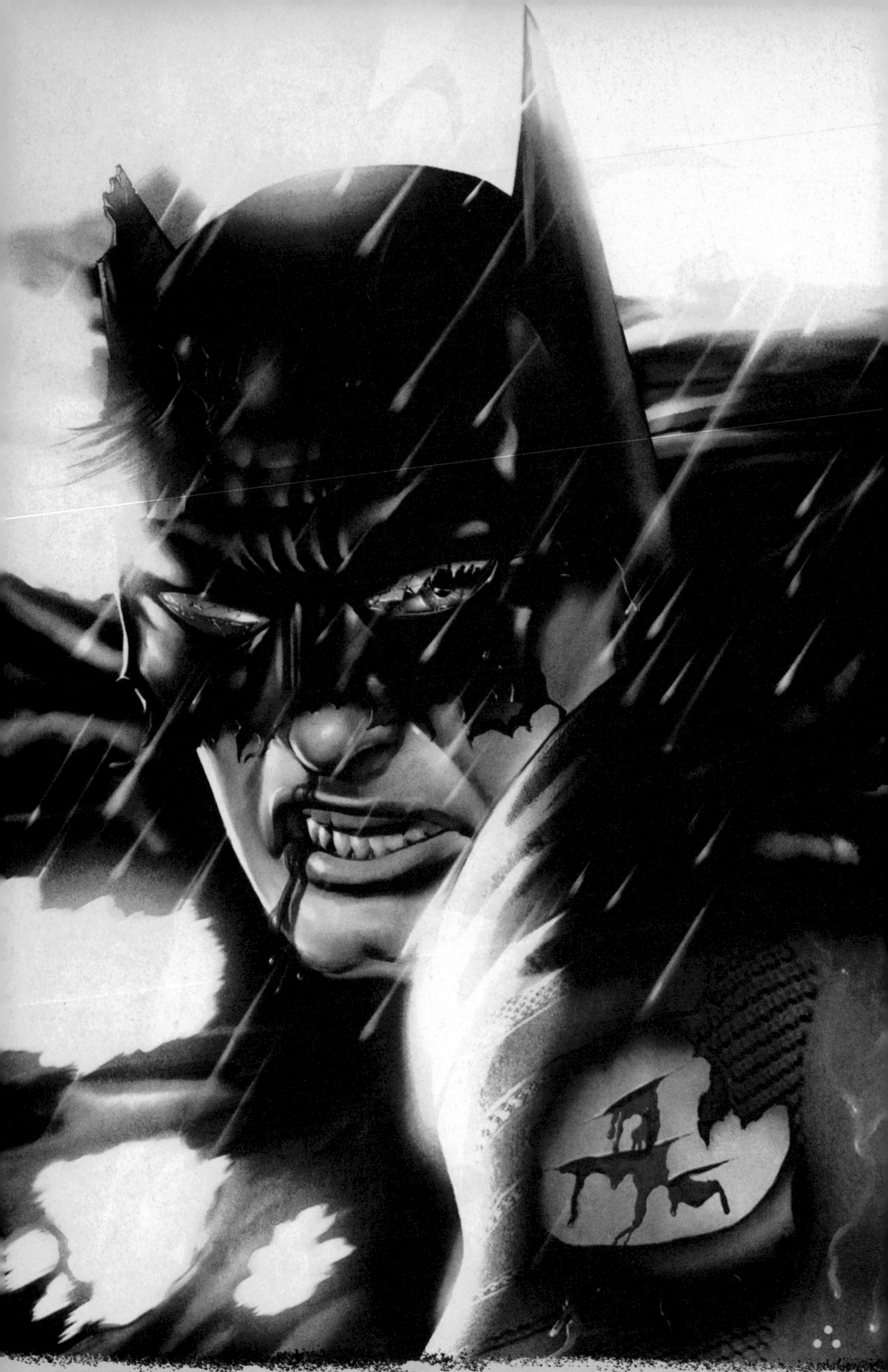

BATMAN: LEGENDS OF THE DARK KNIGHT #184 Cover by Brian Haberlin

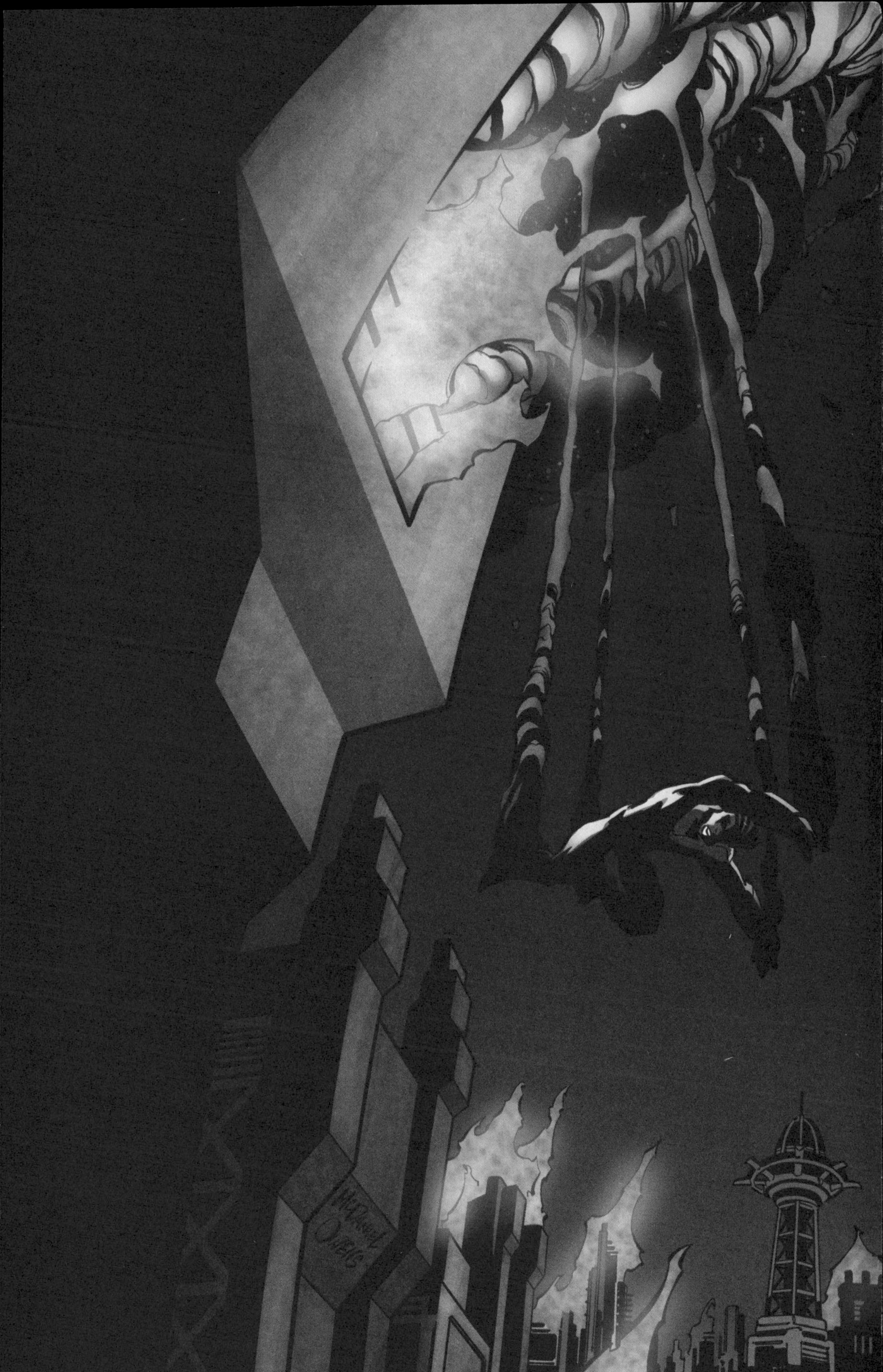

NIGHTWING #98 Cover by Scott McDaniel & Andy Owens

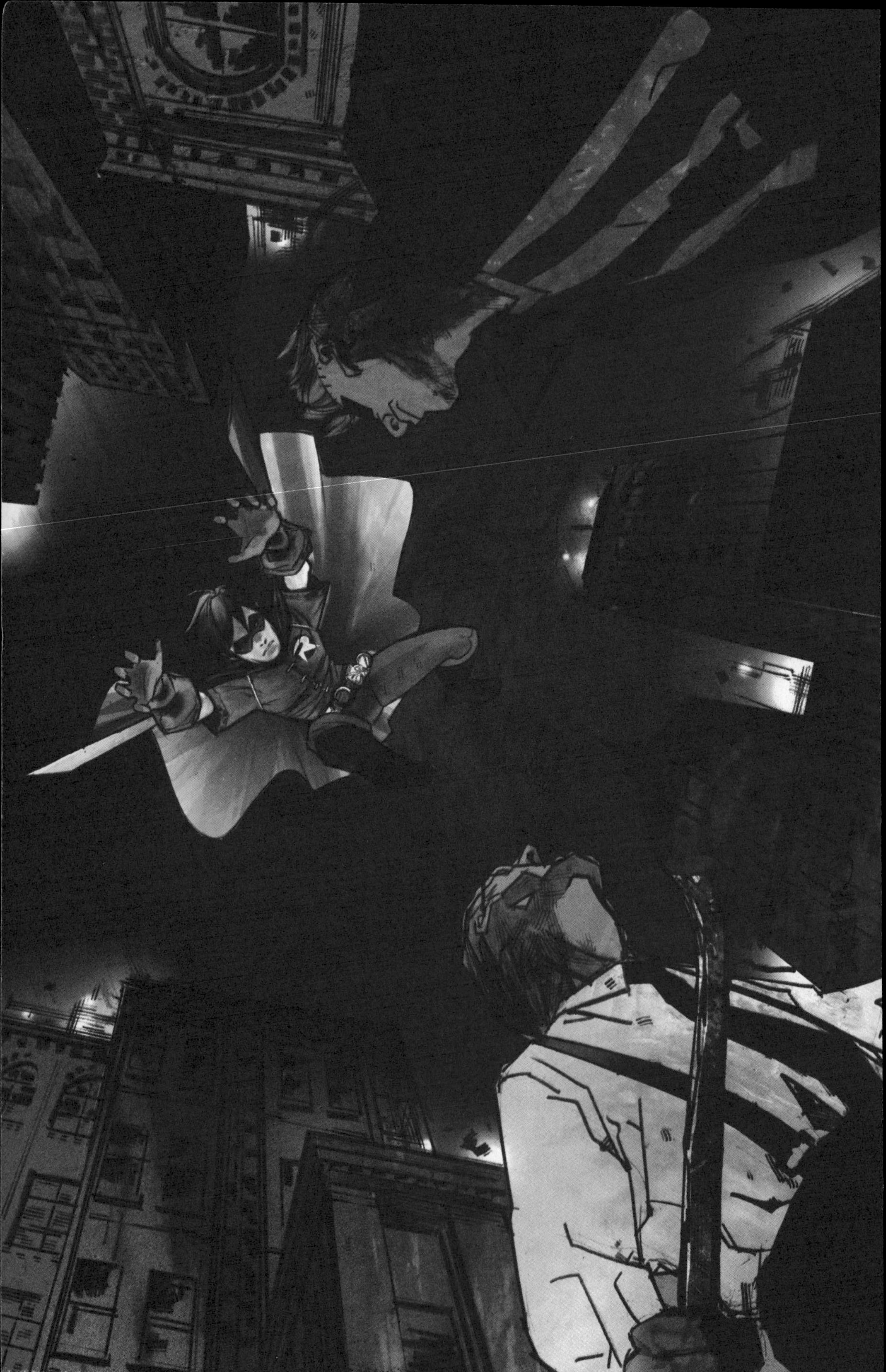

ROBIN #131 Cover by Dustin Nguyen

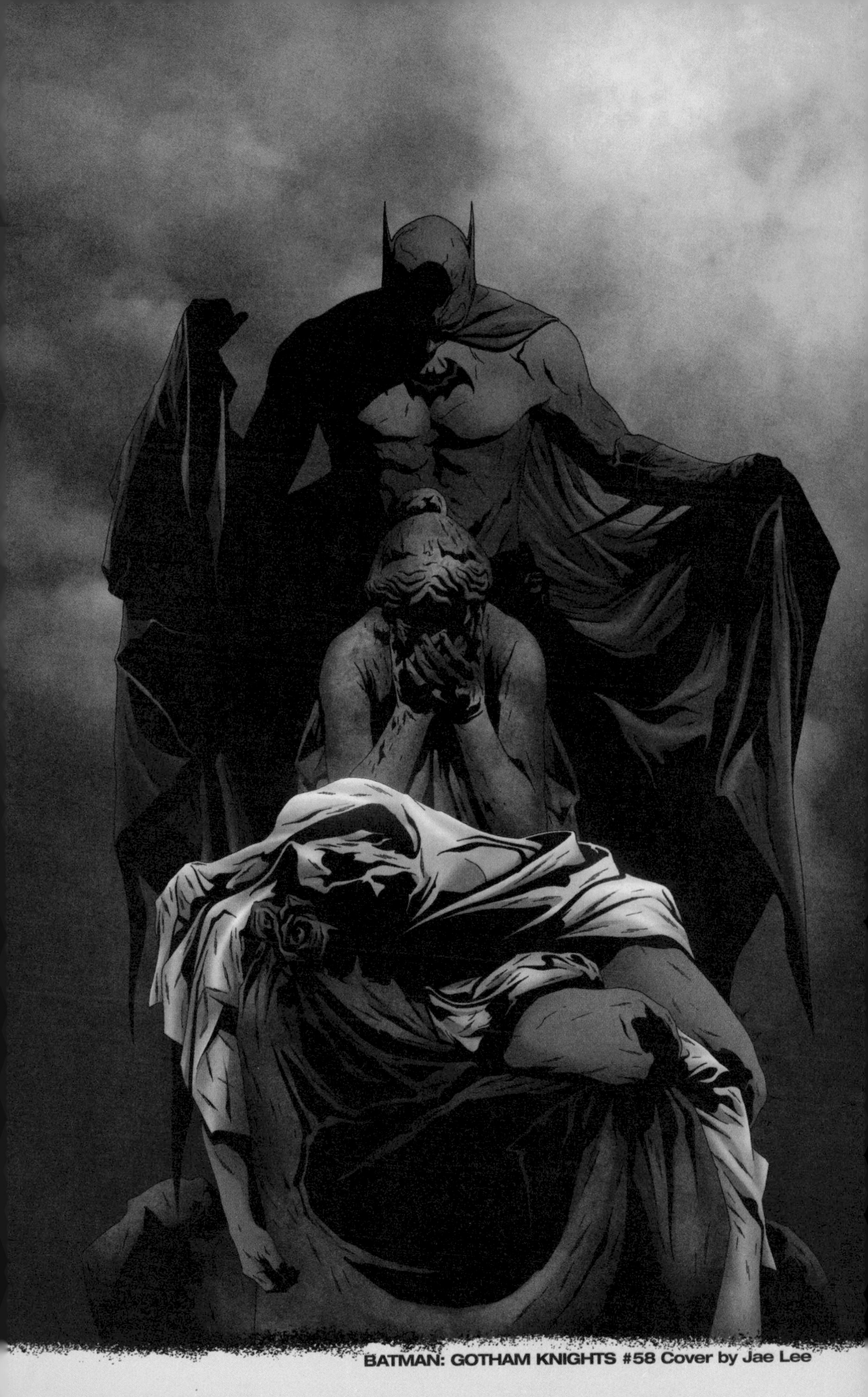

BATMAN: GOTHAM KNIGHTS #58 Cover by Jae Lee

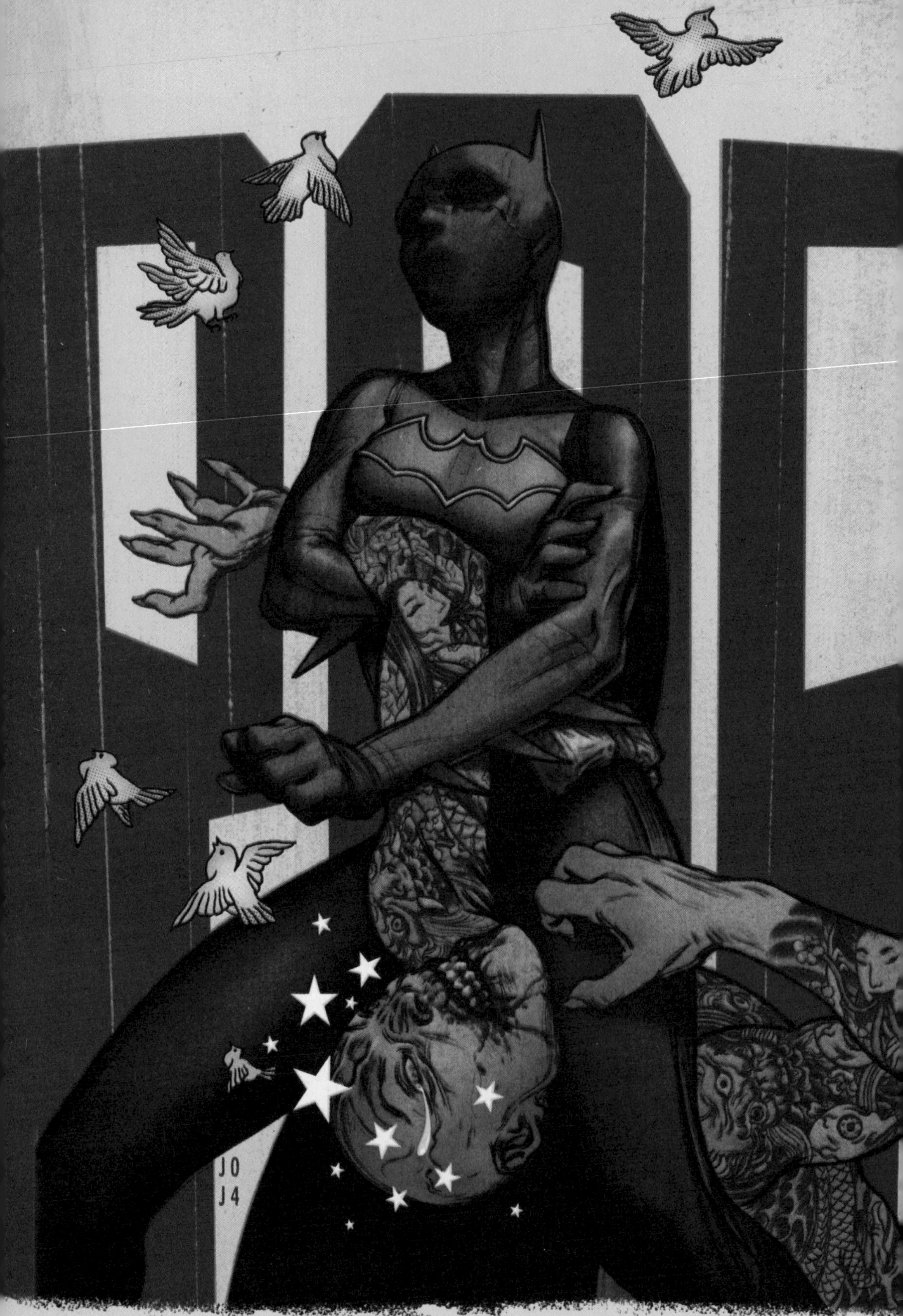

BATGIRL #57 Cover by James Jean

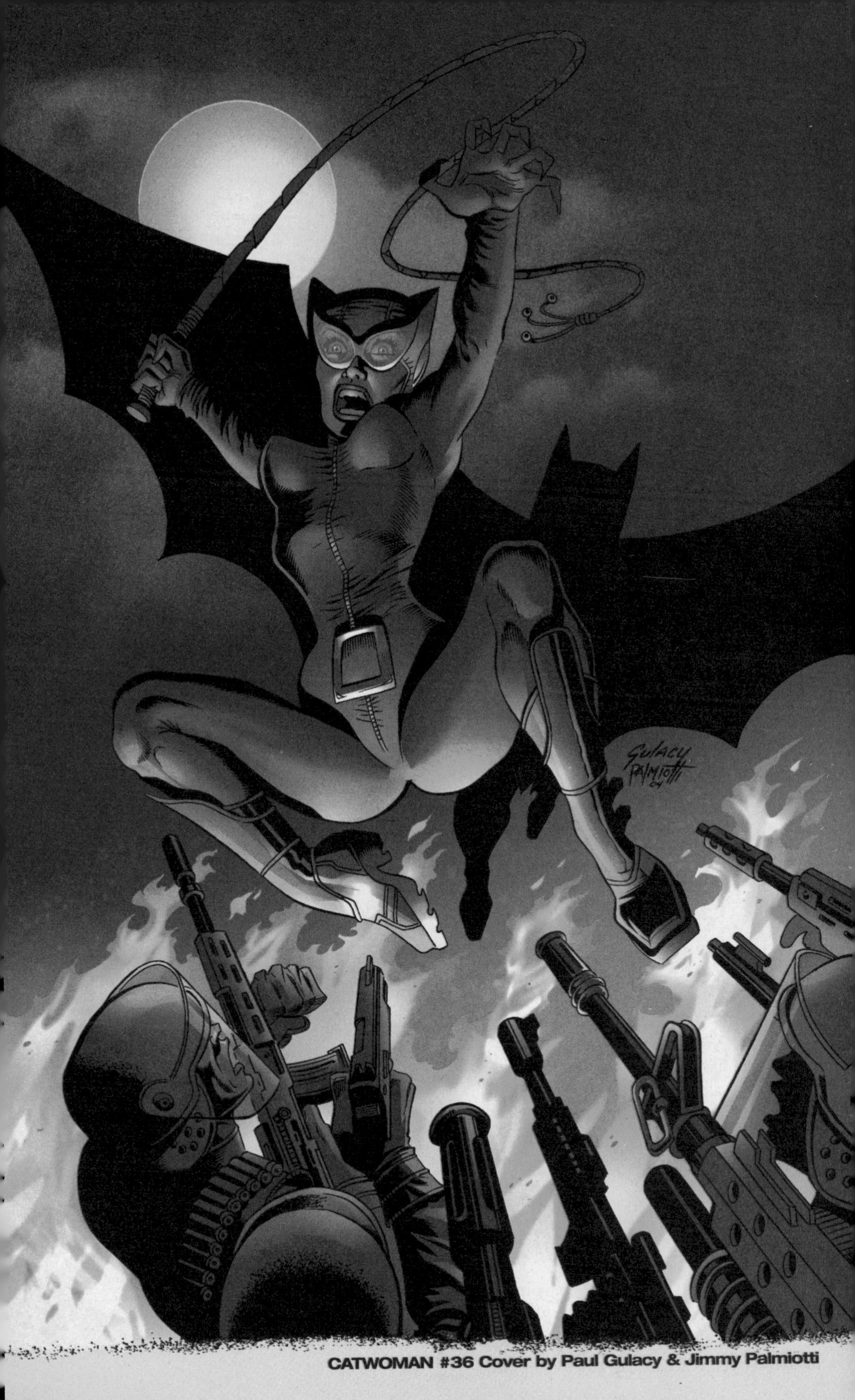
GULACY
PALMIOTTI
04

CATWOMAN #36 Cover by Paul Gulacy & Jimmy Palmiotti

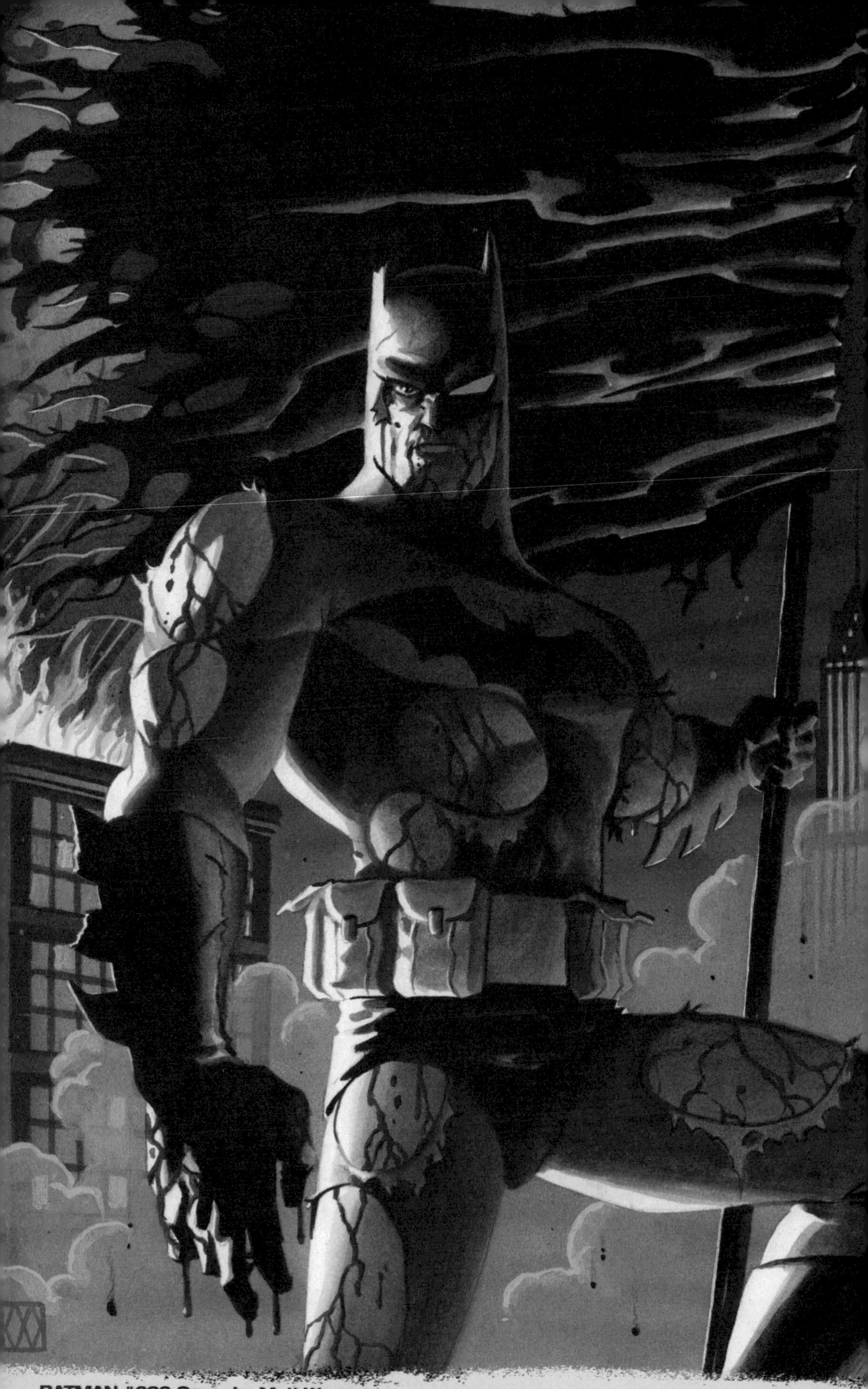

BATMAN #633 Cover by Matt Wagner

READ MORE OF THE DARK KNIGHT DETECTIVE'S ADVENTURES IN THESE COLLECTIONS FROM DC COMICS:

BATMAN

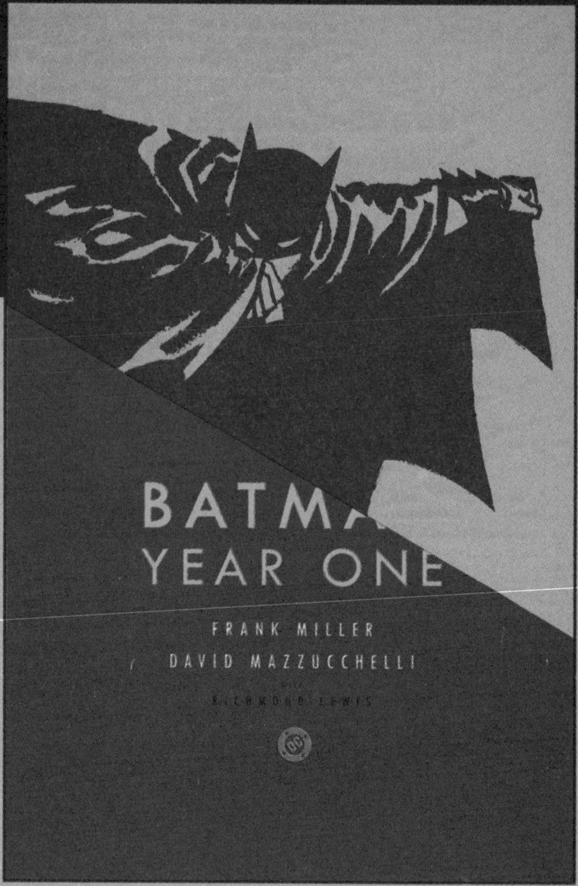
BATMAN
YEAR ONE
FRANK MILLER
DAVID MAZZUCCHELLI

BATMAN: YEAR ONE

One of the most important and acclaimed Batman tales ever — written by **Frank Miller** and illustrated by **David Mazzucchelli** with painted color by **Richmond Lewis.**

"..AN UNUSUALLY AMBITIOUS AND GRIPPING CRIME NOVEL..."
— ROLLING STONE

BATMAN: THE DARK KNIGHT RETURNS

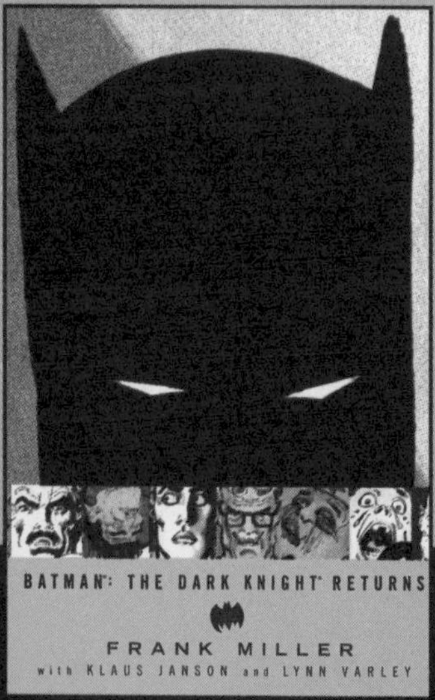
BATMAN: THE DARK KNIGHT RETURNS
FRANK MILLER
with KLAUS JANSON and LYNN VARLEY

FRANK MILLER
KLAUS JANSON
LYNN VARLEY

BATMAN: THE DARK KNIGHT STRIKES AGAIN

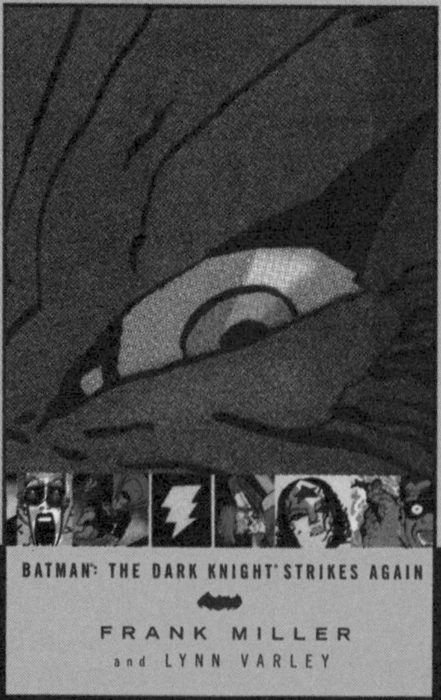
BATMAN: THE DARK KNIGHT STRIKES AGAIN
FRANK MILLER
and LYNN VARLEY

FRANK MILLER
LYNN VARLEY

BATMAN: THE GREATEST STORIES EVER TOLD

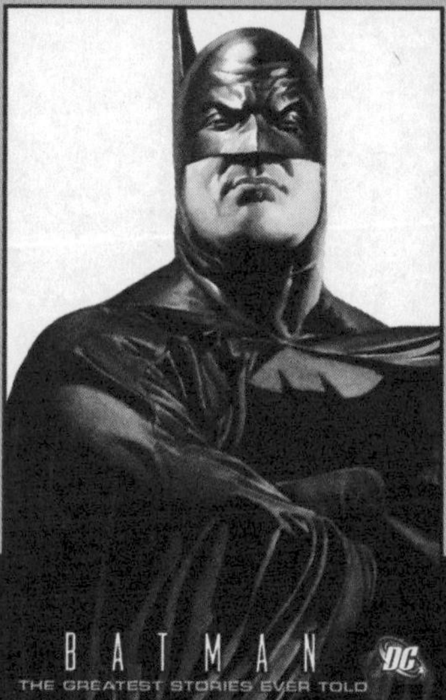
BATMAN
THE GREATEST STORIES EVER TOLD
DC

VARIOUS

BATMAN:
THE LONG HALLOWEEN

BATMAN
THE LONG HALLOWEEN

JEPH LOEB
TIM SALE

BATMAN:
DARK VICTORY

BATMAN
Dark Victory

JEPH LOEB
TIM SALE

BATMAN:
HAUNTED KNIGHT

JEPH LOEB TIM SALE
BATMAN
HAUNTED KNIGHT

JEPH LOEB
TIM SALE

BATMAN:
SCARECROW TALES

BATMAN
SCARECROW TALES

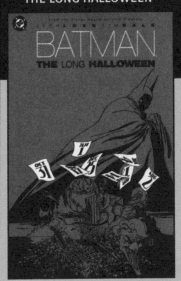

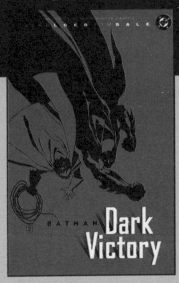

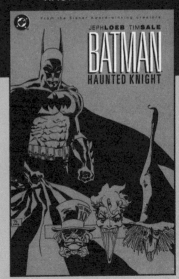

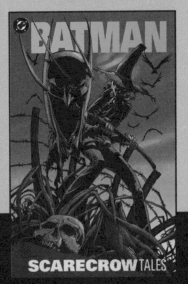

VARIOUS

BATMAN:
BLIND JUSTICE

BATMAN
BLIND JUSTICE
SAM HAMM
DENYS COWAN
DICK GIORDANO

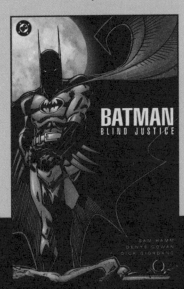

SAM HAMM
DENYS COWAN
DICK GIORDANO

BATMAN:
BROKEN CITY

BATMAN
BROKEN CITY
BRIAN AZZARELLO
EDUARDO RISSO

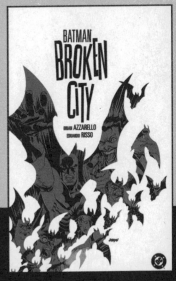

BRIAN AZZARELLO
EDUARDO RISSO

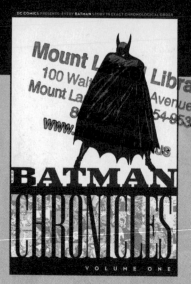

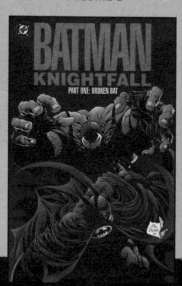